Dare Call it Treason

Dare Call it Treason

Richard M. Watt

DORSET PRESS
NEW YORK

2001 Dorset Press

ISBN 0-7607-2240-4 *paperback*

Printed and bound in the United States of America

01 02 03 04 MP 9 8 7 6 5 4 3 2 1

BVG

Introduction

FROM 1914 THROUGH 1918, it was the proclaimed conviction of the Allied powers that "We stand at Armageddon, and we battle for the Lord."

In the end there was at least one event which suggested that Providence did, indeed, favor them. In the spring of 1917, the French Army —in size and aggressiveness the mainstay of the Allied cause—collapsed in despair, confusion and mutiny. Between the Germans and Paris there was a mere screen of faithful die-hards pretending to be an army, grimly awaiting the major German offensive which they could not hope to hold. Behind them was the wreck of an army, misused and punished into "collective indiscipline"; behind it was France, almost sold by self-seeking politicians who could see no treason in accepting money or the promise of political support from German agents. It was an immediate question whether the French Army—or France herself—would fight again.

A prompt German offensive could have swept into Paris. Thus decapitated—as in 1940—France probably would have collapsed. The English, already overextended in northern France, could have done little. The United States was represented in France by only a single infantry division (which constituted a large part of its regular army). What roads history would have followed thereafter can hardly be guessed. Certainly, somewhere along the Channel coast, the British Expeditionary Force would have faced its equivalent of Dunkirk. The result might have been anything: a negotiated peace, with France under the rule of a totally corrupt, pro-German, anti-English clique; a subsequent joint Anglo-American invasion of the European continent with some earlier De Gaulle to help rally those Frenchmen who still believed in a free France; or fates now somewhat unimaginable.

But, by a "crowning mercy"—which even today can only seem a providential miracle—the Germans never learned of their opportunity. Clemenceau gave France her first strong civil government in years; Pétain rallied and rebuilt the French Army. Both were fallible men. The first would die bitterly disappointed; the second, a disgraced prisoner. Yet for a few months glory touched them; they saved France.

Every army in history has had its tales of mutiny. That of the French Army in 1917 has long been considered the outstanding example, but it was an orderly protest compared to the dissolution of the Russian Army that same year, or to the scenes in Germany a little over a year later. In fact, it was more of a "soldiers' strike" than an out-and-out, large-scale mutiny. The Army failed France less than the French high command and civil government had failed their army. Nevertheless, its mutiny endangered both France and the Allied war effort, and so Pétain dealt with it firmly as well as justly.

Mr. Watt is the first to make the story of this "mutiny" into a definitive historical study, packed with lessons for soldier and civilian alike. Had this book been written thirty years earlier, the likelihood of France's collapse in 1940 could have been foreseen. French history has shown few Clemenceaus, and a political system which insisted on cherishing a Caillaux, a Malvy and a Laval can only be termed irresponsible at best.

It is in this last sense that this book must be read. As the author repeatedly cautions his readers, the French system of government, the French sense of political responsibility and the interrelationship of the French government and the French Army are unique. The similarities to their American counterparts are more a matter of semantics than of spirit; actions which are logical in one environment make little sense in the other, to the frequent confusion of the average American. This is a history of Frenchmen and French institutions in a time of peril and bewilderment. They must be judged by their own standards. We shall be judged by our success in applying the lessons of their misfortunes.

—JOHN R. ELTING
Colonel, U.S.A.

West Point, 1962

CONTENTS

Introduction by Colonel John Elting   *v*

1. THE YEARS BEFORE   *2*
2. THE ARMY AND THE NATION   *20*
3. FRANCE MOBILIZES   *35*
4. THE FIRST MONTH   *58*
5. 1915   *72*
6. COLONEL PÉTAIN   *93*
7. G.Q.G.   *106*
8. 1916   *114*
9. THE TROJAN HORSE   *131*
10. PRELUDE TO CATASTROPHE   *146*
11. THE MAY MUTINIES   *175*
12. THE JUNE MUTINIES   *197*
13. PÉTAIN AND THE SUPPRESSION: I   *214*
14. PÉTAIN AND THE SUPPRESSION: II   *231*
15. *L'Antipatriotisme*   *246*
16. THE LAST MUTINY   *266*
17. "I WAGE WAR!"   *277*
18. AFTERWORD   *295*

Illustrations following page *184*
Maps
FRENCH TRENCH SYSTEM 75
FRENCH FIRING TRENCH *(cross section)* 77
BATTLE OF VERDUN, 1916 *118*
THE WESTERN FRONT, 1917 *346*
NIVELLE'S ORIGINAL PLAN *348*
NIVELLE'S OFFENSIVE, SPRING 1917 *349*

Author's Note *305*
Acknowledgments and Notes *307*
Bibliography *323*
Index *331*

THE COMING OF SPRING had brought no lift to the hearts of Frenchmen. Even the ending of the winter—cold, wet, dreary, coalless—brought none of the customary vernal elation, only a sort of sullen relief. Though 1917 was only five months old, already in this third year of the war a ruinous military defeat had robbed the nation of the only thing which was sustaining it—hope.

Across northeastern France there ran a jagged, looping scar. From the air, or on the maps in the newspapers, it looked like a furrow cut out by the hand of a monster plowman. It was the front. And for more than thirty months the French Army had battered itself against the trenches of its German enemies with no perceptible results—only that in every attack many more Frenchmen died than Germans.

From time to time there had been great hopes. Huge offensives had been mounted which were to crack through the German front. But all these had failed. And after the catastrophe of mid-April past, few Frenchmen could be got to believe in them any more.

So now the nation was plainly dying. A succession of vacillating and confused governments had failed to offer the despairing nation any alternative other than a slow slide over to the parties of the left, which, even though their leaders might be accused of fomenting defeatism, at least offered a plan for peace.

This, then, is an account of a nation in a state of near-collapse. It is a story of treason and of faithless men whose personal ambitions exceeded their patriotism, of politicians who played on the despair of a nation exhausted by three years of defeat and generations of fratricidal strife.

1

And, too, this is a book about military mutiny on a huge scale—the story of millions of French soldiers, whose individual bravery and devotion equaled or exceeded that of their enemies, but who had been bled of hope and determination in a thousand fruitless minor battles punctuated by a series of major holocausts.

Finally, this is the account of the greatest moments in the lives of two men, one of them a politician whose task it was to suppress a well-organized campaign of treason, the other a general who had to put down mutiny within his collapsing army but who, in so doing, had to find a better method than the conventional blood bath.

And this story of treason and mutiny begins fifty years before the event.

1

THE YEARS BEFORE

LE PREMIER DU MONDE! Overwhelming pride in France and a certain contempt for anything not French is a national characteristic which has for centuries distorted the minds of France's citizens, tormented her friends and, upon occasion, humbled her enemies. It is a predominant characteristic of a truly unique nation, but nowhere is it so evident as in her Army.

To begin with, the French Army always regarded itself as the master of war—privy to all the secrets of battle and the principal repository of its glory. There was, of course, considerable justification for this conviction, because, until the Franco-Prussian War of 1870, an immense array of allied nations had always been required to subdue the French Army. And, apart from its victorious past, the

French Army could also point to the fact that France originated countless basic military theories which had survived to become standard practice among the nations of the world. Had not the French kings created the world's first standing armies? Had not the French conceived the idea of conscription and "total war" in 1789 and formed a mighty citizen army which defeated in turn almost every major European power? And had not Napoleon, the world's greatest soldier, conquered the entire European continent and displayed the military superiority of the Frenchman at war? Certainly there could be no question among right-thinking men of whatever nationality that militarily France was *le premier du monde*.

Until 1865 this confident frame of mind was based on a solid foundation: the French Army was supported by the largest and wealthiest political entity in continental Europe. But in 1866 Prussia burst from its Baltic seclusion, trounced the Austro-Hungarian Empire in a lightning campaign, secured the leadership of the horde of minor Germanic principalities and kingdoms and established itself as the most dynamic power in Europe, backed by an economic and military potential which would rapidly exceed that of France. It was inevitable that France and Prussia would soon go to war to settle the question of the leadership of Europe.

The Franco-Prussian War was a devastating military fiasco for the French Army—most of it surrendered within a few months—as well as a political catastrophe, since it resulted in the final union of the Germanic states under the Hohenzollern King of Prussia. From the instant when the victorious King William of Prussia became William, Emperor of the Germans, in 1871, France would never again achieve the position of military pre-eminence it had held for centuries before. A European age had ended.

But for France and its Army, the position of a second-class power was unthinkable. The Army burned for revenge, and the nation throbbed with the desire to reconquer the provinces of Alsace and Lorraine, which had been taken by the Germans. And if there was one single point upon which all Frenchmen would then agree, it was the necessity of rebuilding the Army. "Give us back our legions!" [1] the representatives of the people had cried from the parliamentary tribune, and the nation hurried to respond to the call. As for its humiliation in 1870, the Army wasted little time in self-recrimination. It was obvious, to the generals at least, that the defeat had been only the end result of years of legislative parsimony and the lack of adequate conscript reserves. Now the French Army would rebuild itself for the inevitable next war, when it would recover Alsace and Lorraine and would revenge itself upon the Germans. And, in rebuilding the Army, confidence, courage and an awareness of its glorious past and its invincible future would sustain both the Army and the French nation.

In reality, though, something more than determination and a desire for revenge was required to rebuild the French Army to the point where it could match the German war machine. Economic strength, a spirit of self-sacrifice, both political and national unity, and a sustained popular confidence in the Army were necessary. And unfortunately for France, the years between 1870 and 1914 did not supply these necessities.

The French defeat of 1870 had been followed by the bloody uprisings of the Paris Commune and the ultimate creation of the Third French Republic. There then came a period of utter confusion. From the right wing of the political spectrum, the powerful royalist and monarchist elements contended for power against the covey of factions whose aim was the firm establishment of a republican government within France.

At first, it almost seemed as if the right might succeed in strangling the Third Republic at its birth. It was able to force the adoption of a form of government which would make easy a quick transition to a monarchy and to stock it with a President of the Republic and a Senate in which the right was predominant. And, even more important, the Church and the leadership of the Army were firmly in the camp of reaction. But then the right paused to bicker and feud within its own ranks, and suddenly, in 1876, it found that its moment had passed. A republican majority was in control of the Chamber of Deputies and, however bitterly these republicans might quarrel among themselves, it was clear that they would throw France into a civil war before they would permit the coronation of another king.

By the mid-1880s the Third Republic was settling down into the political form which it carried into World War I. Through a series of republican laws, the authority of the French Senate and the President of the Republic had been curtailed sharply. The real political power in France rested in the six-hundred-odd members of the Chamber of Deputies, who represented a bewildering conglomeration of political thought—starting with the royalists on the right and proceeding through a welter of republican parties in the center and the left to a small group of proletarian parties on the far left. And among these political parties, the republicans of the center and the moderate left were in the majority. They represented varying shades of republican thought and drew their strength from the working classes and from the political opinion molders who, in the predominantly rural France of the time, were generally the school-teachers and the doctors, whose thoughts were rationalist and radical. But about the only common ground upon which all the republicans closed ranks was their doctrines of opposition to the influence of the Catholic Church (since historically the Church was royalist, conservative and reactionary) and opposition to the restoration of the monarchy. This community of interest was strong enough to ensure that the French ministerial governments would be formed from among the republican parties, but it was not enough to give each government any particular strength or any lengthy tenure in office. The successive governments were almost invariably coalitions based on compromise and generally contained the same faces. It was a system which really satisfied no one—the royalists had no king, the clericals were forced to witness the receding influence of the Church, the conservative republicans could see that their own left was becoming progressively more Socialist, and the parties of the far left knew that they were a very long way from obtaining any real measure of political power. As a result, lacking both direction and purpose, France was constantly torn by a succession of political feuds and shabby governmental scandals.

There is no better way of describing the political and social climate of France in the period before World War I than to follow the life of Georges Clemenceau, one of France's most prominent figures of the time; for in Clemenceau it is possible to observe, greatly magnified, all the complex characteristics of a French political leader of the time—intelligence, abhorrence of compromise, latent greatness, egotism, malicious pettiness, patriotism, ruthlessness. But, more than this, the span of Clemenceau's life included almost the entire life of the Third French Republic, and his effect on it and its effect on him were so great that their lives became almost synonymous. From its birth following the cataclysmic defeat of 1870 until its demise during World War II, the Third Republic managed to weather four tremendous ordeals. They were the Boulanger affair, the Panama scandals, the Dreyfus case and the near-collapse of France in 1917. Georges Clemenceau took an active role in every one of them.

He was born in 1841 in La Vendée, a remote and largely rural province in the west of France. There was a thin strain of inherited wealth flowing through the Clemenceau family which had, for generations, enabled them to take their place as a species of country squire and to indulge in a predilection for both the study of medicine and the practice of republicanism. Clemenceau's father, grandfather and great-grandfather had all been gentlemen doctors who cherished their financial independence, since it allowed them the intellectual freedom to expound their republican principles and, simultaneously, their opposition to the Catholic Church, which they believed was largely responsible for the repeated failure of France to successfully produce a government firmly based on the dreams of 1789.

This was the family pattern which young Clemenceau also followed. He went to Paris in 1860, got his medical degree in 1865 and then set out to visit England and the United States—twin meccas for young French republicans who loathed the atmosphere of the Empire of Napoleon III. Clemenceau lived for three years in the United States, reading, thinking, writing. To support himself, he took a job as riding instructor and French teacher at a girls' finishing school in Stamford, Connecticut. And it was here that he met and married one of his pupils, Mary Plummer.

Clemenceau and his American bride returned to France in 1869. The call of republican revolution had grown too strong for him to resist, and he was determined to be a part of it.

In the summer of 1870 Napoleon III was foolish enough to declare war upon Germany, and, for his folly, two months later he had surrendered both his person and his largest army to the invader. But this did not mean that the war was over. In the absence of the Emperor and the demoralization of his Paris government, Léon Gambetta proclaimed the dissolution of the Empire and the formation of the Third Republic. On the same day Georges Clemenceau was appointed the republican mayor of Paris' Eighteenth Arrondissement, Montmarte.

To young Clemenceau, now twenty-nine, this appointment, his first taste of political power, was a heady thing. Whippetlike he rushed about, preparing his section of Paris for its defense against the onrushing Germans, who were already investing the Paris defenses. But Clemenceau's efforts were of little avail. He was caught up in a movement and a time far too large for him to influence. Although the Parisians rallied to support the revolutionary National Guard and held out for months against the surrounding Germans, the other sections of France suffered a series of defeats and longed for peace at any price. When a French National Assembly was formed to conclude peace with the Germans, the Parisian revolutionaries saw in it merely an attempt to repress the Republic. In the spring of 1871, the Paris revolutionaries defied the Assembly, which had concluded an armistice with Germany, and formed the Commune.

The Commune was a sort of Socialist-Communist affair, proclaimed by a committee of workers and intellectuals for the benefit of the Paris proletariat; and although Clemenceau was not in complete sympathy with it, he supported it on the grounds that from the Commune would evolve the type of rational republicanism he favored. In this he was mistaken. The Commune lasted only ten weeks and spent most of this brief period fighting French troops raised by the conservative Assembly. It was a fantastically bloody civil war in which quarter was neither asked nor given. The Communards, in the agony of their impending defeat, killed countless hostages whom they took to be antirepublican. The Assembly troops, in turn, butchered more than twenty thousand Communards in the week which saw them capture Paris. Meanwhile, at the height of the Commune uprising it had turned to eat its own. Clemenceau had been accused by the Communards of protecting two Assembly generals captured by the Montmartre mob. The generals were lynched and Clemenceau narrowly escaped death. His usefulness was clearly at an end, and, sickened by the excesses he had seen, and hunted by both Commune and Assembly, he fled besieged Paris, pretending to be an American citizen.

For the next five years, Clemenceau lived a life of relative political obscurity. Elected to the comparatively impotent Paris Municipal Council and supporting himself by practicing medicine, he wielded little influence in the creation of the constitution of the Third Republic in 1875. But when the first elections for the Chamber of Deputies were held in 1876, Clemenceau stood for election and won. In the new Chamber he quickly rose to a position of dominance.

He came into French political life at a time when republicanism was still fighting for its life. Pre-eminent in the turmoil was the fact, difficult to grasp for one accustomed to political life in English-speaking nations, that the political opposition to the succession of republican governments was not a "loyal" opposition. The parties of the right were not merely parties out of power who were contending for the leadership of the Republic. Rather, their aim was to take over the Republic and totally change its form. They cared little about how this was to be done—any subterfuge was acceptable. They regarded republicanism as an abortion and would content themselves with nothing less than its destruction. From the right the clericals and the monarchists made alliance; and, backed by the wealth of their supporters coupled with the influence of the Church and the conservative Army leadership, they made ferocious political assaults upon the republicans. To them Marianne, the symbol of the Republic, was "the Whore."

Aiding and abetting this turmoil was the character of the French voter himself. Highly individualistic, unalterably opposed to compromise, and sufficiently intelligent to possess strong opinions on a variety of subjects, he was represented in the Chamber of Deputies by a bewildering mass of parties. As a result, the republican central elements could remain in control of the government only by means of a series of weakening concessions to their neighbors on the right and the left—concessions which all but emasculated their ministries and reduced them to virtual impotence. Ultimately this meant that the French nation lost respect for its politicians, since they never possessed the strength to remain in office long enough to force through a program of sufficient vitality to command that respect.

Finally, the French citizen contributed to the weakness of the Third Republic by his absolute refusal to become too emotionally involved with it. Within the space of less than a hundred years, the French had experienced eight forms of government: absolute and constitutional monarchy, three republics—the first of which had two phases, Convention and Directory—Consulate and two empires. And, like a man who has been too often disappointed in love and is about to embark upon another affair, the Frenchman had the lurking suspicion that his relationship with the Third Republic would have an unhappy ending. So, to prepare himself for eventual disappointment, he held himself aloof from the lady.

This, then, was the political morass into which Georges Clemenceau descended. He was now middle-aged and almost completely bald. His skull had a Mongolian cast, and over his coal-black eyes the lids drooped sleepily. Outwardly he was unprepossessing—but inwardly he was driven by a furious rage. He was absolutely determined to fix onto the collective conscience of the French nation the same ideals of republicanism which he himself held so firmly. And into the no-holds-barred environment of the Chamber of Deputies Georges Clemenceau adjusted perfectly, for he was a species of misanthrope who always found it easier to make an enemy than a friend. Foremost among his personal qualifications was his cynical knowledge of men. Thoroughly and to the core, Clemenceau *knew* his fellow politicians, and to him they were generally contemptible. He was malicious, unforgiving and unforgetting. Clemenceau quickly came to learn the French political system backward and forward, and he used this knowledge of politics and politicians to blackmail, threaten and cajole in any way that seemed appropriate to the circumstances. Peculiarly, for a French politician, Clemenceau was not a skilled speaker; but he was the absolute master of the brief address from the tribune of the Chamber which with malice, perception and wit would bring a government crashing down. Within the space of a few years he destroyed nearly a dozen ministries. And because of his ruthless, slashing style, he came to be called "the Tiger."

As a vehement republican he was, of course, an atheist, and as a patriot he was ardently anti-German. Politically, Clemenceau generally aligned himself with the Socialists—except, curiously, on economic issues, where he pointed out that "the overwhelming majority of French voters are rural voters . . . and the peasantry of France will never be Socialists." [2] Blessed with an excellent memory, he had acquired for himself a good knowledge of history, art, philosophy and literature. He was clever and witty. But his rudeness and frequent malice brought him constant challenges to duels, with the result that he became a feared swordsman and a deadly pistol shot.

To the re-establishment of France as the principal Continental power Clemenceau dedicated his life, both public and private. The story goes that his neglect of his family reached the point where his American wife accused him of having a mistress. "Yes," he is supposed to have cried, "I have a mistress. Come with me and I shall show you her picture." And, seizing her by the arm, he dragged her after him into his study. Pointing to a drawing of Marianne, the symbol of the French Republic, he said, "There is my true mistress, *la belle France*." [3] His wife left him.

But although he was a power in the Chamber of Deputies, Clemenceau constantly refused offers of the premiership and other ministerial positions. He knew that he had made too many enemies ever to be able to form a secure government on the shifting sands of French politics. And, for this reason, he preferred to remain in opposition, where he would never become tainted with the weakness and lack of direction which characterized the governments of the time.

To his enemies Clemenceau was only a "wrecker," a noisy, vindictive politician who manifested his undoubted abilities only as a destroyer of governments; a man who, refusing office himself, preferred the easier and negative path of senseless destruction of what others were trying to build. But to his few friends he represented the salvation of republican France—a statesman whose every waking moment was filled with an obsession to continue the unfinished task begun by the Revolution of 1789 and develop within France and Frenchmen the greatness and glory which a functioning democracy could bring to the oft-disillusioned nation.

Although for years he refused to form his own Ministry, Clemenceau's position as the leader of one of the largest parties, the Radicals, could not be denied. A Ministry was generally formed from among the ranks of the moderate republicans, and it absolutely had to have Clemenceau's support before it could come into office. Although this did not give Clemenceau the power to bring about the changes in the government which he so greatly desired—or to launch a violent attack on the power of the Church and force the abandonment of the government's colonial policy on the grounds that it only served to weaken France at home—his position did give him the privilege of naming an occasional Cabinet member.

One of his nominees almost wrecked the Republic in its first great crisis.

Georges Ernest Jean Marie Boulanger had been a schoolmate of Clemenceau's, but instead of becoming interested in politics Boulanger had entered the Army. There he had served with moderate distinction in various colonial wars; but real fame was not to come to Boulanger until, when he was an obscure colonel, he was sent to the United States for the centennial celebration of Cornwallis' surrender at Yorktown. There Boulanger discovered that the German flag was being flown alongside the French and United States colors, and he refused to take part in the ceremonies until the insult to France was rectified. He returned to France a hero and, in 1881, was appointed to the military command of Tunisia. There he behaved in the same jingoist fashion which had paid him dividends before.

In January 1886, a new government composed largely of moderate republicans required support from Clemenceau's Radicals. To obtain this support, they offered him the privilege of naming the Minister of War. Clemenceau named Boulanger, his hope being that Boulanger, regarded as "the only republican general," would be just the man to give the nation increased confidence and enthusiasm in the Army and to stimulate Parliament to vote increased military appropriations. For a while it appeared as if Clemenceau had been right.

General Boulanger was indeed popular. For the Army he improved rations and weapons and increased furloughs. For the republican government he dismissed all the Orleanist princes from the officer corps and constantly and vehemently denied that the Army, whose head he was, had any ambitions but to be the servant of the government. And for the populace he organized vast military parades through the streets of Paris, parades led by Boulanger himself astride Tunis, his coal-black charger, and followed by an entourage of three hundred generals. In short, Boulanger became extremely popular. Too much so, in fact, because in 1887 when a new Ministry was formed which excluded Boulanger and exiled him to a post in the provinces, the Paris populace rioted to prevent his train from leaving the station. Ultimately, in 1889, adulation for Boulanger reached such a height that he was able to run for the Chamber of Deputies and achieve a spectacular victory.

Boulangism (already it had a name) was a strange phenomenon. Strange because no one, perhaps least of all Boulanger, had a very clear idea where he stood or what he stood for. The republicans thought that he was loyal to them, but at the same time it was becoming common knowledge that Boulanger was engaging in political activity which was being financed principally by the Duchess d'Uzès, a rich royalist. Such was the confusion that among his supporters were Bonapartists, royalists, republicans, nationalists and even anarchists.

If it were not for the fact that the Republic was in deadly danger, the whole spectacle would have been ludicrous; for, indeed, Boulanger had feet of clay. Apart from his good looks—blue eyes and curly blond hair inherited from his Scottish mother—plus a decided aura of glamour, the man was a cipher. His personal life alone should have been enough to ruin him. He was a satyr and would drop anything for a few hours in the arms of almost any accommodating female, even going so far as to arrange frequent assignations with a woman postal employee whom he took in a closed carriage on the street in front of his favorite restaurant.[4] Moreover, politically Boulanger had no discernible program. All he had to offer was a blurred but glamorous focal point around which the manifold opposition to the Third Republic could rally.

But to those who, like Clemenceau, had sincere republican principles, Boulanger represented the danger most acute in the French political system—the damning evidence that the Third Republic had never really fastened itself in the minds and hearts of its citizens, who, in their adulation of General Boulanger, were asserting their contempt for the vacillating political figures of the day and demonstrating their desire for a "man on horseback" who could deliver them from doubt and confusion.

It became clear that Boulanger's plan was to seize power, abolish the constitution and establish an authoritarian "republic." And he had support; a famous French writer laid Boulanger's appeal bare: "Royalists saw in Boulanger their king; republicans, their republic; imperialists, their Caesar; patriots saw the return of Alsace and Lorraine; peaceable people saw order; and all the restless saw an adventure which would solve all the problems." [5]

On the night of January 27, 1889, General Boulanger and his supporters sat in the Restaurant Durand on Paris' Rue Royale. The results of an election in which Boulanger had run simultaneously for four seats in the Chamber of Deputies were coming in and it was apparent that he had won an overwhelming majority. It was widely understood that if he was victorious in this election Boulanger would consider it a popular mandate to demand the dissolution of the Chamber of Deputies. In the streets outside the mobs were in a frenzy. Their *brave général* had won. For the space of a few hours, the Third French Republic literally teetered in the balance. Boulanger had only to mount his horse and lead the way to the presidential palace and he would surely have been installed as a dictator. Only a single, quaking government detective, standing outside the restaurant with a warrant for Boulanger's arrest if he attempted to make a disturbance, stood in the way of Boulanger and a mob of 300,000 supporters. The Republican Guard, mustered in strength supposedly to protect the President against the mob, stood outside the palace ostentatiously reading Boulangist literature and wearing Boulangist buttons on their uniforms. For some men, however, the moment always passes, and such was the case with Boulanger. Instead of becoming dictator of France, he hesitated, let the moment slip past and repaired to the arms of his current mistress. By a hair's breadth, the Third Republic was saved.

It had not been forgotten by Clemenceau's enemies, and they were many, that it was Clemenceau who had first brought Boulanger to prominence. Indeed, Clemenceau had not forgotten it, either. He introduced a series of measures before the Chamber of Deputies which swiftly led to Boulanger's being indicted for treason. But before he could be tried, Boulanger fled to Belgium, where two years later he committed suicide on the grave of his mistress. His death was almost unnoticed, except by Clemenceau, whose characteristically bitter comment was, "He died as he lived—like a subaltern." [6]

The Boulanger affair had shaken the foundations of Clemenceau's prestige, but the edifice still stood. He continued as before, the most influential single power outside the government, never possessing the overwhelming strength which was his stipulation before he would form a government of his own, but viciously, almost spitefully, smashing successive moderate-republican governments on the floor of the Chamber of Deputies and in the pages of the newspaper he edited. Now it was to be his turn, in the Third Republic's second crisis.

Probably the most respected man in France in the late 1880s was Count Ferdinand de Lesseps. To the greater glory of France he had built the Suez Canal and thus established France in the forefront of international scientific repute. And a few years later Lesseps proposed another engineering marvel. He would build a canal in Panama to connect the Atlantic with the Pacific. To finance this monumental project, a company was formed and a vast amount of stock sold. But soon it appeared that the problems encountered in building a canal through the malarial jungles of Panama were quite different from those experienced in Egypt. In a brief time the original capital of the Canal Company was used up.

To raise an additional 500,000,000 francs to complete the canal, the company retained Baron Jacques de Reinach, a man of shady character and unscrupulous past who, however, had considerable experience in the art of influencing politicians. Reinach began to lobby for a license to hold a national lottery to raise additional funds for the canal. To assist him he hired a certain Dr. Cornelius Herz, with the promise that if the lottery license was granted Herz would receive ten million francs for his efforts.

Herz had no difficulty obtaining governmental sponsorship for the lottery license—he promised a Cabinet minister a million francs for it—but he did experience considerable trouble with various deputies who persisted in wondering aloud whether or not the government was simply sanctioning the throwing of good money after bad in the canal venture. To quiet them, Herz distributed bribes with a lavish hand while, at the same time, providing substantial "subventions" to newspapers, who were then expected to build popular enthusiasm and confidence in the lottery—or at least to refrain from exposing the shaky condition of the Canal Company. Ultimately these newspaper bribes were extended to include even such minuscule opinion formers as "The Beekeeper's Journal" and "The Rod-and-Line Fisherman." But despite Herz's efforts the lottery scheme proved a failure. It was simply impossible to hide the fact that the canal could never be built following Lesseps' faulty plans.

Everything went with a rush. The Canal Company went bankrupt, carrying with it the hopes and the savings of thousands of French small investors. Cornelius Herz fled the country and Baron de Reinach committed suicide, after which it came to light that more than a hundred republicans—deputies, senators and government ministers—had accepted bribes. The government fell after a tremendous attack by the monarchists, who characterized the republican group as being all in league in their corruption. And tainted with the tarbrush of corruption was Georges Clemenceau.

From the floor of the Chamber of Deputies an enemy named Paul Déroulède launched an attack on the republican who, he claimed, had been responsible more than any other for the Panama fiasco. There was a man, Déroulède charged, who had known Cornelius Herz much too well. A man who had secured for Herz the coveted rank of Grand Officer in the Legion of Honor, a man who had accepted huge newspaper subsidies from Herz, and a man who, moreover, was a master spy in the pay of the British government. "You all know him," Déroulède declaimed. "His name is on all your lips. But none of you dare say it, for there are three things which you fear: his sword, his pistol, his tongue. Well, I defy all three and I name him: it is Monsieur Clemenceau!" [7]

Although the charge of espionage was readily proved laughably false, Clemenceau could not hide his connection with Herz, and few of his biographers have chosen to defend him on this count. Indeed, the Tiger admitted that years before when he had founded his newspaper *La Justice* he had accepted money from Herz to get the journal established, but he claimed that this loan had long since been repaid; and, in any event, the loan had nothing to do with the Canal Company. "Aoh, yes!" was the mocking moan from the benches of the far right—and this soon became the refrain for a popular song about Clemenceau. (The cry of "Aoh, yes!" was all the more bitter, since it referred to the popular charge that Clemenceau was a British agent.)

In August 1893 Clemenceau stood for re-election from the constituency of the Var. Wherever he went, whatever he said, the once friendly crowds were the same. For a while they listened to him in silence and then they broke into chants of "Aoh, yes!" Mocked, humiliated, even stoned in the streets, Clemenceau was repudiated by the electorate. For the first time in nearly twenty years, he was out of office.

For many men this would have been the end. But Clemenceau was sustained by his patriotism, his ambition and his bitterness. The Tiger said of himself, "I had a wife, she abandoned me; I had children, they turned against me. I have only my claws left, and I use them well."

In the years which followed, Clemenceau became a writer of books and newspaper articles. Although they were popular and widely read, it was generally assumed that he was off the stage of politics for life. As it turned out, he was merely waiting in the wings.

Economically, the Third Republic had firmly established France as a nation dominated by small businessmen who ruled by means of an unwritten alliance with the nation's largest political entity, the conservative peasant landholder. The small farmer and the small businessman combined to elect small-minded politicians who, if nothing else, could be relied upon to protect the status quo and to reflect the spirit of petty materialism which was characteristic of the age. Earlier in the century a phrase had been coined which was to be the watchword of the bourgeois businessman—*"Enrichissez vous,* enrich yourselves." So in this period of its national life France clearly lost its economic dynamism and became characterized by a single-minded desire to maintain things as they were, to avoid risk and to remain content with a bourgeois scale of prosperity.

French agriculture was sheltered by tariffs so high that, on soil which was incredibly poorly suited for it, wheat was raised and sold at prices far higher than it could have been imported. And in return for this the businessman's markets were tariff-protected to the point where he had very little incentive to improve his products or seek new outlets. This type of economic *quid pro quo* was designed to produce economic stability and even a faint blush of prosperity; but over a period of years it meant that France failed to take part in the age of mass production and giant industry which the turn of the century brought to the United States, Germany and Great Britain.

France even failed to make the best use of its capital. The hoarded savings of its thrifty peasants went to buy foreign bonds which built railways in Russia or steel mills in Germany. And while these nations developed an industrial fiber, Frenchmen contented themselves with merely a modest return on their investments.

Equally as serious, the birth rate of the French population had failed to increase, while the death rate had dropped off. What this amounted to was that France was gradually becoming a nation of older persons—a "Nation of Bachelors and Only Sons" is what it was called in the title of a book published in 1896. The French Army was constantly aware of the ominous fact that France, with its static and aging population of 40,000,000, could no longer hope to field an army equal in size to Germany's, which was based on an exploding population that would reach 65,000,000 by 1914.

Until 1893, France, by dint of calling up almost every available man for military training, managed to keep its Army on a parity with Germany's. But after 1893 the expanding German population and increasing German militarism combined to give Germany an Army which was substantially larger than France's in both active and reserve forces. There was no way to solve this manpower deficiency except to enter into an alliance with Russia, whose teeming millions offered an army of almost unlimited size. Accordingly, and although it rankled good republicans, the French government bowed to expediency and negotiated a military alliance with Russia, the largest and most reactionary nation in Europe. It was agreed that if Germany attacked either France or Russia, the other would march to its partner's aid.

But if France was economically stagnant, politically she was in a slow ferment of change. And this was mostly on account of the growing strength of the parties of the far left.

Immediately following the defeat of 1870, the proletarian parties had seemed totally moribund. Contaminated with the failure of the Commune, the leaders of the "red clubs" of Paris had been hounded through France. If they escaped capture, and few of them did, it was only because they had been able to flee to foreign countries. Otherwise they were seized and flung before military courts whose standard sentence was exile to the penal colonies in New Caledonia. Nor did persecution come solely from the right. Even Karl Marx, from the safety of tolerant England, had sharply criticized the French Commune, and this, in a way, was the bitterest pill of all.

But gradually the parties of the far left restored themselves. The proletarian leaders either served out their sentences or were pardoned in a general amnesty; and by the mid-eighties they had begun to achieve a certain measure of influence. Although honeycombed with police spies, there were now "workers' clubs," a few Socialist newspapers, and a growing trade-union movement. Too, the far left found an ally of sorts in the republican center, which, desperate for support against the rich and powerful right, was willing upon occasion to make concessions in return for support from the left.

Of course, like the other sections of the French political spectrum, the far left was slivered into a multitude of factions. The anarchists were one group, and they pursued their own star without regard to any of their confrères of the left. But the biggest of the proletarian groups was the Socialist party—and, again, this too was split into contending factions. Some of them were Marxists, the equivalent of later-day Communists. Others of the Socialist party were much less doctrinaire, progressing to the point where they were simply the equivalent of a modern-day liberal party. In any event, the far left realized that in the France of the waning nineteenth century they had to make some concessions to reality. The first was that violent overthrow of the government was out of the question; France was fundamentally a nation of conservative peasants and small proprietors whose sheer mass made them immovable. Industrialization had not yet brought to France the numbers of politically active factory workers who were necessary for a true Socialist coup. So instead the left wing had to eke out whatever gains it could in terms of social legislation while, in the economic sphere, agitating for nationalization of the railways, banks and mines.

Only slowly did the far left make political gains. And even when it did, these were less due to its own programs than to the scandals of republican center governments. After Panama, for example, the Socialist representation in the Chamber of Deputies jumped from twelve to fifty as the nation registered its revulsion.

And it was at this juncture that there descended upon France the most decisive event in the Third Republic's history—the Dreyfus Affair, the first scandal directly to involve the Army.

Alone among the institutions of the Third Republic, the Army seemed immune to popular criticism. Its prestige had been more than restored since the debacle of 1870, and the nation regarded the Army as both its shield against another German attack and its hope for future revenge. Beginning in July of 1872, a series of laws had created for France a peacetime army based on conscription, along with a huge army reserve which was to be formed of conscripts who had finished their period of active duty. Each youth, beginning at age twenty-one, was required to serve three years on active service with the standing army—generally in an infantry regiment. This active duty was followed by seven years in the army reserve and then six years in a lesser-grade reserve known as the territorial army. Finally, the French citizen passed into the territorial reserve, to which he belonged for nine years. This meant that every Frenchman was liable to active and reserve service for a twenty-five-year period. The details of this system were altered and re-altered by subsequent laws, but it is essentially the system of active and reserve forces which France mobilized in 1914.

Although the French Army system was capable of providing a large mass of reservist manpower, its state of training can be illustrated by the fact that after his period of active duty the army reservist was subject to being called up for training duty for two one-month periods of training during his entire service with the reserve; the men of the territorial army were liable to active service for one period of two weeks; and the aging territorial reservists were subject to active duty of only one day during their entire nine years' service.

Mobilization of the Army for war comprised, of course, not only the active army and the reserve army, but the territorial army and its reserve. Every man in every component had been given orders telling him where and when to report. All he had to do was to walk to a railroad station and board a train to the headquarters of his army corps, where uniforms, weapons and boots, slightly worn so that they would not blister, were waiting for him. Then, according to the mobilization plan, he either was added to an active-army regiment or else joined a territorial regiment led by a mixture of active, reserve and retired officers.

So, despite any deficiencies in the training of reserves, France had succeeded in creating a huge Army. And it regarded this Army with unreserved affection. The principle of universal service had taught the people to think of the Army as "their own," and they waited with confidence for "the day that the drums would beat." Every child could recite "The Ballad of the Sword," [8] every eye was moist when the regiments paraded down the streets of the garrison towns. The officers of the Army were held in universal respect and noted for their fierce pride, their professional abilities and their fervent nationalism. And even though the officers shuddered with unconcealed disgust at the sordid antics of the republican politicians, the politicians outdid each other to pay honor to the Army and its leaders.

Then came the Dreyfus Affair.

2

THE ARMY AND THE NATION

EVER SINCE THE Franco-Prussian War, the counterintelligence staffs
of the French and German armies had been engaged in furious
efforts to fend off one another's spies. Within the French General
Staff this work was handled by a group operating under the cover
name of the "Section of Statistics" of the Second Bureau, the latter
being the intelligence department of the General Staff organization.

Although staffed by a rather mediocre group of officers, the Section of Statistics of the Second Bureau could boast at least two stunning counterintelligence coups. One of these was the identification
of various German agents in France, to whom it was feeding a huge
mass of false or semifalse intelligence data. The other was that it
had managed to insert an agent into the German embassy in Paris.
This agent was a charwoman, a certain Madame Bastian, whose
stupid appearance served as an artful disguise for the fact that she
was collecting the contents of the embassy's wastepaper baskets and
turning them over to her French employers. (In the palmy days of
the nineteenth century, this technique passed for the height of intelligence acumen.) And from pasting together these torn scraps of
paper, the Second Bureau deduced that the German military attaché,
Colonel Max von Schwarzkoppen, was receiving considerable confidential information from an unknown French Army officer. This
threw the French General Staff into a state bordering on panic, since
the Army chose to regard itself as the national repository for the
concepts of duty, patriotism and honor which were substantially
lacking in French political and commercial life. Obviously the guilty

officer must be found at once, following which the whole event could be revealed in a manner which would redound to the credit of the Army.

At this time, the Second Bureau had been employing the services of a French spy named Bruecker. For a variety of reasons, Bruecker had fallen from favor and knew that he must pull a major intelligence coup to put himself back in the good graces of the Second Bureau. Accordingly, on the morning of September 26, 1894, Bruecker walked into the lobby of the German embassy, reached across a low guardrail, took Colonel von Schwarzkoppen's incoming mail from his box and, unnoticed, walked out the door. It was a desperate gamble, but it paid a commensurate dividend, because in Schwarzkoppen's mail was a document which became known as the *bordereau*. Written on one page of paper, the *bordereau* was a handwritten index of secret French Army documents which the traitorous officer intended to deliver to Schwarzkoppen. It was signed only with an initial, which was later alleged to be "D."

Bruecker immediately took the *bordereau* to the Second Bureau, who, horror-stricken, deduced from the items listed in it that the traitor not only was a French Army officer but, in addition, must be a member of the General Staff itself. On the flimsiest of evidence, it was decided that the culprit was Captain Alfred Dreyfus, a brilliant young officer who had only recently been assigned to the Staff. Aside from the evidence, circumstantial and inconclusive as it was, there were several reasons why Dreyfus was a logical man to fix the blame on. First, the Second Bureau was under great pressure to find the traitor and find him fast; accordingly, they were not disposed to look much further than a similarity in an initial for corroborating evidence. Secondly, Dreyfus was a Jew—in fact, the first Jew who had ever served on the General Staff—and France was going through a wave of anti-Semitism which would make unnecessary any embarrassing explanations as to why a traitor should have been admitted to the General Staff. After all, the public would presumably say, what loyalty could one expect from a Jew? Finally, there was the fact that Alfred Dreyfus was an extremely unattractive and unpopular man—a prig and an ingrate with a cold and repelling personality.

So, in due course, Dreyfus was charged with the crime, found guilty by a court-martial and sentenced to exile for life on Devil's Island. It is doubtful that, at the time, the French General Staff knew that they were convicting an innocent man, although there were plenty of irregularities in Dreyfus' trial. And certainly the French populace was in almost complete agreement with the sentence; in fact, the court-martial was widely criticized for being too lenient in not sentencing Dreyfus to death. But, as several years passed, the feeling began to grow that perhaps Dreyfus had been the victim of a strange and horrible injustice. A small group of writers, a sprinkling of political figures and an occasional courageous military man became convinced of Dreyfus' innocence and demanded a retrial. But the Army itself, backed by the power of a Jesuit-directed press and representing itself as the focal point of patriotism and French pride, categorically denied that there had been any error. The irregularities in the Dreyfus court-marital were glossed over as minor procedural matters which had been necessary to prevent the Germans from learning just how deeply the vigilant Second Bureau had penetrated into the German spy apparatus.

By 1897 the case had gone much too far for the Army to admit that a mistake had been made. Almost without exception, the Army's leaders had sworn that categorical proof existed as to Dreyfus' guilt —even though this proof could not be made public. But actually this "proof" either was nonexistent or was sheer fabrication made up by the busy Second Bureau, whose staff had now falsified so much evidence that they operated in a state bordering upon mass schizophrenia.

Ultimately the Dreyfus case reached a point where it stood for much more than just the guilt or innocence of one man. It had become a question of whether the Army, for the sake of its prestige and honor, was to be allowed to make a sacrificial lamb of a French citizen. In short, was France truly a democratic republic where justice was the right of every man?

France split itself asunder on the issue. Although the Dreyfus case became hideously complex, it was generally the rule that those who believed Dreyfus to be guilty adopted as their cry *"Vive l'armée!"* and tended to ally themselves with the conservative-monarchist-clerical-militaristic right. On the other hand, the pro-Dreyfus group used as their cry *"Vive la république!"* and attracted the parties of the left, the anticlericals, and certain dedicated republicans—prominent among whom was Georges Clemenceau.

Nor was the falsification and suppression of evidence exclusively the province of the Army. Many persons now knew that Dreyfus was innocent, but feared to buck the combined influence of the Army and the Church, together with the flood of aroused nationalism which they had whistled up. It was a sickness which infected every level of French society—even reaching as high as Félix Faure, the President of the Republic, who knew that Dreyfus was innocent and who possessed the authority to pardon him.

But on the evening of February 16, 1899, Faure carried his knowledge to his grave. In the afternoon he had received visits from the Archbishop of Paris, an anti-Dreyfusard, and the Prince of Monaco, who was generally regarded as pro-Dreyfus. Hard on the heels of these illustrious personalities came beautiful young Madame Steinheil, the nymphomaniac wife of a noted French portrait painter. Madame Steinheil and the fifty-nine-year-old Faure retired to a boudoir adjoining the presidential offices. An hour later, attendants in an anteroom heard the lady screaming. The locked door was broken down, to reveal Madame Steinheil, totally nude, writhing on the floor alongside a bed on which the President of the Republic lay in a "significant state of undress" and dying of a heart attack. In one clenched fist he clutched Madame Steinheil's hair.[1] With the greatest of difficulty, Madame Steinheil was disentangled, dressed and discreetly hurried from the scene, following which a doctor and Madame Faure were summoned. But it was all too late. Félix Faure died that night. The anti-Dreyfus press claimed that he had died from a poisoned cigarette given him by the Prince of Monaco.

Ultimately, in September of 1899, the Army gave up. It had become glaringly obvious that Dreyfus was innocent, and the pressure of aroused opinion was too strong to deny. Dreyfus accepted a "pardon" for the crime he never committed.

But the case was not ended there. The Dreyfus Affair had lasted for five years during which the Army had been continuously in the spotlight—and many things had been revealed about the Army which the nation now began to feel were profoundly disturbing. Most obvious, of course, was the fact that there was apparently a substantial number of Army officers who were quite capable of lying and falsification of evidence if "the honor of the Army" seemed to demand it. But an even more disturbing situation had been revealed.

To begin with, the French Army of the turn of the century was huge by the standards of the time. It consisted of more than a half-million men under arms at all times. Added to these were the reserves, the conscripts who had served their obligatory three years of active duty and were now civilians again. But the disquiet was not caused by the enlisted men—they passed into the Army and then out again. Instead, the Dreyfus Affair had focused attention on the officers of this huge Army, who, it was apparent, were not truly representative of republican France.

In a way, this was inevitable. For the sons of families with aristocratic pretensions or confirmed royalist sympathies, the Army offered virtually the only possible career. They could not go into the government; the Republic would not have them, nor could they bring themselves to serve it. They could not go into trade; this was the province of the despised bourgeois. So, all other avenues closed, they joined the Army. And the Dreyfus case had shown that the French Army was dominated largely by officers of royalist leanings who were actually in opposition to the republican government they were supposed to serve. The center of this royalist influence was a clique of officers known as the "Postards" because they had attended a Jesuit preparatory school on the Rue des Postes in Paris; after being graduated from this school the Postards generally trained at the French Army's engineering and artillery school, the École Polytechnique, and from there they had little difficulty in obtaining preferment in promotions, appointments to the General Staff and assignments to the choicer duty spots.[2]

In this manner, there had built up within the Army a hitherto unsuspected state within a state over which the Church had attained great power. The wise officer, even if his personal religious proclivities were none too ardent, took care to send his children to Catholic parochial schools and to be seen at Mass on Sunday. This atmosphere of "fashionable Catholicism" and the concentration of conservative and royalist inclinations which accompanied it were so marked that it was rumored on good authority that an influential Jesuit priest, Father du Lac, kept the Army list on his desk and that all promotions had to be cleared with him.[3]

As all this was revealed, the French nation rose up in wrath. From the pages of his newspaper, Georges Clemenceau attacked the Army leadership:

France is now a country with no security for either the liberty, the life or the honor of her citizens. A horde has ganged up on us, a praetorian guard, a host of monks who have destroyed right, justice and law and have savagely scorched all that forty centuries of human effort has accomplished. . . . Generals with nought but surrenders to their names, Jesuits inspired by the spirit of torture, left nothing standing of what France had been but a realm of stupidity and crime. They denounced us as *sans patrie*. They speak more truly than they realize, for they have taken away our homeland. Now let us face each other squarely and see whether we have the guts to reconquer it.[4]

And on this note the republicans set out to bring the Army to heel. Into the office of Minister of War they thrust General André, an officer of proven republican sympathies. The shoe was now on the other foot, and André shrank from nothing. Into his service he recruited the Masons to act as his own source of information concerning the religious preferences and political philosophies of the Army's officers. A secret network of republican officers was established to spy on their brother officers, and their reports—known as *fiches*—were sent directly to the Grand Orient, the grand lodge of Freemasonry in France. Ultimately, in 1905, this despicable system was revealed and it was widely condemned by a horrified public which realized that the repression had gone too far.

But all this scandal and counterscandal had several significant results. As the power of the right diminished, the strength of the Socialists and the other left-wing parties grew substantially. And although antimilitarism had always been one of the theses of the left, it now became a major Socialist dogma. To the nation the left pointed out that the "honor of the Army" was a fatuous lie, that the leaders of the Army were warmongers and proven antirepublicans; anyhow, they said, a large standing army was unnecessary in this age when the brotherhood of man was advancing to the point where a general war would not be supported by the working classes.

Undeniably these preachings had some effect. The Army no longer enjoyed the almost sacred status which it had once occupied in the minds of Frenchmen. It became harder to pass an adequate military budget through Parliament. The period of active service for conscripts was cut from three to two years, and the already skimpy training periods of the reserves were cut further.

Then, too, the Army itself had been thoroughly demoralized by the Dreyfus Affair and the subsequent republican program of anti-Catholicism. In the years between 1900 and 1911 the number of applicants for St.-Cyr, France's equivalent of West Point or Sandhurst, dropped from 1,895 to 871, and the re-enlistment figures for non-commissioned officers fell from 72,000 to 41,000.[5]

And a final corollary to these events was the attitude of the French nation itself toward war. Even to those who were not influenced in any way by the antimilitarism of the left, the prospect of a war of revenge with Germany was losing its attraction. The burning desire to reconquer the lost provinces of Alsace and Lorraine was on the wane, and less and less did it seem that the Army had a valid claim to the unswerving loyalty of the nation. The French Army career officers and enlisted men now found that they had become an estranged minority, their efficiency hampered by political interference and divorced from the sympathy and trust of both their government and a substantial segment of the French population.

So on these foundations of clay—economic stagnation, political confusion, a decreasing military-age population and loss of popular confidence—the French Army had to prepare itself for the conflict with Germany which was to come. It is amazing it did so well.

But now, as the prestige of the Army had sunk to its nadir, there emerged onto the scene a group of young officers who planned its revitalization. They began it with a new theory, which became known as the "School of the Attack," and it all started because of the huge forts which lined the Franco-German frontier.

It would probably be correct to state that at this period France possessed the finest fortress system in the world. In the years following the Franco-Prussian War, a large share of the nation's military budget had been used to create a series of giant concrete fortress complexes masked by rings of satellite outworks. These fortress complexes had been constructed by the military engineering genius General Séré de Rivière and were considered to be unparalleled examples of the military engineer's art.

The fortress system was based on the fortified cities of Épinal, Toul, Belfort and Verdun, along the Franco-German border. Originally the fortresses had been designed to provide an impenetrable barrier to a German attack, except for *trouées,* or slots between the fortresses. For years the French plan had been to allow the Germans to invade these slots in the defenses and then shatter the invaders by a carefully prepared attack on the German flank. This plan, which was essentially a defensive one, was the official French doctrine until, shortly after the turn of the century, the French General Staff fell under the influence of the group of young officers who were no longer content with the acceptance of such a passive doctrine.

The French General Staff had originally been created, as had general staffs throughout the world, as a response to the tremendously successful example set by the German General Staff in the Franco-Prussian War. Although the functions of the French and German general staffs were approximately the same, the French Army had never quite achieved the attitude of dedicated professionalism which was such a feature of the German General Staff.

But beginning in about 1905, the French General Staff underwent a tremendous change as it came to be staffed by young officers whose military attainments were of a considerably higher order. These officers were prepared to study the theory and practice of war on a much more intensive basis than their predecessors. Seeking to learn the real reasons for the rankling defeat of 1870, they discovered that the German General Staff had formulated its basic strategy by intensive study of the Napoleonic Wars. Accordingly, the French General Staff themselves began to restudy Napoleon's campaigns. They used the texts of Clausewitz and Jomini and, from them, they discovered what seemed to be the fundamental secret of success in war—the offensive! The French interpretation of the Clausewitzian analysis of Napoleon's victories was that if there was one common denominator of the Emperor's brilliant achievements, it was the emphasis which he had placed upon the importance of the attack! And the more they read, the more these youthful officers seemed to find justification for the theory that battles were won by the army which could first ram a mass of fired-up troops against its enemy. "The moral is to the physical as three to one," Napoleon had said, and history seemed to prove that the special character of the French soldier was invincibility in attack, vulnerability in defense.

Buttressing this theory were the impressive and widely-read writings of Colonel Charles Ardant du Picq, a French officer who had been killed in the Franco-Prussian War. Ardant du Picq had made a careful study of the experiences of French soldiers in the Crimean

War and again in the brief Italian campaign of 1859. He tracked
down officers who had taken part in various battles and questioned
them closely as to precisely what had happened at the moment when
they made contact with the enemy. And after Ardant du Picq's death
in 1870, the astonishing results of his investigations were published
in a slender volume (*Études sur le Combat*) which had a tremendous
impact upon French military thinking. He had discovered that there
was virtually no such thing as face-to-face combat—instead, at the
instant when a well-led wave of attackers collided with defending
troops, the defenders nearly always broke and ran. In almost no case
could Ardant du Picq find a verifiable instance of true hand-to-hand
fighting. Moreover, his findings seemed proven by the fact that the
vast majority of bayonet wounds suffered by troops in battle had
been in the soldier's *back*. It was obvious to Ardant du Picq (and also
to his readers) that to win battles it was only necessary to develop
the spirit of the troops to the point where they would allow themselves to be led in a furious and utterly determined charge—"No
enemy awaits you if you are determined, and never, never, *never* are
there two equal determinations. . . . No one stands his ground before a bayonet charge." [6]

Foch, Fayolle, Maistre, Maudhuy, and especially Loiseau de Grandmaison, most of them youthful General Staff colonels at the time,
propounded the doctrine of the offensive to both their superiors and
to their students at the War College. Few could be found to withstand the vehemence and brilliance of these young officers' arguments. This was a theory which could retrieve France from impending defeat at the hands of the far larger and better-equipped German
Army. The problem was solved! Attack with dash and boldness; attack with bands playing to stimulate the patriotism of the troops;
attack with what was thought to be the traditional French weapon,
the bayonet, and France would be invincible once again!

There were only a few dissenters. An obscure Major Henri Philippe Pétain, for example, was instructing at the War College and
arguing that infantry could not by itself win ground in modern war.
"In modern warfare firepower will be the predominant factor," he
insisted. For his views, Pétain was snubbed by the youthful en-
thusiasts and promptly dispatched to service in the field with, it is
said, the notation in his dossier, "Not to be allowed to go above the
rank of brigadier general." [7]

Ultimately, the doctrine of *offensive à outrance*, attack at any cost, prevailed, and in the French Army "Regulations for the Conduct of Large Units" of 1912 the theory became dogma: "The teachings of the past have borne their fruit. The French Army, reviving its old traditions, no longer admits for the conduct of operations any other law than that of the offensive." [8]

Of course, the acceptance of the doctrine of the attack involved certain other corollary changes in French strategy and tactics. First, the French fortresses automatically became outdated and virtually useless, since it was accepted that a fort was useful only on the defensive. This concept came to be carried to such an extreme that foreign observers at French Army maneuvers were invariably shocked at the almost complete absence of the construction of field fortifications and earthworks. Secondly, the importance of accurately determining the enemy's plan of attack was downgraded, because, as Colonel Loiseau de Grandmaison pointed out, "For the attack only two things are necessary: to know where the enemy is and to decide what to do. What the enemy intends to do is of no importance." [9] This was a fortunate theory, since, as a result of the Dreyfus fiasco, the French government had cut the budget for the General Staff's Second Bureau to the point where it was largely ineffective as an intelligence agency.

French infantry tactics were also revised to suit the fundamental strategy. Basically, the Army tactics were to engage the enemy at all points possible in order to compel him to develop his forces and to reveal weaknesses. Then the skirmish line was to be built up by feeding in the reserves, and finally the field artillery would set the stage for the attack by a short, sharp bombardment known as the *rafale*. Following this, every infantryman would simply dash forward. Now, since it had been established as dogma that the particular genius of the French soldier lay in infantry attack, and since the French Army rifle of the time was not clip-fed and therefore was difficult to load during an attack, the logical corollary of the thesis of the attack was that it was most properly carried out with the bayonet. This theory also seemed to meet with the approbation of the deified Napoleon, for it was almost an article of faith that most Napoleonic victories had been won with the bayonet. "The French soldier can do anything with a bayonet except sit on it," it was said. The idea of the bayonet attack had still another argument to substantiate it in the eyes of its youthful General Staff proponents. The standard French infantry arm was the Lebel rifle, a bolt-action rifle which had been introduced by Boulanger in 1886. The Lebel was exceptionally long, more than five feet with bayonet fixed, and it came to assume more the character of a lance than a rifle. It seemed that it was the ideal weapon to capitalize on the verve, *élan* and *esprit* which were theoretically the genius of the French soldier.

Finally, the policy of the attack appeared to make certain types of new weapons, for which funds could not be obtained anyway, almost unnecessary. The clumsy new machine guns could not take a significant part in an offensive, and their importance was downgraded. And because heavy artillery could not be moved forward quickly enough to support a fast surging attack, little attention was paid to the development of big guns. Major Pétain notwithstanding, it became the official doctrine that "the artillery does not prepare attacks; it simply supports them." [10] And, for this support, the French Army had its 75-mm. cannon—truthfully the best and most mobile light-artillery piece in the world.

The new General Staff scheme for wartime operations was given final approval in early 1914. Known as "Plan XVII," since it was the seventeenth French plan adopted since 1870, it assumed that the German advance would come either through Lorraine or else possibly through the Ardennes Forest in the extreme south of Belgium. But any German advance was considered to be of only transitory importance. The German attack would be hit in its flank while the mass of the French Army would pour into the stolen province of Lorraine and, from there, into the Saar Basin.

In a way, Plan XVII was not a plan at all. It was simply a vague statement of intent which allowed considerable latitude in its execution. Only in one respect were its executants left in no doubt—at all times and in all circumstances the governing tactical theory would be to attack. If in question as to the enemy's whereabouts, his intentions or his strength—*attack!* If outnumbered, outgunned, or outmaneuvered—*attack!* If taken in flank or rear—*attack!*

In this manner, trading on the peculiar brand of idealistic logic which is the bane and the genius of its nation, the School of the Attack rationalized the Army's weaknesses into strengths and its liabilities into assets. And, confident that it had rediscovered a secret of war which would make it invincible once again, the French Army failed to realize that it was grossly overemphasizing the importance of the offensive, to the point where it was conditioned to do nothing else.

Contrast France's politico-economic position and the strength of its Army against Germany. In the years between 1870 and 1914, Germany had taken gigantic strides in almost every field necessary to make her the pre-eminent continental European power. Economically, Germany leaped from an impoverished nation to the possessor of the largest heavy industry complex in Europe. Politically, Germany was strongly united behind its Kaiser, and it flattered Germans to believe their leaders when they spoke of Germany's predestination to supersede Great Britain as the world's leading power.

Morally, the German nation was superbly prepared for war. A generation of military writers, politicians and economic theorists had conditioned Germany to expect that her destiny was pre-eminent world power and that it was inevitable (*Realpolitik*) that she would have to fight France and Great Britain to achieve it. Accordingly, the German nation was conditioned to expect war and even to welcome it enthusiastically as the prelude to world hegemony.

But it was in her Army that Germany had her trump card. For all its reputation for ruthless discipline, the German people regarded their Army as the core of their national pride and as the instrument for the fulfillment of collective ambitions.

There was no ambivalence in the relationship of the German people and its Army. Although military service was not exactly popular, it was widely accepted as a duty to the fatherland, and the Army was regarded as a common denominator among the German people in which their youth learned the habits of work, discipline and patriotism which were considered essential to the development of the German nation. Also, there was little conflict between the German government and its Army, since the Kaiser himself was the Supreme Warlord; and he and his sons regarded themselves as soldiers, among whose primary duties were to inspire the German nation with a sense of its military destiny and to provide funds for the increase and development of the Army. Finally, it is almost impossible to imagine the prestige which the military profession possessed in pre-World War I Germany. Although the large size of the Army had watered down the once dominant percentage of Junker aristocratic

officers to about one third of the officer corps, there was a definite
German officer caste which drew its tone from the still-substantial
number of the nobility who served in it. To the German nation,
"the military man seemed to be a consecrated spirit—the lieutenant
moved through the world as a young god and the civilian reserve
lieutenant as a demigod." [11]

But, prestige aside, the German Army entered World War I with
three advantages which made it superior to its French opponent.
First, its immediate strength on mobilization was eighty-seven divisions, as opposed to its enemy's sixty-two. And the German reserve
divisions had achieved such a high standard of training and discipline
that they were capable of being used in the opening German attack
in precisely the same manner as regular Army troops! Secondly, in
its Great General Staff, and, indeed, its entire officer corps, the German Army possessed a body of dedicated professionals whose thor-
oughness and meticulous planning had achieved a standard of military efficiency undreamed of by any other nation. They had evolved
basic infantry tactics which differed from the French in that they
laid great stress on developing the greatest possible firepower from
rifles, machine guns and artillery. And instead of regarding the infantry charge as the culmination of the attack, the Germans viewed
it as simply "presenting for payment the check drawn by firepower." [12] Finally, the German Army had a scheme for attacking
France against which the French Plan XVII would prove valueless.

Volumes have been written about the German Schlieffen Plan,
but, quite simply, it called for a gigantic German thrust through
Belgium, well north of the French fortifications. The French Army,
not believing that the Germans could possibly use their reserve divisions in line with field divisions of the regular Army, had not seriously considered the possibility of such a wide German sweep, since
it would require more troops than the French believed the Germans
could make available. But the principal feature of the German plan,
which had been devised by Count von Schlieffen during his tenure as
Chief of the General Staff, was that virtually *all* of Germany's fighting power was to be devoted to this tremendously strong wheeling
movement. Since Germany's mobilization for war was the fastest
in Europe and since Russia's was the slowest, only a light screen of
troops was to be left to delay the expected Russian advance into East
Prussia. France would be conquered before the Russians were fully

deployed, and then Germany would rush its troops to the east and smash the Czarist armies.

Schlieffen was cold, precise, unbending—a man who fits almost too perfectly into the common conception of the German General Staff officer. Every Christmas Eve he summoned one of his generals and presented him with a military problem, the detailed answer for which had to be returned on Christmas Day. But whatever his personal failings may have been, he was a military genius who, around 1892, had conceived the German master plan for crushing the French Army.

The Schlieffen Plan is generally compared to a revolving door swinging with immense weight through Belgium and across northeastern France to capture Paris, and then catching the French Army from the rear and smashing it to bits against the Swiss frontier. It was a masterly conception. Schlieffen required that every senior officer know it completely and in the utmost detail. In the planning and meticulous development of this plan, the German General Staff invested fifteen years of labor. When Schlieffen died, tradition says that his last thoughts were of his brain child; and from his deathbed his final words were, "See that you make the right wing strong." [13]

By the early summer of 1914, the lines were drawn for a European war. On one side, the Central Powers, would be Germany, Austria-Hungary and Turkey. Opposing them would be the Entente, Russia, France and Great Britain, the last prepared to contribute its tiny expeditionary army of a handful of crack divisions to land in France and co-operate with the French by defending their left flank.

On the morning of June 28, 1914, the heir apparent to the Austro-Hungarian thrones, Archduke Francis Ferdinand, and his consort, the Duchess of Hohenberg, were visiting the city of Sarajevo in Bosnia, a disputed province of the Habsburg empire. As they were riding in state through the city, in an open car, their motorcade made a wrong turn and stopped for an instant. Unluckily, this stop was directly in front of nineteen-year-old Gavrilo Princip, a young Serb, part of a gang of twenty-two terrorists who had come to Sarajevo for the precise purpose of killing Francis Ferdinand. Princip stepped from the watching crowd, pulled a Browning 9-mm. automatic pistol from his coat and fired just two shots. They were enough. Both Francis Ferdinand and his pregnant wife died almost instantly.

In the complexities of European interlocking alliances, nothing more was needed. A month later the armies of Europe were mobilized and World War I began.

3

FRANCE MOBILIZES

IT WAS generally conceded that on the date when the first European army mobilized, general hostilities would have begun. The declarations of war would follow as a matter of course. For every European army in that summer of 1914, it was a life-or-death matter to mobilize at the instant that the enemy did.

There was good reason for this emphasis on immediate mobilization. The peacetime European armies, no matter how big they might be, were actually only understrength shells, useless as fighting forces. But this was by design. The peacetime armies had been planned as skeletons which, at the time of mobilization, would be fleshed out by the huge numbers of reservists which the conscription systems had produced. The German Army, for example, had a peacetime strength of about 880,000 men; but when mobilized (and this took only sixteen days) the German Army suddenly became a mighty force of almost four and a half million soldiers. Obviously, if the French Army did not mobilize when, and as quickly as, the Germans did, France would be overwhelmed by the German torrent.

This, then, was the reason why one of the most crucial functions of the Second Bureau of the French General Staff was to report the instant that the German Army began to mobilize. And, correspondingly, for years one of the most important assignments of the Third Bureau, the Operations Section of the French General Staff, was the constant refining of the mobilization plan to make it more effective and to speed it up to match or surpass the German Army's.

But if rapid mobilization was crucial for all European armies of

the day, it was an unhappy corollary that, for France and Germany
in particular, mobilization meant inevitable war. Again, there was a
good reason for this—both the French and German armies planned
to carry the war onto their opponent's soil. The mobilization sched-
ules dovetailed precisely into the Schlieffen Plan or Plan XVII, both
of which prescribed an advance into enemy territory. These mobili-
zations were fantastically detailed—the result of literally generations of meticulous staff work. Neither of the general staffs could
conceive of these plans being varied in any way without the whole
thing flying apart and reducing their army to a shambles. Take the
case of the German Army. For a moment it looked as if war between France and Germany might be avoided, and the German Emperor summoned General Helmuth von Moltke, the Chief of the
General Staff, to announce innocently, "Now we'll simply march
our whole Army against Russia." Moltke was thunderstruck. To revise the German mobilization scheme and junk the Schlieffen Plan
would take years of staff work. He somehow stammered out his
protests to the All-Highest and, in return, received the withering reproach, "Your uncle [Moltke "The Elder" had been the brilliant
Chief of the General Staff during the Franco-Prussian War] would
have given me a different answer." Finally he succeeded in convincing the Kaiser that it simply could not be done. But such was the
shock of the Kaiser's proposal that later in the day the horrible experience caused Moltke to burst into tears and later he admitted,
"Something within me broke and I was never the same thereafter." [1]

Thus, in the summer of 1914, following the assassination of Francis Ferdinand and the ultimatum which Austria sent Serbia, all Europe found itself the prisoner of its treaty obligations and its mobilization plans. The statesmen and diplomatists who had craftily
conceived the tangle of interlocking alliances now found that these
treaties left them no latitude, no freedom of movement whatsoever.
And France, whose people probably wanted war less than any other
European country, watched the unfolding events with horror. If
either Austria or Serbia mobilized, then, by both moral obligation
and treaty commitment, Russia and Germany would have to mobilize. And if Germany mobilized, then France must mobilize—and to
prevent being overwhelmed, France must mobilize as soon as it even
appeared as if Germany was mobilizing.

After a lapse of almost fifty years, the events of that far-off summer would seem almost ludicrous if they had not been so deadly in their result. The nations of Europe were like a file of marching prisoners chained together by their ankles. And as the leader of the file took a step forward, so each of those behind him had to shuffle forward—prisoners of national pride and shackled together by treaty obligation. And willingly or unwillingly, they reached their ultimate destination—war.

For France the lock-step shuffle toward mobilization and ultimate war began on the morning of July 26 when the Second Bureau reported that German troops had been issued their gray field uniforms, a step interpreted to mean impending operations away from their barracks. But even the hint of menace which this implied had to be taken seriously and a reflex move made, and so the French Minister of War halted all further Army furloughs and suspended routine troop movements. At 4 P.M. it was reported that German officers were being recalled from leave; by 4:30 the French Army had issued similar orders. In the evening the Second Bureau reported that the German railroad system had been alerted to prepare for extensive troop movements; instantly the French General Staff sent out an identical notice.[2]

On July 27 the situation had deteriorated even further. The Second Bureau informed the Minister of War that some classes of German reservists were being alerted for call-up to the colors. It was an erroneous report, but events could not await verification in a situation like this. The French Minister of War ordered the Resident General in Morocco to rush back to France most of the troops stationed there.[3] And so it went.

By August 1, 1914, diplomatic efforts to halt the slide into war had failed completely. Every nation found itself to be completely at the mercy of both her own mobilization plan and those of her future antagonists. By this time move and countermove were following so rapidly that both Germany and France ordered mobilization within minutes of each other. Declarations of war would follow a few days later.

The mobilization of the French Army was announced at 5:15 in the afternoon. A clerk raced out of the central post office in Paris and on the notice board hung on the building wall scrawled in chalk: "Ministry of War. Order of Mobilization. Extremely urgent! First day of mobilization is Sunday, August 2." [4] Throughout France mil-

lions of long-prepared mobilization notices were put into the mail
and, almost instantaneously, the already printed posters calling up
"*les armées des terre et mer*" were slapped up on the boardings.

Now it could all start. Now the long-prepared and meticulously
detailed mobilization could begin to function. The young reservists
and the older territorials would leave farms, factories and offices to
join their regiments. They would put on the shabby old uniforms,
shoulder the unfamiliar rifles and, in one of the 4,278 railroad trains
earmarked for troop transport, be carted off to the assembly points.

As a mighty river is the product of a thousand streams, the French
Army, brought to wartime strength by the mobilization, flowed toward its assembly areas. At the various corps headquarters, the Army
was speedily prepared for service in the field—the handful of men
who formed a section; the four sections which formed a company;
and the four companies which formed a battalion. Three battalions
formed an infantry regiment and two regiments made a brigade. An
infantry division consisted of two infantry brigades together with a
cavalry squadron, field artillery groups, engineers and headquarters
troops. Then two divisions were put together to form an army corps
which totaled 44,000 men. And, finally, the army corps were joined
together to form vast groups called armies. The French had five of
these.

In this manner the French Army would mobilize, concentrate and
commence the audacious attack which was Plan XVII. If all went
as scheduled, the signal for the attack would be given, the bands
would play and the ardent infantry would dash forward shouting
"*Vive la France!*" and "*A la baïonnette!*" and fling itself upon a German foe stunned by the *élan* of their enemy. Through the gaps torn
by the vicious bayonet attacks of the infantry, the cavalry would
charge to saber or lance down the fleeing Hun. Such, anyhow, was
the plan.

For the French Army, the first few days of mobilization posed no
problems which had not been clearly foreseen and for which decisions had not been made some time before. But for the French government the approach of mobilization brought forth a number of
questions which demanded agonizing answers. For example, what to
do about Carnet B?

Carnet B, or B List, had been started some years before upon the

emergence of the antimilitarist activities of the far left. It was maintained by the Sûreté Générale, the secret police, who listed in Carnet
B a group of Socialists, anarchists and syndicalists considered "dangerous from a social point of view." [5] By 1914 Carnet B contained
2,501 names and was bound in a blue notebook locked in a safe at the
Fourth Bureau of the Sûreté Générale.

Although Carnet B listed the names of a scattering of known foreign spies, the majority were native Frenchmen of considerable political prominence whose actions and utterances clearly indicated
that, for a variety of reasons, they would do everything they could
to obstruct, if not sabotage, the war effort. (Among them was a
young Socialist politician named Pierre Laval.) Indeed, the reports
of police spies were unanimous in agreeing that there was a plan to
block mobilization by blowing up bridges, inciting the populace to
disorder and agitating disobedience within the Army. However, it
had been accepted as a matter of course by the government that this
plan (if, in truth, it existed) would be ruptured at its source by the
Minister of the Interior, who would order the arrest of those listed
on Carnet B.

But for thirty-eight-year-old Louis Malvy the question was not
so simple as that. Malvy was a rising young Radical politician who
happened, at the moment, to occupy the position of Minister of the
Interior in the government of the day—and to be Minister of the Interior in the Third Republic was to hold a portfolio of no mean con-
sequence. The Minister of the Interior held a virtual veto over any
form of local government. Here is how the system worked: The
lowest unit of local government was the municipality, which elected
a municipal council and a mayor. These worthies could pass laws
and ordinances pertaining to local matters, but on all matters of real
importance their decisions were subject to veto by a representative
of the national government who was known as the prefect. The next
highest unit of local government was the department, which was
nominally governed by a general council elected by all the citizens
of the department. Again, this body had the power to pass laws and
ordinances affecting the department, but it was forbidden to consider anything not placed on its agenda by the prefect; even when
the law was passed it had to meet with the approval of the prefect,
since the prefect controlled all the police and was therefore the enforcement arm for the decisions of the departmental general coun-

cil. Therefore, in essence, there was almost no local government worthy of the name in France—all real power was held by the man who appointed the prefects.[6] And this man was the Minister of the Interior.

But aside from controlling local government in France, the office of the Minister of the Interior had long since come to assume other powers. Through the intelligent use of various discretionary funds allotted to him, the Minister of the Interior could support his government's policies through "subventions" to sympathetic newspapers. In addition, after the Dreyfus Affair the French government had virtually emasculated the counterintelligence section of the Army's Second Bureau and transferred the primary responsibility for counterespionage into the hands of the Sûreté Générale—which was headed, of course, by the Minister of the Interior.

Finally, since French politicians of the time were insatiably curious about one another, the Minister of the Interior, who controlled both the ordinary police and the Sûreté Générale, had only to ask and all types of interesting information could be learned about his ministry's enemies and, if occasion warranted, even its friends. The result was that unless a Minister of the Interior was exceptionally stupid, he had the opportunity to become very well informed. Louis Malvy was most certainly not stupid, but when it came to Carnet B he was very much perplexed. The persons on Carnet B undoubtedly constituted a security risk if not immediately arrested. It was Malvy's responsibility to order their arrest, and as war drew closer it was expected by Premier Viviani and all the other members of the Cabinet that Malvy would do this as a matter of course. But, curiously, Malvy had reasons of his own for *not* wanting to order the arrests. Accordingly, he searched for a plausible-sounding idea which he could present to the Cabinet and which would persuade them to authorize Malvy not to make the arrests.

He soon struck on an idea, which he promptly presented to the Cabinet. Some of those listed on Carnet B, Malvy claimed, were leaders of the Syndicalist party, a militant, far-left splinter party which had the closest possible ties with the working classes. And the enthusiasm of the workers for the war, as Malvy pointed out, was strongly in doubt. If their leaders were arrested, it was conceivable that the workers might call the dreaded general strike which antimilitarists had long threatened in the event of war. And, obviously, if the workers resisted mobilization it would mean catastrophe for France. So Malvy advised the Cabinet that he wished to delay the arrest of those listed on Carnet B until he had determined what the attitude of the workers would be. His ministerial associates, quite naturally assuming that Carnet B contained a much larger number of syndicalist leaders than it did, and impressed by the logic of Malvy's arguments, gave him the authorization he desired.[7]

But this stay of arrest was just an interim measure. Unless Malvy could come up with some prominent support to justify his reluctance to act, the Cabinet would soon insist that he make the arrests as originally scheduled. Accordingly, Malvy journeyed across Paris to call upon Georges Clemenceau.

Since his defeat in the election following the Panama scandals, Georges Clemenceau had experienced a series of violent ups and downs, although he was a prominent journalist who had played a major role in the Dreyfus defense. Then, in 1902, the Tiger stood for election to the Senate, and won. Four years later, to general astonishment, he broke his lifetime rule of never being willing to form a government unless he was in a position to achieve freedom of action. And Clemenceau formed a Ministry which lasted for three years, an incredibly long period for a Third Republic government. But, predictably, Clemenceau's Ministry was a stormy one. He had to contend not only with the right but with the vastly increased power of the proletarian parties of the extreme left. Both hated him—the right because Clemenceau was a republican and a vicious anticlerical, the left because it regarded Clemenceau as a militarist and a Germanophobe, and, moreover, because he had not hesitated to use troops to break labor strikes. By 1910 the Tiger, frustrated and infuriated by his host of enemies, had quit office in a rage and gone back to the Senate and his newspaper.

Everyone agreed that the aging Tiger was finished as a political force. But he still deserved the respect due to a former Premier, and certainly neither his patriotism nor his hatred for France's enemies was open to question. This was the reason that Louis Malvy sought him out. Malvy knew that if he could persuade Clemenceau to sanction leaving the Carnet B list at liberty it would be a potent argument in getting the Cabinet to agree. The youthful Minister expounded to Clemenceau the same argument with which he had impressed the Cabinet. But the Tiger was not a bit concerned about the

syndicalists or their followers. He earnestly advised Malvy to jail
them all.

This was disappointing to Malvy, but it did not defeat him in his
plan. He summoned to his office the Prefect of Paris, whose business
it was to know the political temper of the metropolitan population.
Again Malvy posed the question and again he got the same recommendation—"Jail them."

But from another expert quarter came more welcome advice. The
director of the Sûreté Générale, M. Richard, advised that in his
educated opinion France had little to fear from the pacifist efforts of
those listed on Carnet B. As for the attitude of the workers, Richard
counseled, "When the regimental band passes, they will follow." [8]
The Minister lost no time in advising the Cabinet of Richard's opinion.

Malvy still had one other person to consult. He summoned to his
office a young Paris newspaper editor who went by the name of
Miguel Almereyda. How and why M. Malvy, the Minister of the Interior and the head of French law enforcement, came to know Almereyda is a strange story.

Almereyda, whose original name had been Eugène Bonaventure
Jean-Baptiste Vigo, was an odd character indeed. Born thirty-one
years before, an illegitimate child, in the city of Béziers, he had
passed a miserable, impoverished childhood climaxed by his arrest for
theft from an employer at the age of sixteen, whereupon he had been
tried and sentenced to two months in jail. For most youths, these
two months would have been so much time wasted. Not so with
Vigo, who was more fluent and more imaginative than other boys his
age. He loathed the society which had sent him, a boy abandoned by
both his parents, to prison for stealing a pittance, and he learned
quickly, with the result that when he emerged from jail he was a
confirmed member of the most extreme left. His state of mind and
his rage against society can best be comprehended by the fact that
the new name he chose for himself, Almereyda, is an anagram for
'y a la merde—"Everything is shitty." [9]

His political views are hard to define with precision. He is generally described as a Syndicalist, albeit a cynical one. Almereyda was a
man for sale, drifting in the confused politics of the left. He would
do anything for a price. Thus he was rarely without funds. From
somewhere he acquired a certain literary ability, which he placed at

the disposal of various left-wing journals. Nor did he confine his career to this; Almereyda was extremely active politically, especially in the violent left-wing campaign against "militarism." As a result, his youth was punctuated with prison sentences. In 1901 he was sentenced to a year in jail for illegal possession of explosives; in 1905, to three years for inciting troops to mutiny; in 1907, to six weeks for rebelling and carrying prohibited weapons; in 1908, to one year for insulting the Army and inciting troops to mutiny.[10]

But despite these prison terms, or perhaps because of them, by 1914 Almereyda had become a character of note among certain Parisian elements. He liked to think of himself as a poet, and physically he looked the part—tall, slender, negligently dressed, and with long curling hair drooping down the side of his head. But there was nothing of the poet in his manner; he was part thug, part blackmailer, part revolutionary, part newspaper editor. And within the criminal fringe of the far left he had acquired considerable influence. There were a variety of reasons for this. One was that he was an authentic "mystery man" who was reputed to have political connections at the highest levels; another was that he controlled a gang of militant leftists known as the Young Republican Guard. Given only a few hours' notice, Almereyda had proved to be able to throw into the streets a disciplined shock force of four thousand hard-core leftists ready to brawl with the police or with rightist demonstrators. And within certain elements of the left, Almereyda's power was such that he was regarded as the "chief of the revolutionary police." [11]

The influence wielded by this young man was enhanced by his founding, in November of 1913, a weekly newspaper, *Le Bonnet rouge*, which had become one of the more important voices of the militant left. Moreover, Miguel Almereyda was one of those named on Carnet B for immediate arrest upon the outbreak of war—and this was the reason that Louis Malvy wanted to talk to him. The Minister of the Interior of France was soliciting Almereyda's services as a sort of ambassador to the left, as a go-between who was in a position to pledge that if they were not arrested, those listed on Carnet B, including Almereyda himself, would not cause trouble. Moreover, Malvy offered Almereyda a "subvention"—a subsidy for the *Bonnet rouge* to be paid out of the secret funds of the Ministry of the Interior. Not surprisingly, Almereyda agreed to the bargain.

Malvy's case was now complete. On the afternoon of July 31, the day before mobilization was ordered, he advised the Cabinet that the majority of the names on Carnet B were syndicalists and that he was in favor of leaving them at liberty. To support this course of action, Malvy quoted M. Richard of the Sûreté Générale as having recommended against their arrest. The Cabinet thereupon deferred to the wishes of the Minister of the Interior and permitted Malvy not to arrest "the militant syndicalists." [12]

Malvy now had the authorization he desired. He had been allowed not to arrest the "militant syndicalists," and he stretched the issue a bit and gave orders not to arrest *anyone* on Carnet B, with the exception of the known foreign spies. On the evening of August 1, the day mobilization was announced, he sent the following telegram to his prefects throughout France: "Having every reason to think that all persons inscribed in Carnet B for political reasons may be trusted, desire you arrest no one belonging to these categories. Confine yourself to arresting foreigners inscribed as spying." [13] Almereyda's *Bonnet rouge* broke the news to the left wing the next day. "The Government Will Not Make Use of Carnet B" was the headline.

Years later, in his own defense, Malvy pointed out that events had justified his allowing the Carnet B listees to remain at liberty—that it had never been established that any of them had attempted to sabotage the mobilization. And this is true. But what Malvy did not point out and what is equally true is that his refusal to jail those on Carnet B had set a precedent which was nearly fatal to France. For, from 1914 until well into 1917, it was understood and accepted by the French security police that they could take no action against prominent political figures (and their friends) who agitated against the war. Those listed on Carnet B remained like a latent malignancy deep within the vitals of France. As long as the nation was healthy and robust, the malignancy could cause no trouble. But as soon as her resistance was lowered, as soon as she had lost her vitality on the battlefields of the Somme, Verdun and the Chemin des Dames, then the disease would creep forth, spread and magnify until it brought France almost to her deathbed.

It is, of course, inconceivable that Louis Malvy did not realize that, in not arresting these pacifist and pro-German political figures, he was loosing upon France a Pandora's box of trouble. Malvy was too intelligent a man for that. And it is also inconceivable that, as was later charged, Malvy himself was a spy in the pay of Germany —even though if he had been it is unlikely that he could have done more for France's enemies. Why, then, did he do what he did? Why did he take the apparently contradictory course of letting the pacifists and the pro-Germans remain free while at the same time arranging with Miguel Almereyda to stifle attempts to obstruct mobilization?

The answer to this complex affair is actually quite simple. Louis Malvy was not his own man; he was merely the nominee of and the mouthpiece for a behind-the-scenes figure who was one of the most powerful politicians in France. The reason Malvy could not arrest the Frenchmen listed on Carnet B was that if he did he would be arresting many of the friends and political associates of his own patron. But while he felt an obligation to protect the friends of his master, this obligation did not extend to letting them sabotage the French mobilization and cause Malvy to be dismissed as Minister of the Interior; hence the agreement with Almereyda.

But who, then, was Malvy's master? How did he come to have pacifist and pro-German connections? And why, if he was politically so powerful, was he not a member of the Cabinet in his own right?

His name was Joseph Caillaux and he was a complex person.

At the time the war broke out, Joseph Caillaux was the aging boy wonder of French politics and finance. He had been born in 1863, the son of a wealthy financier-politician. When still a very young man, he served in the Ministry of Finance and speedily demonstrated the species of genuine economic genius which occasionally crops up in French political life. In 1898 Caillaux was elected to the Chamber of Deputies, and almost immediately he commenced a meteoric career which was to see him become the brilliant and energetic Minister of Finance in a succession of cabinets.

Caillaux's achievements extended even beyond positions in the government. His abilities and energies were such that he became the leader of one of France's strongest parties, the Radical Socialists. This requires some explanation. In the morass of French political parties, few names are exactly indicative of the philosophy of the party. Thus, the Radical Socialist party was neither very radical nor very socialist. Instead, the Radical Socialists were a grouping of the middle left who obtained their support chiefly from the landowning peasants, from the lower middle classes in the large cities, from the more obscure professional men and from the second rung of the gov-

ernment bureaucracy. This was a group, of course, which constituted the bedrock of French political life. There were more of this
class than any other. As individuals, they were wildly jealous of the
haute bourgeoisie. They liked to think of themselves as the "original" republicans; and while they were secretly horrified by the doctrinaire Socialists, the Radical Socialists rarely hesitated to join with
the far left when it became necessary to resist the pressures of the
right and the less liberal center.

By 1914 the Radical Socialists had become powerful indeed. In the
May general elections they had succeeded in capturing 136 seats in
the Chamber of Deputies—more than any other party. And their
power was even further magnified by the Radical Socialist tradition
of having "no enemies to the left." [14] This being the case, the thought
of Joseph Caillaux as the leader of the Radical Socialists seems
more than a little bizarre, for Caillaux was a man of great wealth
and exclusive tastes. He was hardly a republican by birth; in fact, it
was said of him that "Caillaux was brought up in the laps of duch-
esses." [15] His manner was as sophisticated as his clothes, and this
haughty man can scarcely have enjoyed rubbing shoulders with his
supporters, whose days were occupied in eking out a bare bourgeois
existence. Once, in the lobby of the Chamber of Deputies, Caillaux
was talking with a well-born friend when a Radical-Socialist Deputy
approached. Brusquely, Caillaux motioned his fellow politician away.
"He is not one of us," Caillaux murmured apologetically.[16] Then too,
on behalf of his party's platform, Caillaux had to propose legislation
which, as a man of wealth, he secretly detested. For example, on the
subject of an income tax, the adoption of which was a basic Radical
Socialist objective, Caillaux wrote privately, "I crushed it while
seeming to give it my support." [17]

But no matter. Like any good politician, Caillaux made his compromises. And Joseph Caillaux was intelligent, immensely ambitious
and an astute observer. Early in his political career he had been a
member of the right; then, perceiving the gradual drift of French political power, he had eased himself over to the middle left. And this
had paid: Caillaux was now the most powerful man in the most
powerful party in France. Indeed, at the time of mobilization he
would have been a Cabinet member or, perhaps, the Premier of
France—were it not for the events of the afternoon of March 16,

1914. For on that afternoon Caillaux's wife emptied the contents of a pistol into the body of the editor of one of France's leading newspapers.

In 1906 Caillaux had married a certain Madame Gueydan, a divorcee with whom he had been having an affair during a period when Madame Gueydan had been encumbered with her then husband. But Caillaux's marriage had not gone smoothly and he had cast a roving eye about, until, in 1909, he discovered that a packet of very compromising letters was missing from a desk drawer in which he had hidden them—intimate letters which showed that he was having a more than casual friendship with a certain Madame Léo Claretie, a divorcee whose maiden name had been Raynouard. They were foolish love letters which had been signed by Joseph Caillaux with the adoring phrase *"Ton Jo"*—Thy Jo.

Caillaux confronted his wife with the fact of the disappearance of the letters and she admitted that they were in her possession. Now, at this period Caillaux was standing for re-election to the Chamber of Deputies, and he knew that his wife was possessed of a number of embarrassing facts about both his private and his political life, facts which his unsophisticated constituents might not understand. And Caillaux knew his wife to be a vindictive woman. At all costs, he had to avoid a scandal. So this proud and haughty man went to his wife, in tears and on his knees, she later claimed, and pleaded for a reconciliation. If she would take him back he would, he promised, completely sever his connection with Madame Claretie.

Madame Caillaux accepted his promise, and on November 5, 1909, the bargain was sealed. In a scene which could probably occur only in France, Madame Caillaux produced the incriminating *Ton Jo* letters, which were solemnly burned to ashes after she swore, in the presence of a witness, that the letters had not been photographed or copied in any way. Caillaux, on his part, promised eternal fidelity.

As soon as he was safely re-elected, however, Caillaux lost no time in divorcing his wife, and after a discreet interval he married Madame Claretie, in 1911. Apparently the incident was closed and he could follow his busy political career without fear of embarrassing disclosures.

In 1911 Germany almost precipitated a crisis in Franco-German relations. Known as the "Agadir Incident" and revolving around

spheres of influence in Africa, it brought the two nations almost to
the point of war. Under the stress the French government of the day
had fallen, and Caillaux was called upon to form a new government
which would resolve the crisis. This was Caillaux's first post outside
the Ministry of Finance, and it brought forth a latent ambition in
him which had never been suspected by any of his political associates. It became apparent that Caillaux's burning ambition in life was
to become known as the man who saved Europe by negotiating a
widespread French *rapprochement* with Germany. Now, if this
seems either laudable or innocuous, it must be remembered that
France suffered from a permanent military manpower inferiority to
Germany and that, despite the confidence of her Army officers in the
military prowess of France, the only thing which had saved her from
a repetition of 1870 was her foreign policy. For years the aim of
French foreign policy had been to build up an alliance of European
nations which, if they had nothing else in common, feared German
militarism. France had been successful in gathering Russia into this
alliance and had also reached an understanding with Great Britain.
Known as the Triple Entente, this bloc considered itself the military
equal of Germany and the allies which it was expected Germany
would gather about herself—Austria-Hungary, Turkey and Italy.

But the Triple Entente was a delicate affair, fragile as gossamer
web. Its principals conflicted in many areas, and their only genuine
community of interest lay in their fear of Germany. For years
France had acted as the co-ordinator and conciliator of this tenuous
alliance. Every French government knew that it must preserve the alliance or France would suffer disaster. For France to reach a separate, widespread understanding with Germany would mean the abrupt end of the Triple Entente—and it could never again be put
together. This policy was accepted by every responsible French politician and formed a cornerstone of French foreign policy. Differences with Germany could be smoothed slightly, but France could
never adopt more than an attitude of cautious reserve.

So when Caillaux became Premier, his colleagues were astounded
to hear him voice a pro-German attitude. As regards Britain, Caillaux announced, "The best policy to follow is to recognize valid
German claims on us, just as in the past we recognized British
claims." [18]

Now, an anti-British attitude was perfectly acceptable as a private view (indeed, many Frenchmen shared it), but as a public statement by the Premier of France it could be disastrous to the entente upon which the life of France depended.

But if Caillaux was anti-British, his attitude toward Germany was quite the reverse. In fact, he proved so anxious to please the Germans that his negotiations concerning the Agadir crisis took on a distinctly suspicious form. Behind the back of his Foreign Minister, M. de Selves, and without the knowledge of even his closest associates, Caillaux entered into direct and secret negotiations with the Germans.

The Germans were elated. They had a "pigeon" at the very highest level. Skillfully they continued sham negotiations with the French Foreign Ministry through the French ambassador in Berlin. But the serious conversations, the talks which could lead to a substantial German diplomatic victory, could be held with the Premier himself! Although Caillaux subsequently denied it, the fact is that during July 1911 he negotiated directly with the counselor of the German embassy, using as an intermediary a certain M. Fondère, a French national.

Perhaps none of this would ever have come to light but for the remarkable efficiency of the cryptographic section of the French Foreign Ministry. As it happened, on July 27 the German ambassador sent two telegrams to Berlin advising his superiors of developments in the secret negotiations, by means of a little-used diplomatic code which the French cryptographers had broken. The intercepted messages were quickly deciphered, typed on green paper (as was the custom with broken cryptographs) and placed before Foreign Minister de Selves. He was appalled, astounded. This was nothing less than treason! Why else would Caillaux negotiate directly and secretly, unless he wanted to make concessions to which his associates would never agree? Why else would the German ambassador end the second telegram with the advice, "Caillaux earnestly requests that none of these overtures be made known to Cambon [the French ambassador in Berlin]." [19]

M. de Selves gave copies of these telegrams—later known as "les dépêches vertes," the Green Dispatches, to Caillaux and also to the President of the Republic, Raymond Poincaré, and with them he ten-dered his immediate resignation. There was entirely too much intrigue in this situation to suit even such an experienced French political figure as M. de Selves.

This brings up another facet of Caillaux's personality. While he craved to be at the core of affairs, to have a stage for his tremendous ambition and racing intelligence, he felt an absolute compulsion to intrigue. He was one of those men who are constitutionally incapable of doing things the easy or accepted way. In an age when intrigue was an accepted feature of French political life, Caillaux abused the privilege. He had always to surround himself with a circle of undercover acquaintances with whom he held constant secret conferences. And the more mysterious, the more bizarre, his acquaintances were, the more he liked them. In this respect, certainly, for all his brilliance and ambition, he lacked even elementary common sense.

At any rate, Caillaux's personal diplomacy with Germany was to bear bitter fruit for him. As soon as he received Selves's resignation and the Green Dispatches, he rebuked the Germans for their carelessness in revealing the *sub-rosa* negotiations and informed them that henceforth discussions must proceed through normal channels. Naturally, the Germans were disappointed. But, at the same time, they found it useful to learn that the French had broken their diplomatic code.

By October 1911, the Agadir crisis was resolved by a Franco-German treaty which recognized French interests in Morocco in return for France's yielding territory in the French Congo to Germany. It was a treaty which really pleased no one. Years of bellicose propaganda had stimulated German public opinion to the point where it regarded any concession to France as unnecessary and incompatible with Germany's position in Europe. France also regarded the treaty as an unnecessary accommodation to German militarism and an affront to French national pride—and, in addition, there arose a suspicion that France had been sold somewhat short by its Premier.

In January 1912 an investigating committee of the French Senate was convened to look into the matter. Although very little could actually be established to prove that Caillaux had stepped beyond the bounds of prudence in appeasing Germany, the more knowledgeable of French politicians speedily came to the conclusion that Caillaux had at the very least been guilty of incredibly poor judgment in the affair. And among the mass of journalists, foreign diplomats and the more aware of the French electorate, there arose the suspicion that Caillaux was Germanophilic to such an extent that he should never again be trusted to deal with Germany.

Under the combined impact of these suspicions, the Caillaux government fell in 1912. But although Caillaux was no longer acceptable as Premier, it was only a matter of months before he was back in the Cabinet occupying his familiar post as Minister of Finance. If this seems strange, it must be remembered that he was still the acknowledged leader of the powerful Radical Socialist group and that a very large number of deputies had obtained their seats through his help. So Joseph Caillaux was still an extremely influential politician, and, besides his own place in the Cabinet, he was allowed to name several other Cabinet ministers. Among his nominees was devoted young Louis Malvy.

There exist a number of photographs of Caillaux which were made about this time. In one he is seated at his desk in the Ministry of Finance. His office is furnished with the clutter of overelaborate furniture and bric-à-brac which French politicians of the time affected. Though he is not physically prepossessing—he is portly, of only medium height and almost totally bald—his eyes radiate a suppressed force as he stares aggressively back at the camera. It is obvious that he is a man who is accustomed to move in exalted circles, just as it is apparent that he is a man of unbounded confidence in himself and his opinions. It is equally obvious that he is not a man to be taken lightly. Temporarily he might be unacceptable as Premier, but times might change. There could yet come a day when a man whom Germany regarded as a friend and secret advocate could be returned to the highest office. And then the price paid him for his return would be high.

But although it appeared that his powerful connections would allow Caillaux to continue his political career in any post short of the premiership, there were those who regarded him as potentially the most dangerous man in France. Among them was Gaston Calmette, the editor of the important conservative newspaper Le Figaro. Calmette assembled his facts carefully and then went after the head of the man he regarded as a traitor, a hypocrite and by no means free from suspicion concerning certain financial peccadilloes.

Beginning on January 5, 1914, Le Figaro ran a sensational exposé series which rocked official Paris. Each article, generally signed by

Gaston Calmette himself, appeared on the front page. *"L'Opération blanche de M. Caillaux," "La Diplomatie de M. Caillaux"* and a long series entitled *"Les Combinaisons secrètes de M. Caillaux"* (The Secret Schemes of Monsieur Caillaux) screamed from the headlines. The attacks on Caillaux continued without letup. Calmette was getting to Caillaux and he knew it. On the few days when *Le Figaro* ran no written attack, a huge cartoon mocked Caillaux.

Rapierlike, Calmette exposed Caillaux's hypocrisy and his appeasement of Germany, culminating the series with an indictment of the Minister's personal life. And to support this last attack, *Le Figaro* began to run facsimiles of the *Ton Jo* letters which Caillaux's first wife had stolen from him! In horror, Caillaux suddenly realized that his first wife had played him as false as he had her. The letters which had been burned had been photographed first, and now Gaston Calmette had the photographs! In fact, although Caillaux did not know it, so complete was Calmette's knowledge of his career that even the Green Dispatches were in the hands of *Le Figaro*.

Ruin was clearly staring Caillaux in the face. The worst letters had not been printed, but obviously he could not count on Calmette's holding anything back. All would be revealed and he would appear as a fool, a hypocrite and a liar. His name would be discredited and his political career would certainly be at an end. In vain, Caillaux appealed to President Poincaré—was there nothing which the office of the President could do to prevent the ruin of his career? But if the President felt he could not interfere, Caillaux's wife was under no such inhibition; after all, her reputation was also being smirched by M. Calmette. One of the *Ton Jo* letters, written, of course, when both she and Caillaux were married to others, had described a blissful assignation at Ouchy and closed with "a thousand million kisses on all your dear little body." [20]

On the morning of March 16, 1914, Madame Caillaux visited the shop of M. Gastinne-Renette, a gunsmith on the Avenue d'Autin. There she purchased a Browning automatic pistol. She asked that it be loaded, and at a target range in the cellar of the shop she fired six practice rounds at a dummy the size of a man. An obliging clerk reloaded the gun for her and she departed with her purchase.

Late that afternoon Madame Caillaux called at the offices of *Le Figaro* and asked to see M. Calmette. He was out, but she waited for an hour until he had returned. Finally she was ushered into his private office.

Calmette rose. "*Bonjour, madame,*" he said.

Madame Caillaux replied, "*Bonjour, monsieur,*" produced the pistol from her muff and shot the editor six times. He died that evening.[21]

The trial of Madame Caillaux for the murder of Gaston Calmette took place in July and will always rank among the world's most celebrated murder trials. The French public, and the world at large, was treated to a legal spectacle of the gaudiest kind. The trial was long, it was complicated, and it aroused the interest and passion of every Frenchman. In fact, on that July when all Europe was slipping toward war, the Caillaux trial almost completely diverted the interest of France from the approaching danger.

Joseph Caillaux had resigned his Cabinet post on the day that his wife shot Calmette, and he devoted all his considerable energies to masterminding her defense. Within the government he still commanded countless loyalties, chief among them Louis Malvy, the Minister of the Interior, but to secure the sympathy of the masses he required newspaper support to present his wife in the light of the avenger of a scandalous deed. And for a man of Caillaux's wealth and political connections, there was no difficulty finding newspapers to support his cause, principally Miguel Almereyda and his *Bonnet rouge*. In fact, the payments which Caillaux made to Almereyda in return for his support enabled the editor to change the *Bonnet rouge* from a weekly to a daily newspaper. Nor was editorial support the only contribution which Almereyda made to the cause of his patron. Through his underworld contacts, Almereyda produced a bodyguard of Corsican thugs known to be tough and quick with a knife. They were called "the Corsican Guard" and they accompanied Caillaux everywhere he went.

And Caillaux needed protection. His wife's line of defense (indeed, the only defense she could offer, since it was indisputable that she had shot Calmette) was that she had merely called upon Calmette to protest the injustice of his attacks upon her husband and that she had taken the pistol merely to show him that she was serious about her warning. Then, suddenly, the pistol discharged itself six times. "It goes off by itself," Madame Caillaux assured the jury.[22] This being

her defense, it became almost inevitable that the crux of the trial
would not be the murder at all but the question of whether or not
Calmette's accusations were truthful. In fact, it is generally agreed
that for substantial periods Madame Caillaux was entirely forgotten.
With each day's revelations, mobs rioted in the streets of Paris. The
left favored Caillaux, the right condemned him as a traitor to France.

Within the courtroom, tempers grew so hot that judicial procedure degenerated to the point of farce. There were constant interruptions from spectators demanding to be heard; Miguel Almereyda was on hand to lead a hired claque of Caillaux supporters; two
of the judges almost came to the point of challenging one another
to a duel; and it became a common occurrence for witnesses to
scream accusations at one another. Finally the question was put to
the jury: Was Madame Caillaux guilty of willful murder? It was too
much to expect that a French jury would send the beautiful lady to
the guillotine for a crime of passion, and on July 28, 1914, the jury
returned a verdict of not guilty.

From the pages of the *Bonnet rouge*, Caillaux's hireling Almereyda congratulated the jury on its scandalous verdict—one of the
few editors to do so. "Bravo, Jury!" was the headline. "Notwithstanding the outrages, the legal attacks, and even outright threats,
the jury of the Seine has done justice. All who have seen M. Caillaux
at the bar [have seen] . . . a man with the rarest qualities. . . .
more than any other, he is a *leader*." [23]

And now what to do with Joseph Caillaux, his friends in the government wondered. Too much dirty linen had been washed. Caillaux's pro-Germanism and the disclosures brought out in his wife's
trial had made it unthinkable that he be given another ministerial
position. The public would never accept him; in fact Caillaux and his
wife were several times stoned in the streets by enraged mobs. So
when war came a few days later, Caillaux, the man who was one of
France's most powerful political figures, was given a position as an
Army paymaster general and packed off to the south of France,
from where he would have to exert his influence at long range. In the
end, he was to do an amazingly good job of it.

With Madame Caillaux's scandalous acquittal, the French nation
was free to turn its attention to a far greater trial—the impending
war. It was as if the end of the Caillaux trial forced France from its

preoccupation with bickering and pettiness. Suddenly it dawned upon Frenchmen of all political shades and social classes that war with Germany was a very real and imminent danger. The Dentists' Association had hitherto regarded the tense international situation as probably nothing more than a vulgar attempt by Germany to sabotage French oral hygiene by denying the dentists their annual August convention in Paris, and the Socialists had worried about missing their August convention in Vienna;[24] now all these petty concerns were seen in their true light. Party friction ceased as the spectrum of French political life, from syndicalist to monarchist, drew together to support whatever course the government had to take to defend the honor and territory of France.

True, it was remarked by foreign observers that the fervor of the French populace did not begin to match the enthusiasm of Germany or Russia. There were no cheers, no crowds surrounding the Élysée Palace to cry "*A Berlin!*," few thundering demonstrations with the mob pelting the departing troops with flowers. Instead, all was quiet, calm and subdued.

But if there were few outward displays of warlike fervor, the simple absence of support for pacifist agitation against war spoke volumes in itself. France, whose enemies had expected she would tear herself apart on the approach of war, displayed an incredible hardening of resolve. The much feared general strike by the antimilitarist left was never called, and even if it had been it would certainly not have been heeded. The force of French patriotism was far too strong, the danger to *La Patrie* far too great to allow class struggle. A doctrinaire member of the left, Jules Guesde, in justifying his support of the government, put it this way: "When the house is on fire it is no time for controversy. The only thing to do is to take a hand with the buckets." [25]

In the closing days of July 1914 France gave a spectacular display of national unity against which any attempts by those on Carnet B to block mobilization, or any counterefforts which may have been made by Almereyda, faded into insignificance. Although the General Staff had estimated before the war that as many as 13 per cent of the reservists would refuse to report upon mobilization, the actual figure was less than 1½ per cent. The Army recruiting offices were mobbed with 350,000 volunteers. Even three thousand deserters from the peacetime army returned to France to rejoin their regiments.[26]

If there was any further need for proof of the fundamental bed-rock of patriotism of the French working classes in the face of war, it was furnished by their reaction to the assassination of Auguste Jaurès, the beloved and dynamic leader of the French United Social-ist party. Although proletarian theory seemingly obligated Jaurès to regard war as a desperate effort by a dying capitalist class to fore-stall its doom, his actual viewpoint was more realistic and tremen-dously more patriotic. He had even gone so far as to exhort his fol-lowers to take their part in a "holy war for our beloved France if ever she were attacked." [27] Nevertheless, at 9:40 P.M. on July 31, 1914, the day before mobilization, a half-witted youth crazed by pa-triotic fervor climbed through the window of a Paris restaurant in which Jaurès was dining and fired a bullet into his head.

Under more normal circumstances this event would have triggered off an immense riot, the Ministry would have fallen and for yet an-other time the Republic would have teetered on the edge of ruin. In-deed, the movement orders for the 2nd Regiment of Cuirassiers were abruptly canceled to keep cavalry in Paris to deal with the an-ticipated mobs.[28] But these were not normal times. The workers re-mained calm, and a London *Times* observer, marveling at the new-found unity of France, reported that "in the darkening hours of the moment it came as a grief even to the most bitter opponent of the Socialist leader." [29]

Even the newspapers, whose columns had tormented the life of the countless ministries of the Third Republic, now formed an almost solid bloc to express themselves as being firmly behind the govern-ment. The reaction of the far-left *Guerre sociale* was probably typ-ical—"Between Imperial Germany and republican France our choice is made. Long live France!" [30] Almereyda, fulfilling his agreement with Malvy, came through with an unaccustomed call to arms in the pages of the *Bonnet rouge:* "Notwithstanding the ardent pacific wishes of the French government, we have now entered into war. My brother Socialists, let us forget 'The International' and our red flag. Our song is now 'The Marseillaise' and our flag is the tri-color!" [31]

Georges Clemenceau struck a higher pitch of patriotism when, from the unsubsidized pages of his journal *L'Homme libre*, he cried, "And now to arms! Everyone's chance will come; not a child on our soil but will have his part in the gigantic battles. To die is nothing;

we must conquer. And for that we shall need every arm. The weakest shall have his part in the struggle." [32] And Clemenceau rushed to the Élysée Palace to offer his support to his bitter enemy, President of the Republic Raymond Poincaré. *"Mon cher ami!"* Clemenceau cried.[33]

And on August 4 Poincaré came before the Chamber of Deputies with his war message. There was no bickering now. The entire Chamber rose and remained standing for the President's martial address, which was interrupted only by roars of applause—especially when Poincaré called for a "Sacred Union" wherein all Frenchmen regardless of party would be "joined together as brothers in a common patriotic faith." [34]

But the ultimate evidence of the solidarity of France in the face of war was to come on the day after mobilization was announced. On that day the French government virtually abdicated in favor of the Army. Under a law dating back to 1878, the President of the Republic had the power to declare a "state of siege" in case of "imminent peril caused by a foreign war or armed aggression." [35] Such a decree had the effect of suspending considerable individual liberties and placing general police powers in the hands of the Army. In actuality, it amounted to a virtual declaration of martial law. It had never been imagined that the state of siege would be declared in more than a section of France. But on August 2 President Poincaré signed a decree authorizing it throughout France and even in Algeria. On August 4 the Chamber of Deputies ratified the decree without discussion. Thus it happened that the politicians of France, who had not really trusted their Army, who had always regarded it as a hotbed of latent antirepublicanism, unhesitatingly gave themselves and the nation into the Army's hands.

Now it was up to the Army to justify this trust.

4

THE FIRST MONTH

FORTUNATE is the general staff which sees a war fought the way it intends. Indeed, if there is one thing which can be counted upon in war it is that you can count on nothing. This the French Army was soon to rediscover.

To begin with, the French Army was commanded by General Joseph Joffre. Sixty-two years old at the time war broke out, Joffre was almost the antithesis of the soldier in appearance as well as in manner. Fat, unbelievably phlegmatic, routine-loving, he had never been accused of being a military genius, but for three peacetime years he had commanded the French Army.

Prior to 1911 Joffre had been primarily an engineer officer. Only once in his life had he held a real field command—in 1894, when he had led a little expeditionary force to Timbuktu to put down a colonial insurrection. Joffre had no reputation as a strategist or tactician, and although in 1910 he became a junior member of the War Council, the job that had been assigned to him in the event of mobilization was the direction of the lines of communication.

But in 1911 General Michel, the designated commander of the French Army in time of war, fell from favor. He had advanced the disagreeable theory that the German plan for invading France involved a huge attack through Belgium and had recommended that the French Army prepare itself to stand on the defensive. This last was, of course, anathema to the influential "Young Turks" of the School of the Attack, whose influence by this time was such that they could pull down even the Commander in Chief designate of the French Army. So Adolphe Messimy, the Minister of War in the government of the hour, looked about for a new Army commander. Several senior generals, notably Joseph Gallieni and Paul Marie Pau, were considered but were rejected for one reason or another. Pau, for example, demanded the right to make his own senior military appointments, a privilege which the distrustful government would not allow. Finally, the most obvious choices having been exhausted, Joffre was selected.

What did he have to recommend him? First, he was politically acceptable—neither an aristocrat (his father was a cooper) nor an ardent Catholic. Second, he was acceptable to the General Staff, which probably regarded him as "a solid shield behind which subtler brains could direct French military policy." [1] At any rate, Joffre well knew to whom he owed his appointment and also the ousting of his predecessor—to the influential young officers of the School of the Attack. Accordingly, Joffre gave his blessing to the development of their Plan XVII, the violent offensive into Alsace and Lorraine.

But although Joffre was, to an extent, beholden to the Young Turks of the General Staff, this is not to say that he was in any way subservient. In his exalted position as ruler of the French Army, he developed a species of Olympian detachment. Solemn, somber, never ruffled, he seemed like a brooding presence hanging over the General Staff and, indeed, the entire Army. His age, girth and imperturbability gave an impression of paternal grandeur which accentuated and reinforced the confidence the French Army had always had in itself. With "Papa" Joffre in command, what could possibly go wrong? With his blessing upon them, how could the plans go awry, how could the tactics be in error?

Immediately upon mobilization the French Army began to put Plan XVII into force. Since it was thought that the Germans would have to divide their forces to meet an attack in the east by the huge Russian Army, the French saw no insurmountable difficulty in carrying out their own attacks. So Joffre began a series of tentative assaults which were designed to clear the way for the audacious drive into Alsace and Lorraine. But before these offensives had the opportunity to gather headway, there was ominous news from the north. The Germans had burst across the Belgian frontier and, using immense howitzers of a size unknown to other armies, were reducing the vaunted Belgian fortress system into so much crushed concrete.

Now, prewar French doctrine had been to completely ignore the enemy's activities in favor of pursuing Plan XVII. This procedure, it was held, would rapidly place the Germans in such a position that they would have to abandon any offensive of their own in favor of countering the French thrust, and thus the French would retain the initiative with the privilege of directing their attack where and when they wanted. In practice, this theory was found to be valid—but it worked the other way. The Germans outnumbered the French by three to two, and it was only a matter of days before their drive began to exert tremendous pressure.

For the first two weeks of the war, Joffre attempted to follow the doctrine of the offensive. The German incursion into Belgium was officially ignored; it was regarded as a feint or a cavalry raid. How could it be anything else? It was obvious that the Germans could not possibly have enough troops to provide the necessary manpower for a serious attack through Belgium. Moreover, the Second Bureau had advised that the German railheads opposite Belgium were too small to support anything more than twenty-two divisions.

But gradually and sickeningly it became clear that the German thrust into Belgium was no mere smash-and-grab raid. It was nothing less than the most powerful military offensive the world had ever seen, mounted by five German armies which totaled nearly two million fighting men. And its aim was to debouch on the French left, outflank the entire French Army (together with the handful of divisions which the British had brought across to support their allies), roll it up, smash it, and then transfer the German troops east to deal with the ponderous Russian forces. The Germans had found enough manpower by training and arming their reserve divisions to a far greater degree than the French thought possible. The proficiency of the German reserves was such that they were being used in almost the same manner as the active divisions.

But, despite this evidence of the immensity of the German offensive on his undefended left, Joffre continued with the attacks envisioned in Plan XVII. A French drive into Alsace and Lorraine was thrown back; in its stead, Joffre launched two other armies into the Ardennes Forest where he foresaw no serious German opposition. He could not have been more wrong. The German Fourth and Fifth Armies were just beginning their own scheduled advance and the two forces met head-on. On one day, August 22, four bloody engagements were fought—Virton, Ethe, Rossignol and Neufchâteau. The French lost them all.

Under the circumstances, it would seem apparent that the logical, the prudent, the accepted tactics for the French Army would have been to conduct a series of rear-guard actions: to beat a slow retreat, pausing along a river, a height, or some other naturally defensible terrain feature and to dig trenches (they had proved their value in the Balkan War of two years before), site artillery and machine guns, string barbed wire and shred the advancing German columns in a blast of firepower. But so steeped was the French Army in the School of the Attack, in the idea of the irresistible bayonet attack that, as Winston Churchill pointed out, "Though the Germans invaded, it was more often the French who attacked." [2]

This, then, was the way the French Army fought. In nineteenth century massed formations, the troops were assembled in fields or on roads in full view of the efficient German artillery observers. There was no attempt at surprise or concealment—indeed, the French infantrymen, with their bright red trousers and dark blue coats, were superbly visible.

When all was ready, bayonets were fixed and the attack began. Flags snapping in the air, regimental bands playing "The Marseillaise," the officers in white gloves and twenty paces forward, they swept forward to the sound of bugles—full tilt into the massed firepower of the twentieth century.

And now a ghastly truth became evident. No amount of *élan*, no Napoleonic traditions, no exhortations by officers crying *"En avant!"* and *"À la baïonnette!"* could save from slaughter the troops charging over open fields at the hands of an entrenched, numerically superior enemy which possessed machine guns, modern magazine rifles and long-range artillery.

A British Army officer was horrified. "Whenever the French infantry advance," he wrote, "their whole front is at once regularly covered with shrapnel and the unfortunate men are knocked over like rabbits. They are very brave and advance time after time to the charge through appalling fire, but so far it has been of no avail. No one could live through the fire that is concentrated on them. The officers are splendid; they advance about twenty yards ahead of their men as calmly as though on parade, but so far I have not seen one of them get more than fifty yards without being knocked over." [3]

But somehow the German onrush had to be checked and a spirited charge was the only method the School of the Attack knew. Every man was thrown into the battle. Even cavalrymen, dismounted and with their horses either dead or exhausted, made suicidal charges on foot across the fields, their only weapons their long lances. The French artillery was helpless against the entrenched Germans—"What were they to fire at, anyhow, when all that could be seen of the enemy was a few faint gleams of well-aligned cannon?" [4] To a French corporal the German machine guns seemed "like a coffee mill—*tac-tac-tac*. The bullets stream past; it is an infernal uproar. For each bullet that I hear I think, That one is for me." [5]

By August 25, the tremendous force of the Schlieffen Plan had become evident to Joffre in its fullest scope. Plan XVII was dead. An irresistible mass of Germans was pouring across the Franco-Belgian frontier, well north of the French armies. Now it had become a matter of the starkest necessity for the French to avoid being outflanked and encircled.

So, for day after day during the hottest summer in years, the French Army retreated southward and westward. Always in danger of being outflanked and caught in reverse, the French streamed back in long, dusty columns. Every road was filled with men, guns and horses—and hanging over the exhausted troops like an invisible pall was the knowledge that in a few hours, a few days at most, these same French roads would be filled with the gray-clad, spike-helmeted Germans.

It is a difficult undertaking to rewrite tactical doctrine in the midst of a war. It is almost impossible to rewrite it when an army is in full retreat, when it is deathly tired, confused and decimated and utter ruin is looming. Nevertheless, the useless sacrifice of the French Army to the gods of the Attack could not continue and Joffre sent the following modifying instruction to his army commanders:

> The engagements which have taken place so far have served to display the admirable qualities of our infantry. Without in any way wishing to impair this dash, in which lies the principal factor of success, it is of the greatest importance, especially when it is a question to carrying fortified positions, to learn to await artillery fire and to prevent the troops from exposing themselves hastily to the enemy's fire. . . .

As many guns as possible should be engaged from the beginning of an engagement. The attacks will be all the more successful, all the less costly, in proportion to the care with which they have been prepared.[6]

Thus, as Plan XVII had proved a failure, so did the theories of the School of the Attack. And still the German offensive rolled onward while, tottering with exhaustion, the French armies fled before its enveloping thrust. The world stood aghast. Could Paris possibly be defended? Could the French Army possibly come back from this great retreat which by now had left northeastern France naked to the invader?

By August 30 the rumble of German guns in the northeast was audible in Paris and the city experienced its first air raid. A German plane let loose five bombs on the Rue Albouy and the Quay Valmy, and with the bombs a message was dropped. Signed by a Lieutenant von Heidessen, it said: "The German Army is at the gates of Paris; there is nothing left to you but to surrender." [7]

On September 2 the situation had become desperate and the French government fled Paris for Bordeaux, announcing: "If this formidable struggle is to be given all its dash and efficiency, the government must remain free to act. . . . The government, therefore, transfers its residence to a spot where it can remain in constant communication with the whole country." [8] The announcement closed with admiring references to the Paris population and recommendations of "calm and resolution." Nevertheless, more than a third of the citizens of Paris saw fit to flee the oncoming Germans. The railroad stations were mobbed with refugees and the roads filled with carts and automobiles heading south.

To explain the stunning defeats of August 1914, it is customary for apologists for the French Army command to complain that the Germans possessed great superiority in artillery and automatic weapons; anyway, they say, the French Army gave as good as it got. To proffer this explanation is to deny the facts. Agreed, the Germans possessed the heavier artillery. This was the reason why the French armies came under long-range artillery fire to which they could not even reply. Yet in their 75-mm. artillery piece the French had a quick-firing weapon which in most respects was superior to its German 77-mm. counterpart and which, if they had grasped the secret of its proper use, should have helped to even out the German edge. With regard to automatic weapons, the French and German armies were alike in possessing two machine guns per battalion. But the Germans invariably used theirs better, probably simply because they had faith in their effectiveness and the French School of the Attack did not. Finally, while it is true that the Germans suffered severe losses, it is probable that at no time did their casualty totals exceed two thirds of the combined French and British—this despite the fact that the Germans were the invaders.

No, the inescapable conclusion is that the French Army theorists, while convinced that they had grasped the secret of success in modern warfare, had in reality seized upon its antithesis. They had actually done their unwitting best to destroy their Army. And, almost symbolically, one of the dead was the high priest of offensive action, Colonel Loiseau de Grandmaison, killed leading an infantry brigade charge. Now the French Army could be saved only by the one quality the Army theorists did not believe their troops possessed— tenacity on the defensive.

To the neutral observer in August 1914, it seemed as if nothing could save France. But, actually, there was still a glimmer of hope. Even though the French Army had been disastrously defeated in almost every battle, it had not been routed. Though the troops had been marched to the point where they were in a stupor, though the Army had lost more than a third of its effectiveness, it still existed as an organized force. Each corps had always taken the right road in its retreat, fewer than ten thousand unwounded prisoners had been taken by the Germans,[9] and the cry of "Every man for himself" had never been raised. The Army had been pushed to the brink, but it still was capable of marching and fighting another day. And as long as this was the case, the French had not yet lost the war. Moltke, the Chief of the German General Staff, realized this, and when gleeful subordinates came to tell him that the Schlieffen Plan was victorious and that the French Army was routed, he said, "Don't let's deceive ourselves. . . . When armies of millions stand facing one another, the victor has prisoners. Where are our prisoners?"[10]

By September 3 the German armies were nearly at the gates of Paris. A few more days of uncontested marching would have finished the war. But Joffre had taken a number of steps to prevent this from happening. First, on the insistence of the Minister of War, he had appointed General Gallieni as the military governor of Paris. Gallieni was an old and respected French soldier, passed over in favor of Joffre as Commander in Chief but possessed of imagination and energy all out of keeping with his sixty-five years. In the absence of the government, Gallieni became undisputed master of Paris. There had been some official discussion of evacuating Paris and declaring it an open city. Gallieni would have none of it. He posted the following announcement:

To the Army of Paris and the Population of Paris

The members of the Government of the Republic have left Paris in order to give a new impulse to the national defense. I have received the order to defend Paris against the invader. This order I shall fulfill to the end. GALLIENI [11]

He then busied himself with readying Paris for a siege. Out of the half-deserted city he dragooned up masses of manpower and marched them out to the ring of fortifications which surrounded Paris. There they began to dig rifle pits, repair crumbling masonry and clear fields of fire. Gallieni remembered the siege of Paris in 1870, when the animals in the zoo and the rats in the gutters had been eaten, so the Bois de Boulogne, the infields of the race tracks and every park he could find were filled with cattle ready for slaughter.

But more had been done to defend France than simply placing Paris in an attitude of defense. At the French Army's Grand Quartier Général—G.Q.G.—Joffre was slowly evolving his answer to the Schlieffen Plan. Somewhere, sometime, he theorized, the Germans would make a mistake. For the moment he must continue his retreat, get his troops out of the German grip, reorganize them and then give battle. In addition, to strengthen his left flank, which by now was almost bent back to Paris, Joffre had been shuffling reserves over from his fortress-defended right. Finally, he had formed two new armies to supplement the two he already had in the field. One of these, the Sixth Army, was based in Paris and originally consisted of a handful of reserve divisions, but shortly it was stiffened by the arrival from Algeria of two first-class regular divisions.

In all of this, the imperturbability of Joffre was astounding. Granted, the man was no strategic genius, but his nerve was phenomenal. This Commander in Chief who had not won a battle and whose enemy had already conquered an area containing a sixth of the population of France gave not the slightest evidence of the awful strain which any normal man would have felt. Every night Joffre retired punctually at ten, leaving strict instructions that his slumber should not be disturbed. His meals were eaten with a gourmet's zest and with a calm which his anguished subordinates found shattering.

In a way, Joffre's *sang-froid* had some justification. Much had begun to go wrong with the Schlieffen Plan, especially with German communications. Radio messages were a haphazard thing, and in the line of the German advance the French cavalry patrols had cut telegraph wires in countless places. The result was that neither the German Supreme Headquarters nor any of the five German armies slicing into France had a very clear idea where the others were or what they were doing.

Even more important was the fact that the German commander, General von Moltke, had tampered with the purity of the dead Schlieffen's scheme. One of the keys to its success had been the intentional weakening of the German left flank so as to draw the French right wing out of its fortifications. But Moltke had been unable to resist the urgings of the commanders on the German left to strengthen their forces. The result was that these armies had actually driven the French back into their fortresses, thus unintentionally giving Joffre the reserves of manpower which he was now railing to his own left. Moreover, two of the five German invading armies had been weakened by detachments to defend East Prussia against the advancing Russians and were now becoming too small to carry out their task.

And finally, it must be recalled that the German thrust was a wheeling movement, which meant that the outer sections had to move a much greater distance than the inner. This imposed a tremendous strain upon the flankers—the armies on the outside.

It was the two outside German armies, the First Army, commanded by General Alexander von Kluck, and the Second Army, under General Karl von Bülow, who were to prove weak links in the German chain.

These two armies had marched so far and so fast that they were now fully as exhausted as their French and British adversaries. Moreover the Allies, in their retreat, had pretty much broken contact with the Germans, who did not have a clear idea where they had gone. Kluck in particular was in a quandary. He seems not to have realized that Joffre's new Sixth Army was forming on his flank. Thus Kluck thought that he was outside the Allied forces and that his flank was secure. In addition Bülow was urging him to wheel inward to help crush the French Fifth Army. Thus, lacking information and direction from Moltke, Kluck edged out of his assigned path and began to march south and east. This was tremendously significant. The German "wheel" had now been pushed in. The hitherto sacred Schlieffen Plan had been drastically altered and instead of passing *behind*, or to the west of Paris, the German armies were altering their direction to pass *in front*, to the east of Paris. Thus the arc of the German wheel was made smaller by some eighty miles, and this was to prove its undoing.

The change in the German plan rapidly became clear to Gallieni in Paris. He now had the newly formed Sixth Army with him, and, he realized, he would not have to use it to defend Paris, for Paris was not going to be attacked at all. And, in a flash of brilliant strategic insight, Gallieni saw that as they crossed the Marne River all the German armies were simultaneously presenting their flanks in front of him. The German flanker was himself now ouflanked and "in the air." So, on September 4, Gallieni ordered the Sixth Army to attack the German flank and, in what must surely be one of the most fateful of military telephone conversations, had his Chief of Staff call Joffre's Chief of Staff (Joffre himself would not speak to Gallieni on the telephone) to urge in the strongest possible terms that the entire French Army cease its retreat and go over to the offensive without delay.

Whatever Joffre's attributes, speed of reaction was not one of them. He realized that the French Army had only one more battle in it. If this failed, all was lost. The heat of this September day was intense and Joffre wandered outside his headquarters, now in a school at Bar-sur-Aube. In the shade of a tree, he sat alone astride a chair and pondered Gallieni's message. All through the hot summer afternoon he sat in the dusty schoolyard. Then as evening drew near he got up, lumbered into his headquarters and sent an urgent message to his armies. They were to halt their retreat, turn about and attack.

The Battle of the Marne started in earnest on September 7 and, on a front of nearly 150 miles, the fighting quickly reached a tremendous pitch. For the oncoming Germans, the French turnabout was a bolt from the blue. They had not dreamed that the French armies, which they had thought to be totally disorganized, were capable of a battle of this scope. And as the battle developed, the shaken nerve of the German Commander in Chief began to collapse. To be sure, it was not only this battle which was undoing Moltke; he seems never to have quite recovered from the shock of his horrifying interview with the Kaiser on the day of mobilization. Then there was the terrifying suspense of not knowing precisely what his armies were doing and where the Allied forces were. And now there was this. To Moltke the situation seemed ominous, the reports from the field too sketchy, the fighting on the Marne too violent. And Moltke was in the most frustrating position a commander can be in—isolated from the battle. At Supreme War Headquarters in Luxembourg only the vaguest of messages filtered back to him and they all seemed to indicate one thing: defeat. By mid-morning of September 8 Moltke could stand it no more. He summoned his intelligence chief for France, Lieutenant Colonel Richard von Hentsch, and, in a moment of desperation, dispatched him on a tour of the German armies to see what the situation was and, apparently, to co-ordinate a retreat if it had already begun. Countless conflicting accounts have been written about his tour of the armies—and in retrospect, the whole thing seems incredible.

Moltke had given Hentsch no written orders, with the result that the colonel was left to implement what *he thought* were the wishes of his distracted chief. He seems to have set out in a reasonably optimistic frame of mind. In turn, he visited the headquarters of the Fifth, Fourth and Third Armies and found them doing quite well. But when, on the night of the 8th, Hentsch arrived at the headquarters of Bülow's Second Army, he found quite a different atmosphere. The sixty-eight-year-old Bülow was clearly at the end of his emotional string. He had no more reserves and, moreover, a gap had opened between his army and the First Army which was on his right. The general was desperately apprehensive and, doubtless, Hentsch's appearance was a godsend. Here was a representative direct from Supreme Headquarters, a junior officer but at the same time a member of the deified General Staff and one clothed with vague but seemingly sweeping authority from Moltke. Bülow voiced his fears and, apparently, received Hentsch's acquiescence to a Second Army retreat.

Now the gap between the Second and First Armies was threatening to become a yawning void. On September 9 Hentsch again got into his automobile and set out for the headquarters of Kluck and the First Army, but by this time he had lost his earlier optimism. The roads he traveled were filled with panicky stragglers, the flotsam and jetsam of any battlefield, but something which Hentsch had never seen before. At times his car was slowed to a crawl by mobs of skulkers or transports blocking the roads, and Hentsch could only force his way through by drawing his revolver. By the time Hentsch reached Kluck's headquarters, he was personally somewhat demoralized.

The First Army had faced about to the west and were dealing very successfully with the French Sixth Army's attack against them. But there was the widening gap between the First Army and the retreating Bülow. And in this gap the little British Expeditionary Force had reappeared, making a tentative and halting advance which could cut off the First Army from the rest of the German forces. Hentsch wasted no time. He did not even bother to consult with Kluck personally but spoke only to the First Army Chief of Staff, who was also a General Staff member serving his obligatory term in the field. Hentsch directed the First Army to retreat and, for the French, the Battle of the Marne was won.

But all of this, the fatal alteration of the Schlieffen Plan and Colonel Hentsch's automobile ride (which German apologists have used in an attempt to establish that the Battle of the Marne could have been won had only the First and Second Armies been ordered to stand still and fight it out) cannot detract a whit from the valor of the French armies.

The Battle of the Marne was really an amazing feat and fully deserves to be known, as the French have always called it, the Miracle of the Marne. The French troops were exhausted and their armies almost decimated. The German troops were better trained and had the advantage of the initiative. But still, under this pressure, the French managed to revise in mid-course their disastrous infantry tactics and to learn to take advantage of artillery support in their attacks.

Conditions being what they were, the Battle of the Marne must be considered more of a strategic than a tactical victory. The German Army had not been defeated on the field of battle so much as they had been placed in a position where they had to retreat hastily to avoid catastrophe.

By September 11 the Battle of the Marne was over. The situation suddenly became fantastically fluid as the Germans beat an orderly retreat while simultaneously staving off Allied attempts to pursue them.

It is often argued that, had the French and the British pressed the German retreat more vigorously, it might have developed into a rout and the war would have been won within a few weeks. But it is questionable whether this could have been done. During the first six weeks of the war the French Army had been tremendously shaken. Of the approximately 1,300,000 French troops who formed the field armies at the time of the great retreat and the Battle of the Marne, almost half, 600,000, were killed, wounded or captured.[12] It is a magnitude of violent disaster which has rarely been seen in the history of warfare and from which few armies have ever survived.

Even more ghastly was the number of casualties among the French officers. In the last analysis it is the platoon leaders, the company and battalion commanders who make out of the huge congregate mass which is a modern army a slashing weapon. And now they were dead or wounded. Whole St.-Cyr classes almost ceased to exist, and it is probably a conservative estimate that *two thirds* of the French infantry officers in the engaged divisions were casualties within the six-week period which encompassed the great retreat and the Battle of the Marne.

And now the war was entering a different phase. The retreating Germans had not really given up their original efforts to outflank the French and, as they gradually established a line of resistance along the River Aisne, they constantly extended their own right toward the north. Always seeking to outflank the French, the Germans seeped north of the French defensive lines—and always the Germans were barely held in check. Military correspondents of the day accorded to this lengthening of the lines the dramatic title "The Race to the Sea," but really it was more of a shuffling side step toward the English Channel. The Germans usually arrived on the scene first, seized the heights and the most defensible ground, and dug in to face the French or the British, who arrived on the scene "a corps and a day too late." [13]

In this manner, the front was established, along a line extending about four hundred miles across the richest provinces of France. And as the armies met and fought one another to a standstill, the troops began to dig—first shallow rifle pits, then small trenches, then deeper ones. They dug, of course, to protect themselves—but for the men of 1914 the trenches were to be what they so closely resembled: a mass grave of fantastic size.

During 1914 the French Army suffered casualties—in killed, wounded, prisoners and missing—totaling 754,000 men.[14]

5

1915

B Y THE BEGINNING OF 1915 the glorious illusions of the previous summer had been completely dispelled. It had become apparent that war on the western front had become a sort of vast siege operation, the type of campaign which armies had years ago conducted around fortified cities into which enemy forces had shut themselves. And now it was taking place again, a siege with all the traditional characteristics—strong fortifications, huge artillery, masses of men and a terrible slowness as every inch of ground was contested again and again.

It is this last characteristic of war in the trenches which made World War I the horror story it largely is and ultimately led to the shredding of the once-high morale of both troops and nations. The awful slowness, the terrible futility, of trench warfare can hardly be overstated. Under the hail of machine-gun bullets, whole battalions, regiments, divisions died in windrows for the sake of an attack on a tiny terrain feature which had no real military value except that it overlooked the next tiny terrain feature. In a war for which almost the entire world mobilized every resource of manpower and technology, prepared to fight in every quarter of the globe on a scale which had never before been dreamed of, it seemed grotesque, almost ludicrous, that the decision could be made only in a few churned miles of earth in France. If there was one common aim of all the top military commanders in World War I, it was to restore a war of movement, to break out from the frustrating and unanticipated vise of trench warfare into which they had been forced.

War is always full of surprises for one side or the other, but the development of the trench war was one which almost no one on either side had foreseen and for which no nation was really prepared. It is a time-honored aphorism that war offices are always preparing for the last war, and, indeed, there seems to be some truth in it. But in the case of World War I, the general staffs had not even had the dubious benefit of a recent war to which they might look for guidance. The "Pax Britannica" had prevailed too long and too well, with the result that the only major European conflict that had occurred in over a century had been the brief Franco-Prussian War in 1870, fought forty-four years before and replete with misleading conclusions for both France and Germany, who, in preparation for war, resolutely followed the elusive star of a war of movement, maneuver and quick victory. And the British, whose most recent conflict had been the Boer War fought at the turn of the century, had been woefully misled when they thought that they had learned the secret of modern warfare on the South African veldt. They put a heavy emphasis on infantry marksmanship and cavalry. It seemed inconceivable that a bullet could stop a charging cavalry horse. A prominent British military figure, Sir Evelyn Wood, had once seen a crazed London cab horse dash down Pall Mall and knock down an iron lamppost and two stone pillars. "If it were possible," he pondered, "to obtain the same sort of determination from riders as that which inspired the unfortunate horse . . . all cavalry charges would succeed in spite of every sort of missile." [1] And no army (least of all the offensive-minded French), had practiced much at digging trenches or field works. At a British Army maneuver just before the war a colonel who had ordered his troops, the 20th Hussars, to entrench on a vital height had earned himself a stinging public rebuke. "I hope," the British Army Commander in Chief had announced, "that I shall never see such a horrid sight again as cavalry digging." [2]

Why, then, did the armies of World War I remain bogged down in trench warfare, when none of them planned for it, none of them wanted it and all of them hated it when it came about? Was it, as many propose, that the generals on both sides were so stupid or unimaginative that their mental processes simply could not conceive of any method to get them out of the trench stalemate? The basis of this proposition is the indisputable fact that for a period of almost four years the German and Allied armies lay in close proximity to each other and neither side was able to move more than a few miles. This fact is, of course, a damning one; still, the factors that brought about the stalemate in the first place merit thoughtful analysis.

Chief among these factors was the effectiveness of the machine gun in stopping infantry attacks, even though the attacks were usually supported by artillery fire—and even though the latter actually accounted for more casualties in the war than did the machine gun.[3] Cheap, light, requiring few soldiers to man it and firing 450 rounds per minute of a relatively lightweight ammunition which posed no very difficult supply problem, it was able to stultify almost every offensive from the winter of 1914 to the spring of 1918. It is certainly not too much to say that if the machine gun had not been invented the war of the trenches would never have taken place. Even more than its companions the magazine rifle and barbed wire, it forced the combatants into the trenches and kept them there.

The basic reason why the generals were unable to get them out— were unable to open up the trench war into a war of movement— lay in the state of technology in the early twentieth century. The development and manufacture of firearms could be indulged in at a modest cost by almost any government or armaments firm. As a result, the science of small arms was almost a perfected art (so much so that most of the small arms used as late as World War II bore turn-of-the-century patent numbers). In efficiency and reliability these weapons were far ahead of the only thing which could really overcome them, an armored vehicle combined with and driven by an internal-combustion engine—the creation of which required a much greater technical effort and the need for which had been much less obvious.

World War I, then, came when the nations involved were at a peculiar stage of technological development. Because they were not far enough advanced, they did not have the weapons needed to break the trench stalemate. But because they were as far advanced as they were, they were able to create, arm and maintain a solid defensive system stretching for more than four hundred miles; and whereas in other wars the troops had had to suspend fighting in the winter and go into quarters, now the armies were well-enough supplied to spend the year round in their fortifications, improving, deepening, making even more permanent the omnipresent trenches.

The generals are to be blamed not so much because they failed to

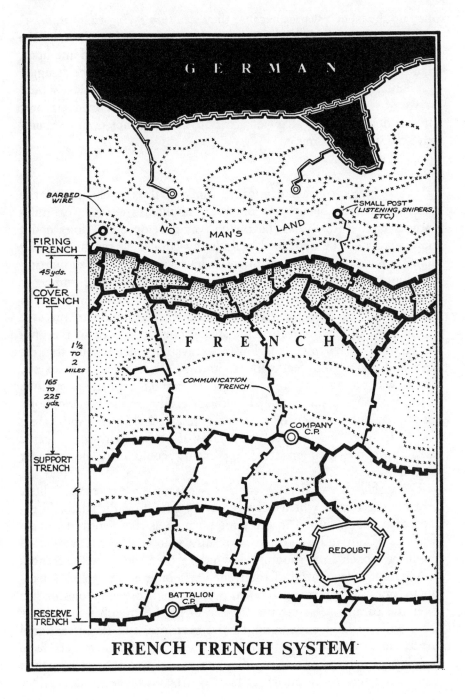

FRENCH TRENCH SYSTEM

open up the trench war as because they *went on trying to do it,* wasting thousands of lives with each attempt, long after it should have been apparent that they could not succeed with the old methods. Had they faced reality, they might have recognized that the struggle was actually going to be a war of attrition. In the end, the war would be won by the Allies because they followed (however inadvertently and inefficiently) a strategy of attrition, although not even to themselves would they admit it.

It is a common misconception to think of the trench lines of the western front as being two opposing ditches extending for miles without end. Actually, as the trench war developed, the lines could more accurately be described as a closely connected series of strong points which formed a continuous belt, reinforcing and supporting one another by means of flanking fire from their machine guns.

This is what a typical French Army "strong point" was like in 1915, by which time the trench system was beginning to mature:

The forwardmost works of the strong point consisted of the "firing trench," a narrow, laboriously excavated gulch about six feet deep and about four feet wide at its top. Directly in front of the trench was the parapet, a sandbagged or earthen rampart about one foot high which was studded with carefully concealed loopholes through which riflemen or machine-gunners could fire. And a few feet in front of the parapet was a mass of barbed wire many yards deep through which an attacking enemy could only flounder at length.

The inside of the firing trench was cut up by "traverses," little bends in the trench which occurred every four to eight yards. In effect, these traverses served the same purpose as the watertight bulkheads of a ship and prevented an enemy who captured a section of the firing trench from shooting down the whole length of the trench.

Against the front wall of the trench was built a "fire step," a banquette on which riflemen stood to peer through the loopholes or fire over the parapet. Against the back wall of the trench small niches were built to hold ammunition, hand grenades, and flares to signal the artillery. And also against the back wall of the trench were little openings which led down into dugouts, the more elaborate of which were ultimately to be buried twenty feet beneath the ground under

4'-0"

BARBED WIRE

PARAPET

PARADOS

APPROX. 1'-0"

2'-0"

AMMUNITION NICHE

FIRE STEP.

5'-8"

1'-8"

2'-4"

1'-4"

3 FEET

CROSS-SECTION OF
FRENCH FIRING TRENCH

alternate layers of dirt, concrete, stone and steel rails and could be made safe even against a direct hit from a six-inch shell.

About forty-five yards behind the firing trench a "cover trench" was generally built, similar to the firing trench but designed to shelter troops during a violent bombardment and grenade attack on the firing trench, following which the troops from the cover trench could rapidly reinforce and provide fire support for any of their beleaguered mates who might still remain alive in the firing trench.

From 165 to 225 yards behind the cover trench was the "support trench"—again similar in construction, but usually containing the company command post and offering support for the firing and cover trenches, or, if they were lost to a successful attack, providing another trench barrier to the continuation of the attack.

Generally placed behind the support trench was the "redoubt," a small field fortification which was completely surrounded by wire and within which a platoon of troops was placed with orders to defend it to the last man in the event of an enemy break-through which punctured the firing, cover and support trenches.

Finally, behind all these works, about two miles behind the firing trench, was the "reserve trench," in which was located the battalion command post and which served as the final barrier to an enemy. The vital feature of the reserve trench was the fact that, protected by its distance from the front line, it was out of range of most of the enemy's artillery, which could reduce the foremost trenches to a rubble but which could never deliver a mass of field artillery fire on the reserve trenches. A typical large-scale attack would, after days of furious bombardment, carry the forward trenches, but was almost invariably stopped by the relatively unscathed reserve trench.

Connecting all these defenses, from the firing trench back to the reserve trench, were "communication trenches" similar to the other trenches except for being wider and often without fire steps.

But all of this took some time to evolve. Since no army had foreseen the development of trench warfare, no army had been even remotely prepared for it. And the first winter was a horror of lack of material, compounded by lack of knowledge. Both the Germans and the Allies sensed that only artillery could reduce the trench systems which had by then begun to proliferate almost spontaneously under the necessity to find shelter from the hail of bullets fired by the omnipresent machine guns. But both sides had gone into the war with a supply of less than 1,500 rounds per artillery piece;[4] this stock was almost exhausted in the opening battles, and it took endless months to build up the supply to a point where a really effective bombardment was possible. Yet the Germans had an advantage in their artillery: although their field gun was qualitatively inferior to the French 75, they had entered the war with a substantial quantity of medium and heavy artillery and howitzers designed to fire in the high, looping trajectory which was so valuable for trench warfare. The French, on the other hand, had desperately little heavy artillery and were dependent on the less suitable flat trajectory of their 75 plus obsolete heavy artillery dredged up from various fortresses.

So new was the need for specialized weapons to fight the war of the trenches that the quantities required were anyone's guess. When Lloyd George, the British Minister of Munitions, was told in 1915 that he should plan on furnishing four machine guns per battalion, he scoffed at this figure, which the military men had supplied him. Instead, he gave instructions to "square that number, multiply the result by two, and when in sight of that, double it for good luck." [5] Fantastically, this proved to be almost precisely the number of machine guns which the British Army ended up needing.

Aside from making clear the shortages in armaments, that first winter of 1914-15 brought out woeful deficiencies in methods. Everything was somewhat catch-as-catch-can, with too many problems and details left to be solved on the basis of *système D*, a French Army expression derived from the verb *se débrouiller*, meaning "to muddle through." Take, for instance, the trenches themselves. For many months they were badly revetted, with little lumber available to support the sides or for duckboards on the bottoms. As a result, during the rainy seasons the trenches were a ghastly Calvary for the unfortunates who inhabited them. Freezing mud up to the troops' knees compounded "trench foot" with the commonplace horror of having the partial remains of a corpse, buried by previous artillery bombardment, exhume itself through the pressure of the mud and slither into the trench to become food for the enormous rats which multiplied in the fighting sectors.

From time to time the poorly revetted trenches would collapse. If this happened at the same time to troops on the two opposing sides, the situation became faintly ludicrous. A young British liaison officer with the French Army witnessed a simultaneous collapse of both the French and German firing trenches at Vimy. "It was as embarrassing as if a lady's bathroom had burst open as she was getting into the tub. Both sides were horribly *gêné*. . . . No one fired, it was too obviously a checkmate." [6] Both French and Germans fell to digging furiously while their sentries glared at one another over the few hundred yards separating them. Within a few hours, shallow trenches had been completed, the troops jumped into them and the war started again.

But as the months of trench warfare dragged on, the trench systems became more and more elaborate and more professional. The trenches were better built, with concrete poured to form pillboxes for the ever-multiplying machine guns; dugouts were enlarged and deepened until they could hold whole companies of men with safety under even the most violent bombardments; roll after roll of barbed wire was added to that already there; finally at points of sensitivity or danger it became standard practice to duplicate the trench systems, so that for miles behind the foremost firing trench the ground was sliced into trench after trench.

As the defenses grew in complexity, the problems of supplying and manning them multiplied. A host of complicated and hitherto undreamed-of services spawned and multiplied. For the French Army, at the top of the hierarchy stood G.Q.G., the Grand Quartier Général, commanded by Joffre and located now at Chantilly, with an enormous staff of more than five hundred officers and nearly a thousand clerks, plus guards, escorts, dispatch riders, etc. This vast retinue disposed of French military operations throughout the globe and, as a result of Joffre's tremendous prestige as the "Savior of the Marne," gave tacit direction to its allies.

For all its size, G.Q.G. could not possibly handle all the manifold technical problems connected with supply, military movements and tactical direction of the more than one hundred infantry divisions which composed the mass of the French Army. To supply these essentials there evolved an elaborate chain of command which pyramided down through army groups, armies and army corps, all devoted to interpreting and amplifying the basic strategic decisions of G.Q.G., as well as providing the infantry with such arms and services as corps artillery, engineers, cavalry and aircraft.

Subordinated to—indeed, sometimes buried by—this mass of staffs and services were the infantry divisions themselves. They were commanded by a general and possessed their own artillery and engineers, but at this time they consisted principally of two brigades of infantry which were subdivided into regiments, battalions and companies.

"The company," stated the French Army manual for platoon commanders, "is the organization which appeals most to the soldier. It is the largest unit in which all the grades and men can be personally acquainted. It is the smallest one that can be charged with elementary tactical operation." [7] This being the case, it is worthwhile to follow a French infantry company into the trenches.

As constituted on paper, the company consisted of a captain, three lieutenants, and two hundred men subdivided into company staff and four platoons. In practice, after a company had been in action for a time its numbers often fell to 150 or even 100 men and it became very difficult to build the company back to full strength.

This is how a French infantry company lived and fought in the trenches:

Coming from rest or reserve billets well behind the trench lines, the company relieves another which has manned the trenches for a week or ten days. Generally all reliefs are made at night and in strict silence, to avoid the enemy's observing the operation and shelling the inviting target of trenches packed with double their normal complement. The company being relieved sends an officer and four enlisted guides back to the beginning of the communication trenches, and they escort the relieving company up to the sector they are to hold, generally a strong point consisting of a few hundred yards of trench. At the company command post the two commanders confer:

"How far are the Boche firing trenches from ours?"

"Three hundred yards. Where are his machine guns sited?"

"Here and here and here"—pointing to the map.

"How's our wire?"

"Pretty good, but this afternoon our artillery stirred up a Boche barrage and they cut the wire here and here. You'll have to get out a wiring party tonight. Any mining going on?"

"None that we've heard. But the next company north thinks they're being mined under. Last night one of their patrols heard some digging just outside their own wire. A bad business. That's all, then?"

"Yes. If you'll relieve me, we'll get out. Maybe we'll be taking over from you next week, so try to keep the trenches cleaned up. I had to practically rebuild the cover trench when I took over."

"Don't fear, my boys always leave a trench in good shape. Maybe we'll even dig a couple of dugouts."

"Au 'voir."

"Au 'voir."

The relieved company files rapidly out—no point in taking too long and being killed by a stray shell on one's way to rest billets.

The newly arrived company quickly disperses itself along its sector of the trenches. In the firing trench, the cover trench, the support trench and the redoubt the four platoons take their places. Contact has been established between the adjoining companies on the right and left. Sentries are posted every few yards in the firing trench; standing on the fire step, they peer cautiously through the camouflaged loopholes in the parapet. The rest of the troops file into the dugouts, except for a group of ten men and a corporal told off as a wiring party. They will leave the trench on the company's left, crawl along repairing the wire, and re-enter by the trench on the company's right. The officer in charge of the company's section hurries down the firing trench to alert the sentries not to fire on their own men.

Faces blackened, the wiring party climbs up a scaling ladder and creeps out into no man's land. The older troops among them are sweating nervously, for the Germans know that the French wire was cut in the afternoon's bombardment and it is obvious that the French will have to repair it tonight. When they are part way along the wire, they hear a hollow explosion from the German trenches a few hundred yards away, and the more experienced members of the wiring party throw themselves flat on the ground. The lemon-colored light of a flare bathes the ground with flickering glow. One soldier, an eighteen-year-old of one of the new classes, feeling nakedly exposed on the ground in view of the German trenches, starts to get up in order to jump over the parapet and back into the haven of the firing trench. He gets no farther than rising to his knees, as a hail of machine-gun bullets lashes accurately across no man's land. "Damn kid," the troops say to themselves. "If you keep still they'll never see you, no matter how bright the flare. Now we're in for it—we'll be caught out here for hours." A cluster of German flares soar up and the machine guns keep up a slow traverse over the ground.

Now the French are manning their trenches in force. The friendly machine guns open up; here and there rifle bullets stab across, carefully aimed at the flickering German machine guns. There is a spark as machine-gun bullets hit a strand of barbed wire, and for a moment the wire gives off a soft blue glow. The fire fight continues for twenty minutes, gradually loses intensity, dies away to nothing. The German flares stop; the wiring party hurriedly tumbles into its trenches. It has left two men dead—the boy who tried to run and an experienced soldier who was unlucky enough to be hit by blind rifle fire. The company's bleeding in the trenches has started.

Morning routine in the trenches never varies. Since no one knows what the dawn's light will bring—maybe a mass of German infantry crouched just outside the trenches, or the flash of German bayonets in the opposite trench as a surprise assault is launched—dawn is always the most dangerous time. For this reason, well before first light the sergeant of the guard in each of the trenches has brought the company to stand-to. Every loophole is manned, all the troops are awake and waiting in their dugouts or sitting on the fire step with loaded rifles in hand. Miles in the rear the artillerymen stand by guns loaded and registered on the enemy trenches and no man's land, The telephone circuits are manned, flare pistols are handy. A half hour passes. The sun has come up and one of the lieutenants has cautiously raised a periscope above the parapet and swept the length of the enemy trench. There is no sign of life either in no man's land or in the German trenches. Another half hour passes. The roll is called, the men are released for breakfast in their dugouts, except for the sentries and the snipers on the parapets.

Now commences the tedium of trench life. Working parties are told off to bring up ammunition and food; other groups begin the constant drudgery of deepening the dugouts and repairing the trenches. Throughout the trench system millions upon millions of sandbags are in use as parapets, trench walls, traverses, etc. Each of these sandbags has been filled by hand; they weigh about forty-five pounds each, and a squad of ten men can fill only about 150 bags an hour. It is slow, backbreaking drudgery, made worse by the fact that in their work the troops must remain completely unobserved by the enemy. Any sandbags to be put up on the parapet will be placed after dark, the entire trench system, from Switzerland to the English Channel, is under the closest possible scrutiny during every daylight hour. Unceasingly, binoculars and periscopes scout the opposing trench lines for the slightest unguarded movement. Does a faint trail of smoke frequently rise above a certain point in the trench? Then, obviously, there must be a concealed loophole in the parapet and behind it a nervous sentry smoking his pipe. Binoculars carefully study and restudy the parapet until the tiny loophole is found; a sniper sights in on the loophole and in a moment it is all over with the careless sentry.

In another section of the trench, the French see a shifting movement in the German sandbagged parapet. A working party is obviously repairing the trench or replacing rotted sandbags. The attention of the French company commander is called to it. Clearly, this is an opportunity that is too good to pass; at least a dozen men must be working in one congested spot in the German firing trench, and although they are under cover from rifle and machine-gun fire they can be reached by high-trajectory weapons.

The company commander snaps out a few orders, and from the trenches in the rear a sergeant and a few men run forward. They are carrying a trench mortar—an antique, almost comic-looking little cast-iron weapon, looking very much like a crude piece of drainpipe secured on a metal base. The soldiers set the piece on a floor of the trench and pour the contents of a few packets of powder into the mouth of the mortar. A mortar "bomb" is carefully dropped into the mouth of the mortar, its fuse lighted, and a lighted stick thrust into the mortar's touchhole. With a sharp bang the bomb sails up into the air, describing a high loop, and by a lucky happenstance the first shot drops directly into the German trench. There is a dull explosion; most of the German working party is now probably dead or maimed. But now retribution must be expected. Trench mortars are so vicious that the enemy always replies in kind, and for this reason they are hated by every infantryman. Within a few moments a German trench mortar speaks. The bomb is clearly visible as it curves up from the trench, rises in its flight, stops, then falls down toward the French trenches. But its progress is noted by few; every wary soldier has taken cover within a dugout or is flat on his face in his trench. Only the sentries must stand in their partially sheltered niches and take it. They press themselves against the parapet, praying that the dreaded mortars will soon let up.

Whether by trench mortars, by an occasional artillery shell, by snipers' bullets, or by machine guns firing on night patrols or wiring parties in no man's land, the constant wastage of men goes on. "The war of the trenches," it is written in the French Infantry Manual, "is neither a relaxation nor guard duty; it is a phase of the battle. It is necessary that the adversary feel in front of him a vigilant hatred and know that we wish no rest before his defeat. It is necessary that each hostile company go back from the trenches with a loss of at least twenty men." [8] The staff officers at G.Q.G. have even invented a name for it; they call it "maintaining moral ascendancy." The pursuance of this precept cost the French Army about 1,500 casualties a day.

But day-in, day-out losses, bad as they were and senseless and futile as they seemed to the men in the trenches, were as nothing compared to the horror of a full-scale offensive. For these, preparations began months in advance. As it became apparent that only artillery could blast a path through the barbed wire (experience evolved the precise formula that 150 shells from a 75 were necessary to cut a ten-yard breach in a wire entanglement twenty yards thick), [9] the preparations for an offensive assumed the form of a stupendous logistics problem. Not only must vast quantities of shells be brought into the area, but immense amounts of rifle and machine-gun ammunition had also to be brought forward. And, compounding the problem, there was the matter of supplying hand grenades. Since so much of the fighting was done at relatively close quarters, and since the defenders were usually sheltered in the wreckage of dugouts and trenches partially shattered by the pre-assault bombardment, it was found that the best weapon for blasting one's way into a trench was the hand grenade. At the beginning of the war its use had hardly been contemplated, and the supply was almost nonexistent. But the obvious utility of this simple bomb, which could be thrown over a traverse or tossed into a dugout, soon made it such a favorite that almost half of a French infantry company were "bombers" rather than riflemen. However, the problem of supplying an advancing front line with these bulky objects rapidly became a major one, and it was common for an advance to peter out due to the lack of grenades.

Aside from logistics problems, the question of tactics was a major assault consideration. The experiences of 1914 had made evident the fact that men could not advance in dense masses and survive against enemy machine-gun fire no matter how badly the machine-gun nests might be shattered by artillery fire. So a better way, an entirely new set of tactics, had to be evolved.

Drawing on both its own experience and the most successful features of German attacks, the French Army developed an assault system the main features of which were looseness and flexibility. The assault formation consisted of a series of three waves, the foremost being a loose line of riflemen and "bombers" known as the "assault wave." Consisting of two platoons, or roughly half the strength of an infantry company, the assault wave dashed forward on a front of about two hundred yards, filtered its way around various strong points and concerned itself principally with gaining ground. Approximately thirty yards behind the assault wave the "Moppers-Up," or "trench-cleaning wave," followed. Generally, these men were drawn from a unit reserve and were not formally a part of the attacking company. It was the job of the moppers-up to kill off the Germans remaining in the trenches overrun by the assault wave. Usually this was accomplished with hand grenades, the moppers-up proceeding down the length of the trench and tossing grenades over traverses.[10]

Finally, following the moppers-up by about fifty yards was the "supporting wave," comprising the balance of the company. As the assault wave became casualties or completely lost momentum in its advance, the supporting wave passed through it and continued the advance. And, in turn, as the company became decimated or exhausted, successive companies took over and continued the advance.

As this tactic became refined, and as more artillery and more shells became available, it became possible for French commanders almost to count on the capture of a section of the German firing trench and maybe even the support trenches a few hundred yards back. True, vast quantities of artillery ammunition had to be expended, and one had to be prepared to accept the almost complete loss of the first few waves in the assault; but, provided one could summon the moral resolve to spend enough lives, the thing could be done. Purely and simply, it was a matter of gathering together more men for an assault than the defenders could kill with their machine guns and artillery.

For days in advance of an attack, battalions of infantry are gathered by night and moved up to dugouts immediately behind the trench lines. Then on the night before the attack they are hurried up through the communications trenches. They dash across certain dangerous spots, known trench crossing points which German artillery is ranged in on and shells at murderously unpredictable intervals. Now the forward trenches are jammed with troops. In the darkness stretcher-bearers and messengers can scarcely make their way through. The French artillery has opened fire now, and a few of the waiting infantrymen stand on the fire step and peer over the parapet to see if their artillery is beginning to cut through the German barbed wire. From the French trenches, small parties creep out to snip paths in their own barbed wire.

Nervously, the troops await daybreak. The complexities of a trench warfare assault are such that it is almost impossible to attack at night. The men are quiet, apprehensive, irritable. The troops of the first waves know that their chances of surviving the morning are not good. The sergeants call the roll and then call it again—a procedure which is thought to help dispel nervousness. The corporals check every man's equipment; the riflemen carry their weapon plus 120 cartridges, six hand grenades, gas mask, entrenching tool, shelter half, rations for three days, two canteens (one with a liter of brandy in it), and five empty sandbag sacks. Identification tags dangle from every man's neck and wrist.

Too soon daybreak comes. The artillery fire has reached its zenith and the company commander constantly glances at his wrist watch. Now it is *l'heure H*, the captain blows his trench whistle and the officers spring up the scaling ladders and dash out into no man's land, followed by their troops. The artillery has checked its fire, and each company of attacking troops spreads out to form "waves" which begin to trudge toward the German lines. They cannot move very fast—the battlefield is a morass of shell holes and remnants of barbed wire.

Now the Germans have recovered from the bombardment. From their trenches machine guns stitch bullets across at the attackers. The German artillery opens up. In the attacking waves, men begin to crumple. But they reach the first German lines, toss countless grenades into the trenches and the dugouts and bayonet the defenders. Then they regroup and advance against the second German line.

But now the whole grisly procedure begins to fall apart. The rearward German trenches have been, by design, constructed far enough back from the front lines to be out of the range of most of the French artillery. And now the French attackers are exhausted—only a few minutes of combat are enough to tire an attacking force. There are no more grenades; too many officers are killed or wounded; some French units have moved quickly through the first German lines, while others are still held up by a particularly stubborn machine-gun nest; the noise of the battlefield is fantastic and no one can hear the orders of the surviving officers. Ahead the undestroyed German trench line flares with the massed firepower of machine guns and rifles. The attackers are now completely disorganized. In their rear the French general commanding the attack is himself confused. No messenger can get back to him; he does not know how far his assault waves have got. Should he commit his reserves now, when it may already be too late, or should he cut his losses and then perhaps find out that only a few more companies might have saved the day?

And now the attacking waves, cut to pieces, have had to go to ground. They cannot possibly assault the undamaged German second lines. They collect themselves into disorderly little groups and either occupy a captured German trench or else begin to dig frantically to prepare for the furious German counterattack which always comes. Long gone are the days when entrenching tools were considered unworthy of the French soldier. Now it is officially acknowledged that the troops must entrench at once. "When he [the soldier] has gained an advantage at the price of blood, if he counts only on his gun to hold it he will be cruelly deceived." [11]

There is not enough time to entrench adequately. There is no barbed wire in place. Ammunition runs short because it cannot be brought across the shambles of the battlefield. The German artillery is pouring shells into the newly won French positions. The French artillery is now out of range, and the shell-pocked battlefield is an almost impenetrable barrier to the guns being moved rapidly forward —and anyway, it would not dare give close support because the French artillerymen do not know where their own troops now are.

From the German trenches waves of gray-clad Germans begin a counterattack. Resisting desperately, the French are turned out of their dearly bought positions. By nightfall it is all over. With the exception of a few hundred yards of German firing trench to which they may still be able to cling, the French are back in their original lines.

So it went. During 1915 the French launched endless series of infantry attacks, assaults consisting of attacks by companies, then battalions, then divisions. They failed almost uniformly—gaining a few hundred yards at first, then losing it in a German counterattack.

And as the months dragged on, the French infantryman came, like the chameleon, to adapt the protective coloration of his surroundings. Gone were the red trousers and the cloth cap of a few months before. Now infantrymen had somehow begun to achieve a curious shabby sameness. Muffled in muddy horizon-blue greatcoats, constantly smoking pipes, generally bearded, they came to be labeled *poilus*—"hairy ones"—a sobriquet in which they took a perverse pride. Their pleasures were few and simple. In off-duty hours during their turn in the trenches they would organize ratting parties to corner and kill the immense rodents which infested the trenches and which had grown to the size of small cats from feeding on the unburied dead in no man's land. And always, constantly, the men prayed for the time when their division would at last suffer the one-third loss in effective strength that was almost mandatory before it would be pulled out of the trenches and sent to rest billets, or else to man the quiet sectors of the front opposite Alsace-Lorraine, where communications were so poor that assaults were rarely mounted.

Although discipline was strict in the French Army, it rarely manifested itself in overbearing commands or humiliating spectacles—at least not in the personal relationship between the company-grade officers and their men. There was a good reason for this. A prewar policy had compelled French candidates for St.-Cyr to spend at least one year in the ranks. It had been a concession to republicanism demanded by the government after the Dreyfus Affair, and now it stood France in good stead. The junior officers knew their men well; it was a tradition in the French Army for the officer to use the familiar *tu* in speaking to his men. It was also a tradition that on the day when an attack was to be made, *le jour J,* it was the captain or one of the lieutenants of the infantry company who blew the trench whistle to signal the moment of attack and led his men up the scaling ladders with the cry, *"En avant!"*

At this period, during 1915, about 50 per cent of the company-grade officers from the prewar active army were still alive.[12] But their ranks were thinning fast and replacements had to be found, so a number of schools were set up to train promising enlisted men into officers. In this, France was inadvertently fortunate. Although it had been something of a prewar scandal, there were vast numbers of educated Frenchmen who, had they been in the more caste-conscious German or British armies, would certainly have been officers, but who chose to serve their period of conscript duty as enlisted men and later had been mobilized as such. ("Your grandfather commanded armies, you drive generals," a high-ranking officer had remarked to his wellborn military chauffeur.)[13] But now these men were available, and they were combed out of the ranks and sent to the various officers' schools which had been set up to give quick training behind the lines.

Although he may have been hastily trained, the French officer was blessed with good human material with which to work. The poilu was intelligent, amazingly patriotic and, though sometimes cynical, quick to respond to courageous leadership. And the French infantryman had a sense of humor which served to make almost bearable the troglodyte existence of the trenches. When the Germans set up a sign outside one of their trenches reading, "Soldiers of the north, you are all cuckolds—we are sleeping with your wives!" the instant reply from the French trenches was the sign, "We don't give a damn—we all come from the south." [14]

For all their humor, though, the troops had a number of serious complaints. One was the pitifully small amount of time which they were given for furloughs—only seven days out of every four months, and even that subject to cancellation whenever an offensive was scheduled. Another was the almost criminal inefficiency of the French Army Medical Service, which was chronically understaffed, undersupplied and woefully inept.

The officers on the staffs—G.Q.G., the armies and the army corps —also came under the infantryman's scorn. The poilu knew, since it was he who was dying in the fruitless assaults, that these attacks would always be bloody failures until the staffs learned that the only way to gain any ground at all was to prepare the attack with more artillery—vast masses of it, huge calibers of it, and alps of ammunition to be fired by it. This was the only way to success, the poilu thought. Raw courage, the bayonet and the legendary *furia francese* had been tried and had failed. Now they must have artillery to cut the enemy barbed wire, to blow in his trenches, to seek out and smash the ubiquitous machine guns. And because it seemed to the troops that the staffs could not see this or did not get it produced fast enough, and because the staffs, as if in horror at what they had created, seemed constantly to move their headquarters back a little farther to the rear, the enlisted men grew to hate them and called them *embusqués*, slackers.

Nor did it help when Joffre himself described his strategy as *"Je les grignote"* [15] —I am nibbling at them. This was a monumental indiscretion, because the French lost more men than the Germans in almost every battle—and the loss was compounded by the fact that, whereas Germany's population was large enough to make good her losses and even increase the size of her Army, the French Army could scarcely make good its losses even by drafting boys of seventeen and men over forty-five. Joffre had not realized it when he spoke of "nibbling," but it was exactly this aspect of the war which would almost crush the morale of both the French Army and the French nation. The true horror of World War I was not in its maimed and killed, not in the length of the war, and not in its barbarism or atrocities—it was in the fact that *so many men died and achieved nothing by it*. And no nation suffered proportionately more than France.

Aside from faulty tactics and occasionally faulty leadership, the reason for the suffering of the French lay in the difference between their position and that of their German adversaries. The difference was this:

For the Germans, it was not strictly necessary to attack. They already occupied French soil; they had carried the war to their enemy; and they held the high ground and the most readily defensible areas which they had first seized in the "Race to the Sea." As long as the Germans did no more than repel their adversaries' attacks, they could be considered to be winning the war. Probably at almost any time after the beginning of 1915, the Germans would have been happy to conclude a negotiated peace leaving them in possession of the part of France they now held; had this been done, it would have rightly been regarded as an immense German victory and an overwhelming French defeat.

The French, on the other hand, were faced with a more complex problem. To win the war, or even to turn the tide of battle in the Allies' favor, it was necessary that there be at least a modicum of progress toward recapturing that part of France held by the invader. And this could be accomplished only by the tremendously costly "nibbling" at the German trenches, or else by finding leadership and techniques to make the "nibbling" more productive and less costly. And this was only 1915; strong as the German trench systems were now, they would grow vastly stronger in the months to come. So, in essence, it became a race to find generals with ability and ideas before the best and bravest of the French troops had died in the shell holes of no man's land or in screaming agony on the barbed wire of the German firing trenches.

During 1915 the French Army suffered casualties—in killed, wounded, prisoners and missing—totaling 1,549,000 men.[16]

6

COLONEL PÉTAIN

I T IS AN OFT-NOTED FACT that the generals who command armies in time of peace must frequently be replaced when war breaks out. It seems to hold true in the armies of all nations and gives rise to a whole host of complex theories as to how officers should be selected, trained and promoted.

Actually, the problem is an almost inevitable one. The reason why many generals fail in war is simply that they are totally inexperienced, that for all their exhalted rank their only qualification for their position is success in what can be only a distant approximation of what war really is.

When one stops to think about it, the whole thing is really amazing and not a little unfair. Alone among the professions, the military man is expected to prepare himself, to devise plans, to assume responsibility for the lives of thousands or millions of men, all without any previous *practical* experience in battle. And, warfare being what it is, actual battles cannot be arranged merely for the purpose of educating the generals. Accordingly, the closest thing to practical experience that a general may get is in maneuvers.

Now, maneuvers are all well and good. They give officers the experience of handling troops in the field and they give the troops valuable exercise in certain basic military skills. And they help to weed out the utterly incompetent officer. But maneuvers have the disadvantage of having almost preordained results. There are so many known governing factors that there is relatively little stress or strain on the commanders. Little occurs which is unexpected, and

93

there is always the comforting knowledge that on the last day of the maneuver the Blue Forces will triumph decisively over the Red Forces—as the last day of German Army maneuvers always ended with the Kaiser personally leading thirty squadrons of cavalry on a "victorious" hell-for-leather charge through the simulated enemy positions, a charge which had not the faintest similarity to anything that could be expected in time of war.

But for a make-or-break test of military leadership there can never be even a close substitute for actual warfare. Once the battle starts, a thousand unforeseen and never before experienced pressures impinge themselves upon the commander. Although he is generally free from any actual danger of being shot at, he is correspondingly divorced from the battlefield physically. He can know what is happening only through the agency of reports by his subordinates, reports which may or may not arrive and which may or may not be accurate, and on the basis of these reports he must issue orders which may or may not reach their destination.

The commander orders troops to move to a threatened spot and they seem to take a treasonably long time getting there—if, indeed, they get there at all. Bad weather turns the battlefield into a lake of mud. Trusted subordinates are killed or wounded and their places taken by officers who are not well known to the commander, and who may not fully comprehend the commander's plan. He is the recipient of frantic pleas for reinforcements from sectors of the line which are, or perhaps only imagine themselves to be, undergoing violent attack. He receives wildly contradictory reports from various areas under his command, reports which show that enemy troops have appeared in spots where it is *almost* impossible that they can be. Should he ignore these reports? Should he send troops to deal with the enemy and then probably find that the "enemy" is actually nothing more than some farmers working in a field? Or should he send a staff officer to ascertain the true picture and then find that he is too late to deal with a strong enemy incursion on his flank or in his rear?

All the while, and however efficient are his staff and his subordinate officers, the commander must deal with the development of the battle, must strive constantly to enforce his will and retain his initiative against the enemy. And, at the same time, he must divine the enemy's plan and develop his own counter for it.

As all this is going on he must plan or at least pass on the plans for supply, billeting, replacement of casualties, movement of dumps and depots and countless other details. Thousands of men are waiting for his orders. Innumerable decisions must be made, each interacting with another, while simultaneously he must keep his subordinates aware of his intentions and, in so doing, must see that the orders sent to them are clear-cut, direct and not susceptible of alternate interpretations.

Under these circumstances, it is hardly surprising that many commanders snap under the stress. A general who is "successful" in peacetime may owe his elevated station to such fundamentally nonmilitary factors as social or political acceptability, academic brilliance or an appealing personality; but when a war begins, and especially when it begins disastrously, peacetime criteria are dispensed with in a mad scramble to find generals who can withstand the stress and *win battles.*

Among all the nations who fought on the western front in World War I, the French Army probably suffered the most from the failure of generals to live up to expectations. In the first six weeks of the war, Joffre retired three army commanders, ten corps commanders and thirty-eight division commanders who, it was found, either were incompetent or simply collapsed under the pressure.[1] A perfect example of this occurred in the largest of the five French field armies, the Fifth, which at mobilization mustered almost 300,000 men. The Fifth Army was commanded by General Charles Lanrezac, who was thought to be one of the French Army's best and most dynamic generals and a true apostle of the offensive spirit. But when the Schlieffen Plan erupted upon Lanrezac (he was holding the French left, and therefore the Germans debouched on *his* left), he suffered a form of personal collapse. Under the unexpected German attack he became comatose, was incapable of making positive decisions, and completely lost confidence in his troops and himself. All thoughts of blocking the German advance or striking at the enemy flank fled from Lanrezac's mind. All he could think of was to retreat southward. When Joffre proposed a fighting stand, Lanrezac presented such an aspect of lethargy, despondency and hopelessness that Joffre, who was probably looking for a scapegoat in any case, relieved him on the spot. In this manner, too, went many of Lanrezac's former subordinates. The Fifth Army at the outbreak of the fighting had contained twenty-two generals who commanded either divisions or

corps; within six weeks twelve of these twenty-two had been relieved.[2]

If large numbers of generals were to be dismissed, replacements
had to be found for them. Generally, these replacements were officers who had been commanding divisions, regiments or even brigades
which quickly distinguished themselves in the early fighting. For a
French officer who possessed cool nerve plus the ability to adapt
himself to the wholly unanticipated conditions of trench warfare,
the French Army of 1914-15 offered the possibility of meteoric advancement.

It was found that several types of officers possessed the requisite
intelligence, experience and nerve to achieve some measure of success
in trench warfare. One type was the thoroughgoing butcher—the
species of commander whose psychological make-up permits him
unhesitatingly to expend the lives of masses of troops without qualm
or compunction as long as the objective is gained. The classic example of this type of soldier was Charles Mangin, a brigadier general at the start of the war. Short, burly, fantastically energetic,
Mangin speedily proved himself to be a well-trained, adaptable
ramrod under whose lash even the most comatose subordinates became imbued with fighting spirit. And when it came to trench warfare, Mangin possessed the "advantage" of being able to view men
as an expendable mass—a point of view doubtless conditioned by
the fact that he had spent most of his military career alternately
fighting and training the natives of France's African colonies.

In a way, Mangin could be regarded as a typical product of the
system of generalship which developed during World War I. There
is no question but that one of the requisites of a successful general is
a certain indifference to the suffering of his troops. In war it is inevitable that many will be killed or maimed, and the commander
responsible for launching his troops into battle cannot concern himself with this to the point where his powers of decision or judgment
are crippled by the thought of the suffering of his men. It is for this
reason that generals should live in a certain seclusion, protected from
seeing too much of the awful human debris of battle. But, of course,
this can be carried to an extreme, and the endless slaughter of World
War I tended to breed too great an indifference to casualties on the
part of the upper levels of command. Winston Churchill, in a not
unsympathetic portrait of Sir Douglas Haig, wrote that the British

Commander in Chief "presents to me in those red years the same mental picture as a great surgeon before the days of anesthetics, versed in every detail of such science as was known to him; sure of himself, steady of poise, knife in hand, intent upon the operation; entirely removed in his professional capacity from the agony of the patient, the anguish of relations, or the doctrines of rival schools, the devices of quacks, or the first fruits of new learning. He would operate without excitement, or he would depart without being affronted; and if the patient died, he would not reproach himself." [3]

This, then, was the attitude at the very highest levels of command. Perhaps it was necessary. Certainly there was no room for squeamish commanders. They had to learn to live in semioblivion of the horrors of the trenches. And in many cases they adjusted quite nicely. Joffre, for example, managed to preserve his equanimity without apparent strain. Amid the bustling activity of G.Q.G., Joffre was an island of calm. He napped after lunch and during car rides, and he slept soundly every night. His office was bare, no papers on his desk, no maps on his wall. Few things excited him, and these only trivia—for example, the high cost of his personal mess accounts; or when someone other than himself touched his fountain pen. And once at luncheon on Good Friday when he noted that there was no meat listed on the mess menu he announced in a rage, "I am a republican general!" and stopped service of the meal until a hastily prepared meat dish could be brought on. [4]

But even if this apparent unconcern with the drawn-out suffering at the front had an excuse at G.Q.G., it had an unhappy corollary effect in the lower ranks of command. The new "butcher" type of general coming to the fore calculated success in terms of lives lost. If losses were high, then the attack, however otherwise fruitless, could be represented as having been "pressed home with vigor and élan." But if losses were light, then, somehow, it was thought that the troops had "failed in their duty." In this way, a premium came to be placed upon the nerveless commander who could order wave after wave of troops to certain death. And in this, during the first year of the war at least, the French system of military justice played a significant part.

The military discipline of any army is, of course, inseparably bound up with the system of trial which the army uses. For the French Army, one of the manifold reactions to the Dreyfus case had been the overhaul of the court-martial system. In 1906 a series of reforms, made principally at the behest of the republicans and the parties of the far left, had ensured to accused members of the Army a fair trial by a seven-judge court-martial. Coupled with this was a system of appeals and reviews by higher courts. But this was only a peacetime system; at the outbreak of war military justice was administered by *conseils de guerre* which conducted speedy trials and greatly restricted the accused's right of appeal. Even they were thought to be too slow under certain circumstances, so on September 6, 1914, the government established by decree a supplementary system of *cours martiales*. These *cours martiales* were designed to try only certain types of crimes—looting, desertion and self-mutilation. They consisted of three officers who could be appointed on the spot, convene the court immediately and then try the accused, who, if found guilty, was punished without delay.[5] It was a system so quick that it speedily lent itself to the grossest of abuses. It put every enlisted man totally at the mercy of any superior who had the rank to convene a *cour martiale*, especially if the officer was disposed to ignore the stipulation that only certain categories of cases could be brought before such courts.

Inevitably, the *cours martiales* became the essential instrument of all the "butcher" generals, who used them to set an example of their own implacable determination. The case later to become well known as "the affair of the four corporals of Suippes" was typical of these executions *pour l'example*.

In March of 1915, the 336th Infantry Regiment was in the lines at Perthes-les-Hurlus in Champagne. For days the troops had been sent forward in successive company-strength attacks in an effort to find a weak spot in the German lines. Every attack had been a failure. The French artillery preparation had been so limited that the barbed wire in front of the German trenches was still uncut, although it was sagging with the weight of dead French infantrymen. By March 9 the infantry was exhausted and the attacks were sluggish and dispirited. But this served only to infuriate General Reveilhac, the frustrated commander of the infantry division to which the 336th belonged. He now ordered the 21st Company into the firing trenches for another assault.

The 21st Company was not a good choice. It had been shot through in a useless attack two days before, and now through loopholes and periscopes the men could clearly distinguish the rotting bodies of their comrades. So when, *l'heure H*, 5 P.M., came and the company commander blew his whistle and dashed up a scaling ladder, he was followed only by another officer and a few N.C.O.s. None of the enlisted men, it appears, joined them.

The attackers were met by a storm of German fire, and it was only by great good luck that they were able to fall back into the trenches. Even if the enlisted men had taken part in the assault, it seems agreed, they could not possibly have gained any ground, such was the volume of the German fire. But to Reveilhac, watching the attack from a command post, this was clearly mutiny. In a rage he telephoned his divisional artillery commander, a Colonel Bérube, and ordered him to commence fire on the *French* trenches, where, Reveilhac said, "the officers have advanced and the men are not following them." Respectfully but firmly, Bérube declined to follow his chief's instructions; to fire on Frenchmen was murder and Bérube would not do it without a written and signed order from the general.

Even though balked from this quarter, Reveilhac was determined to bring the 21st Company to heel. Peremptorily he ordered the company commander to send four corporals and sixteen men out into no man's land immediately to cut the barbed wire in front of the German trenches. Now, this was an operation which even at night was considered close to suicide, and in this case it was still daylight and the German trenches were thronged with alert defenders. It was tantamount to a death sentence. But an order like this could not be disobeyed, and Corporals Maupas, Girard, Lefoulen and Lechat were selected, together with sixteen privates.

The second they clambered over the scaling ladders, they were pinned to the ground by furious machine-gun fire. To reach the German barbed wire, a hundred meters away, was absolutely impossible. The men crouched in shell holes until nightfall, when, many of them wounded, they tumbled back into their trenches.

Now Reveilhac had the excuse he wanted. Here was an opportunity to make an example of what happened to troops who would not advance. A *cour martiale* was convened at Suippes on March 16 and the four corporals and the sixteen privates were brought before it on charges of refusing to obey orders in the face of the enemy. The colonel who was senior officer of the court obviously had his instructions from Reveilhac, and all accused would speedily have been found guilty were it not that the general now, apparently, had second thoughts about the affair. To shoot the privates might be overdoing things; perhaps it would be enough to shoot only the corporals. Accordingly, the privates were acquitted with the excuse that they had "not heard any orders to advance" and the four corporals were found guilty and condemned to death.

The following day Maupas, Girard, Lefoulen and Lechat were shot. The 336th Infantry Regiment, outraged at this callous injustice, teetered on the edge of revolt, and a unit of cavalry dragoons had to be brought up to maintain order. At the execution, the shaken firing squad could not, or would not, aim properly. Two of the corporals were only wounded and had to be finished off by the pistol of the officer commanding the squadron—a grisly operation which was completed only seconds before the order for the postponement of the execution arrived, signed by the now remorseful Reveilhac.[6]

The four corporals of Suippes were by no means the only victims of injustice served up by the *cours martiales* at the behest of wrathful generals. There exist well-authenticated accounts of many other cases—such as that of a company of the 45th Brigade whose attack on April 19, 1915, was checked by heavy German fire. The division commander, a General Delatoile, announced to his staff that it was his intention to shoot the whole company "to set an example." Horrified, his subordinates succeeded in getting this number cut down to seventy-five victims, then to twenty, and ultimately to six. The only way these could be selected was for the whole company to draw straws to determine who would be the propitiatory six. Those unlucky enough to draw the short straws, an N.C.O. named Morange and five privates, made a brief appearance before the tribunal, after which the court was recessed. The next morning a priest arrived at the prison stockade and advised the men that in their absence the court had reconvened, found them guilty and sentenced them to death. Within minutes they were executed by a firing squad assembled from another regiment.[7]

There were, however, French generals who made their way up from obscurity without becoming butchers. One of these was Robert Nivelle, who during the open field warfare of September 1914, when he was a lieutenant colonel of artillery, had command of a group of guns attached to the 63rd Infantry Division. Under heavy

German pressure at the Battle of the Ourcq, the infantry broke and ran. Obviously an extreme measure was required and Nivelle seized the opportunity. He limbered up five batteries of 75s and personally led a charge through his own infantry *toward* the advancing Germans. It was a fantastically daring act, for instead of being protected by the infantry Nivelle's artillery was now in front shielding the shattered troops. But the gamble paid off—the astounded Germans were stopped by a hail of short-range artillery fire and the revitalized French infantry charged forward to a successful attack.

But of all the ambitious officers who catapulted upward, none advanced further then Henri Philippe Benoni Omer Joseph Pétain.

Countless tales have been written about the typical peasant farmer of the north of France. Shrewd, taciturn, practical, stubborn, dour, he is the antithesis of the gay Parisian boulevardier of song and story. Doubtless these tales have more than a shred of truth about them. Philippe Pétain possessed, in great measure, all of these traditional qualities. And precisely because he possessed these qualities, Pétain saved the French Army.

No one could have started out more inconspicuously. When World War I began, Pétain was a simple colonel of infantry—actually, the commander of the 33rd Regiment of Infantry, although temporarily also in command of a brigade stationed at St.-Omer. He had no political connections, no independent income, no family background which would open doors for him. Pétain was simply a highly competent officer who was good with troops in an age when it was not particularly fashionable to be the type of officer who is good with troops. In the normal course of events, since he was fifty-eight in 1914, he would have reached mandatory retirement age in only one more year; it was by no means certain that he would become even a brigadier general, for among the 211 colonels of infantry in the French Army he stood only fifty-first in seniority.[8] So doubtless Pétain was already making plans for his retirement. He would have to look back on a career filled with frustration. His only solace would be the cold comfort of his reputation as a meticulous officer whose theories regarding the use of artillery in conjunction with infantry had made him the leader of a tiny group of like-minded officers, all of whom had fallen into official disfavor through their resistance to the arguments of the predominant School of the Attack.

Pétain had been born in 1856, the fifth child of a moderately well-off farmer in the rural Pas-de-Calais department in northern France. His early education was at a local Jesuit school and was followed by several years at a Dominican college outside Paris. When he was twenty he was accepted at St.-Cyr, and after his graduation two years later he was immediately posted to the 24th Battalion of Light Infantry. He was totally wrapped up in his career (he never married until well after the end of World War I) and soon became known as an officer who possessed a high degree of technical knowledge, especially about artillery support for infantry. But, for all his study and all his competence, Pétain did not rise either fast or far. He did not have the ability to make many friends of either his superiors or his equals and, for this reason, never acquired the patrons in high places who could have secured him preferment in advancement or duty station. Nevertheless, he exhibited enough stubbornness to insist on the rightness of his own opinions, however counter they might run to the thoughts of his superiors.

Aside from technical proficiency, there was only one military characteristic which distinguished Pétain—his appearance, which was everything that an officer's should be and rarely is. He was a tall man, with very blue eyes and a fair mustache, and a lifetime of soldiering with troops had given him a physique which compared favorably with that of men many years his junior. His imperturbable demeanor accentuated his quiet confidence. "He is silent, calm, cold, the enemy of too prompt resolutions," reported the general commanding the XVth Corps, under whom Pétain served. Another commanding officer said, "Never talks uselessly." [9]

Pétain's professional competence prevented his career from being spent entirely in a succession of obscure troop commands, although he had more than his share of these. For a while he even had a rather posh job as an aide to the military governor of Paris, and later, as a major, he was assigned to duty as an instructor at the School of Fire at Châlons. The doctrine being taught at Châlons was a faithful reflection of the preachings of the Young Turks of the School of the Attack—that artillery and rifle fire were merely subordinate adjuncts to an infantry assault. Pétain could not agree with this. Notwithstanding the fact that he was an infantry officer, he propounded that "artillery conquers, the infantry occupies." [10] There could not be two doctrines at the school, so Pétain was abruptly sent back to an infantry regiment. Later, when he was again an instructor, this time at the War College, his abrasive views on the need for powerful artillery support brought him few converts, although in his dossier there was a grudging comment by a superior that "in matters of infantry firepower" Pétain was "one of the two or three leading authorities in France." [11]

Pétain's advancement was slow indeed: a second lieutenant for five years, a first lieutenant for six, a captain for ten. The years crawled on, and it became apparent that he had passed the age when military reputations can be made. Occasionally there would be a brief moment of recognition: his undoubted competence and reputation as a commander of troops led to his ultimately being assigned to command the 33rd Infantry Regiment, one of the crack units in the French Army; and in 1912 a brilliant St.-Cyr graduate, Lieutenant Charles de Gaulle, had the opportunity to select any regiment in the Army and chose to serve under Pétain. For all practical purposes, however, Colonel Pétain's career was over. In thirty-six years of soldiering, Pétain had never heard a shot fired in anger until August 1914.

But then, searching desperately for qualified officers to command divisions in the place of dismissed incompetents, the eyes of Joffre's staff fell upon old Colonel Pétain. It was noticed that in the course of the great retreat Pétain's brigade had performed most creditably. His troops were marching well and fighting well, their casualties were remarkably low in relation to the results they achieved, and Pétain seemed neither flustered nor unnerved at the unfortunate way things were going. Very well, Pétain would do. And on the night of August 31 Pétain was promoted from colonel to brigadier general and from a temporary brigade commander to the command of the 6th Division. He received the news in the tiny town of Tavaux, where his unit had paused during the retreat and where he was quartered in the residence of the daughter-in-law of a long-dead French general named de Sonis. It is said that, because there was no opportunity for Pétain to purchase a general's insignia, Madame de Sonis cut the stars from her dead father-in-law's uniform that night and sewed them on the coat of the man who, three years later, would save France.[12]

Now, with a modicum of rank, came the opportunity for advancement which Pétain had long been denied. Sheer ability plus an awesome knowledge of troop psychology brought him success both on the field and at the conference table. His grasp of the new problems posed by trench warfare brought him to the attention of Joffre, who variously described Pétain as possessing a "highly developed tactical sense," a "profound knowledge of infantry" and an "exact sense of realities." [13]

Promotion followed promotion in dizzying succession. On October 20, 1914, Pétain was made commander of the XXXIIIrd Army Corps; and eight months later, in June of 1915, he became commander of the Second Army, with the rank of full general—a dazzling rise for the obscure colonel of eight months before. "He was always successful," a British observer wrote later, "for at every stage of the war he was just a little ahead of the practice, theory and thought of the moment." [14]

Foremost among Pétain's attributes was his ability as an organizer. Again and again he reviewed every detail. Before an attack he would sometimes personally visit the troops and, walking among them, question every N.C.O. to ensure that he completely understood the assault plan. He set up schools in the rear of the Second Army where new tactics were developed, refined and taught to officers and men from the front. And always he harped on more artillery, more ammunition, more material. Once all the corps commanders in the Tenth Army were asked how many additional hand grenades would be needed for a proposed assault. The most that any other corps asked for was five thousand; Pétain demanded fifty thousand.

The net result was that Pétain consistently got more results for fewer men killed than almost any other general. He husbanded his troops' lives with all the avarice characteristic of his peasant background. And, unlike other generals, he was not the slightest bit hesitant in criticizing a faulty assault plan which his superiors had worked up and demanding that the attack be canceled. But however demanding he might be, Pétain was a fighting general; in fact, during 1915 it was the meticulously conceived assaults he launched which *almost* succeeding in rupturing the German trench system in Champagne.

Now the *"méthode Pétain"* got a respectful hearing at the highest echelon. President Poincaré, describing a conference with Pétain, wrote in his diary on July 6, 1915: "For the moment, the general is not favorable to further offensives. He feels that as the war is dragging on it is indispensable to economize our forces and wait until we have acquired heavy artillery and munitions. All of this is said with great calmness, force and lucidity. There is at most a slight nervous movement of the eyelids to show, from time to time, that under the outward appearance of great self-possession the general hides an ardent and secretly emotional nature." [15]

G. Q. G.

THE MEMBERS of the headquarters staff of a World War I army were rarely designated by simple assignment. Unlike the officers of an infantry company, who were either casually promoted into their jobs or else jerked from a file of officers of suitable rank and grade, the staff officer was the product of an entirely different system of selection. He had usually been personally selected by a general upon whom he made an agreeable impression; and such being the case, the staff officer led a life closely akin to the servitor of a great king in an ancient Oriental court. In the name of his general he implemented decisions of a momentous nature. On orders drafted by the staff officer, huge numbers of men instantly advanced or retreated; masses of materials were directed from one place to another; vastly senior officers plummeted into obscurity. And no matter how lowly the staff officer's rank, it was known that he sat on the right hand of great power, so, as he traveled away from headquarters, he was received in splendor and his favor courted assiduously.

But this coin had another side. No matter how exalted was his own rank, the staff officer was nothing more than a walking extension of the power and prestige of the general whom he served. And once the power of his general was curtailed or diminished, so likewise was that of the staff officer, who then found himself a member of an inferior command, despised by his former sycophants and far removed from opportunity and distinction. Thus it was to every staff officer's benefit constantly to strive to enhance the power of his chief. And, in particular, thus it was at the Grand Quartier Général of the French Army.

By the end of 1914, G.Q.G. was firmly settled in the little town
of Chantilly. The location had been selected with great care. A
former resort center, Chantilly lay twenty-five miles north of Paris
and about an equal distance from the trench lines. Grand Quartier
Général itself was situated in a requisitioned hotel, the Grand Condé,
into which had been jammed all the paraphernalia of a modern gen-
eral-headquarters staff. The hotel's former American Bar (the sign
still hung over the entrance) housed the military-police offices; in
the lobby waited coveys of orderlies in smart uniforms who rose
en masse and saluted as every officer passed; and elevators manned by
sprucely turned-out enlisted men waited to whisk visitors to the upper floors, which had been turned into offices. It was becoming a
huge establishment jammed with officers of every grade and service.

But within this luxurious hotel the staff officers of G.Q.G. lived a
monastic life. No one was allowed to bring his family to Chantilly,
nor were any visitors allowed, for fear that this would permit a host
of female spies to flood the little town. Aside from horseback riding,
which was available to the cavalry officers, there was no recreation
whatever. It was even forbidden to be on the streets of Chantilly
between the hours of 8 P.M. and 6 A.M. Accordingly, there was almost nothing left for the staff officers to do but work.

They worked incredibly hard, but still they had time to spare—
and ambitions to feed. Endlessly they calculated and recalculated
their own ranks vis-à-vis their classmates at St.-Cyr or the École
Polytechnique. Ceaselessly they bickered over the medals and promotions which their acquaintances had won and speculated as to
how they had obtained them. But there was one subject on which
there was no debate: to a man they chorused their horror at the
Paris politicians, who, they felt sure, were attempting to diminish the
authority of Joffre over the conduct of the war. The total incompetence of the individual politician in military matters was an inex-
haustible joke, and any advice which the government might have the
temerity to proffer to G.Q.G. was received with either outrage or
barely concealed disdain.

Jealousy of the Army's power and contempt for *les civiles* were,
then, the only luxuries which Grand Quartier Général and its master,
Joffre, living in taciturn splendor in a villa across the road, permitted themselves. "After the victory of the Marne," an observant
G.Q.G. officer later wrote, "there was in reality only one power

in France, that of Joffre and his staff." [1] And it was nothing less than the truth.

The underlying basis for Joffre's almost total control of the French war plans and policy lay in the fact that during peacetime the war had never been conceived of as anything other than a short, sharp clash of arms culminating in a quick victory. In contemplation of this, the government had no hesitancy in turning extraordinary powers over to the Army. After all, it was thought to be only a matter of a few weeks before Plan XVII would prevail, and it seemed that the wisest course was to clothe the Army with full powers for the period. But now, as the war dragged on for month after month, the politicians began to wonder if perhaps too much authority had not been given to Joffre and G.Q.G. Their suspicions were heightened by the fact that the Army gave no sign of being willing to give up any of the extraordinary powers which the state of siege and various other decrees had given it. Truly, it was an unusual situation. In military matters Joffre was not noted for great cleverness or powers of dissimulation, yet in his dealings with the government he suddenly revealed himself to possess an almost Oriental guile. It was a cunning totally unlooked for in this paunchy, sleepy-eyed man who was generally regarded as a "republican general" and who owed his position not so much to ability as to the government which had selected him over the heads of generals much better qualified.

The politicians were now to learn that power, once relinquished, is not easily retrieved. The "abdication" of the civil government in the early days of the war had made Joffre the virtual dictator of France; and when, just before the Battle of the Marne, the government had fled Paris to take refuge in Bordeaux, it seemed as if his patent was confirmed. Joffre and his officers at G.Q.G. had savored delicious months of power completely free from tiresome governmental questioning or tedious ministerial restrictions. As the "Savior of the Marne," Joffre had come to enjoy fantastic prestige, both within France and abroad. He was at liberty to direct the war as he wished and to influence France's allies as he desired. Naturally, neither he nor his subordinates cared to share this intoxicating power, and with cunning and skill they struck back at those who would encroach upon their authority.

The government had finally straggled back from Bordeaux at the end of 1914. Its flight had done nothing to enhance its prestige in the eyes of either the Army or the nation. Although Joffre and Gallieni had been delighted to have the ministers leave Paris and thus further enhance the Army's authority, even Gallieni had grum‑ bled that "at least one of them ought to stay behind," if only for the sake of appearances.[2] As for the forsaken Paris population, it had coined a spiteful little parody on "The Marseillaise" describing the government's flight:

> To the railroad stations, citizens!
> Board the trains! [3]

But no matter, the government was back and was now squarely faced with a neat question which many democracies have never been able to solve: How much and what type of control should the civil‑ ian government exercise over its Army in time of war? It is, after all, the civilians and not the soldiers who have been elected by the people and charged with the responsibility for the nation's affairs. But, despite their responsibility, the civilians generally lack the neces‑ sary military knowledge and, in France at least, the trained staffs required to supervise the Army completely. Even if they did not, his‑ tory is replete with examples of awful catastrophes resulting from undue interference in military matters by civilians. So the democratic government usually withdraws itself from matters of tactics and strategy, except in the broadest sense, and contents itself with the "general direction of the war effort." However good this may sound in theory, in practice it is found to have a serious flaw, because for the nation involved in a gigantic war there is no clear‑cut line between military matters and general policy. Only a few months of World War I fighting had demonstrated that a failed offensive, faulty tactics or poor military leadership could easily cost close to half a million casualties. And a catastrophe such as this, although technically a "military affair," was simultaneously a matter of the highest national policy.

This, then, was the question which bedeviled both the French Ministry and Parliament. Where did their responsibility end and how should they discharge it? But in Joffre's mind there was no question about this. His back stiffened by his ever watchful subordinates at G.Q.G., Joffre would not tolerate the slightest interference. He de‑ manded total authority in military affairs, conceding archly that "the Commander in Chief is responsible only to the government, who can replace him if they do not approve of his actions." [4] This was a hollow concession. Joffre well knew that his prestige made him unassailable; and, secure in this, he demanded "full liberty of action concerning the direction of operations." [5]

Nor did he stop there. He developed several clever techniques with which he put teeth in his desire to be left free from interference. One method was simply to deny the government anything but the skimpiest details regarding his future plans. Under the pretense of ensuring secrecy, he had early in the war advised Gallieni of his method of dealing with the government: "In the accounts which I send them, I never make known the aim of the operations under way or my intentions." [6]

The corollary to this was Joffre's policy of prohibiting inspection trips to the front by members of Parliament. Only with the express permission of G.Q.G. could a deputy or a senator visit the fighting zone, and even then he was closely escorted by a member of Joffre's staff who followed a rigid itinerary designed to show the politician only what G.Q.G. wanted him to see. Joffre frankly admitted that this policy was aimed at preventing Parliament and the government from becoming "the grand inspector of everything which takes place in my armies. That is inadmissible. . . . Never would I accept it." [7]

The uncertain members of the government quailed in the face of such forthright determination, and some of them, notably Alexandre Millerand, the Minister of War during most of the first year of the war, apparently conceived their duty to be the complete support of Joffre in whatever he desired to do. Many members of Parliament, however, viewed the matter differently. They were not content to remain mere onlookers while France fought for her life. Parliament knew that it had a valuable function in the war—only it could vote funds, stimulate the flow of weapons and explain to the people what was required of them. But Parliament could not exercise these duties, together with its larger obligation to ensure proper direction of the war effort, unless it had at least some knowledge and control of the Army's activities. The politicans recognized, of course, that it was impossible to discuss secret military affairs in open session, but they had another idea. In both the Chamber of Deputies and the Senate there existed parliamentary committees known as Army Commissions, and the legislators now endowed these commissions with power to inspect the fighting front and to discuss their findings among themselves in secret meetings. This, they thought, would provide at least some measure of parliamentary control over the Army.

But they reckoned without Joffre. At almost every turn he blocked the efforts of the Army Commissions to inspect the front without restriction. G.Q.G. bluntly threatened to arrest commissioners who went to the front lines without Army authorization. Even so fearsome a character as Georges Clemenceau, who was the chairman of the Senate's Army Commission, experienced great difficulty in visiting the front. Nor was Joffre content with that. Any general who permitted himself to be interviewed by a commissioner was made to feel the sting of official displeasure.

In retaliation the frustrated Parliament resolved to clip the Army's wings. On September 1, 1915, a measure was passed which, in substance, revoked much of the power granted to the military by the state-of-siege decree.[8] But even this did not work out as it was planned. Two "zones" had already been established—the Zone of the Armies, which comprised the twenty-five French departments through which the front lines ran, and the Zone of the Interior, which was the rest of France. The abrogation of the state of siege referred only to the Zone of the Interior, a situation which scarcely troubled Joffre; he cared nothing for the Interior—let it only supply him with men and supplies for his armies and he would be well content. Skillfully G.Q.G. maneuvered to harden its grip over the Zone of the Armies. Parliamentary visitors found it even more difficult to obtain permits to visit the front, and Millerand, the cowed Minister of War, frankly declared, "There are two well-marked spheres . . . the Zone of the Interior, which depends upon the Minister, and the Zone of the Army, which is not in my province. It depends upon General Joffre. General Joffre does not want it invaded by civilians." [9]

In all this contention, the role of the staff at G.Q.G. cannot be overlooked. Coupled with their natural desire not to see their chief's power, and hence their own authority, diminished was the re-emergence of the old conflicts between the Army and the government. The politicians never truly trusted this military hierarchy which might produce a Caesar, and the officers could rarely bring themselves to regard the politicians as being able to make a serious contribution to the direction of the war. Even though Joffre would not permit his officers to criticize Parliament in his presence, there is no doubt but that many of his attitudes toward the government grew out of the unspoken disdain in which his subordinates held the politicians.

Typical of the attitude of G.Q.G. toward *les civiles* was that shown when a certain Lieutenant Colonel Buat returned to Chantilly following a tour of duty at the Ministry of War in Paris. To his surprise, Buat found that his fellow staff officers regarded him with a certain suspicion and half seriously advised him that he would benefit from the "purer air" of the Zone of the Armies after his "impure" association with the civilians. At first Buat came to the defense of the Zone of the Interior, but so pervading was the anti-Parliamentism at Chantilly that only a few days later he was admitting that his duty at G.Q.G. "had made him well again and had enabled him to rid himself of parliamentary miasmas." [10]

The year 1915 ended with Joffre clearly ahead in his battle against parliamentary supervision. He had even succeeded in banishing General Maurice Sarrail, an officer of great prominence who was regarded as being the only true republican general and, as such, commanded strong support from the parties of the left. "Sarrail is a flag," it was said. "Removing him from his command would be a slap at Parliament." [11] Yet Joffre flung the gauntlet at the politicians and relieved Sarrail. Notwithstanding this affront, the government was still intimidated by Joffre. On December 2, 1915, his powers were enlarged. Previously he had commanded only the front in France. Now he was made "Commander in Chief of the French Armies" and in one bound assumed direction of French forces everywhere.

There was now only one chink in G.Q.G.'s armor. Serving in the French Army were hundreds of members of Parliament. By law they could go on leave to attend parliamentary sessions as often as they liked. In this manner, then, and only in this manner, was Parliament able to find out enough of what was going on at the front to enable it to exercise even a modicum of direction of the war. Joffre hated it, but he was helpless to prevent the soldier-deputies from journeying back and forth between their regiments and Parliament.

And it was one of these soldier-politicians who was to point out a mortal danger for France in 1916.

8

1916

IN DECEMBER 1915 Joffre and Sir Douglas Haig, the British Commander in Chief, began a conference at Chantilly to complete their plans for 1916. As the senior of the two generals, and because the French Army was much larger than the British, it was tacitly agreed that Joffre and his staff would take the lead in developing the Allied strategy. Sir Douglas Haig was well aware of G.Q.G's thinking in regard to the conduct of the war; indeed, he shared and endorsed it. Both the allies exuded confidence. Victory, for them, was always just around the corner. The formula was simple: By a series of attacks designed to chew into the German lines on a broad front, large pieces of invaluable terrain would be won and the German armies crushed to death by the simple application of sound military strategy.

Granted, their reasoning went, the first seventeen months of the war had not proved too fruitful, but doubtless this had been because they had attempted to do too much with too few men and guns. Now the lesson had been learned, the troops were veterans and the munitions had begun to flow forward in quantity. Now was the time to set vast plans afoot.

Joffre suggested, and Haig agreed, that the campaign for 1916 should take the form of a huge frontal attack on the German trenches in the Somme River area west of Péronne at about the center of the front. As originally proposed, the battle was to cover a front of about fifty miles and was to be a combined Franco-British operation, with the French contributing the majority of the manpower. Although

114

the attack would not start until June, a full six months off, every minute was desperately needed to increase the size of the Allied armies and the quantity of heavy artillery and shells, since the principal feature of the offensive was to be vast numbers of men (nearly a hundred divisions), plus a prolonged artillery bombardment to flatten the German barbed wire and knock out the ubiquitous machine guns.

But in planning attacks on the western front for 1916, Joffre and Haig were not alone. With Russia almost neutralized, the Germans too were attempting to solve the riddle of trench warfare in France. And in December 1915 they too came up with what they thought was the answer.

The report of the new German Chief of Staff, General von Falkenhayn, to the high command began by summing up the current military situation: Among Germany's enemies, Russia was mortally weakened, Italy was nearly comatose. Who, then, remained? Only France and England were serious adversaries, and "France has been weakened almost to the limits of endurance." In truth, then, the real enemy was England, who was sustaining the war by the "enormous hold" which she still had on her allies and who was "obviously staking everything on a war of exhaustion."

Candidly, Falkenhayn declared that over the long run the Allies were more likely to grow in strength than were Germany and those nations following her flag. The decision was then obvious: Germany could no longer play the passive role of the defender, however profitable it had been to date. She must lash out at the English, destroy their armies and ruin their hopes; only then would the war be over.

But how to do this? The English, Falkenhayn admitted, were virtually impregnable in their island nation; and the geography of the western front prohibited a really stunning assault against the British-held sections of the trenches. The only remaining alternative, the German general reasoned, was to strike an indirect blow at Britain by inflicting a total defeat on Britain's major ally, France. If France could be knocked out of the war, "England is left to face us alone, and it is difficult to believe that in such circumstances her lust for destruction would not fail her."

But how to deal a war-ending assault on the French trench positions? The question was indeed a complex one, because, Falkenhayn wrote, the lessons to be deduced from the failure of our enemies' mass attacks are decisive against any imitation of their battle methods. Attempts at a mass breakthrough, even with an extreme accumulation of men and material, cannot be regarded as holding out prospects of success against an enemy whose morale is sound and who is not seriously inferior in numbers. The defender has usually succeeded in closing the gaps. This is easy enough for him if he decides to withdraw voluntarily, and it is hardly possible to stop him from doing so. The salients thus made, enormously exposed to the effects of flanking fire, threaten to become a mere slaughterhouse [for the attacker].[1]

Where, then, to attack the French? There was only one answer, Falkenhayn reported—*find a spot which the French Army could not give up, and start a smashing attack at this spot.* Then, instead of retreating trench line by trench line and selling ground dearly, the French Army would be forced to throw every corps, every division, every man onto an anvil on which it would be hammered to death by a German Army which would be superior in manpower, guns and tactics. It was not necessary to capture the spot under attack, although it would be a desirable outcome, Falkenhayn theorized. It was only necessary to draw the French Army to the area and crush it under conditions of a forced defense.

So far, so good. Now all that remained was to find a position which the French simply could not give up and which would be the most difficult for them to defend. Again the remorseless logic of the German Generalstab: there was one spot which the French regarded as a position from which, for reasons of strategy, morale and national pride, they could never retreat even if every man in the French Army had to die in its defense, and on this spot the German attack was prepared. It was the fortress of Verdun.

Since this was to become the bloodiest battlefield in the history of the French nation, it is important to describe it carefully. Verdun was an old fortified city which had been regarded for a hundred years and more as one of the principal defenses against German invasion. Following the Franco-Prussian War it had been intensively fortified, a process which continued up through the early 1900s until the French School of the Attack disparaged the use of fortresses as encouraging a defensive spirit. Nevertheless, it had been well armed and amply manned through the first year of the war. Then, because the Verdun fortress complex was so large that it seemed immune from German attack, and since the sector was very quiet, the majority of the troops and guns were sent elsewhere to feed the insatiable maw of the trench system. But even though it was a quiet front and comparatively lightly manned, Verdun was actually the hinge and the pivot for the northern half of the Allied trench system; and, more to the point, over the years Verdun had been built up in the minds of the French populace as being absolutely impregnable. Its loss would be a strategic and moral disaster of such staggering proportions that G.Q.G. refused to consider it—and so they dismissed the possibility from their minds.

Physically, the Verdun fortress complex in December 1915 was a salient jutting out like an elbow into the German lines. It consisted of the city of Verdun and about twenty concrete-and-steel forts surrounding it in a rough circle about five miles from town. Although these forts contained subterranean living quarters, magazines, and gun galleries, and were as solid and well constructed as French military engineering could make them, the speedy pulverization of the apparently similar Belgian fortresses in 1914 had given rise to the impression that concrete-and-steel fortresses had become obsolete in the face of the German seventeen-inch howitzers. For this reason the forts were now almost untenanted, and the principal defenses now consisted of a slender trench line which was poorly dug and poorly protected by wire. There would come a time when General Herr, the French commander at Verdun, would be criticized for his failure to have a series of trench defenses constructed. But he had a good excuse: Verdun was so drained of troops that there were not enough men to dig the trenches.

Fortunately for France, among the handful of units at Verdun in that winter of 1915-16 were some chasseur battalions commanded by Colonel Émile Driant, a respected fighting officer and also a member of the Chamber of Deputies. The disreputable condition of the defenses at Verdun was a source of constant anxiety to Driant, who knew that his superiors had made frequent fruitless appeals to G.Q.G. for more men and for an improvement of the miserable road and rail communications to Verdun. In every case Joffre had

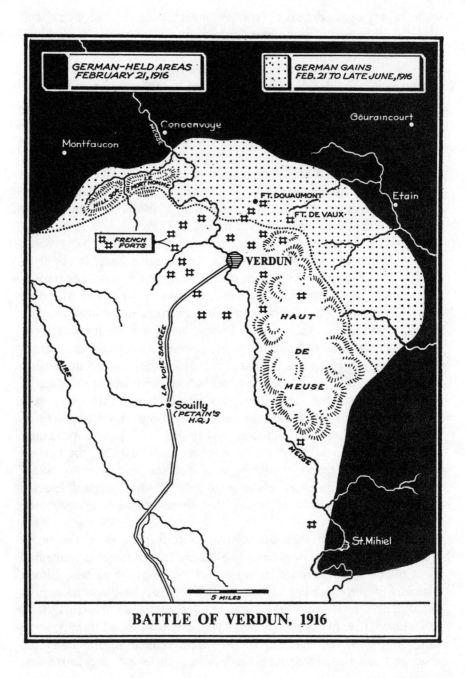

GERMAN-HELD AREAS
FEBRUARY 21, 1916

GERMAN GAINS
FEB. 21 TO LATE JUNE, 1916

Consenvoye

Gouraincourt

Montfaucon

MEUSE

HILL 304

MORT HOMME

FT. DOUAUMONT

Etain

FT. DE VAUX

FRENCH FORTS

VERDUN

HAUT

DE

MEUSE

AIRE

LA VOIE SACRÉE

Souilly
(PETAIN'S H.Q.)

MEUSE

St. Mihiel

5 MILES

BATTLE OF VERDUN, 1916

rejected his subordinates' appeals. "You will not be attacked," G.Q.G. had said. "Verdun is not a point of attack. The Germans do not know that Verdun is disarmed." [2]

Finally Driant (who, incidentally, was the son-in-law of General Boulanger) resolved to take matters into his own hands. In November 1915 he requested leave, journeyed to Paris and appeared before his fellow deputies at a session of the Chamber's Army Commission. Driant's account shocked the commissioners, and the upshot was that they called upon General Gallieni, who had recently been appointed Minister of War, to ascertain what the true situation of the Verdun defenses was.

On December 16, 1915, Gallieni wrote Joffre: "From different sources have come reports on the organization of the front, calling attention to certain defects in the defenses." [3] It was a letter which triggered off the most violent response from Joffre. He rose up in wrath and, curtly addressing his reply not to "*M. le Ministre de la Guerre*" but simply to "*le Ministre de la Guerre*," [4] advised categorically, "Nothing justifies the fears which, in the name of the government, you express in your dispatch of December 16." Nor did Joffre's reply end there. He knew that Parliament's information had come from a soldier-deputy and demanded that the reports "be communicated to me with information as to their authorship. . . . I cannot admit the continuation of this state of affairs." [5]

Under this blast the government retreated somewhat, assuring Joffre that it had "full confidence" in him.[6] But as the weeks went by it became more apparent to many persons in the government that the condition of the Verdun fortifications was far from good and that, despite Joffre's wrathful assurances to the contrary, there was a very real possibility that Verdun might soon be attacked. Finally even Joffre at G.Q.G. became somewhat concerned about it; but now there was a matter of face involved. The Army Commission of the Chamber of Deputies had dispatched members to inspect the situation at Verdun. Obviously, G.Q.G. could not now admit that there was any possibility of a mistake. So the members of the Army Commission were deliberately deceived. They were taken on carefully conducted tours of the few fortifications in decent condition and were shown aerial photographs which proved that the enemy trenches, in some cases a half mile from their French counterparts, were completely unsuited for launching an attack; it was an unheard-of distance for troops to advance over open ground, and the Germans had shown no sign of digging assault trenches closer up. Nor were there any of the other normal indications of a preparation for an offensive—increasing numbers of aircraft making photographic and observation flights, enemy artillery registering on future targets, or huge masses of men and material brought up to the front.

Yet there really were ominous straws in the wind for the observer who could view them without preconceptions. On other sections of the front, German attacks flared and flickered, as if their only purpose was to focus French attention away from Verdun; German fighter planes were unusually active, driving French observer aircraft away from the Verdun area; the Germans closed down their Swiss border, always a sign that a big operation was impending. Now even the Second Bureau at G.Q.G. caught the scent; it reported that some of the German formations opposite Verdun included *Sturmtruppen,* crack assault troops of a suspiciously high quality for that supposedly somnolent sector. Finally, the commander at Verdun reported that German deserters had begun to cross over to the French lines with reports of a huge offensive about to begin.

Gradually G.Q.G. hedged its bet slightly. Reluctantly, another division was moved into Verdun and a regiment of engineers was sent to improve the trench system. And then a corps and still another corps were put in motion over the miserable roads toward Verdun. Reinforcements were on the way, and the only question was whether they would get there in time.

Early in the morning of February 21, 1916, the Battle of Verdun began. All at once the sky in the east, still dark in the lingering dawn of this winter morning, lighted up as more than three thousand German guns commenced an artillery bombardment on a fantastic scale. The volume of fire was stupendous—nothing approaching it had ever been seen in the history of warfare. Almost at once the single slender French trench line was blotted out, and communications with the rear areas ceased to exist. To the French troops huddling in the sketchy dugouts and flattened trenches, it seemed that they were the lone survivors in a world of mud pulverized by unending explosions.

Finally, at four-fifteen in the afternoon, the initial German advance began. But it was not the massed frontal attack of the type used in previous years. Instead, the German onslaught was spearheaded by small parties of scouts who probed the wreckage of the French trenches looking for signs of serious resistance and, when these spots were found, retired to call for renewed artillery bombardment. When this was completed, the first wave of the German advance came forward. This first group consisted of a thin line of troops armed principally with hand grenades and flame throwers to blast or burn the remaining defenders out of their dugouts. Following this first line came the main body of the German advance, riflemen picking their way through the craters in an extended single file to deal with French strong points that the artillery could not reduce and to establish a forward line from which the German advance would jump off the next day.

Night finally closed on a day which had left the Germans in the positions they needed to widen their attack. They had smashed the middle of the French front and reduced French communications to a jumbled mass. And among the French units which they had destroyed were the battalions of the farsighted Colonel Driant, who had lost eighteen hundred of his complement of two thousand men. When the pitiful remnant of Driant's unit withdrew it was covered by a tiny rear guard, which was overwhelmed and killed to a man; among this rear guard, dead with a bullet in his forehead, was Colonel Driant.

The next day, February 22, the German infantry attack began in earnest, and in the shell holes and the blasted trenches the remnants of the French forces, now beginning to be reinforced by new divisions rushed in by an alarmed G.Q.G., put up a frantic delaying action. But by the twenty-fourth the situation had become desperate. The Germans had committed eighteen divisions to this attack which was remorselessly chewing up the defenders. The next day they would capture a principal French fort, Douaumont, which gave them a superb artillery observation post as well as a propaganda victory of immense proportions. Indeed, French prospects looked so bleak that the French commander on the spot wanted to conduct an extensive retreat which would virtually give up Verdun to the Germans.

But more French reinforcements were on the way, and almost as important as the hundreds of thousands of troops set in motion toward the battle was one man in a staff car splashing down the highway between Bar-le-Duc and Verdun. It was Pétain. The full import of the German attack had finally registered with Joffre, together with the realization that if the Verdun defenses were to be held they had to be commanded by the best France had to offer. So on the evening of February 24 he telephoned Pétain to come to Chantilly. Pétain arrived at eight the next morning and was given orders to proceed to Verdun and take command of the battle, which he did at midnight on February 26.

Anyone who was at Verdun in that dismal February will testify to the fact that Pétain was the very heart of the defense; it is possible that no one else could have done what he did. More important than anything else, he utilized his awesome knowledge of practical military affairs to render order out of what had been almost chaos. After he had set up headquarters in the town hall of the little city of Souilly, a few miles southwest of bombarded Verdun, his first act was to divide up the battlefield among energetic subordinate generals. With a piece of charcoal he sketched out four sectors on a map pinned up on the wall, and to these sectors he ordered Generals Duchêne, Balfourier, Guillaumat and Bazelaire, each with his own artillery and each with instructions that he was to fight to the last man but never retreat. But just in case any of the sectors was overwhelmed, Pétain made sure that seven successive lines of defense were entrenched. And, disregarding the theory that the concrete-and-steel forts were worthless shell traps, he consigned to each of them a garrison with a fourteen-day supply of food and water and instructions never to capitulate.

Next Pétain turned his attention to the matter of supply. Verdun was served only by two supply routes not cut by the enemy—a single rail line which was under frequent enemy artillery fire, and could never handle more than eight hundred tons a day, and the road from Bar-le-Duc to Verdun, which was only twenty feet wide and already disintegrating under the strain of the heavy military traffic. Very well, the principal supply route must be the road, and thousands of territorials were brought in to widen it and keep it in repair. In this way the Bar-le-Duc road, later known as the Voie Sacrée, the Sacred Way, became the central artery which was to handle a volume of traffic that ultimately reached a truck every fourteen seconds.

Now the organization was set up, the battle lines were drawn, the supplies and reinforcements set in motion. The Battle of Verdun soon rose to a mighty crescendo. Both sides made the most profuse use of their artillery—the Germans because they had planned to decimate the French at little cost to themselves, and Pétain because he always believed that firepower conquers the battlefield and that infantry only occupies it. To this end, Pétain had two thousand guns in action. When his generals came to him to report, his first words always were: "What have your batteries been doing? We will discuss other points later on." [7]

Nevertheless, for a battle which started out as fundamentally an artillery engagement on a vast scale, Verdun speedily degenerated into a succession of wild infantry melees which were distinguished only by the vast numbers of troops who died and by the valor displayed by both sides. Every attack, every minuscule gain in ground, was met by a counterattack. Fresh divisions were fed into the battle, remained in action for a few days and emerged from Verdun grotesque fractions of their previous strength.

The trench systems had been sketchy to begin with, and, since they had to be improved under a hail of artillery and small-arms fire, they never became as deep or as complex as those in the other sections of the front. For both the French and the Germans, the trench systems were mainly a series of connected shell holes filled with the debris of the battlefield—ammunition crates, broken equipment, rolls of rusty barbed wire, countless rotting corpses.

As the battle stretched out, week after week, month after month, the artillery on both sides became tremendously proficient and fantastically prodigal with ammunition. An attack would be scheduled and artillery supports arranged. Days before the attack the artillery would begin to register on the enemy trenches; as each gun was brought into position, it fired a few rounds under control of an artillery observer to establish accuracy. Then, as the attack date grew closer, the volume of artillery fire became greater. Shrapnel swept the defender's communication trenches to keep reinforcements back. High-explosive shells burst along the main trench systems to flatten the barbed wire and crush the defenders' strong points. Finally, on the day of the attack, the bombardment swelled to a crescendo of fire. The defenders huddled in trenches which were now just partially blown-in shambles. Then, at the precise moment when the barrage lifted—moving toward the defenders' rear to prevent reinforcements from coming forward—whistles would blow in the attackers' trenches as a signal for the assault troops to clamber up scaling ladders, pick their way through lanes cut in their own barbed wire and, at a dogtrot, wend around the welter of shell holes toward the enemy lines a couple of hundred yards away.

Meanwhile, suddenly relieved from the storm of shellfire, the remaining defenders would cautiously peer over the shattered parapets of their trenches. Through the gloom caused by smoke shells or gas they would spy the attackers. "Here they come!" "Get the artillery at them!" No use calling for support on the telephones, the lines were cut days ago by shellfire. Quick, the flares! A volley of colored flares soars into the air, and, well behind the defenders' lines, out of reach of the attackers' artillery, the waiting gunners slam shells into breaches. Every second counts; the guns have already been registered on the neutral ground, the no man's land between the trench lines, through which the attackers must pass. The defenders' batteries begin to fire frenziedly, and seconds later the attacking troops are swept by a hail of shrapnel. But the defenders' artillery has been just a fraction too late. The first enemy wave is already at the defenders' trenches. They have suffered terrible casualties, most of their officers are dead or wounded, but they are at their enemy. The attackers crouch above the trench and toss grenades over the parapet; then they jump into the trenches. Many of the attackers' first wave have not carried rifles; instead they are armed with steelbound clubs or trench knives, which are less unwieldy in the confined trenches. The attackers range down the trench. From time to time they are halted by a traverse behind which a group of defenders have organized themselves. The attackers attempt to squeeze past the traverse and are bayonetted by the defenders. But grenades loft over the traverse, and at last the trench is taken.

Now the attackers must collect themselves, since they know that they, in turn, are about to become the defenders. Their own second wave has been halted by the bombardment, and as a result they are too few to press on to attack the second trench line. Feverishly they grapple sandbags from the parapet in front of the trench and throw them up on the back. Now the enemy artillery knows the first trench line has been lost and begins bombarding it. Through the smoke and the awful explosions, the newly arrived occupants of the trench see waves of counterattacking troops advancing upon them. It has all started over again; by nightfall the trench will probably be retaken. Nothing much will have been gained or lost—except for a few thousand men dead or dying in shell holes in the neutral ground.

In this manner the Battle of Verdun continued without interruption for four months. In certain respects it was apparent that the German offensive was fulfilling its aims. The French had, as Falkenhayn predicted, reacted to the German offensive by summoning to Verdun every possible man and every possible gun. By June, sixty-six French divisions out of the little more than one hundred which existed had passed through the horror of Verdun. The German strategy of subjecting the French Army to a "forced defense" under unfavorable conditions had brought results. From February to June of 1916 the French Army had suffered a staggering total of 410,-000 casualties, as opposed to the German total of around 245,000.[8] To this extent, the first months of Verdun were a German victory.

Still the Germans had not quite achieved their ultimate objective at Verdun, the destruction of the French Army. There were a number of reasons for this. First, the Germans found that they had grossly underestimated the tenacity and courage of the individual French soldier and officer, Second, the Germans had been, to an extent, hoist with their own petard. They had started out to force the French to defend a spot which was important mainly for morale reasons and then found that the German populace began to attach almost as much importance to the capture of Verdun as French public opinion did to its defense—thus preventing Falkenhayn from exercising the degree of battle selectivity and manpower economy which was the keystone of his original plan.

Finally, there was a group of circumstances which were working against ultimate German success and which it had been impossible for the Germans to foresee. They could not have known that the French concrete-and-steel forts would turn out to be much better constructed than their Belgian counterparts (the concrete in the French forts had been placed in one pour, which left no weakening construction joints) and would provide invaluable shellproof shelter for vast numbers of French troops; they could not have predicted that the French heavy artillery would succeed in blowing up the German ammunition dump near Spincourt which held nearly a half-million fused shells; and no one could have foreseen the impact that Pétain would have in organizing, inspiring and directing the battle.

From the steps of his headquarters at Souilly, Pétain watched the truckloads of troops jolting down the Sacred Way, and the mere presence of this silent man gave the soldiers hope. Undoubtedly one factor contributing to the sturdiness of the French was the fact that Pétain kept his troops in the line for shorter periods than did the Germans. Each French division stayed at the front for only a few days and was then pulled out to rest and replenish its ranks. The Germans used fewer divisions, but left them in "the furnace" for weeks, by which time they were complete wrecks. And, too, Pétain never ceased to inspire his men with a sense of glory. Once, when the fighting reached a peak, he drafted a famous message to the troops which ended, "*Courage—on les aura* [we'll get them]!" [9] It was not good French, but the poilus picked it up and the phrase swept through France.

Even so, by the end of June 1916 the Germans had chewed enough tiny bites from the French defenses to be almost in possession of Verdun. It is difficult to avoid the expression that the war literally teetered in the balance. The French Army was physically and morally tied to Verdun. It had given its best, spending its blood like water in the defense of countless little woods and heights. Hill 304, Le Mort Homme, Le Bois Camard and the Belleville Height were carpeted with French corpses. It was a blood bath unequaled since the first horrible weeks of the war. The best divisions were exhausted, the best men killed or maimed. Now, if Verdun fell, all the sacrifice would have been for nothing. The Germans would have achieved a moral ascendancy from which the French could never recover. If the Germans could take Verdun, France's traditional bastion against their enemy, then the French could not stop them anywhere.

But somehow the French Army held. Backed to the point where the loss of just a few hundred yards would have meant collapse of the front, they stopped the last German attacks at the end of June. And then, in Picardy some 130 miles to the northwest, was heard the sound of British guns. On a twenty-five-mile front extending north and south of the Somme River, the British, with French support, were launching an offensive eastward toward Péronne and Bapaume. The Germans could not fight two major battles at once. As if turning off water at a tap, the German high command shut off the reinforcements for its Verdun forces. The pressure behind the German wave was shut off. It washed once more—and then it was silent. The French Army still held Verdun. Although grievously, almost mortally, wounded, it had won.

The Battle of the Somme had originally been planned as predominately a French offensive. The only reason for waiting until summer to start it had been to allow the British to add a certain amount of weight to it with their "New Armies," which had been recruited during 1914-15 and would not be trained or equipped to go into the line until the middle of 1916. But now, under the impetus of the French, who desperately needed to have German pressure drawn off them at Verdun, and under the stimulus of British General Headquarters, which was anxious to prove to the doubting that given enough men, guns and ammunition the Allies could win the war on the western front, the offensive in the Somme sector was somewhat revised. Although the French contributed substantially, the most important role both in men and in material was to be played by the British.

The high ground, the crucial topographical feature of the area—a section of France which is notably flat—was held by the enemy. The German defenses were exceptional in that their lines were built on or into a series of hills which commanded all the Allied trench system. As a result, the German observers could watch, spread out below them as in an army school sand-table exercise, every British movement for almost thirty miles—and there was much to observe. As spring advanced, the British built new roads and rail lines into the area; laboriously, miles of communication, assembly and assault trenches were dug; tremendous quantities of artillery were moved up, together with hundreds of thousands of shells; troops by the scores of thousands were brought in, and, out of range of the enemy artillery, cities of tents were erected to house them. And as the German observers watched these obvious preparations for an attack, the German troops toiled night and day to improve their already strong fortifications.

The result of this German activity was that by the summer of 1916 the German defenses in the Somme area were probably the strongest field fortifications ever built in the world. Not only was there the customary main trench line backed up by additional trenches, but this system had been duplicated so there were really two separate systems of trenches which the Allies would have to overrun. In fact, it was impossible to draw straight lines bisecting the German defenses without crossing at least thirteen separate trenches.[10]

Most of the trenches were, in the report of the British Commander in Chief, "protected by wire entanglements, many of them in two belts forty yards broad. . . . The numerous woods and villages in and between these systems of defense had been turned into veritable fortresses. The deep cellars usually to be found in the villages, and the numerous pits and quarries common to a chalk country, were used to provide cover for machine guns and trench mortars. The existing cellars were supplemented by elaborate dugouts, sometimes in two storeys, and these were connected up by passages as much as thirty feet below the surface of the ground." [11]

The objective of the Allied attack on this fantastically strong defense system was, in retrospect, absurdly optimistic. It was no less than to crash through the German trench lines on a front of twenty-five miles, then wheel and roll up the exposed German flanks. Meanwhile, the cavalry was to charge through the gap and raise havoc far in the German rear. (In this connection, it must be observed that Sir Douglas Haig was a former cavalryman and retained up to the end of the war a touching, if unrealistic, faith in his old arm.)

A principal feature of the Allied attack was an artillery bombardment on a vast scale. It began on Sunday, June 25. The artillery, massed so that there was an average of one gun for every twenty yards of front, roared day and night. The German trenches were marked by a continuous heaving line of dirt as countless shells fell on them. To the British observers, it seemed as if the barbed-wire entanglements had been severed in a thousand places.

At precisely 7:30 A.M. on the first of July, a hot, cloudless summer's day, the slam of the artillery stopped for a moment—and then resumed as the gunners lengthened their range to put a steel curtain across the German communication trenches in the rear. Simultaneously, whistles sounded in the packed Allied trenches as nineteen divisions poured over the parapets.

The French had learned of the power of modern automatic weapons during the first month of 1914, a lesson bought with blood and relearned at Verdun. Now it was the British turn to learn. As they rose from their trenches, each British battalion formed into line abreast and marched stolidly across the battlefield. And each line was closely followed by a second, a third and then a fourth wave.

Now the slaughter started. Secure in their deep dugouts, the German troops had been largely unaffected by the week-long Allied bombardment. Although their first system of trenches had been reduced to a shambles, the Germans poured out of their shelters and swiftly set up machine guns in shell craters. And as the British lines came to within a hundred yards, the Germans opened a cataclysm of fire upon the attackers.

The carnage was so terrible that it cannot be grasped in the aggregate but must be reduced to more readily intelligible proportions. Winston Churchill recounts the experiences of the 8th Division, which was one of the fourteen British divisions taking part in the July 1 assault. The 8th Division threw 8,500 men, virtually its entire infantry strength, across no man's land against the German lines at the Ovillers ridge. Opposing the 8th Division was the German 180th Infantry Regiment, with only 1,800 men, or two thirds of its strength, present in the front lines. The British attack was violent and well directed. The German defense was stubborn and ingenious. The attack was over precisely ninety minutes after it began. Out of the 1,800 German troops engaged, the casualties totaled eight officers and 273 men. Out of the 8,500 British engaged, the casualties totaled 300 officers and 5,274 men.[12]

By nightfall of July 1, the British attack had been brought to a standstill. Only in one small area did the onslaught bring even a modicum of success. On their right the British had succeeded in capturing some German trenches and advancing the line about a mile. But what had been the cost? Of the approximately 140,000 British troops who climbed over their parapets that hot summer day, nearly 60,000, almost half, were killed, wounded or prisoners. It was, and still remains, the greatest number of casualties the British Army ever sustained in a single day.

It would have been well if it had been all over then. Certainly the casualties had been steep enough, and there was even a modicum of success to report: the French, by means of surprise and heavier artillery and by adopting the German method of attack—small units utilizing ground cover—had succeeded in capturing a substantial number of German trenches and actually took six thousand German prisoners. Instead, the offensive was prolonged. Haig was convinced somehow that the German defenses were almost crushed and that just a little more pressure would bring about their collapse. Month after month it went on, a series of wearing, small-scale actions punctuated by full-scale attacks.

Finally, in November, it ended. Each side had lost more than half a million casualties. The Allies had gained a few miles, but as fast as the Germans lost a trench line, they were easily able to dig another. And when the winter rains put a stop to the attack, the Allies were left clinging to a tiny tongue of mud that extended into the German lines, a perfect "shell trap" into which the Germans could pour flanking fire at any time they desired.

During the first ten months of 1916, the French Army suffered casualties—in killed, wounded, prisoners and missing—totaling 861,000 men.[13]

9

THE TROJAN HORSE

THE UNION SACRÉE, the political and social unity which President Raymond Poincaré had proclaimed at the beginning of the war, had been a phenomenal occurrence, as well as a testimony to the fundamental patriotism of the French people. For France, torn apart as it had been by internecine feuds and rivalries, closing ranks behind its government was a spectacle which was witnessed only in brief and infrequent intervals during the life of the Third Republic.

Within this framework of solid resolve, the pacifists and the various political factions of the far left were, at first, completely impotent. But as the war dragged on and victory seemed further away than ever, the wonderful unity of the Union Sacrée slowly eroded. To be sure, the fundamental patriotism of the people was undiminished—it was *"Pour la France!"* which returned the indomitable poilus to the attack time after time—but within France all the old social and political divisions were slowly reasserting themselves. And by 1916 these divisions had begun to take frightening forms.

Most serious were the developments within the United Socialist party, France's second largest political group and the possessor of one sixth of the seats in the Chamber of Deputies. Before the war this party had been the leader among the left-wing groups which had threatened a general strike in the event of mobilization. Many of the prominent figures within the United Socialists had been on Carnet B. But in the confusion caused by the murder of Jaurès, the head of the party, and the general patriotic fervor of the war's beginning, the United Socialists had supported the Union Sacrée.

131

Some of its leaders had even accepted Cabinet positions as a demonstration of solidarity.

By 1916 the United Socialist leadership had begun to pay the price for its seeming abandonment of Socialist principles. As the war dragged on, a sizable proportion of the party membership had come to regard its moderate leaders as traitors to the cause, and the party had split. The more militant and doctrinaire Socialists now rallied under the leadership of Jules Longuet, the grandson of Karl Marx. This group paid only the barest lip service to the Union Sacrée. A prominent contemporary Socialist thus described these Frenchmen: "In all good faith [they] stood to their views that under the capitalist system nothing could justify the workers of one country in killing the workers of another. They had no interest in their own nation which was worth defending in the field. The past of France was for them a record of class oppression, the present of France the continuance of chattel slavery in disguise, the future of France no better than the permanence of penal servitude for life as wage slaves to the bourgeoisie. German domination could be no worse for them than the economic tyranny of their own capitalist countrymen." [1]

To this group of Socialists, and to the anarchists and syndicalists who gathered about them, it seemed that the path of duty lay in preserving their international contacts and working for peace at almost any price. At party rallies they vehemently attacked the prolonging of the war, an old Socialist, Vaillant, stating, "Oh, if only I can outlive the war by six months—just six months—so that I can tell the people: Very well, there you are, you have seen into what a terrible ordeal they have led you—your capitalist society of financiers and armament makers!" [2]

Even more significant was the French attendance at international Socialist conferences where representatives of the French far left met with fellow Socialists from all over the world, including Germany. In September 1915 the first of these wartime conferences was held, in the little Swiss town of Zimmerwald outside Berne. Lenin was even in attendance. The upshot of the conference was a statement signed by both the French and the Germans that "we German and French Socialists and Syndicalists affirm that this war is not our war!" [3]

A second conference was held at Kienthal in Switzerland a year later. And at this meeting the Socialists went on record as calling for "the end of this world-wide butchery." [4]

The pacifist activities of this group of militant Socialists were made more effective by the fact that they served as a rallying point for the various minor parties of the far left. Then too, the very militance of their Socialist viewpoint had brought this group into positions of great prominence among the workers in the armaments industries, where the trade unions, such as the Federation of Metals, were rapidly mushrooming into a size and influence undreamed of in prewar days. A left-wing-backed Committee for the Resumption of International Relations sprang into existence, and a series of pamphlets calling for peace began to flow from clandestine printing presses. And now, as the unions began to feel their strength, labor unrest began to manifest itself. Industrial strikes in France increased from none in 1914 to 98 in 1915 and to 314 in 1916.[5]

In retrospect, it is impossible to avoid the conclusion that the various wartime French governments, through weakness, vacillation and want of energy, brought upon France the host of internal troubles which shortly visited it. At any time, the government in power could, by displaying vigor and ruthless determination, have cut out this pacifist cancer which was beginning to eat at France's vitals. A series of quick arrests would have emasculated the Socialist leadership and cowed their trade-union followers. Indeed, the Socialists themselves were terrified of the prospect. Once, just before the conference at Zimmerwald, a small group of Socialist deputies met on the terrace of a Paris café with Leon Trotsky, who was then living in Paris and editing a revolutionary Russian-language newspaper. All the deputies spoke in pacifist platitudes until it was mentioned that those attending the Zimmerwald conference might possibly need false passports in order to leave France. Much to Trotsky's amusement, this thought so horrified the Frenchmen that the check was quickly called for and the deputies scuttled off.[6]

But instead of using their police powers, the various governments hesitated and attempted to compromise and conciliate in the interests of political harmony. They gave the Socialists their passports to Zimmerwald, the government hesitated, the Socialists grew stronger, bolder and more vehement in their demands. And aside from the activities of the militant Socialists and their adherents, there were other manifestations of the gradual breakup of the Union Sacrée.

One was the reversion of the newspapers to their prewar practices of sniping at the government in power. Generally, this took a novel form. In the early days of the war both patriotic fervor and censorship had combined to reduce almost to the vanishing point the actual news value of the great daily papers; only the most absurdly optimistic reports were printed, together with glowing panegyrics on the various French military leaders. Rapidly it came to the point where the intelligent reader discounted most of what he read. In the trenches, copies of Swiss newspapers or the London *Times* became prized by the French troops, who read them because these journals "tell things as they are in truth." [7] Now, as the early flush of adulation waned, the French newspapers found it possible to damn with faint praise and still stay within the bounds tolerated by the censor. Some newspaper editors, in their desire to stimulate the government to greater energy, went even further, and among them was Georges Clemenceau.

At the beginning of the war his newspaper had been titled *L'Homme libre* ("The Free Man"). But his criticism of the conduct of the war had been so forthright that the government had finally invoked its privilege of military censorship to suppress *L'Homme libre*. It was a futile move. Almost immediately Clemenceau was publishing a new paper, mockingly entitled *L'Homme enchaîné* ("The Imprisoned Man"), and it rapidly became tremendously popular, with a circulation ultimately exceeding 100,000 copies a day.

Almost every day *L'Homme enchaîné* ran a two-column front-page editorial. From his editorial offices on the Rue de Taitbout in Paris, the Tiger thundered out at the lack of bold action and dynamic leadership on the part of the government. Recognizing that Clemenceau was irrepressible, the government contented itself simply with censoring his more violently critical attacks; huge white spaces appeared under such intriguing headlines as "The Dream—The Reality" and "The Military Situation." [8] Cartoons attacked the muddling *système D* under which troops in the Zone of the Armies were given leave but no trains were assigned to carry them back to their homes,[9] or depicted shivering citizens huddled before a coal-yard closed for lack of supply, with the caption, "The ministers change, but the problem remains the same." [10]

Chief among Clemenceau's themes was that the government was too comatose, that it was allowing France to slip back into the habit of politics as usual. Its appeasement of the Socialists appeared to him to be outright treachery; the military failures seemed to Clemenceau to be an obvious manifestation of the government's incompetence, and most issues of *L'Homme enchaîné* concluded with the bold-type statement "The Boches are at Noyon!"—a reminder to all France that the front line was as close to Paris as the little city of Noyon, only fifty miles from the capital.

Clemenceau was now an old man in his mid-seventies. Despite his gout and the white string gloves he habitually wore to hide an incurable skin infection, he enjoyed almost perfect health. It was as if his whole life had been a preparatory schooling for this event. He literally churned with energy. As a senator he delivered impassioned speeches damning defeatists and faint hearts. Everything, Clemenceau thundered, must be devoted to war—every nerve, every muscle, every thought. Total war was his message. He was the dominant force in the Senate's Army Commission. And implied but never stated as he wrote, spoke, or visited the troops in the trenches was the Tiger's own burning conviction that he and only he could save France from defeat.

There were only a few who agreed with him. Through the years, Clemenceau's outspoken attacks had left him with a host of enemies, for the very violence of the old man's emotions made others distrust his judgment. President Raymond Poincaré summed it up: "I am always rather nervous, perhaps a little too nervous, of his whims, his very versatility, and his fine contempt for everybody except himself. . . . It is certainly not for mere ambition that Clemenceau wants to be in office; it is because he is convinced that he will save the country and that he alone can do so. If ever the real moment comes, I shall call on him without hesitation. . . . The more I think of the matter, the more I say to myself: 'So long as victory is possible, he is capable of upsetting everything!' A day will perhaps come when I shall add: 'Now that everything seems to be lost, he alone is capable of saving everything.' " [11]

But Georges Clemenceau was not the only newspaperman attacking the conduct of the war. Anarchist Miguel Almereyda's *Bonnet rouge*, thanks largely to the secret subsidies being given it by Minister of the Interior Louis Malvy, had become a powerful voice among the militant left wing. Gradually the little two-sheet evening newspaper had backed off from the position of archpatriotism which it had professed in the first days of the war, and now, by 1916, Almereyda's *Bonnet rouge* was being recognized as the veiled voice of pacifism. The *Bonnet rouge* articles were clever and sardonic, but beneath their seeming humor there was generally found either an attack upon the futility of the war or else a gibe at France's British allies, who were represented as foot-dragging cowards. But so skillfully written and ambiguous were these articles that most of them got by the censors. Indeed, it would have been difficult to censor an editorial which ostensibly called for a greater war effort in the following words:

> Germany still has numerous reserves. Thus the French nation knows where it stands. It can appreciate how great are the sacrifices still to be expected of it, especially if told to hold out for the realization of uncertain and remote aims.[12]

Or an article slyly attacking the courage of the British troops which told of the pleasure which the editor experienced

> upon learning that the British were shelling the German trenches vigorously and had penetrated the enemy lines at several points without committing the imprudence of going too far forward and installing themselves in an advanced position. . . . Be assured that they [the British] will act with the coolness and calm so characteristic of their temperament . . . No foolish rashness—oh, no! [13]

Nor did Almereyda's activities stop with the editorship of the *Bonnet rouge*. Inexplicably, this young, debonair anarchist had acquired a substantial amount of money. He owned several automobiles, had two mistresses set up in expensive apartments, and was becoming a heroin addict. Increasingly, the day-to-day editorship of the *Bonnet rouge* was being left to other hands. But this only allowed Almereyda more time to devote to his friends on the left. Trading on his past services to Caillaux and his peculiar friendship with Malvy, Almereyda came to be regarded as the "ambassador of the left." He was constantly interceding to free pacifist comrades of the left who had been swept up by Malvy's police subordinates. At first Almereyda had run newspaper appeals on behalf of his arrested friends and then, upon their release, carried front-page articles of appreciation with headlines such as "Thank You, M. Malvy," and going on to explain that his, Almereyda's, "appeal has not been in vain." [14]

But in time the Ministry of the Interior had come so deeply under Almereyda's influence that he could directly intercede with its operations at almost any level. For example, in a letter to M. Leseyeux, assistant to M. Paoli, secretary general of the Prefecture of Police, he wrote: "Enclosed is a list of some poor devils who have been arrested and whom, in accord with M. Malvy and M. Richard [Director of the Sûreté Générale], I ask you to release. If I thought that there would be any danger or embarrassment for the country, I would not even make this request." [15]

The close relationship between Malvy and Almereyda was a source of wonder to Malvy's ministerial associates. One of them, Gallieni, visited Malvy's office and noted, "He has, it seems, been obliged to obey the editor of the *Bonnet rouge*, a bad type, whom I saw waiting in the antechamber." [16]

In addition to Almereyda there were a number of other strange characters loose in France at the time. The Germans had come to recognize the importance which newspapers could play in the subversion of France, and they established agents in neutral Switzerland to arrange for purchase of French journals through third parties. Once the newspapers were purchased, their editorial policies could gradually be altered to support the pacifist line. The principal German representative in Switzerland was a former banker, a man named Marx, who before the war had had extensive business dealings with various Frenchmen who could be relied upon to do anything for a price.

One of these Frenchmen was a forty-seven-year-old international swindler and confidence man named Paul Marie Bolo. Born the son of a poor café owner in Marseilles, Bolo had, at an early age, determined to rise above the economic and social milieu of his parents. In succession he had become a hairdresser, dabbled in dentistry, failed as a restaurateur, done fairly well as an embezzler and ultimately succeeded in contracting a series of bigamous marriages with a covey of wealthy women. Capitalizing on his wives' money and his own suave good looks, he gained access to the smart world of prewar Paris society; his wealth even procured him the Legion of Honor. But, as successful as he might be socially, Bolo was a catastrophic failure in the series of international stock frauds in which he tried to interest his new-found friends. By July of 1914 he was teetering on the edge of bankruptcy when, in Switzerland, he met Abbas Hilmi, the former Khedive of Egypt, whose hatred for the British had led him to become a German agent. Vastly impressed with this smooth-talking, distinguished-appearing Frenchman, the Khedive was inveigled into making Bolo his sole agent for financial affairs in Europe; and in order that Bolo might have a suitable title for business negotiations, the Khedive bestowed upon him the Ottoman rank of pasha.

Thenceforth known as Bolo Pasha, the ex-hairdresser became the chief importer of German funds into France following the outbreak of the war. The Khedive received money from the Germans in the form of checks drawn on Swiss and Italian banks. The funds, which amounted to about two million francs per month (nearly a half-million dollars at the current rate of exchange) were then given to Bolo, who was to use them to buy an interest in various prominent newspapers. The Germans regarded Bolo as ideal for the job; his lavish scale of living and his previous speculative activities provided a perfect cover for an investor in French newspaper stocks.

The whole scheme would have worked beautifully had it not been for Bolo's greed. Of the vast fortune given him, only a paltry amount was ultimately to find its way into purchases of newspapers. Most of it stuck to Bolo's own fingers as, with the consummate artistry of the experienced embezzler, he, the traitor, betrayed his employers.

But despite occasional setbacks, the German plans for the subversion of France were proceeding more or less according to schedule. For each of their enemies, France, Britain, Italy and Russia, the Germans had long since worked out a scheme for treason from within. The plans all bore a rough similarity: first, discord by means of the parties of the far left; next, pacifist articles published by defeatists either paid or directly inspired by Germany; and, finally, the establishment of an understanding with a prominent political personality who would ultimately take over the weakened enemy government and sue for peace. They allowed Lenin to return to Russia in 1917. For Britain they apparently intended to use the Irishman,

Sir Roger Casement, to stir up internal strife. And for France they picked Joseph Caillaux.

Ever since his wife's acquittal in July 1914, Caillaux had brooded on the tricks of fate which had quashed his meteoric career. Although he still had many friends in Parliament who were indebted to him, and although his nominee Louis Malvy was still the Minister of the Interior, he could never live down the twin stigmata of his wife's scandalous trial and his reputation for having appeased Germany in the Agadir incident of 1911. When war came he had joined the Army as a paymaster. Predictably, he asked to be assigned to the staff of the darling of the left wing, General Sarrail. As his assistant Caillaux took with him a young staff writer from Miguel Almereyda's *Bonnet rouge* named Ceccaldi. The way for Caillaux's appointment to the Army had been personally paved by the then Minister of War, Messimy, who wrote Joffre, "There is no use in either of us creating political difficulties for ourselves; that is why I ask you most urgently to authorize this assignment. If it is not made, once peace returns, or even before, both you and I will have real enemies on our hands." [17]

But again Caillaux's haughty lack of discretion led him astray. Rumor, apparently based on solid fact, reached Paris to the effect that Caillaux, in uniform, had addressed a gathering of front-line troops from his constituency, offering to secure them easier duty if they wanted it. When this came to G.Q.G.'s attention, it was indicated to him that, should he care to return to civilian status, the Army would be pleased to process his resignation. Nor had Caillaux been forgotten by the French populace. Several times, in Paris and at his country residence in Mamers, he and his wife were recognized by crowds in the street and hissed or stoned by mobs crying, "Death to the German spy!" [18] Under these conditions it was impossible for him to remain in France, and so he secured his release from the Army and, through his still-excellent political connections, was appointed to head a vaguely defined official mission to South America. On November 14, 1914, Caillaux and his wife sailed from France.

Caillaux's subsequent tour of South America was to be a strange, almost incredible one, explicable only by the fact that he was so aflame with thwarted ambition and so devoured by his love of intrigue that he devoided himself of both patriotism and common sense. As he traveled through South America, Caillaux extended himself to make contact with German diplomatic officials, to whom he expounded his hatred of England and his desire for a lasting friendship with Germany.

Caillaux had no difficulty in making the acquaintance of German functionaries. He was even helped in this task by a young phony nobleman, "Count" James Minotto, a newly appointed member of the foreign department of the Guarantee Trust Company of New York, who also operated as a German spy. Using Minotto as a go-between to the Germans, Caillaux left no doubt as to his views. France, he declared, would be bled white and ultimately crushed by the German Army. Then, as in 1870, France would have to sue for peace. At that precise moment, it would be necessary for the French government to be revised to make room for a powerful political figure who could sweep aside Parliament and impose his will in an authoritarian manner. Of course, such a man would have to be acceptable to the German victors—and Caillaux made it unmistakable that he was the man who would be suitable in every respect.

For almost two months Caillaux toured South America, spreading his message of defeat. The Germans, of course, greeted him with delighted incredulity; here, speaking of the impending German victory, was the man who had once been France's Premier, who still enjoyed official position as a deputy, and whose nominee was Minister of the Interior. The German press began to make oblique reference to Caillaux as "the only reasonable French statesman." [19]

Berlin was kept fully informed of Caillaux's tour. A dispatch from Count von Luxburg, German ambassador to Argentina, was later deciphered by Allied cryptographers.

Caillaux has left Buenos Aires after a short stay and is going direct to France, evidently on account of the [group undecipherable] scandal, which he regards as a personal attack on himself. He speaks contemptuously of the President and the rest of the French government, with the exception of Briand. He sees through the policy of England perfectly. He does not anticipate the complete overthrow of France. He sees in the war now a struggle for existence on the part of England. . . .

Caillaux welcomed indirect courtesies from me, but emphasized the extreme caution which he is obliged to employ. . . .

He warns against the excessive praise bestowed upon him by our press. Our praise injures his position.[20]

And the next day the German ambassador to the United States signaled Berlin:

Steamer *Araguaya* left Buenos Aires January 30. The captain is carrying important papers. Capture very desirable. Caillaux is on board. In case of capture, Caillaux should, in an unobtrusive way, be treated with courtesy and consideration. Can you inform our cruisers? [21]

But the German raiders missed the *Araguaya*, and Caillaux, back in France, retired to his country residence. Although still a member of the Chamber of Deputies, he kept his appearances in Paris as brief as possible. The Germans had telegraphed from South America that Caillaux "fears fate of Jaurès if goes Paris." [22] Nor were Caillaux's fears unfounded. Once when he appeared on the streets of Vichy a mob of two thousand persons drove him to take refuge in a police station, from which he had to be rescued by a contingent of troops from the nearest garrison. A contemporary diarist, marveling at this, wrote: "The case of Caillaux is amazing. He has firm friends and admirers, with strong support in the Chamber." [23]

But although much of Caillaux's time was spent in the provinces, he was far from forgotten. A procession of dissimilar persons made their way to Mamers to render homage to the frustrated politician. Minister of the Interior Malvy paid his respects to his patron; Miguel Almereyda showed up from time to time, as did Bolo Pasha; a certain Madame Duverger, the mistress of a German agent stationed in Brussels, arrived to present Caillaux with messages offering her paramour's services in establishing contact with the German Foreign Office; and an anonymous Swiss banker appeared one day bearing a slip of paper which stated, "I am at your disposal and am authorized to establish the relations you desire," [24] and giving the address of Marx, the German spymaster in Berne.

Although there is no evidence to establish that Caillaux ever accepted any of the German offers to enter into direct negotiations with them, it is damning enough that he never conceived it his duty to inform the French counterespionage bureau (a part of Malvy's Ministry of the Interior) of the German overtures. Most certainly, Caillaux was not guilty of being a spy in the pay of the Germans. Had money been offered him he would have recoiled in horror. Yet his ambition and lack of common sense were leading him along the path of treason. Somehow he never realized that France, in deadly embrace with Germany, was now no place for the political machinations of prewar days. "His crime," a fellow deputy was later to observe, "was not to have believed in victory; to have gambled on his nation's defeat." [25]

Perhaps even more heedless than Caillaux's activities were those of his nominee, Louis Malvy. By January 1916 Malvy was in complete charge of French counterespionage in the Zone of the Interior. As part of the conflict between Parliament and G.Q.G., Malvy had succeeded in persuading the Ministry of War to close down the Army's Second Bureau counterespionage operations everywhere except in the Zone of the Army.[26] Yet from the very first days of the Carnet B the Ministry of the Interior had been amazingly tolerant of the activities of the pacifist and defeatist left wing. This was all the more striking by virtue of the fact that while governments came and went, Malvy was always retained as Minister of the Interior. In succession the governments of Viviani, Briand and Ribot were organized, were reorganized and then fell. Only one man, Louis Malvy, appeared in every Cabinet in the same post. He owed his astounding continuance in office not to his efficiency—he was widely regarded as negligent in the extreme—but, rather, to his superb position in the French political spectrum. As a member of the Radical Socialist group, with its tradition of "no enemies to the left," coupled with his inaction toward the pacifist activities of the militant left, Malvy had come to be very popular with a substantial segment of the Chamber of Deputies. Moreover, Malvy's status as Caillaux's "representative" in the government gave him an additional grip on his office.

But the activities of political pacifists, ignored as they were by Malvy, did not go totally unwatched. The Army's Second Bureau had been driven out of Paris, but the core of the section devoted to political counterespionage had been re-established at G.Q.G. itself, safe within the Zone of the Army. This section operated under the cover name of "Service du Moral" and was headed by a shrewd young lieutenant named Bruyant[27] whose interest was immediately directed to M. Malvy, to the *Bonnet rouge* and to the various pacifist agitators. Another object of concern was M. Caillaux.

From a variety of sources whose reports would not pass through the hands of the Minister of the Interior, the Service du Moral collected information. In particular, Bruyant and his staff kept a close eye on the activities of Joseph Caillaux, and, being Frenchmen, they of course compiled dossiers.

Skilled hands opened letters from Caillaux to Bolo and Almereyda, letters thanking them for their support at one juncture or another. From a trustworthy source they learned that under the name Reynouard (his wife's maiden name) Caillaux kept a safe-deposit box in the Banca d'Italia in Florence, into which he had put papers outlining his plans for assuming the premiership by a *coup d'état* when the last French offensive had failed. And when, in December of 1916, Caillaux and his wife traveled to Florence and then on to Rome, an alarming report of his visit was made by Admiral de Saint-Pair, the French naval attaché in Rome, in a private letter to the chief of staff at the Marine Ministry in Paris.

MY DEAR FRIEND,

The day when you were in Rome, the Ambassador [Camille Barrère] informed you of the acts and behavior of M. Caillaux. Since your departure, our information as to the dealings of this personage has been considerably increased, and today, having a good opportunity, the Ambassador entrusts me with the duty of informing the ministers of the situation. I give you below a summary of our news. . . .

On December 17 M. Caillaux expected to meet M. Salandra [the Italian Premier] at the house of M. Brunicardi. M. Salandra avoided the meeting and sent M. Martini [the former Colonial Minister] in his place. The conversation was a two hours' monologue. M. Caillaux explained that the Briand Ministry [the current French government] was finished.

M. Caillaux considered that the time for him to take power had not arrived. He expected a Clemenceau-Barthou Ministry, which could live only by intensifying the war. But it was evident that this Ministry could live only two months, France being unable to continue her military effort beyond the end of the spring. Then M. Caillaux would assume power and sign peace. He promised that the whole world would be astonished by the advantages which Germany thought of giving to Italy and France; all the bill would be paid by Russia and the Balkans. . . . Immediately peace was signed, France would conclude a treaty alliance with Germany and Spain against England and Russia, who were our real enemies. . . .

M. Caillaux did not confine his visits to a few politicians. He has also been to the Vatican. In spite of statements to the contrary by M. Sonnino, it is certain that he has seen neither the Pope nor Cardinal Gasparri; but Mme. Caillaux has seen the latter prelate several times. M. Caillaux saw at the Vatican the most pacifist of these prelates who are so pacifist, notably Mgrs. Misciatelli, Migone, and especially Pacelli, most impetuous of peace-at-any-price pacifists. [Monsignor Pacelli was, of course, later to become Pope Pius XII.] He strongly urged these prelates to make a bigger campaign than ever for peace, telling them that if Italy concluded a separate peace France would be forced to withdraw from the struggle. . . .

I need not tell you how serious M. Barrère considers the situation to be. M. Caillaux repeated on several occasions that immediately on his return to Paris he was going to bring B. [Briand] down and was going to replace him by Léon Bourgeois. Naturally it is not this detail which is worrying M. Barrère, but—as are all the Entente ambassadors and Italian statesmen who have supported the present policy—he is rightly alarmed by these German intrigues coming to light with such violence. He desired that our Minister should be informed. I have made for him this short summary, which is a truthful reflection of matters. . . .

Goodbye, my dear friend. Whenever there is a safe opportunity I will keep you informed as to the development of this drama.

Yours affectionately,

G. de Saint-Pair [28]

Five days later it was the turn of Major Noblemaire, the assistant French military attaché, to report. His message took the form of a cryptographic dispatch to General Louis Lyautey, the newly appointed Minister of War. When decoded, it read:

This telegram is very secret. In the absence of Colonel François [the French military attaché], who is absorbed in the preparations for the mission to Epirus, I beg to report as follows.

I have not so far told you anything of the presence in Italy of M. Caillaux nor of his movements, because, in the first place, I hoped that the subject might remain more political than military; secondly, because I knew that the Admiral, our naval attaché, had been authorized by the Ambassador to send the first information by courier on the 22nd of December to Admiral Lacaze, then Interim Minister of War; and finally, because I knew that the Ambassador was giving a report to the President of the Council [Premier Briand]. But during the last three days I have noticed in military circles, where, as everywhere else, people speak too much of it, such a feeling as the result of M. Caillaux' language, and perhaps more as a result of the freedom which is apparently given him to make such utterances, that I consider it my strict duty to acquaint you with this feeling. It goes so far as a fear that France will conclude a separate peace, and in the comments which I hear I see more pessimistic deductions as to the exhaustion of the material and moral resources of France . . .

I am in a position to give you on this subject, if you wish it and as soon as you express the wish, very precise and detailed information.[29]

Trustworthy hands brought these reports to the personal attention of Aristide Briand, the French Premier of the time, and his instructions were solicited. Clearly, this was too critical a situation to let develop. But it was also delicate. Caillaux was a former Premier of France and an acknowledged leader of a major political coalition in the Chamber of Deputies. While it was increasingly clear that he and his left-wing supporters were paying only lip service to France's war effort, it was also clear that to arrest on charges of treason a former Premier and a covey of influential left-wing leaders and journalists, besides dismissing the Minister of the Interior himself, would be such a blow to French national morale that it might mean the collapse of France. The troops would never again trust a government which had shown itself so near treason.

It was clearly a dilemma. But before it was resolved, the harassed government would have a graver problem on its hands.

10

PRELUDE TO CATASTROPHE

As the winter of 1916–17 approached, it became painfully apparent to the French government that two and a half years of war had got France almost nowhere. The fruitless battles of 1915, the siege of Verdun, the offensive on the Somme—the never-ending "nibbling"—had all been completely barren of results, except that the nation and its Army had almost bled to death. By December 1916, some 1,300,000 Frenchmen were killed, dead of wounds, in prison, or missing—wastage of more than one life for every minute of the war.[1]

And now the politicians had completely lost the feeling of blind acquiescence which they once displayed toward their generals. For two and a half years they had provided G.Q.G. with all it had desired, they had accepted the diminution of the government's prestige in favor of General Joffre, they had unhesitatingly placed the blood and treasure of France in the hands of the military, and what had they been given to show for it? Only a series of battles, ill-conceived, as they seemed in retrospect, and with the butcher's bill higher in each successive fight. At the opening of the war the Army had declared that it had only to attack and victory was certain; but, as it turned out, the Army was wrong. Then G.Q.G. had said that the Army must launch a series of frontal attacks to wear the Germans down; now it seemed apparent that it was the Allies who were being worn down. Finally, Joffre had said there was no danger at Verdun —and an unprepared Verdun had almost fallen in a bloody battle of fantastic size. Clearly, the politicians said to themselves, affairs could not be allowed to continue in this manner. Beneath this military bungling the nation would collapse.

France could no longer make good her losses. Already the military depots were almost empty and replacements for the hundred-odd infantry divisions could be obtained only by juggling the bookkeeping—reducing divisions from twelve battalions to nine, converting a couple of divisions of territorials into first-line infantry, or calling up the next class of conscripts early and thus providing 200,000 youths none of whom was over eighteen.

In the trenches and on the home front, France was ready for collapse. There had to be a change in tactics and strategy. But how to effect this? Since the beginning of the war, the direction of military action had been almost completely in the hands of Joffre, cloistered at his Grand Quartier Général in Chantilly. He had steadfastly refused the counsel of the government, had demanded the right to pursue his own strategy with complete independence, had created at Chantilly what amounted to a second government for France. All of this, much as it grated on the politicians, could have been tolerated if only it had brought victory. But it had not, and the laurels of the Savior of the Marne were now permanently tarnished.

The despair of the nation had given birth to a host of bitter and wholly untrue stories about Joffre and his staff. "What is the difference between a staff officer and a Chinese vase?" "Nothing, they are both decorated before they undergo fire." [2] And the airtight secrecy at Grand Quartier Général enabled scandalmongers to hint at vast orgies taking place at Chantilly.

It was clear that Joffre and his strategies had lost the confidence of the nation when, early in the winter of 1916, the Chamber of Deputies and the Senate each held secret sessions to debate the progress of the war. Freely the deputies and the senators castigated the conduct of the war, pointed to the immense casualty lists, ridiculed the optimistic predictions of G.Q.G. It was with difficulty that Premier Briand succeeded in obtaining a vote of confidence, and when it was finally obtained it was clearly conditional upon the government's dismissal of Joffre.

So, in a complicated face-saving arrangement, Joffre was promoted to the rank of marshal and then "retired" as the Commander in Chief of the French armies.

Now Joffre was gone. The politicians were stunned by the ease of it. Suddenly the awesome and terrible teeth of the Grand Quartier Général had been pulled. But now whom to put in Joffre's place? The most obvious choices lay among the three army group commanders. One by one the government considered them. Foch was rejected out of hand—for a variety of reasons he had fallen from favor and had made too many enemies among the politicians; Castelnau was set aside as being too religious to suit the anticlericals; and Pétain's cold personality and blunt statements had won him few friends to support his candidacy.

Attention turned to one prominent military figure—indeed, the only general who enjoyed the glamour and prestige of a recent resounding victory. Robert Nivelle had risen fast and far since the early days of the war when, as a heroic lieutenant colonel, he had charged forward with his guns to save the day at the Ourcq. In April of 1916, while the Allies were preparing for the Somme offensive, Joffre had begun to be dissatisfied with Pétain's direction at Verdun. Although it was conceded that Pétain was "the heart and soul of the action," [3] he had revealed a distressing tendency to pessimism which was to plague him for the balance of the war. Constantly Pétain demanded floods of fresh troops and torrents of artillery ammunition. It was useless for Joffre to point out that all the available reserves were desperately needed on the Somme. Ultimately, the only way that Joffre could solve the problem was to promote Pétain to the command of the Group of Armies of the Center (G.A.C.), from which it was hoped he would "take in the situation with a clearer view." [4] And in Pétain's place Nivelle had been appointed.

Immediately the young general had done much to arrest the final German attacks. (The famous phrase "They shall not pass" was really Nivelle's, although generally credited to Pétain.) Nivelle had then turned his attention to rolling back the Germans, the keystone of whose defense was the symbolic Fort Douaumont, captured in their initial Verdun attacks and now supposed to be impregnable. Together with Charles Mangin, the fearsome general who functioned as Nivelle's key subordinate, a meticulous and incredibly audacious plan had been conceived.

Into the area overlooking Fort Douaumont, Nivelle had brought more than five hundred artillery pieces of the heaviest caliber, together with immense stocks of ammunition. Three crack infantry divisions plus three battalions of fierce African troops had been taken out of the line, rested and brought up to full strength following which they had been given weeks of training on terrain features built to simulate those surrounding Douaumont. The troops had been formed into assault parties, each given a separate and specific objective and drilled and redrilled until they could find their way almost in the dark. Previous theory had been thrown to the winds, and the men had been trained to disregard their flanks and imbued with the idea that their only mission was to follow close behind a rapidly moving artillery barrage and then strike with the utmost speed and violence at their assigned objective.

As soon as all was ready, the French artillery began a tremendous bombardment on Fort Douaumont and on the German batteries which defended it. The guns thundered for days, and then, at 2 P.M. on October 22, the French bombardment suddenly ceased and shifted to a rolling assault barrage. Immediately, 630 German artillery pieces which had been skillfully concealed from the French artillery observers flung aside their camouflage and commenced a furious counterbarrage against the expected attack.[5] But there was no assault —the French barrage had been a feint. Instead, the location of each of the hitherto hidden German guns was quickly noted and the French artillery resumed its counterbattery fire. Two days later nearly half of the defending German batteries had been destroyed. It was then—following a tremendous bombardment by vast numbers of the deadly little trench mortars—that the French infantry dashed forward, shrouded by a heavy fog. Unhesitatingly the assault parties smashed through to their separate objectives, using compasses to find their way. The Germans were stunned and confused by the violence and precision of the attack. In two hours, Fort Douaumont had been recaptured.

It had been a resounding French victory—quick, cheap in lives and loaded with prestige. More to the good, Nivelle had followed his success at Fort Douaumont with a series of quick attacks on a similar imaginative pattern, until, in the space of a few weeks, the Germans had at some points been pushed back almost to the line from which they had begun their assault on Verdun many months before.

Reflecting on these victories, in which they hopefully saw the seeds of more to come, the government debated no more. Robert Nivelle was appointed Commander in Chief to replace the fallen Joffre.

When Nivelle journeyed to Chantilly in mid-December of 1916 to assume command of the French armies, his subordinates saw a man who in every way looked and acted like the man of the hour. Tall, spruce, appearing much younger than his sixty-one years in spite of his gray hair, the general radiated charm and confidence. Speaking of the "Verdun Method," the name instantly attached to the tactics which had brought him to his present eminence, he said, "The experiment has been conclusive. Our method has been tried out. I can assure you that victory is certain." [6]

Nivelle's elevation would have aroused the resentment of the many senior generals over whose heads he had jumped had it not been for his happy gift of always being able to utter the well-turned phrase. Indeed, the man was amazingly fluent. Unlike the dour and uncommunicative Joffre, Nivelle had the ability to express himself perfectly, to convey his enthusiasm and conviction in a line of cogent argument which demolished the misgivings of the less articulate. What is more, as the son of a French father and an English mother, Nivelle spoke flawless and idiomatic English, an incalculable asset when dealing with France's principal allies.

Of course, Nivelle knew that he owed his appointment to his stunning successes at Verdun and that more of the same was expected of him. He also knew that success had to come quickly, because through the agency of the Second Bureau and of Postal Control, a section of G.Q.G. which censored and regularly analyzed the mail sent by the men in the trenches, it was authoritatively reported to him that "the man in the ranks is no longer aware of why he is fighting. He is completely ignorant of anything happening outside his own sector. He has lost both faith and enthusiasm. He compares his life with that of a convict. He carries out his duties mechanically. He may become the victim of the greatest discouragement, display the worst weaknesses." [7] Obviously there was little time to lose, and Nivelle resolved to deliver to France a smashing victory based on the audacious pattern which had served him so well at Verdun.

In early January 1917 the leaders of the Allied governments met in Rome for an interallied military conference. The disillusionment of the various governments with the results which had been obtained by their military leaders was evidenced and underlined by the fact that, for the first time, the generals were left in the background. The government leaders, Prime Minister Lloyd George of Great Britain and Premier Briand of France, together with the Italians, discussed military plans for 1917. Nothing very definite was concluded except that none favored the resumption of the grinding horror of the Somme, which had been planned by Joffre and Haig before Joffre had passed from the scene. The only other area of agreement which the Allies found was the conclusion that Italy would probably collapse as a combatant if the Germans and the Austrians were given the freedom to develop serious pressure on her. Obviously a Franco-British offensive would have to be mounted on the western front. But what shape it would take and how it would differ from the fruitless blood bath of the Somme the politicians could not clearly see. It was all very discouraging, and the Allied leaders left Rome much depressed.

As Lloyd George journeyed northward back to London, his train was stopped at the Gare du Nord in Paris, where Robert Nivelle waited to introduce himself to the British leader. Swiftly and informally Nivelle outlined his plans for a totally new sort of offensive, brief and crushing and patterned on the successes at Verdun. He had only a few moments to state his case, but it was enough to intrigue Lloyd George, who had heard sketchy but glowing reports about this dynamic Frenchman. The British Prime Minister invited Nivelle to come to London the following week to discuss the plan more fully.

Nivelle's trip to London on January 15-16 was a tremendous personal success for the French general. The British civilian leaders were vastly impressed with this soldier who, unlike their own military men, could express himself with fluency and enthusiasm—and, what was more, he spoke flawless English! There seemed to be no end to the attributes which this spruce dynamo possessed—it even transpired that he was a Protestant. And, of course, the fact of his half-British parentage ruled out the possibility of any latent Anglophobia, the suspicion of which had always faintly tainted relations between French and British generals.

Skillfully, Nivelle outlined his plan to Lloyd George and his associates. They were aware of the novel military methods used to recapture Fort Douaumont? Good. Then only envision an attack of the same type, conducted by meticulously trained troops used in immense quantities. Imagine, also, that instead of simply bombarding the forward German positions, enough artillery was gathered so that *all* the enemy lines could be shelled simultaneously. And then, after this was done, the infantry, which would be trained to move at a far faster rate than ever before, would smash completely through the German positions in a matter of hours! The key to his success, Nivelle implied with becoming modesty, was that he and his subordinates had dared to introduce unorthodox tactics and had developed the ability to think on a much larger scale. The fault with the previous Allied tactics was that they had been too ponderous, trying to capture one German line at a time rather than simply slamming through the entire depth of the enemy front in one bound. None of this "nibbling" for Nivelle. In his Verdun Method he had developed a tactical system of such violence and speed that henceforth the Allies could plan in terms of daring offensives crowned with the greatest of results.

All who listened to Nivelle were enthralled. Obviously, this handsome general standing before them was the prophet of the future. Here was a new voice positively sparkling with fresh confidence and new ideas! It seemed to his listeners that France had produced a major military genius. Only the British Imperial General Staff were not overwhelmed with Nivelle's arguments. It was one thing, they pointed out, to raid an isolated strongpoint like Douaumont; it was quite another to repeat the performance on a broad front against the main German trench system.

But to Lloyd George this merely proved that Nivelle had the imagination which his own generals lacked. If the Imperial General Staff had a better plan, then let them come up with it—but let it first be understood that the government would tolerate no more Sommes. The only plan which the British military could offer was that which had been decided upon months before by Haig and the now deposed and discredited Joffre, and it consisted of renewing the attack on the Somme. To the British government this was even less appetizing than it had been to the French politicians. The decision was made; the British would wholeheartedly support a Nivelle offensive in the spring of 1917, even support it to the point where Sir Douglas Haig and his forces in France were placed under orders to "conform to the views of the French Commander in Chief" and to "carry out the orders of all that relates to the conduct of operations." [8] This last was heady wine indeed; in effect, it amounted to the subordination of the British to Nivelle and gave him a formalized authority over the British which even Joffre with all his prestige had never been able to achieve. Such was the charm of Nivelle's personality and the magic of his victory appeal.

The co-operation of the British having been assured, Nivelle then turned his attention to the morale of his troops. On the western front the troops were enduring the coldest winter in years, which, coupled with the bloody stalemate at Verdun and the slaughter on the Somme, had served admirably to prepare the soldiers for an onslaught of pacifism from the rear. Nivelle wrote to Minister of War Lyautey:

I have the honor to inform you that I have reported the following pacifist intrigues to the Minister of the Interior. Faced with this grave threat to the morale of the troops, I am persuaded that serious measures must be taken. I should be obliged if you would get in touch with M. Malvy in order to decide on measures for putting an end to these intrigues immediately.

The volume of pacifist propaganda in the Army is increasing.

Pamphlets. For more than a year, there have been pamphlets—pacifist brochures and papers—getting into the hands of the troops. Their distribution has now reached epidemic proportions. In a two-week period now we are catching up with more than were ever seized during a three-month period in 1916. . . . They furnish doubts as to the justice of the cause for which the soldiers are fighting. They find excuses for Germany, affirm the impossibility of victory, and claim that peace alone will resolve the problems of coal and the high cost of living. Others are full of the most dangerous information and the worst kind of advice. . . . These scurrilous publications undermine the battle spirit of the soldiers, unnerve and dishearten them.

Soldiers on Leave at Meetings. While on leave, a certain number of soldiers attend meetings where, under the pretext of discussing corporative questions, the leading trade-unionists and anarchists air their pacifist theories. When they return to the trenches, the soldiers repeat to their comrades the arguments they have heard.

Soldiers in Touch with the Ringleaders. Some soldiers keep up a regular correspondence with the individuals suspected of running the propaganda. The letters which they send to them acknowledge receipt of papers, pamphlets and sheets which they admit having transmitted to others or distributed. . . .

Proposals: The pamphlets should be seized in the works where they are printed; meetings where discussion is not limited to strictly professional matters should be forbidden; the revolutionary paper *Natchalo* should be suppressed; Sebastien Faure, Merrheim, Hubert and the dozen or so agitators who support them should be vigorously opposed, the pacifist propaganda smashed, and normal working conditions enforced in the war plants and arsenals.[9]

Nivelle next directed his attention to his own command. He knew that G.Q.G. at Chantilly had acquired a reputation as a hotbed of jealousy, backbiting, and antigovernment intrigue. So, to disassociate his command from the previous one and to emphasize its new character, he caused the entire huge establishment to be transferred to Beauvais. And within the confines of G.Q.G. itself a shake-up took place. The ideas, plans and policies of Nivelle were meeting with a certain obstructionism, which was quietly but mercilessly rooted out by the new commander and the key subordinates he had brought with him to his new post.

Chief among Nivelle's energetic juniors was his *chef de cabinet*, a certain Colonel d'Alenson. In the British and American military hierarchies there is no post exactly equivalent to that of *chef de cabinet*. It combines the functions of a confidential secretary with some of the prerogatives of a chief of staff. No one is closer to the commander, no one is in a position to influence him more, than the *chef de cabinet*, who has his superior's ear at all times and, being greatly trusted and privy to all secrets, is usually privileged to speak with the utmost frankness. Historically, French military men have found a *chef de cabinet* to be of great value in acting as a sounding board for their plans and aspirations. But in Colonel d'Alenson Nivelle fell under an influence which was distinctly unhealthy, and which merely served to accentuate and distort his inflexible belief that a furious attack on the largest possible scale was all that was needed to achieve victory.

D'Alenson has been described by an English liaison officer as "one of the strangest characters thrown up by the war," an "immensely tall, loose-limbed man" whose "cavernous face, prominent cheekbones, and receding forehead were covered by a sallow skin, and the top of his head by closely-cut hair the colour of a fallow deer." But the physical characteristics most often mentioned were d'Alenson's eyes; they sparkled with a strange, unnatural glitter, explicable only by the fact that d'Alenson was dying and knew it. He had less than a year before he would succumb to tuberculosis, and the knowledge infused this ambitious man with the relentless drive and distorted vision of a fanatic. "His energy," the British officer noted, "was contagious, his illness he forgot, and this one dying man, guided by the false light of his fever, fearing above all things the inexorable passage of time, feeling that everything must be compressed within the narrow limits of his own lifetime, urged constantly, such was the frenzy of his haste, that the tempo of the attack and the speed of preparations should be increased, until the impression one gained ceased to be that of high authority prescribing dispatch, but rather of an uncontrolled force like a swollen torrent rushing madly onward." [10]

Under these circumstances, the reason of his closest aide being somewhat unhinged and acting as a goad for his already impatient nature, Nivelle jammed forward the preparations for an early attack. The French Army had been divided into three army groups—the Group of Armies of the North (G.A.N.), under Franchet d'Esperey; the Group of Armies of the Center (G.A.C.), under Pétain; and the newly formed assault army, the Group of Armies of Reserve (G.A.R.), under Micheler, whose enthusiasm for Nivelle's tactics had won him the command of the attacking forces. Later a fourth army group was formed, the Group of Armies of the East (G.A.E.), under Castelnau.

Ceaselessly Nivelle bombarded the army group commanders with his dynamic conceptions of tactics. "I insist," he wrote, "that the stamp of *violence*, of *brutality* and of *rapidity* must characterize your offensive; and, in particular, that the first step, which is the *rupture*, must in one blow capture the enemy positions and all the zone occupied by his artillery." [11] (The italics are Nivelle's.)

In brief, the Nivelle plan was this: The Battle of the Somme had succeeded in pushing a slight dent into the German lines, a dent just south of which the German lines bent east and west along the River Aisne. Thus, the German front projected in a huge bulge which could be attacked by the British from the north and the

French striking up from the Aisne in the south. It was anticipated that the British attack would open a few days before the French and thus draw the German reserves north to meet it, following which the French would erupt violently on the southern flank of the German salient and crush through it, opening a gap of approximately seventy miles in the German trench system through which the Allies would flood and end the war.

Strategically, it was not a bad plan; the Germans were in an extended position in their salient, and their infantry had been cruelly mauled in the Somme battle of the preceding summer. In fact, the only fault with the plan was that to pull it off required the ultimate in surprise—and here Nivelle could not help but fail.

Among the keys to the success of his Verdun Method were, first, arousing the enthusiasm of his troops by the prospect of a crushing, war-ending victory and, second, preparing both officers and men for the offensive by giving them a thorough understanding of their role in the operation. But, given these hypotheses, it became almost impossible to expect that surprise could be achieved as it had been in the much smaller Verdun attacks. The troops had been deliberately aroused to expect final victory in the forthcoming offensive, which, they were told, would take place as soon as the weather moderated in the spring. Indeed, the poilu had only to look around him in that winter of 1917 to see that something very big was in the air.

Division after division was moved into the G.A.R. area south of the German salient, and there, in vast camps, the troops were trained in the Verdun Method. They exercised with the new tanks, a British invention from which promising results had been obtained the preceding fall. They practiced following a rolling barrage similar to that which had been used in the Somme attacks, but with one important difference: Nivelle had stressed lightning speed in the advance so as to overrun the German guns before they could devastate the offensive. Accordingly, the various Army commanders had been queried as to how fast the French rolling barrage, and hence the troops who advanced just behind it, could travel. A premium was put on the most wildly optimistic estimate, and the prize was won by the ruthless firebrand Mangin, who declared that his troops could advance at the phenomenal speed of better than thirty yards a minute and keep it up for mile after mile. Troop commanders who demurred that this speed could not possibly be kept up over the cratered ground of a battlefield were made to feel the wrath of official displeasure.

As the tempo of training picked up speed, various new weapons and tactics were tested. To clear away machine-gun nests, the infantry companies were to carry forward their own artillery in the form of the lightweight 37-mm. cannon which would be handled by only two men. And, since the attack would culminate in a speedy debouchment into open country, the troops were exercised in open-field warfare, the tactics of which had been almost forgotten in the years of static struggle in the trenches. The use of the grenade, a principal weapon in trench-to-trench attack, was de-emphasized in favor of rifle practice.

The troops learned to attack in relays, with fresh divisions passing through exhausted ones in a continuous rolling offensive, the maxim of which was "Keep moving." "The infantry must be through the rearmost German positions seven hours after *l'heure H*," the G.A.R. was told.[12] And as the troops trained, they watched new roads, gun emplacements, airfields and supply dumps being built. Over the fields the cavalry cantered, preparing for the moment when the German lines would be ruptured and the charge would be sounded.

Truly, these were great days. From both what they were told and what they saw, the troops gradually gained the heartening impression that they were part of an irresistible host which, once launched, could not be denied until they had smashed the German lines. For there were not only Frenchmen in the training areas. To strengthen the attack to its ultimate, Nivelle had ordered in the Senegalese. Thirty-five battalions recruited from among the Peul, Bambara, Malike and Tukulör tribesmen of French West Africa were to be used in the offensive. Early in the war a series of legends had grown up about the Senegalese. It was said that they were blindly devoted to their white officers, who spoke their native tongues; that they possessed unbounded courage and never missed the opportunity to throw themselves on the enemy, whom they terrorized with the three-foot-long curved knives called *coupe-coupes*. True, experience had shown that the Senegalese could not stand cold weather and that, illiterate, uneducated and understanding little French, they could not absorb any complicated tactics. Nevertheless, their moral effect was substantial and they were to take their place in the first wave of the offensive.

Nor was that the end of the strange sights to be seen in the build-up area. There were even a couple of Russian brigades which had been brought to France. The morale of the Russian troops might not be what it should, since they were riddled with the discontent which was infesting their revolution-infected motherland; but, stiffened with French officers who wore Russian uniforms, these strange brigades were counted upon for valuable service.

Probably the troops were never officially told it, but certainly they were allowed to believe that the war would be "over by Christmas," and so as the masses of men streamed toward the River Aisne the spirit of August 1914 began to return and the blue-clad marchers once again sang "The Marseillaise."

But all these preparations could not but become known to the Germans. In the little cafés in the Zone of the Armies the troops talked of nothing but the impending attack. It was too much to believe that more than a million men can be made privy to a secret and then have it remain such. Faithfully the German spies reported what they had heard to their contacts in Switzerland.

But the biggest blow came in the middle of February. In his desire to stimulate enthusiasm and to diffuse the necessary knowledge of tactics and objectives, Nivelle had allowed orders to be circulated right down to battalion level. This was absurdly audacious and was repaid by a German trench raid which captured plans, orders and maps on the body of a French officer.

Now the offensive stood revealed in considerable detail. Now the Germans knew that their salient would be attacked, and they hastened to make preparations for it.

On the western front the Germans possessed about 150 divisions facing 180 of the Allies. It was instantly apparent to the Germans that they could not possibly withstand a two-pronged attack on their exposed salient. But to know the French plan was to know how to counter it. All they had to do was withdraw from the salient, to straighten their line and thus eliminate the danger of being attacked on both flanks while simultaneously economizing manpower by having a shorter line to defend.

It was a strategic decision of the very highest order. Ground, even a few pitiful miles of it, had been purchasable only at a phenomenal cost in lives, and Nivelle had never even considered the possibility that the Germans would voluntarily withdraw from the salient.

Truly, the German decision was an awesome strategic gamble. Now it remained to see what effect it would have on the French plan.

The German withdrawal from the salient began on February 9 with the commencement of "Operation Alberich," a demolition program appropriately named after the malicious dwarf in the Nibelung saga. Although they were resigned to giving up this conquered territory, the Germans resolved to deliver it as a desert, a land which would take months of work before it could be used as a staging area for an attack, and throughout the seventy-mile width of France which formed the salient they fell to in an orgy of calculated destruction. Thousands of houses were pulled down, every fruit tree was sawed through, wells were poisoned, reservoirs were blown up, railheads and bridges destroyed. Meanwhile behind the salient the German engineers readied what the Allies called the Hindenburg Line, (after Falkenhayn's successor as Chief of the German General Staff), a magnificently strong defensive position into which they would retreat. The Hindenburg Line ran south from Arras to a ridge of hills which overlooked the River Aisne at the point where the G.A.R. was assembling for its assault. At this juncture the German defensive system curved off in a westerly direction following the ridge, which was known as the *Chemin des Dames*, the "Ladies' Road," after an old carriage route which had been hewn out for the daughters of Louis XV.

Both the Hindenburg Line and the connecting Chemin des Dames took advantage of the most readily defensible and most easily supplied ground. Unobserved by the Allies and unscathed by Allied artillery fire, the Germans labored furiously to make these positions into what can truthfully be described as one of the strongest defensive lines ever constructed.

As Operation Alberich began in earnest, it became evident to the British and French troops in the front lines that the Germans were preparing to abandon the salient. At night the flames of villages being razed by the Germans were clearly visible in the Allied trenches. Back to Nivelle at Beauvais sped messages that the Germans were going to withdraw—there could be no possible doubt of it. Now, the front-line commanders urged, was the time to strike, while the Germans were weakened, while their heavy artillery had been pulled back out of range and while they had converted their own rear into an impassable shambles. But to Nivelle and his staff, the reports of the German withdrawal seemed almost treasonous. The French offensive had been predicated upon striking at the German salient, and it was unthinkable to be told that there was now to be no salient. Nivelle was far from stupid. He was aware that the complete alteration of the German defensive system might well spell the end of his cherished offensive. All, now, would have to be changed. The contraction of the German line by a withdrawal would free more than a dozen divisions for the defenders, and many of the laboriously prepared French gun positions, roads and bivouacs would be useless. The prospect was too depressing to think about, and so all the frantic reports of the impending German withdrawal and all the pleas for permission to attack fell on annoyed, unbelieving and indifferent ears at G.Q.G. Nivelle did not want to believe it, and so he simply closed his mind to the evidence.

The actual German retreat from the salient began on March 15 and was finished on March 19. The withdrawal was conducted in a series of steps. At midnight the reserves pulled back; at 4 A.M. the main body left the trenches. Behind them was a light rear guard of machine-gunners who could keep up a furious fire, if necessary, until 6 A.M. when they too withdrew.

Slowly the advancing Allies pushed into the smoldering devastation of the salient. They could neither move fast nor far. The German demolition teams had done their work well. There were booby traps everywhere to mangle the unwary souvenir collector. Bridges and roads had to have mines removed and then be laboriously rebuilt. Shelter and food had to be found for the liberated French populace, whom the Germans had crammed into a few of the larger towns. And everywhere, gorged on the offal of battle and destruction, were huge rats. The fields and shattered trenches were alive with them, and at night their eyes glittered red as they caught the reflection of the headlights of trucks grinding their way slowly along the ruined roads.

For the French nation, the reoccupation of the salient, represented as it was in the guise of a brilliant French victory, provided a momentary shot in the arm to counteract the general gloom. But at Grand Quartier Général the facts were too well known to permit any illusions. Obviously the entire strategic basis of the planned attack had evaporated, and it was generally assumed that the scheme was at an end. But G.Q.G. was reckoning without the unquenchable enthusiasm of its master, stimulated as he was by the firebrand optimism of d'Alenson. To the amazement of his staff, Nivelle announced that the attack would come off as originally planned, the only change being that, instead of pinching off the now nonexistent salient, the offensive would be mounted directly against the Chemin des Dames at the southern extremity of the Hindenburg Line.

In effect, Nivelle chose to regard the German withdrawal as nothing more than a serious inconvenience. But it was an inconvenience which would shortly be compounded from another quarter, because on March 19 the shaky Ministry of Aristide Briand fell and was replaced by that of Alexandre Ribot.

The Ribot Ministry was probably no stronger than any of those which had preceded it. Ribot was eighty years old, and Louis Malvy was still Minister of the Interior in deference to his supposed position of influence with the workers and the parties of the extreme left. But there was one important difference: the kaleidoscope of French politics had thrown up Paul Painlevé as Minister of War, a man who, unlike many of his predecessors, determined that if he was to accept responsibility for the conduct of the war, then he would insist upon being fully informed of all of the plans being developed at G.Q.G.

Paul Prudent Painlevé was in every respect an unusual minister. At fifty-three this short man with the high, piping voice had not been a politician for very long. Early in life he had achieved fame as a brilliant mathematician; then, becoming absorbed with politics, he had put his incisive and remorselessly logical mind at the service of France. He neither possessed nor desired to acquire the powers of dissimulation and intrigue which characterized so many of his confreres. His personal ambitions, perhaps because they had already been gratified by his internationally acknowledged genius as a mathematician, were distinctly subordinated to his determination to serve his nation in an honest and honorable manner.

Painlevé's first move as Minister of War was to meet with Nivelle and learn at first hand the plans of the French Commander in Chief. He prefaced his interview with the general by stating plainly that, had he been Minister of War at the time of Joffre's dismissal, he would have selected Pétain as Commander in Chief. But what had been done was done, and Painlevé expressed himself as intending to give the fullest support to any well-conceived plan which Nivelle might develop. He assumed, of course, that Nivelle's plans for an offensive had been canceled by the German withdrawal—as well as by the fact that Czar Nicholas II had abdicated on March 15 and it was expected that the Russians would shortly make peace with the Germans, thus liberating a large number of German divisions to reinforce the western front. Moreover, Painlevé advised that before he assumed office he had heard complete details of the Nivelle plan bruited about in Paris. Even the exact date for the launching of the offensive, April 8, was well known. Obviously secrecy was hopelessly compromised.

To his astonishment, Painlevé heard Nivelle assuring him that his plan for a crushing spring offensive had changed only in minute detail. The only alteration would be that the objective of the attack was no longer to bite off the salient but, instead, simply to crack open the German line, after which the French forces would spread out in the open country beyond and the rupture of the entire German trench system would inevitably ensue. The German defenses would be overrun with only trifling losses; the German reinforcements meant nothing, because, Nivelle said, "I do not fear numbers. The greater the numbers the greater the victory." [13] To every objection raised by Painlevé, Nivelle had a glib, optimistic and reassuring answer.

Finally the interview concluded itself and the perplexed Painlevé retired to consider the matter at length. Although there was no denying that Nivelle's confidence and argumentative powers were soothing, Painlevé could not help feeling that somehow the picture was not so rosy as it had been painted. More and more this offensive began to sound like the familiar type of attack which Joffre had mounted for two barren years. This was shrewd judgment on Painlevé's part, because he could not know of the influence wielded on Nivelle by the dying fanatic d'Alenson, just as he could not know then of the misgivings which were beginning to creep into the minds of Nivelle's top field commanders. Acting on his own hunches, Painlevé resolved to learn more for himself.

As soon as it leaked out that he was undertaking a personal evaluation of the Nivelle offensive and that he remained to be convinced of the soundness of the attack, a number of persons came forward to air their private doubts in the matter. Repeatedly it was brought to Painlevé's attention that in the months since the original conception of the Nivelle plan the whole Allied military situation had changed vastly. Not only had the German withdrawal affected the plan, but there was now the matter of the impending collapse of Russia. And, much more importantly, it now looked as if the United States would be coming into the war—which would mean that, instead of having to defeat Germany in an immediate battle, France could wait until the Americans had a chance to add their power to the Allied cause in an overwhelming offensive. Finally, there was a real question as to whether the Nivelle plan had ever been any good. Painlevé learned that his predecessor as Minister of War, Lyautey, had ridiculed the plan as of the sort that one would expect to have been dreamed up by "the army of the Grand Duchess of Gerolstein." [14]

Through private sources, Painlevé received much disquieting information. It was rumored that the chief of G.Q.G.'s Third Bureau (Operations), a certain Colonel Renouard, actually opposed the offensive and had gone so far as to state his objection in writing, only to have it torn out of the files by d'Alenson. And, too, it was learned that General Micheler, the commander of the G.A.R. and the man to whom the responsibility of implementing the major attack had been given, had definitely cooled toward the plan. But the final blow to Painlevé's confidence in the Nivelle plan took place on March 25, when Charles de Freycinet, a vastly respected French political figure whose advanced age put him completely beyond suspicion as wishing to further his own ends, brought him a memorandum written by a senior staff officer attached to the G.A.R. and reportedly reflecting the views of every responsible officer on that staff. In the memorandum Painlevé was advised that there was no question but that the Germans knew of the French offensive and were speeding every effort to prepare for it; and, further, that should the Germans succeed in preventing the French from breaking through, "the best corps in the Army, the Ist, XXth, IInd Colonial and XXXIInd, and more besides, will be decimated." [15]

By now the offensive was only weeks away. If Painlevé was to exert any effect on it, he had to do it soon. In his quandary, he resolved to take a highly unorthodox step. To his presence he summoned the three army group commanders, Nivelle's top fighting subordinates, and separately he questioned them: What did they think of the forth-

coming offensive? On March 28 he interviewed General Micheler.
From the start of the meeting it was clear that Micheler did not
hold out the hope for a war-ending victory which had been promised by his chief. He dwelt on the many changes in the general situation which had taken place since the plan's conception in December.
For example, until the German withdrawal Micheler had been faced
with the problem of breaking through an enemy position which was
two systems deep. Now, from what was known of the improved
German line, it appeared that this defensive position was four systems deep. But when the question was put to him point blank,
"Should the attack be given up?," Micheler was evasive. He outlined the difficulties involved in giving up the attack: The Germans
would be left with the initiative, and the French concentration on
the Aisne had left other sections of the Allied trench system weakened or in too poor repair to resist an attack. Even more dangerous
was the weakness on the other Allied fronts, such as Russia, now
clearly in her last gasp, or Italy, whose condition was not much
better. If the Germans were free to direct their reserves against
either of these two fronts, then there might be a catastrophe for the
Allies.

Next Painlevé summoned Pétain. Predictably, Pétain's advice was
direct, forthright and tinged with pessimism. It was sheer folly to hope
that the troops could break through; the German trench system was
simply too strong and the area which the artillery would have to
bombard was too big. Better give up the breakthrough idea, Pétain
counseled, and concentrate on just capturing the first couple of German trench positions in a limited attack which would punish the
Germans severely at a moderate cost in French lives.

Lastly Painlevé consulted with Franchet d'Esperey, the determined
commander of the G.A.N. D'Esperey was clearly unenthusiastic
about the offensive. The subject of the German defensive system
was raised. Nivelle had stated flatly that the German lines were
weak and far from complete, but d'Esperey said he believed the enemy trench system not only was completed but was immensely
strong as well. He felt that the Germans had constructed this line
along entirely novel principles and, moreover, had prepared a new
type of defense for the French attack, the existence of which the
Germans could hardly be unaware of.

These interviews left Painlevé completely at sea. He knew that the offensive was due to start in only a matter of days; he knew that preparations for it had been virtually completed and that even now the artillery was firing its preliminary bombardment of the German lines. And, more than anyone else, Painlevé knew the compelling necessity that this offensive should be a success. It was the last great spurt of French blood and morale.

Painlevé, in the vise of his dilemma, saw no other course open to him than to throw a new light on the facts for Nivelle and to attempt to get him to alter his plan. So on April 3 he invited Nivelle to Paris for an evening dinner meeting at which the current situation of the war could be reviewed so that Nivelle himself might propose modifying the offensive. The dinner was served at the War Ministry, and following it those present adjourned to the minister's study, against one wall of which extended a huge map of the western front. Besides Nivelle and Painlevé, the meeting included Premier Ribot and several others, one of them André Maginot, the Minister of Colonies, who had earlier in the war served as a sergeant in the Army and had lost a leg in battle, and who years later was to build the defensive system which would bear his name.

Painlevé opened the meeting by reviewing recent events—the German withdrawal, the fact that Russia had virtually collapsed, and the impending entry of the United States into the war. Did not, he asked, these events require a reappraisal of the forthcoming offensive? Finally, besides these alterations in affairs, was there not a possibility that the offensive might fail anyhow?

Nivelle jumped to his feet. Really, he implied with scorn, this was too much. He had been selected as commander of the French forces on the western front presumably because he knew something about the military art. Did the government think that all the apprehensions had not been reviewed beforehand, and by *experts?* Did they not realize that his staff at G.Q.G. was meticulously studying every change in the front? As for the offensive, it simply had to take place or the Germans would use the breathing space to administer the *coup de grâce* to either the Russians or the Italians, perhaps both. Then where would France be? As for the Americans, surely it would be endless months, perhaps years, before their tiny Army could be expanded and their weight felt. And, for good measure, he could categorically assure the government that the German defenses were far weaker than was generally supposed.

Nivelle was magnificent in his courage, and there is no question but that his fluency and confidence swept his listeners along. He paused dramatically in his oration, strode to the wall map and, with an imperious gesture, pointed out the huge territory which his lightning offensive would capture within its initial few hours. And under the spell, desperately *wanting* to believe, Painlevé too walked to the map and laid his hand on the area which Nivelle had indicated.

"General," the little mathematician said, "if your offensive resulted only in giving us back this vast territory and all it contains, the government and the nation would consider it a great victory and owe you an immense debt of gratitude."

Nivelle smiled graciously at Painlevé. "That would be nothing," he condescended, "a poor little tactical victory. It is not for so meager a result that I have accumulated on the Aisne one million two hundred thousand soldiers, five thousand guns and five hundred thousand horses. The game would not be worth the candle." [16] And on this note the conference adjourned.

Although, without question, what carried the day was Nivelle's superb confidence, buttressed by the general feeling that events had gone so far that some sort of offensive had to be mounted, there is much reason to believe that his confident mien was largely assumed. Those who knew him well began to get the impression that he had come to have doubts in his own plan. Consider now the state of mind in which Robert Nivelle, a man who had neither the experience nor the temperament to ready him for this pinnacle of power, must have found himself—his agony of apprehension when he discovered that he was shackled to his grandiose commitments and clasped in the dying embrace of the embittered genius d'Alenson. His gnawing apprehensions had begun to reveal themselves in a detachment and preoccupation which he seemed unable to shake and which served to reduce his efficiency. At this vital period it is probable that many of Nivelle's command functions were actually in the hands of Colonel d'Alenson. Men who knew both of them claim that the driving determination of the dying colonel can be readily detected in the tenor of the instructions issued from G.Q.G. in the last few days before the offensive. On April 4 this message went out over Nivelle's signature: "It is necessary to see the larger view . . . , to decentralize . . . , to cultivate initiative . . . , to encourage subordinates, to infuse all with the spirit of action . . . , to act in accordance with the Napoleonic maxims of energy, activity and speed." [17]

By now, preparations for the attack had reached their zenith and it was evident that, whatever doubts the generals and politicians might have, at least the morale of the troops could not be higher. The prospect of victory at last had filled the troops with an implacable resolve. The despond of the previous months had been cast off and the censors reported that, in their letters home, "all the fighting forces speak of gigantic preparations going on before their eyes. . . . The unanimous opinion is that the war will be over this year. . . . The spirit which dominates them all is the firm desire to do their duty no matter what it may cost. To sum it up, the general impression is very gratifying." [18]

The preliminary artillery barrage had begun, and along the length of the front the French heavy artillery crashed with heartening regularity as the big guns commenced pounding the German lines. Behind the huge front the French divisions moved up into temporary bivouacs. In immense numbers they filled every road with never-ending files of horizon blue. It was a vast assemblage of manpower; the depots had been swept clean, the hospitalized had been returned to their regiments with their wounds still fresh. And as they marched forward the troops marveled at their own numbers. Truly they were invincible. How could it be otherwise? Behind them, the comforting crash of the huge cannon; around them, virtually the entire armed might of France; ahead of them, victory!

In a series of preliminary attacks designed to clear the way for the main offensive, the troops showed magnificent courage and confidence. By now Nivelle's plan had been revealed to them in the fullest detail. But they were soon to pay a bitter price for this knowledge. On April 4 the Germans launched a large-scale raid in the vicinity of Sapeigneul where they overran the French forward trenches and captured a number of prisoners. Among these was a French sergeant of the 3rd Zouaves who was carrying a satchel, within which the Germans found maps, plans and details that revealed almost every aspect of the offensive. Originally these documents had been in the hands of a French captain, a company commander, who, when his position was being stormed by the Germans, had given the vital orders to the sergeant with instructions to flee to the rear. Ironically, the captain ultimately made his way back to safety, while the sergeant was captured.

It can be argued, and with some justice, that the capture of the French plans at Sapeigneul really made little difference in the German plans to meet the French offensive. For many weeks the Germans had been preparing a series of surprises for the French offensive. The Hindenburg Line and the Chemin-des-Dames defenses had been constructed on an entirely new concept. Instead of being the now familiar series of trenches packed with men for a depth of a mile or so, they were designed to provide a proliferation of mutually supporting machine-gun nests made of concrete. Behind these was a solid defensive position into which an immense number of dugouts had been built and natural caverns had been adapted to house troops in safety during a bombardment, following which they would emerge to act as "counterattack divisions." Known to the Germans as an "elastic defense," this system was specifically designed to stop the Nivelle type of attack. The machine guns in their concrete pillboxes were expected only to hold up the French offensive, to sell ground dearly until the counterattack divisions ruptured the French assault with a series of violent counterstrokes.

In addition to novel defenses and new tactics, the Germans had yet another surprise for the French. Originally the Nivelle plan was predicated on superiority of numbers, and the Germans were supposed to have only nine divisions to meet forty-four French. But by early April the Germans had stripped their other fronts and had amassed forty-three divisions along the Aisne, and so now the French attackers were barely equal to them in manpower.

All of this, as it became known at G.Q.G., was ignored by Nivelle. His courage goaded by the determination of d'Alenson, he put the finishing touches on his offensive, which was now scheduled for mid-April.

There was to be only one more obstacle for Nivelle to surmount before the attack was to begin. The troublesome Painlevé began to experience renewed apprehensions. From all sides the little Minister of War was being bombarded with supplications to exert his authority and cancel the offensive on the grounds that it could not possibly succeed. Seeking to overwhelm Nivelle with the concern which the government felt, Painlevé arranged another meeting with the general. This time the group included the august figure of Raymond Poincaré, the President of the Republic. The meeting began at 10 A.M. on April 6 in the private railway car of the President, on a siding at Compiègne, the town to which G.Q.G. had recently been moved in preparation for the offensive. Only the most exalted military and political figures were invited, and, in order to promote frankness, there were no minutes taken.

Nivelle knew what they had come for and the atmosphere was tense and cool. Poincaré opened the meeting by observing that the forthcoming offensive was utilizing the last scraps of French manpower, and tactfully, almost deferentially, he suggested that it might be wise to consider altering the plan in the light of recent developments. Painlevé then spoke in the same sense.

Finally it was Nivelle's turn to reply. Acidly he observed, "The offensive alone can give victory; the defensive gives only defeat and shame." He indicated that he bitterly resented this continued lack of confidence on the part of the government, based as it was on rumors, observations solicited by his inferiors and "the lucubrations of some reserve officer or other." Nivelle stressed the imperative need for this offensive, morale having already been brought to fever pitch in anticipation of the war's end. If this offensive was canceled, did not the government realize that the growing pacifism and war weariness in France would never permit another large-scale attack? Warming to his subject, he conceded the danger of becoming bogged down in a long battle of attrition and promised categorically, "I will not, under any pretext, get involved in another Battle of the Somme." In fact, he went on, unless the offensive was successful within forty-eight hours after it was launched he would stop it then and there. This was a positive promise.

All this was received in silence. Then the politicians turned to Nivelle's subordinates, the army group commanders. All, in the presence of their Commander in Chief, were evasive—except Pétain, who, when asked what the chances were of rupturing the German lines, replied crisply, "We have not the means to carry it out. . . . Even if it were to succeed, we could not exploit it. Have we five hundred thousand fresh troops to make such an advance? No. Then it is impossible." [19]

Nivelle, shuddering with fury, interrupted. It was evident, he said, that he had lost the confidence of the politicians. "Since I am in

agreement neither with the government nor with my own subordinates, the only course open to me is to resign."

This statement struck the politicians with sudden horror. How
could they conceivably explain to the nation the resignation of the
western-front commander at this critical hour? If Nivelle was allowed to depart, then civil and military morale would collapse. In a
flash it became clear to them that they had a tiger by the tail. The
plans and hopes of the Army had been advanced and stimulated to
such a degree that the offensive simply had to take place as scheduled. Besides, they rationalized, even if Nivelle's plan was a trifle too
grandiose, it seemed to promise at least a modicum of success. And
there seemed to be nothing risky about it, since Nivelle had promised
to stop the operation if his plan did not meet with success within
forty-eight hours.

Nivelle, having made his dramatic resignation announcement, had
risen to his feet. Immediately he was surrounded by Poincaré, Ribot
and, more reluctantly, Painlevé. Placatingly they urged the general
to remain. "Resign on the eve of a great battle? There is no question
of resigning, but of coming to an agreement." And in a few more
moments the government had given its final approval of the attack.

Winston Churchill has put the whole situation in an accurate light:
"So Nivelle and Painlevé . . . found themselves in the most unhappy positions which mortals can occupy: the Commander having
to dare the utmost risks with an entirely skeptical Chief behind him;
the Minister having to become responsible for a frightful slaughter
at the bidding of a General in whose capacity he did not believe, and
upon a military policy of the folly of which he was justly convinced. Such is pomp of power!" [20]

The night of April 15, the eve of the attack, brought sheets of
rain mixed with sleet, and the troops, toiling their way into jump-off
positions, were rapidly exhausted by the mud and the cold. As they
reached appointed positions, either in the assault trenches or in countless muddy fields behind the lines, they were called into dripping
circles around their company commanders, who read Nivelle's order
of the day: "The hour has come! Courage and confidence! Long
live France!" [21] (On the German side, the well-informed Kaiser had
sent a message to Crown Prince Rupprecht of Bavaria, "Your armies are undergoing heavy artillery bombardment. The great French

infantry attack is hourly awaited. All Germany is expectantly watching her brave sons. Greet them for me. My thoughts are with them.") [22]

At 6 A.M. the whistles blew in the French assault trenches and the leading battalions went over the top. Behind them the immense reserves breathed a sigh of expectation and began their shuffle forward.

Immediately it became clear that the gloomiest prognostications had been correct: the French guns, despite their number, had been unable to cover the vast ground to be bombarded. In many places the German barbed wire was hardly touched and the attacking troops piled up before it, perfect targets for the defenders' machine guns, which were now revealing themselves in unheard-of numbers. At other sections of the front, where the French guns had succeeded in cutting the wire, the defenders fired volleys of yellow flares and, almost instantly, the German artillery laid down an accurate curtain of shrapnel across the front.

And the French rolling barrage was of little assistance. As predicted, it had been set to move too fast. The assaulting troops, forcing their way through the rain, the tormented mud and the churned shambles of the battlefield, could not keep up with their barrage, which, useless, disappeared into the distance. Instead of racing forward almost unscathed to bypass strong points and thrust rapierlike into the German defenses, the French attackers in many cases could not even leave their own trenches, on account of the torrent of machine-gun fire lashing accurately across from the German side. All this, of course, while one of the principal features of the Nivelle plan, the continuous forward movement of reserves, was remorselessly jamming an additional series of fresh battalions into the assault trenches every fifteen minutes.

Secure in their headquarters, the generals commanding divisions, corps, armies and army groups could not know that the attack was failing on a widespread basis; each assumed that his men were being held up by a few company commanders who were intimidated by a handful of troublesome machine guns. Ruthlessly they attempted to goad, drive or exhort their troops forward. Mangin, whose Sixth Army was charged with spearheading the attack in its most critical sector, sent forward orders: "Our artillery preparation cannot have allowed the enemy to establish a continuous line of machine guns. You must take advantage of the gaps and pass through the islands of resistance." [23] But there were too few gaps, and these peremptory orders served only to pile up more dead on the German wire.

By noon the weather had deteriorated further and the rain had turned to a mixture of sleet and snow. Aircraft observation was impossible and all visual communications had collapsed. The French batteries now had no idea where their own troops were. Some artillery commanders, hearing vague reports that the troops had not yet left the trenches, brought their barrages back to the starting points. And for the troops who had advanced this was the final horror. Shielding their eyes against the sleet, they saw the line of exploding French shells slowly reappear and roll back over them.

During the afternoon tanks were introduced into the battle. Immediately they became a target for the superbly directed German artillery and drew so much massed fire that the infantry companies which followed the tanks were slaughtered almost to a man. Then, precisely at two-thirty in the afternoon, the German counterattack divisions began their own attacks, which served to pile the already telescoped French formations back into one another, causing a fantastic jam-up. In the rear the roads congealed with cavalry, artillery trying to move forward and infantry divisions waiting for their scheduled advance.

One aspect of the first day of the offensive went as planned. The gallantry and *élan* of the troops had been magnificent. Only the Senegalese had been disappointing. The cold weather had numbed them to the point where they could only shamble aimlessly through the slush. They could not hold their rifles in their frozen hands, so they dropped them or threw them away and, weaponless, lurched forward into the attack. Speedily their ranks were decimated and their white officers killed. Then, leaderless, the black troops began to drift aimlessly back toward the rear. They could not be stopped, and in their search for warmth and shelter they invaded the various headquarters, wandered into hospitals and climbed aboard hospital trains. Wherever they went they spread fear; and, since much had been expected of them, their obvious defeat brought sudden despondency throughout the rear areas.

But the worst aspect of the failed offensive was the complete collapse of the always incompetent French Medical Service. The medical corps had been instructed to prepare for ten or fifteen thousand wounded. Instead, on the first day of the offensive it received more than ninety thousand. Lack of the most elementary equipment kept the wounded lying unsuccored in the rain and untended in the hospitals. And as the reserve divisions filed forward they witnessed the unspeakably depressing spectacle of countless wounded dragging themselves through the freezing mud in a pitiful search for medical care.

As night fell on the first day of the great offensive, the situation was this: Instead of bursting through the German lines and pausing for the night a prescribed six miles behind the Chemin des Dames, the French Tenth Army, a battering ram comprised of five army corps, was still stacked up behind a front which it had not dented more than a few hundred yards. Only in a few places had the French attack carried any ground at all, and in these areas it was only a ludicrous fraction of what had been promised. Instead of being miles behind the German lines, the French were barely clinging to toeholds in the enemy defenses. And in the night sky the flares of the Germans bloomed out in bright-red clusters as they called for their artillery to lengthen its range in preparation for the assault of the counterattack divisions in the morning.

Huddled together, awaiting the morrow with despair and apprehension, the French troops endured another night of rain and sleet. "It's all up," they said. "We can't do it, we never shall do it."

The G.Q.G. communiqué of that evening was studiously imprecise. It stressed the stubborn resistance of the Germans and told of heavy fighting still continuing. Unsaid, but fully understood by the whole Army, was the fact that Nivelle had failed to make good on even one of his grandiose promises. And in the weeks to come he had to renege on still another. If the offensive was not a success, he had averred, he would stop it within forty-eight hours. Now he was to learn that a general offensive such as this could not be shut off all at once. Too much had been committed, too many troops lay exposed on impossible terrain and must either be withdrawn or, somehow, advance to a more tenable area. The lines must be straightened and the divisions that had made some headway must be succored. So for weeks the dreary battle persisted. The troops, now completely exhausted and totally dispirited, were flung against various German strong points along the Chemin des Dames, some of which they carried, some of which they did not.

And miles behind the lines, at G.Q.G., there was combat of a different sort. In the frustration and humiliation of the failure of his offensive, Nivelle cast about frantically for a scapegoat on whom to place the blame. Shamelessly he leaked word to influential members of the government that it was all the fault of General Mangin. Indignantly and successfully, Mangin repudiated the charge.

Finally, in a last desperate effort to shore up his position, Nivelle journeyed to Dormans, the headquarters of General Alfred Micheler, commander of the G.A.R. Within the hearing of a room filled with Micheler's subordinates, Nivelle commenced to castigate him for his failure to make the attack a success. But this was criticism which Micheler was in no way prepared to accept. Furiously he turned on Nivelle; rank was forgotten; counteraccusation followed accusation as the two generals screamed shrilly at one another. The junior officers writhed in silent embarrassment at the disgraceful scene. It ended with a furious warning by Micheler that Nivelle had better be resigned to accepting the blame for the failure. "You wish to make me responsible for this mistake—me, who never ceased to warn you of it!" Micheler cried. "Do you know what such an action is called? Well, it is called cowardice!" [24] Completely beaten, knowing his career was at an end, Nivelle left the room. Witnesses to his departure say that he reeled as if drunk as he climbed into his car.

So the great gamble had been tried and now it had failed. The troops had been exhorted to give their all, and, as always, they had given it generously. The Army had been promised victory, and, as always, the promises had been lies. Now the troops learned that they had been sent into a battle the success of which had been doubted by almost every one of their leaders.

So perhaps this was the end, and three years of fighting, bleeding and dying had been only for this—to be dashed to a pulp in another series of hopeless attacks against the hills near the bend of the River Aisne. Perhaps it had all been useless—the hopes of victory, the welling pride of patriotism, the sacrifice of countless lives. Perhaps it would be better to give up now. And in the slough of despond, morally betrayed by their highest commanders, the victims of indecision in their own government and demoralized by the defeatists in the rear, the troops turned against their Army and their nation.

On April 29, 1917, the French Army began to mutiny.

11

THE MAY MUTINIES

M UTINY was in the air. No one spoke of it, for an army mutiny
is like a horrible malignant disease and the chances that the
patient will die an agonizing death are so great that the subject cannot ever be mentioned aloud. Yet the imminence of revolt was obvious. It was apparent to the company commander who dared not even
speak to his slovenly troops when they passed him by without a
salute. It was apparent to the battalion commander who visited the
squalid rest camps where the soldiers wandered about dirty, dishev-
eled and drunk.

"It's all over," the men wrote home. "We did not get the Boche
this time. We'll never get them." Or else, "Perhaps 'they shall not
pass,' but neither shall we." And Postal Control, screening the mail
from the Zone of the Armies, reported to G.Q.G. that even the officers were bitter and cynical. "They are giving us citations and
medals, but we feel like throwing them back in the faces of the
high command and telling them, 'Keep the medals, but have done
with this stupidity.' " [1]

At the front the vaunted Nivelle offensive had had its objectives
compressed to the point where relays of attacks were being launched
merely in an effort to secure a few topographical features on the
ridge of the Chemin des Dames. (Nivelle wrote to the British, "Although the progress of the attack is less rapid than we had hoped
. . . I anticipate no halt to the operation.") [2] But the failure of the
April 16 attack had calamitous effects on the subsequent fighting.
The jam-up of troops, horses, guns and supplies for the abortive as-

175

sault resulted in a collapse of organization. *Système D* had bred its inevitable result. Whole divisions were lost to G.Q.G. Supplies were erratic and everything was confusion in this muddy jumble in front of the Chemin des Dames. In the trenches some exhausted divisions were called upon to fight incessantly; others were put into the line on April 19, were ordered to attack on the twenty-third and had the attack postponed to the twenty-fifth, then to the twenty-ninth, then to May 3, and finally to May 5.

Worse even than the delays and the confusion was that the men recognized the Chemin-des-Dames attacks for what they were—a last, erratic, barren attempt by Nivelle to salvage something of his threadbare reputation.

On the night of April 21-22 the 1st Colonial Infantry Division was being brought back in trucks from the fighting front. These colonials had always been considered steady troops and good fighters, and they were favorites of General Mangin, who used them to spearhead assaults. But now, on this April night, they had suddenly become a screaming mob. The backs and sides of the trucks were jammed with shouting men who leaned out and shook their fists at the other infantry units moving forward toward the front. "Long live peace!" and "We're through with killing!" they screamed.[3] Their officers did nothing to stop them. Either they were powerless or else they did not care. They stood in the jolting trucks tight-lipped and impassive.

Within a few days it had become apparent that this scene was not to be an isolated case. General Micheler's huge G.A.R. had been broken up on April 24 and its demoralized subarmies distributed among other commands. One of these, the Sixth Army, now came under General Franchet d'Esperey, the commander of the G.A.N., who was very much concerned at what he found. The Sixth Army had been the army of General Mangin, who had used it remorselessly in his unsuccessful attempt to batter his way into the German lines. But now Franchet d'Esperey, who was preparing an attack at the north end of the Chemin des Dames, found it necessary to report to G.Q.G. that there were many "symptoms of unquiet" among the troops of the Sixth Army. His complaint merely was brushed aside by Nivelle, who told him to ignore any disturbances unless "those who make them are to be part of the attack."[4]

This report was to be the last one which could be shrugged off by the high command. On April 29 the first full-fledged mutiny was reported. The 2nd Battalion of the 18th Infantry Regiment had virtually ceased to exist as a formed unit after the April 16 offensive. It had been in the forefront of the attack and had made perhaps a quarter of a mile of headway into the German elastic defense before being hit full tilt by the pile-driving attack of one of the enemy counterattack divisions. Broken into fragments, the battalion had been reduced to the scattered groups who were able to find their way back into the French lines. When the roll was called in the morning, it was found that only some two hundred men were alive and uninjured out of nearly six hundred who had attacked the day before. The best and bravest had vanished—were dead or dying somewhere out in the hell of the churned-up battlefield. Many of the company commanders, most of the platoon leaders, the best of the N.C.O.s, were gone; only the battalion commander and his staff were alive to lead the pitiful remnants of the companies, more stumbling than marching, through the rain back to a billeting area outside Soissons.

For the survivors, the horror of the experience had been almost too much. For the first few days the shell-shocked troops drifted aimlessly about their miserable, water-soaked billets. Rumors circulated that the battalion would be suppressed, its few survivors distributed as replacements and a fresh battalion moved in from the reserve. But for the French Army there were now no more fresh battalions in reserve. In fact, there were no more Frenchmen with whom to raise new battalions; instead the Army was actually shrinking.

So from the depot and from the other battalions in the regiment a few officers and men were shifted, and the 2nd Battalion was fleshed out to an approximation of its former size. The next step, and one eagerly anticipated by the hapless battalion, was its transfer to the Alsace front, the quiet sector in the east of France known as the "sanitorium of the western front" where, on account of the rugged terrain and the undeveloped lines of communications, the war was almost totally stagnant. Here, away from everything except minor patrol activity, the battalion would recoup from its agony and slowly recover its confidence, *esprit* and determination. Here, too, the officers and their men would come to know one another, and from among the shattered ranks the most promising men would be selected to fill the yawning void left by the dead N.C.O.s.

But the 2nd Battalion did not know, nor could it be told, that the French Army was totally exhausted—that it was almost a corpse scrabbling in reflex agony against the barbed wire of the Chemin-des-Dames defenses, that the attack which Nivelle had promised to call off within forty-eight hours if it had not succeeded could not now be called off without leaving the troops exposed in totally indefensible terrain. No troops could be moved out of the battle sector. And so the 2nd Battalion, having already sacrificed itself in vain, was called upon to repeat its sacrifice.

On April 29, less than two weeks after it had been pulled out of the line, the 2nd Battalion was ordered back to the front.

The men could not believe it. They had been promised that they would be sent to Alsace. They had been through too much, and now these new officers whom they did not yet know, trust or respect, and who they suspected were the incompetent dregs of other units, were ordering them to fall in with full field equipment. When the initial shock had worn off, the troops raged through their miserable encampment. The wine ration which had been issued to them was speedily drunk up, and, from hiding places in the wretched huts that sheltered them, hoarded bottles were produced. It took only a little wine to turn men in their exhausted and demoralized state into a drunken mob which refused point blank to march and screamed, "Down with the war!"

But by midnight the alcohol had worn off and discipline began to reassert itself. The battalion commander himself, in company with a platoon of military police, had come to order the men to assemble. The sullen, now sober troops were collected, and by 2 A.M. the battalion had been put on the road toward the thundering front.

Only a few men were left behind when the 2nd Battalion moved forward. As the troops assembled and began to march off down the muddy streets, the military-police platoon picked out a score of soldiers who were supposed to have been the ringleaders of the mutiny. Little care was used in selecting these men; indeed, in the hurry and with the dark streets lighted only by lanterns, it was probably inevitable that many of the wrong men would be selected. In any event, time was pressing, the battalion was late in marching and no one was disposed to worry too much about the justice of accusations.

About a dozen men were pulled out of line and thrown into the stockade.

It is difficult to say who was more frightened or panicky, the officers on the *conseil de guerre* or the enlisted men who faced them. But there is no doubt that the outcome of the trial was the result of fright and panic. The officers knew only that the 2nd Battalion had, even if temporarily, mutinied. And they knew that for the sake of discipline an example had to be made, with the result that, of those selected as ringleaders of the 2nd Battalion mutiny, all were found guilty and sentenced to imprisonment in French Guinea—except for five men who were sentenced to death, Privates Cordonnier, Didier, Garrel and La Placette and a corporal named Moulia.

Several officers had been brought back from the front to act as witnesses, and it is easy to suppose what their frame of mind must have been. Certainly they were not inclined to be much concerned with the niceties of legal procedure. The men on trial had taken part in the rebellion, had they not? They had refused to march when ordered, was this not true? Then, clearly, the men were mutineers and some of them must be sentenced to death. It was difficult to collect evidence properly, and, very probably, some of the men were unjustly accused. But if a few mistakes were made it was unimportant compared to the compelling necessity of ensuring that the rebellion would never recur. Only in cases of obvious and gross injustice were any charges dropped. Corporal Cronau of the 5th Company had been arrested on a report that "a big blond corporal" had been one of the leaders. Cronau was big and blond, but was also able to prove that he had been in the hospital at the time and could not possibly have taken part in the disturbances. Reluctantly Cronau was released and short, dark Corporal Moulia, a soldier with an excellent battle record, was thrust into his place.[5]

The executions took place only a few days later. Of the five men sentenced to death, only Moulia escaped. On June 12 as he was being led to the firing squad an unexpected barrage of long-range German artillery fire began. In the confusion, Moulia broke away and fled into a nearby wood. He was never recaptured, and twenty years later he was rumored to be living in South America.[6]

Despite Moulia's escape, the mutiny of the 2nd Battalion of the 18th Infantry Regiment had been quickly suppressed and relentless discipline restored. Outwardly it had meant little, only one infantry battalion out of more than a thousand in the French Army. But actually it had been significant, if only for one reason—it was the harbinger of a host of similar revolts which would, in the weeks to follow, sweep through the French Army like an insidious disease.

The next outbreak took place on May 3 in the 2nd Division of Colonial Infantry, part of Duchêne's Tenth Army, billeted outside Soissons. Like the other French infantry divisions, the 2nd Colonial had been effectively bled of its sturdiest troops by the years of ruinous attacks; and its officers and N.C.O.s whose morale and physique had never failed were long since dead, their places generally filled with boys of eighteen or men who were really past their prime for this sort of work. And now, on this rainy afternoon of May 3, the men of the 2nd Colonial Infantry had been ordered to assemble from the villages around Soissons, preparatory to marching forward to again take their place in the front lines.

As the troops fell in, filling the fields and roads in the ruined northern suburbs of the little city, the officers were worried. In the last few days a flood of *papillons*—a term for pacifist leaflets—had been found in the camp. Although, months before, Nivelle had appealed to the Minister of the Interior to suppress the pacifist pamphleteers, nothing had been done. And now the camps were flooded with these *papillons* calling for an immediate end to the war and the overthrow of the system which had sponsored it. No one knew how these pamphlets had found their way into the 2nd Colonial's camp, and, too, none of the officers knew how the men would react to them. But now, it seemed, the officers were suddenly faced with a matter of more immediate concern.

There was no question about it, many of the men were drunk. To be sure, not so drunk that they couldn't fall into a loose assembly formation, but drunk enough so that their voices were loud and their movements stiff and clumsy. Of course, this had happened before when the division was due to move up into the trenches for an assault; no matter how vigilant the officers and N.C.O.s tried to be, the men always managed to find a little more than the daily wine ration. Usually no one thought much about it. The older men, elderly survivors of the trench warfare in 1916 or 1915, and maybe even a lucky few who had been mobilized in that far-off August of 1914 and had miraculously lived through nearly three years of war in the trenches, drank to rid themselves of the feeling of impending death that was always with them as they returned to the front. The young troops, the boys of eighteen with only the horrible experience of the fruitless and costly attacks of the last few weeks to guide them, drank to give themselves courage to face the trial awaiting them. And always before, while perhaps not strictly sober, the infantry regiments which comprised the fighting core of the 2nd Colonial had fallen into long blue-clad ranks and had marched off in a fairly good humor, or at least with ungrudging resignation. A few of the younger troops might even start singing "The Marseillaise," although that would stop quickly under the cynical amusement of the veterans, who had lately come to prefer a sardonic chant which gibed at the once-coveted Croix de Guerre:

> *Ah, you'll get it, you'll get it . . . the Cross.*
> *If not the Cross of War,*
> *You'll get a cross of wood.*[7]

But now, on this gray, rainy afternoon, the troops took their own time about falling into line. The platoon commanders, looking anxiously at their watches, began to shout for their sergeants to hurry things along. Of course, they didn't shout in the peremptory manner they would have used only a few weeks before, and certainly not in the way they had been taught to give orders at the officers' training schools. No, with the temper of the men being what it was, it seemed better to be a little less demanding, to couch commands in a voice which was not so harsh. So they called, "Let's go, my boys," or "Come on, hurry up there."

Slowly, but very slowly, the muddy roads began to fill with troops. The companies started to take form at their usual intervals —only this time there was something very strange about most of the companies. Many of the men were not carrying their rifles or wearing their packs.

And now the startled platoon officers notice it. "Sergeant, where are the men's rifles?"

The sergeant stands mute, his eyes studying the ground at his feet.

The officers turn to the men in the ranks. "What's going on here, my boys? This is no time for making jokes. Where are your weapons?"

Finally from the rear of the ranks, obscured in the mass of men,

a wine-thickened tongue replies, "We're not marching, my lieutenant."

Now the companies began to break up into formless groups, generally circling a gesticulating speaker who was exhorting, "Down
with the war!" and "Death to those responsible!" The baffled officers
and the senior N.C.O.s attempted to call the men back into ranks
but, generally, were ignored. In response to their questions, the bewildered officers were told flatly, "We're not such fools as to attack
against uncut barbed wire or unshelled German trenches."

Now the truth was out. The men had learned that they were to
take part in one more large-scale attack on the Chemin des Dames
and they were not willing to undergo another blood bath like the
one they had endured during the April 16 attack. Toward their officers they showed a certain respect, none was personally insulted,
and a direct order was usually obeyed—but they would not fall in
ranks with their weapons and packs, and they would not march to
the front.

It was the same in every regiment and in almost every battalion
of the 2nd, so there was nothing for the thunderstruck officers to
do but to assemble at the headquarters of the division commander
and appeal to him for instructions. But all was in an uproar at headquarters. During the morning a gang of perhaps two hundred soldiers had appeared before division headquarters itself, shouting, "We
won't march!" The mob was too large to be arrested and could be
dispersed only by threats from the gendarmes of the headquarters
guard.

Finally a plan of action was developed. Although it contradicted
every basic tenet of military discipline, it might work. Certain officers who were known to be well liked and respected by the troops
were to go among the men and explain that it was the sacred duty
of the 2nd Colonial to relieve another division which had already
been in the front lines for too long. Quickly these officer delegates
were selected and hurried out to the troops. For hours they toured
the division's encampment. Everywhere they met the same situation:
the men were basically loyal, they were willing to defend the
trenches, but they were not willing to engage in another fruitless onslaught against the Chemin des Dames. All thoughts of victory had
fled, the men had lost confidence in their Commander in Chief, and,
everywhere, they voiced a demand for peace.

But the officers' plea to duty was not ignored. With the exception of a few enlisted firebrands who continued their attempts to arouse the troops to defiance, the officers were successful in gathering the rebellious companies together and appealing to their sense of comradeship—"The troops in the line are exhausted, they await your coming anxiously. We must not fail Frenchmen who are your comrades —they have never failed you."

Finally it worked. In the dusk of the ending day, the now sober troops gathered again in company formation, this time with packs and rifles. Only a few, the ringleaders of the rebellion, refused to fall in and were hustled away by armed N.C.O.s. In silent ranks, the troops tramped down the roads toward the ominous bulk of the Chemin des Dames distantly visible against the skyline. The 2nd Division of Colonial Infantry would take its place in the trenches, but not for the attack; other, more reliable troops would somehow have to be found for that. Even though, seemingly, this rebellion had been suppressed as quickly as in the 18th Regiment, there was actually a tremendous difference. The situation of these troops plodding along the night-shrouded roads was different from that of the 18th Regiment: *there were too many of them to be punished*. And the soldiers sensed with an ominous thrill that they could defy their officers, could shrug off the faceless inevitability of discipline with near-impunity, could refuse to attack. In short, it was up to the troops themselves whether they would live or die. And, marveling at this simple but heretofore unsuspected truth, they marched forward to share it with the Army.[8]

The French offensive against the German fortifications on the Chemin des Dames is generally considered as having ended on May 9, 1917. Accounts vary widely as to the total number of casualties suffered by the French Army, but it is fairly definite that there were almost 100,000 during just the first few days of the Nivelle offensive in April; and to this must be added at least 30,000 men for the period until May 9. Certainly these were heavy casualties, but equally certain was the fact that the Germans had stiff losses to reckon with—losses both in troops and in ground on the valuable Chemin-des-Dames ridge, the capture of two miles of which represented the principal French achievement in the entire series of battles.

It probably would have been possible for G.Q.G. to have argued that this fighting had not been in vain and that, while admittedly the offensive had not achieved its expectations, the battles had been at least as successful as the abortive attacks of 1915, or the fighting at Verdun and on the Somme in 1916, none of which had been followed by a mutiny within the Army. Perhaps it would have worked; perhaps if the troops had been told what the situation truly was, together with an honest announcement of the casualty figures, there never would have been an Army mutiny. But instead an apprehensive G.Q.G. refused to admit failure and declined to release the casualty figures until many weeks later, and even then they were obviously falsified. The outcome of this was that the troops had to believe any distorted figures which were told to them. Wild rumors of fantastic casualties swept through the Zone of the Armies. "A hundred thousand *killed*," some said, "and another two hundred thousand wounded!" These were the statistics generally believed by the troops.

So in the absence of any firm figures, sensing only that they had suffered a catastrophe of the most awful magnitude, the French Army suddenly began to flicker into mutiny.

The revolts began as they would continue—spontaneous mutinies without a realizable objective, devoid of organized leadership, and without individual heroes or villains. It was a drama without characters, for this was a convulsion within a mighty army, and the individuals are submerged in the anonymity of this blue-clad wave dusted lightly but significantly with the gray of the Russian brigades.

It was not, obviously, that every French division mutinied simultaneously, or even that every French division mutinied at all; during this early May of 1917 it was still possible to find dependable infantry divisions to move up to the front lines. But the agonizing problem was that it had suddenly become almost impossible to separate dependable troops from those who might all at once refuse to move up to the trenches. And from frightened commanders in almost every camp and on every front there had suddenly begun to come reports telling of floods of pacifist leaflets and newspapers, of infantrymen who were constantly drunk and surly, and of political meetings where the troops waved the red flag and spoke of international social revolution and immediate peace with their "German comrades."

Only certain infantry divisions of glorious history, the seven cavalry divisions and, of course, the military police, the *gendarmerie*,

Joseph Caillaux.

Miguel Almereyda, editor of the *Bonnet Rouge*. This photograph of him was taken in his cell at *La Santé*, after the court had condemned him to three years of prison for insulting "the Fatherland and the Army" in 1909. *(Courtesy of the Hoover Institution on War, Revolution and Peace)*

Front page of the *Bonnet Rouge* for October 14, 1916. Note the blank spaces where articles have been heavily censored. The piece on the left ("Where Are the Pacifists?") has been drastically mutilated, and consists of an ironic attack on pacifists and pacifism, obviously designed to be read as a disguised statement of the newspaper's own pacifist position. *(Courtesy of the Hoover Institution on War, Revolution and Peace)*

Joffre.
(Wide World)

Nivelle.
(Courtesy of Sir Edward Spears)

Pétain. This photograph of him was taken on January 14, 1919, outside U.S. Army HQ. He is wearing the U.S. Distinguished Service Medal, and the *grande plaque* of the French *Légion d'Honneur*. (*U.S. Army Signal Corps photograph*)

Joffre, talking to French officers. (*U.S. Army Signal Corps photograph*)

Clemenceau, acknowledging the cheers of the 33rd (British) Division, Cassel,
April 21, 1918. *(Imperial War Museum)*

King George V decorates Pétain, July 21, 1917. *(Imperial War Museum)*

Clemenceau, arriving at the Chamber of Deputies.

Aerial photograph, showing section of Western Front after heavy artillery bombardment. Note high concentration of shell craters. German first line (A-A') has been demolished by shellfire. Arrow indicates a shell exploding. Region: Cornillet, May 1917. (*U.S. Army Signal Corps*)

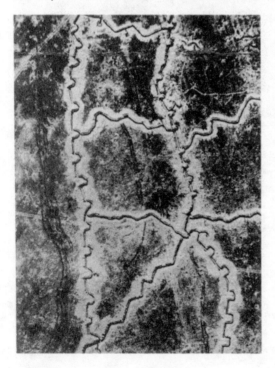

Aerial photograph of forward section of German trench system, Somme region, October 1915. The German front-line firing trench is at the left in the photograph. The black "bands" in front of the trenches are belts of barbed wire. Communication trenches connect the firing trench to the support trench. Compare with diagram of 1917 French trench system, page 75. (*U.S. Army Signal Corps*)

could be absolutely relied upon. As for the run-of-the-mill divisions which comprised the bulk of the Army, one day the troops were docile and well-behaved, the next day they might flame into full-fledged revolt.

Such was the spontaneity and the unpredictability of these outbreaks that even the most experienced commanders were caught unaware. General Maistre, the highly competent commander of the Sixth Army, had just advised G.Q.G. that he could assure them of success on a projected attack since it was to be executed with "such troops of the first order as those of the XXIst Army Corps." Two days later the supposedly sturdy XXIst Corps erupted in mutiny and Maistre was writing, "The operation must be postponed. . . . *We risk having the men refuse to leave the assault trenches.*" And when he asked for fresh and rested troops to conduct the battle, Franchet d'Esperey sent him five divisions but warned, "They are in a state of wretched morale." [9]

As the month of May drew on, the reports to G.Q.G. of "collective indiscipline"—a euphemism which came to be adopted to cover the ugly word *mutiny*—rose in an awesome crescendo. Nor were the revolts confined just to decimated infantry divisions. On May 20 at the XXXIInd Corps replacement depot, a group of soldiers destined for the 162nd Regiment suddenly erupted into rebellion. Arm in arm they marched down the company streets singing "The International." Surrounding the headquarters of the depot commander, they shouted for him to appear and listen to their demands—more pay, more leave, better food. The officers were powerless to deal with this mob, which that evening elected three delegates to present their ultimatum; and when morning came, the men refused to fall into ranks when ordered. [10]

A few days later, on May 26, four battalions of the 158th Division burst into mutiny when ordered from their rest camp to the front. They elected "deputies," on the style of the Soldiers' Councils which had just been created in the Russian Army and news of which had filtered down to the troops through the distorted prism of pacifist leaflets sent out from Paris. When the division commander refused to receive the "deputies," the battalion mobbed the general's headquarters and could not be driven away. Finally, long after the time scheduled for the troops to move up to the trenches, a small column of loyal troops and N.C.O.s was formed and to this column the mass of the rebels attached themselves, shouting pacifist slogans as they marched unhindered by the now thoroughly frightened officers.[11]

This, then, typifies the situation in which the officers found themselves. Almost overnight the entire basis of discipline had evaporated. The officers suddenly found that they were not in control of their men but were only scurrying about on the perimeter of what had become a huge, disorderly mob. Sometimes they were able to guide the crowd toward the place where they, the officers, wanted it to go. Sometimes they merely shouted commands at a group of unlistening and unreasoning men who had in a flash become a drunken gang. Suddenly the thin tissue of convention on which military discipline is ultimately based had become transparent to officers and enlisted men alike.

The traditional, the accepted method of putting down a military mutiny is by brute, naked force. It is a technique which has become classic during the thousands of years in which military forces have existed. The rebellious troops are surrounded by an overwhelming display of loyal military might, are cowed into surrender and are summarily shot. It is basically a simple operation, one which any strong-willed military commander can handle and one which has been, at one time or another, employed in almost every army. But the prompt and ruthless suppression of a military rebellion is totally dependent on one stipulation—that the majority of the army, the nonmutinous mass, is maintained in good discipline. When it is not, the heretofore simple problem is made hideously complex. Any army is but a flicker away from becoming an armed gang. The only thing that prevents this is military discipline, which is actually an incredibly flimsy institution, if its subjects but knew it. Military discipline is totally dependent on its willing acceptance by the mass of the enlisted men—most importantly, by the noncommissioned officers, who occupy positions of immense influence over the men.

Suppose a small group of dissident infantry mutinies, refuses to march when ordered, perhaps even threatens its officers. In this case an officer shouts a few commands, and a master sergeant, a few armed N.C.O.s and a file of troops with bayonetted rifles suffice to remove the mutineers to a stockade and, ultimately, to the firing squad. But suppose that the *whole* regiment of more than two thousand men mutinies, that the division to which they belong is teetering on the abyss of rebellion, and that there are no disciplined troops nearby. Then the problem becomes an entirely different one. The officers themselves cannot arrest the whole regiment; they are outnumbered one to twenty. The master sergeant cannot be appealed to; if he is not in actual mutiny himself, either he is unwilling to perform his duty or else too few of the noncommissioned officers will follow him. Now military discipline has entirely evaporated. An officer who shouts orders at his men is regarded only with sullen insubordination, is rewarded with hoots of derision. There are far too many mutinous troops to put in a stockade—indeed, there would be no one to guard them. To court-martial two thousand men is ridiculous and impossible, to contemplate shooting two thousand mutineers is unthinkable. Where could enough firing parties (each consisting of twelve trustworthy men) be obtained?

Recognizing the *fait accompli*, the frightened officers decline to expose themselves to ridicule or actual physical violence by shouting orders at the troops. They tend to let the troops alone, to try not to antagonize them. Instead the officers gather around the regimental headquarters while their superiors try to discover some way to bring the troops back to discipline.

The best example of this kind of helplessness of the officers in the face of mass mutiny was seen in the repeated revolts at Soissons. Although there were mutinies throughout the Zone of the Armies, it was probably inevitable that they would be the most serious in the areas immediately behind the Chemin des Dames, where most of the Army was concentrated and to which the majority of the shattered regiments had returned from the front. And in the heart of this crowded area lay Soissons, the ugly little city which was to become the focal point of the mutinies.

Soissons had always been a depressing place, but in May of 1917, it was more dispiriting than ever. The battles that had several times raged back and forth through the city had made a muddy shambles out of its cobbled streets, and artillery fire had shattered many of the city's dank stone dwellings, stores and factories. Most of Soissons' twenty thousand peacetime inhabitants had long since fled the city, but this did not mean it was deserted. Owing to its location, sixty-five miles northeast of Paris and only about five miles behind the main battle front, and the fact that it was a major railhead, Soissons had become a busy military center.

In its buildings were housed the staffs of a number of division commanders, as well as those of at least two army corps—the XXIst, under General Pont, and the XXXVIIth, under General Émile Taufflieb. The narrow streets of Soissons were crowded with trucks and guns, while the masses of troops were billeted in the decaying little farming villages which comprised the suburbs and in *casernes*, barracks, in the city itself. These troops belonged principally to the XXIst Army Corps and either had just been brought back from the front or else were at "rest," awaiting reassignment to the fighting lines. Jammed together as they were, these exhausted units resembled nothing so much as a mass of tinder ready to catch any spark; and the repeated violent mutinies at Soissons were to demonstrate just how difficult it was going to be to stop the inevitable conflagrations.

Most of the mutinies took place at night or early in the evening. General Taufflieb has given a graphic account of one of them. At five o'clock on a mid-May afternoon, when Taufflieb and a captain of his staff were walking down a street near his XXXVIIth Corps headquarters, several shots were fired at them by a marksman they could not see. Taufflieb and his companion did not pause to find out where the shots had come from. They sprinted back to the corps headquarters, calling for the major in charge of the corps' *gendarmerie*. Within minutes the major assembled a patrol and sallied forth into the now darkening streets. He came back a short while later to report that a XXIst Corps battalion of infantry stationed in a nearby barracks had mutinied. Plainly drunk, the men had barricaded themselves in their quarters and posted guards with fixed bayonets at the entrance, and they were now holding a meeting in the courtyard. In the surrounding dusk they could be heard singing "The International," and from the windows of the barracks they occasionally fired random rifle shots to keep back any officers who might be so brash as to attempt interference.

There was no telling what these troops intended to do. Taufflieb thought they might even try to storm his headquarters. He ordered his chief of staff to gather all the corps' gendarmes inside the headquarters, arm them heavily and have them guard the two entrances to the building. While this was being done, Taufflieb himself telephoned General Pont at the XXIst Corps and learned that Pont was fully aware of the situation but could do nothing about it.

Suddenly, outside his headquarters, Taufflieb heard the sound of shouts and rifle fire. Running to one of the heavily guarded entrances, he looked out. At the end of the street he could make out a mob of marching men; the mutineers had left their barracks and were headed down the road toward Mercin, a little town just east of Soissons and on the railway route to Paris. They carried torches, and in the flickering glare Taufflieb could see that most of the men also carried their rifles, which they occasionally fired into the air. As they marched they chanted "The International," but through the hubbub of the sound the general could clearly hear cries of "Peace!" and "To Paris!"

Gradually the noise of the marching men receded into the May night as the troops streamed toward the railway station at Mercin. There they hoped to seize a train and ride to Paris. But in this their desire was thwarted; the railway station had been closed down and no trains were present. Raging with disappointment, the men then directed themselves along the narrow road toward the little town of Pernant, where they expected to find troops of a similar inclination who would join them in a march on G.Q.G. at Compiègne, twenty miles to the east. But again they were frustrated. A regiment of territorials had been hastened up to block the way, and these old "papas" were determined. They would not attack the mutinous battalion, but neither would they allow it to pass down the road toward Pernant and Compiègne. There was nothing for the men to do but turn aside and wander south toward the tiny town of Saconin, where they drank the remains of the wine they had brought with them in their canteens. Then, its effect worn off, they began to straggle back toward Soissons and their barracks.[12]

Only a few nights later Soissons again erupted in mutiny. In the morning the troops of the 370th Infantry Regiment, another unit of the XXIst Corps, had been notified that they were to be sent up to the front lines shortly after midnight. It was what they had been dreading for days, and the news brought forth a volley of inflammatory speeches from ringleaders urging the troops to refuse to board the trucks. By 11 P.M. the men were milling about the streets. A gang of soldiers had smashed into a canteen and, almost to a man, were drunk on looted wine. Clearly, the 370th Regiment was primed for rebellion and needed only the slap of a firing pin to set it off. And this too was provided when two trucks belonging to the 17th and 36th regiments snorted down the streets. The trucks were filled with soldiers waving red flags and screaming wildly,

"*A bas la guerre!*" The vehicles pulled to a stop in one of the crowded streets, serving as ready-made platforms for orators gesticulating in the feeble light of the lampposts.

In wine-thickened voices the speakers ranted about the butchery of war, about the peace offers spurned by a French government in the grip of the profiteers, about the politicians who callously sent troops to their death merely to prevent the inevitable encroachment of a truly socialist system. Instead of the 370th Regiment moving forward to attack the Chemin des Dames, it might be better employed in cleaning out the nest of vipers who were the government in Paris!

For a moment the men around the trucks were silent, and then there began an ominous roar. "We march on Paris!" Get the deputies out of Parliament!" "*A bas la guerre!*" In another moment the drunken mob of five hundred men was surging down the cobblestone streets toward the railroad station.

On the way the mob swelled and shrank. Some of the men, faced with the sudden jarring realization that this was open rebellion, made their way to the edge of the throng and disappeared into blackened alleys and side streets. But other troops, witnessing the shouting crowd surging down the street, fell in to march with the mutineers. Many of the soldiers had their rifles, and, weapons slung over their shoulders, shouting and screaming defiance, they half ran, half marched to the station.

Only twice did they break their stride. Once they encountered a regimental physician, who, to the men, symbolized the hated incompetence of the French Army Medical Service. A dozen men surrounded the unfortunate doctor and beat him to the ground with rifle butts, kicked him where he lay and left him broken and bloody in the gutter. Again the mutineers stopped when their path was blocked by three gendarmes, the hated military police, who valiantly but ill-advisedly ordered them to halt. With a roar, the mob charged them and seized their weapons, and in a few minutes the three gendarmes were left beaten almost to death and dangling by their feet from lampposts.

At the railway station the troops found a train with steam up about to leave for Paris. As they stormed toward the locomotive, the civilian train crew leaped from the engine and fled for their lives. Somehow there were a few poilus with railway experience in the mob, and these were pressed into service to drive the locomotive while the troops piled aboard the train. And thus, screaming imprecations against the war and Parliament and firing rifles into the air, the 370th Regiment set out for Paris to disperse the government.

Of course, this scene could not go unobserved in Soissons. The regimental adjutant of the 370th, aghast at what he had seen, sprinted to the regimental headquarters, where he phoned the headquarters of General Rendeau of the 170th Division. They, in turn, telephoned the headquarters of a cavalry division located in reserve in Villers-Cotterêts, a small town on the railway line, through which the mutineers had to travel to get to Paris.

Villers-Cotterêts is surrounded on three sides by a dense forest. Into this forest, on the east side of the town, the well-disciplined cavalrymen were deployed. They had been turned out from their beds in furious haste, since there were only minutes to spare before the mutineers' train would arrive. Like cavalrymen in every army, they felt superior to the plodding infantrymen, the slime of the trenches; and, conversely, the infantry had little respect for the cavalry, which had been only lightly engaged and had suffered relatively little ever since open-field warfare had ended in 1914. Thus, the cavalry, filling the role of tightly disciplined professionals who regarded themselves as the "policemen of the Army," were the best troops—indeed, perhaps the only troops—who could be relied upon to halt the mutineers and even, if necessary, to shoot to kill their fellow Frenchmen in the cause of discipline.

By the time the train appeared outside Villers-Cotterêts, the cavalrymen had managed to throw logs across the tracks and to site machine guns in an arc around the roadbed. So when the train ground to a halt at the obstruction, the mutineers had little choice or chance of resisting. A cavalry officer, tall and imposing, stepped out from the darkness and ordered them out of the train. By now the stimulating effects of alcohol and the novelty of freedom from discipline had evaporated for the men of the 370th Regiment. They recognized their defeat in the muzzles of the carbines held by the cavalry troopers, and sullenly they dropped down from the train to be disarmed and rounded up. A few who resisted were shot on the spot. Only a handful escaped—a few men who broke away from the cavalrymen, fled into the woods and were able to make their way to a nearby village, where sympathetic peasants hid them for a few days until they too surrendered.[13]

Throughout the mutinies there was a curious sameness about the preoccupation of the troops with railroads. Again and again they sought to storm the stations and seize trains for Paris, where somehow, they seemed to think, they could throw out the government and declare peace. Some of this was obviously just a normal desire to get home, strip off their uniforms, see their families—in short, to shed the horror of the trenches and of death on the barbed wire of the endless battlefields. Yet there was certainly something else that exerted the magnetic attraction toward Paris, and almost surely this was the impression that in Paris they would find sympathy, help and a populace which was also sickened by war and would rise up with them.

This was why so many mutinies centered around railway stations —such as that which took place in the evening of May 27 in the little city of Fère-en-Tardenois, fifteen miles southeast of Soissons. The 18th Regiment, after its mutinies of late April, had been returned here for three weeks of rest, and now an attempt was being made to load the men into trucks for their return to the trenches. Most of the men were drunk, and it was proving difficult to get them into the trucks. Then suddenly through the streets of the rest of the camp a few troublemakers began to run, firing their rifles and shouting, "To Paris! To Paris!" From the rolling mass of one battalion they succeeded in persuading 150 men to join them in an attack on the nearby railway station, where a train was about to depart for Paris. Storming the railroad station, they seized the train, from which they could not be ejected until after a night of confused brawling with a hurriedly summoned force of gendarmes.[14]

But if there exists a single "classic" example of the May mutinies, it was that of the 128th Regiment, part of the 3rd Division of the IInd Corps. Even after the defeat of the Nivelle offensive, the morale of the 128th had remained high, and on April 29 the regiment had been put into the line on the Chemin des Dames. The troops were ardent and well led, and in an attack launched on May 4 they were able to seize at least a part of the German trench system in front of Mont Spin. To succeed in taking even the smallest section of these heavily held trenches was a victory of the first magnitude, and the

128th was showered with congratulations, most particularly from the general commanding the brigade, who categorically promised "a long rest" for this heroic regiment once it could be withdrawn from the front.

For the next ten days the 128th Regiment huddled in its trenches during tremendous German bombardments and then rose to fight off determined German attacks. Every day was an agony, every night was a hell. And to the rear the litter-bearers brought a constant trickle of dead and wounded as the 128th Regiment pumped out its life-blood in defending the ground it had won.

Finally the regiment was relieved by another. But as the men marched to the trucks waiting in the rear, they could hear the crash of another German attack beginning and the word filtered back that this time the defense had not held. The exhausted troops were furious. What was the use of it all? Why should they, the infantry, fight and die to hold a little tongue of land which would soon be lost anyhow? And where was the French artillery which was supposed to blast a path for them and then to protect their gains against German counterattack? Why did the German planes always have command of the air, and never the French? Why, indeed, were they fighting at all?

In this ugly frame of mind, the 128th went into a ramshackle rest camp in Prouilly, a village west of Reims. The camp was too small to hold even this decimated regiment, and a few companies had to be sent to billet with the nearby 120th Regiment and the 117th Territorial Regiment. Despite the fact that they were supposedly at "rest," morale fell steadily within the 128th. Most depressing of all was the fact that there was no leave allowed. It had been months, in some cases more than a year, since the men had had leave, and they were desperate to see their families again. Instead the 128th was immediately plunged into a round of exhausting training exercises in an attempt to assimilate four hundred replacements who had been sent up from the depots to fill the gaps left by the regiment's ordeal in the line. But these replacements were different from any that the 128th had seen before. These were men who had come from depots and other regiments where they had seen strange sights, been witnesses to hitherto unthought-of acts. They had seen mutiny, and had seen that it went largely unpunished.

Then, on May 20, the 128th Regiment received orders to prepare

that afternoon to move up to the front. The men were first stunned
and then infuriated. They had been promised a long rest, and now,
only five days after they had come out of the trenches, they were
being sent back again. And it was not even their turn! They knew
that the 120th Regiment had been in rest camps longer than they.
But when the companies of the 128th that had billeted with the
120th returned to the regiment's camp, they learned why they were
being sent to the front. Originally the 120th had been ordered to
move up, but now it was in mutiny.

At once the camp at Prouilly flared into rebellion. At least two
companies refused to board the trucks for the front. The rest
gathered around various orators. As Painlevé later described it,
"Some spoke of the exhaustion of the troops; others, of the scandalous privileges of the *embusqués* in the rear echelons; still others, of
the incapacity of the staffs, who accepted honors and privileges but
failed to give the troops the victory which each day had been promised them; and, finally, other orators spoke of the news from Russia [where the troops were refusing to continue the war] and
pointed to the Russian soldiers as an example." [15]

Only on the next day, and after a personal appeal by the corps
commander, backed by a huge force of gendarmes, could the 128th
be prodded into leaving. Even then about sixty men at first refused
to march with the regiment, but they finally decided to rejoin their
comrades. This left the officers of the 128th with a problem:
obviously there had to be some victims *pour l'exemple*. They chose
the sixty who had refused to march, and from these, apparently by
drawing straws, five men were selected to be tried. A *conseil de
guerre* was convened and two of these men, Privates Breton and
Lamour, were condemned to death. [16]

These, then, the 18th Regiment, the 2nd Colonial Division and
the 370th and 128th regiments, were typical of the early revolts, the
May mutinies. But as May came to an end it was apparent that they
had sown the seed well and truly. Throughout the Zone of the
Armies the units which could be persuaded to march forward to the
trenches were baaing in imitation of lambs led to the slaughter, and
their officers were helpless to prevent it. [17] Yet it was still possible to
man the front lines, sometimes with dismounted cavalry, sometimes
with still-reliable divisions, sometimes with the splinters of once-

mutinous regiments—although these last were never considered truly trustworthy.

If the harassed generals could find one consolation amid the horror of mutiny and revolt, it was that the first month of rebellion had served to disclose a kind of rough pattern to the outbreaks. This much had become obvious: the French Army was not a totally defeated mob, abandoning the trenches and streaming in terror to the rear—not yet, at any rate. Instead, the soldiers had suddenly flared into a kind of "professional strike," [18] a strike stimulated by the fact that they had suddenly and completely lost faith in their generals and their generals' strategies and were no longer willing to entrust their lives to a high command which they felt was indifferent and careless of their suffering.

Toward their own junior officers the men felt no particular ill-will, and it was rarely that any of these were physically assaulted. But staff officers were a different matter. The men called them *les buveurs du sang*, "the drinkers of blood," and toward them the troops had developed a distinct animosity—so much so that most staff officers prudently ceased wearing the distinctive striped armbands which were their identification.

And there were other common denominators of revolt. For example, the pattern of the May mutinies indicated that this was almost entirely a revolt of the line infantry divisions, which was understandable because the other arms—the artillery, the cavalry, the territorials, even the machine-gun companies within the infantry divisions themselves—had suffered nowhere near the proportion of casualties that the infantry had. Moreover, by the end of May it had come to the point where a mutiny could even be predicted with a certain degree of exactitude. It would take place generally in an infantry regiment which had suffered severe losses in the Nivelle offensive or in the subsequent Chemin-des-Dames fighting. The Sixth Army was the most mutinous, followed in order by the Fourth, the Tenth, the Fifth, and the Second.[19] And the mutiny would be triggered off when the regiment had been out of the lines a short period of time and then was ordered back to the front.

As for the role of the defeatist pamphlets, the example of the Russian Revolution, and the pacifist agitation of the left-wing political parties, all these probably played a distinctly secondary role in initiat-

ing the mutinies. This is not to deny their importance or the growing influence that the pacifist-defeatist group was to gain among the
troops. But it is most certainly a fact that at the end of May the troops
that were revolting did not constitute a *revolutionary* force, as was
later to be claimed. Rather, they were the symptoms of an almost
mortal disease within the Army: the disease of despair.

There was still a tough crust manning the trenches and capable of
defending France from attack. But behind this crust the Army was
soggy with revolt. Moreover, this was only May—and what lay
ahead no one could tell.

12

THE JUNE MUTINIES

IT WAS NOW early June. From everywhere Grand Quartier Général was receiving reports of large-scale mutinies. All three regiments of the 9th Division burst into revolt upon being ordered up to the front. They shouted, "We want leave!" and flatly declared, "We will not move up." The same day the 5th Division caught the spark; its troops hurled invective against their government which was "refusing to make peace with the Germans" and threatened, "We will march on the Chamber of Deputies." In the camps of some of the most famous of the army corps, mutineers seized the barracks and promised to shoot any officers who might try to arrest them.[1]

There seemed to be no limit to the revolt. Most frightening was the fact that four weeks of mutiny had succeeded in contaminating the troops manning the front lines and they had begun to threaten their officers: "We will defend the trenches, but we won't attack." "We are not so stupid as to march against undestroyed machine guns." "We have had enough of dying on the barbed wire."[2]

Now the front could be manned only by patching with bits and pieces of once sturdy divisions, even with loyal splinters of regiments and battalions, while the rebellious remnants were left in the rear. On the Chemin-des-Dames ridge it was now the Germans who were attacking; and once when an exhausted French division gave way under the pressure, no replacement was available except the 70th Division, itself quivering with mutiny. There was no help for it, the division had to be sent forward. But before the troops entered the trenches, the 70th's commanding general toured the

197

ranks, desperately appealing to his troops' pride. "There are bad elements among us, but they are not found in this division. I am counting on the overwhelming majority of our good troops to inspire any weak characters with a sense of duty. So, in entrusting you with the care, the discipline and the honor of the division, I am taking the best way to your hearts as Frenchmen and as soldiers." [3] The appeal worked and the 70th held the gap.

But regardless of whether or not a sound unit could be scraped up to fill a hole in the trenches, the mere existence of these mutinies was placing France in desperate danger. Painlevé pointed out that with the Germans lying only "100 kilometers from Paris, the single fact of not being certain that an order given a regiment will be executed automatically is a grave peril. Imagine a duelist engaged in a mortal struggle who cannot be sure that a muscle he may need quickly will not fail him." [4]

Over the entire Zone of the Armies, G.Q.G. had thrown the tightest possible clamp of secrecy. Even in its reports to the government, which the Army never truly relied upon when it came to security matters, references to the mutinies were studiously vague. They spoke of disturbances in the 36th Regiment, in the 129th Regiment, then riots at Dormans in which the troops shouted, *"A bas la guerre et vive la révolution russe!,"* and finally admitted that five army corps had "been contaminated." [5]

But, of course, the Ribot government had its own sources of information. Wandering through the chaos of the Zone of the Armies, aghast at what they saw, were various senators and deputies who, as members of certain parliamentary commissions, had received permission to visit the front. G.Q.G. no longer had the power to keep them out, although the various area commanders did their best to prevent the politicians from seeing too much. But in this they could not but fail. There was simply too much to see. Deputy Aristide Jobert, for example, was received in a corps commander's headquarters the walls of which were stitched with machine-gun bullets fired by mutineers. [6]

In some ways the harried generals were the strangest sight of all. Unwilling to admit military failure, they had succeeded in convincing themselves that the mutinies were almost solely the product of defeatism from the Zone of the Interior, and they sought to press this opinion upon the appalled politicians. "There exists," General Fran-

chet D'Esperey assured Deputy Henri Gallichet, who had just witnessed a night of renewed rioting in Soissons, "an organized plot to
dissolve discipline. . . . The ringleaders among the troops are in contact with suspicious elements in Paris. They scheme to seize a
railway station so that they may transport themselves to Paris and
raise the populace in insurrection against the war. The Russian
Revolution has served as their model. . . . The troops are in a continual state of excitation kept up by the newspapers, which are filled
with details of the events in Russia, by parliamentary criticism of
the generals and by the exaggerations of pessimists. . . . Why do
you close your eyes to this? . . . Unless it is stopped we will have
no Army and the Germans can be in Paris in five days!" [7]

And suddenly, both from their own reports and from those of
G.Q.G., it became evident to the Ministry of War that between
Paris and the front there were only *two divisions* which could be
"absolutely and completely relied upon." [8]

The revolt was even finding its way to the rear, borne on a flood
of desertion. In 1914 there had been only 509 desertions; in 1915
there were 2,433; in 1916 the figure was 8,924; [9] now, in 1917, the
troops were deserting at the rate of 30,000 men a year.[10] And it was
in the unit from which men were deserting that men would mutiny.
Even in the chasseur battalions, a kind of elite group of light infantry, one battalion of which was attached to every division, mutiny and desertion marched together. The 57th Chasseur Battalion
listed 145 mutineers and 98 deserters; the 60th Battalion, 300 mutineers and 75 deserters; the 61st Battalion, 250 mutineers and 25 deserters.[11]

Many of these deserters were, of course, troops on leave who simply refused to return to their regiments; and this touches on a particularly ugly aspect of the mutinies. The spontaneity of the mutinies was such that the majority of the troops who revolted did so
in relative ignorance of the fact that other regiments had also risen
up. But when soldiers from one division met soldiers from another,
it was inevitable that they would share experiences and learn that
mutiny was widespread within the Army. And this, in turn, triggered
off more riots. Nowhere was this interchange of information more
likely to happen than in the slatted boxcars of a train of *permissionnaires*, men on leave. Here, in these trains which always moved at an
agonizing snail's pace in deference to almost every other type of

rail traffic, the troops had ample leisure to learn of mutiny in one another's regiments. As a result, by the time the trains arrived in Paris, which was the switching point for most traffic from the front, the leave trains were a teeming madhouse of rebellion. The interiors of the cars were torn to splinters, their occupants either waving hastily contrived red flags or, in the case of an estimated 60 per cent of the troops, dead drunk.[12] And upon their arrival at the railway stations the men were sure of a welcome; hordes of leftist agitators descended upon them, inviting them to pacifist meetings held in the guise of trade-union gatherings or distributing the ubiquitous pacifist *papillons*.

Getting the men to return from leave proved even more difficult. They would do anything, it seemed, to delay the trains. At such major railway marshaling yards as Troyes, the troops unhooked the cars, opened water tanks and threw rocks at the railway employees who attempted to stop this sabotage—for, indeed, there was no other word to describe it.

Sunday, June 3, 1917, was a beautiful day throughout France. The rains of the preceding days had passed on, and now the air was warm and soft. "A sky like silk," one Parisian wrote in his diary, "boats on the canal, soaring plumes of water [from the fountain display at Versailles]—a brilliant display of festivity and pleasure, and the war so far away." [13] Yet this beautiful Sunday was tinctured with the strain of crisis for many. At the Élysée Palace, the Cabinet of Premier Ribot was holding an extraordinary session to discuss events of the most desperate concern. Coupled with the agony of the avalanching mutinies had come a flood of strikes and of pacifist orations in Parliament, and a covey of new defeatist newspapers. One of these last was a new weekly called *La Tranchée républicaine*. It had been started up by a member of the *Bonnet rouge* staff, using funds supplied by Almereyda. *La Tranchée républicaine* was edited as a journal of the far left designed to appeal to the troops at the front. Its current issue featured attacks on "the war profiteers," had extensive coverage of the political activities of the syndicalist and militant-Socialist parties, and gave front-page assurances of support for "our Russian friends" in their revolutionary activities.[14]

Among those attending the meeting in the Cabinet chambers of the Élysée Palace was President of the Republic Raymond Poincaré. He had just been informed that yesterday in a session of Parliament a deputy named Augagneur had made a speech attacking the war. Augagneur had claimed that the recent Russian Revolution, coupled with the fact that the Americans "would arrive too late," meant that all was lost. Amazingly, this speech had been received with considerable applause in the Chamber of Deputies, not only from the militant Socialists but from the less doctrinaire political friends of Joseph Caillaux as well.

The strikes of the trade unions had also become an increasing problem to the harassed government. The day before, Poincaré himself had witnessed a strike demonstration by several thousand women armament workers. In a mob they had marched down the Champs Élysée, turned off on the Avenue Alexandre III and demonstrated outside the Élysée Palace. "Their clamors rose up for more than two hours," he wrote in his diary.[15]

At the Cabinet meeting Premier Ribot was bitterly critical of the police for allowing the striking women to get as far as they did. A demonstration like this, Ribot pointed out, could "degenerate rapidly into dangerous troubles and even riots." So among the matters on the Cabinet's agenda were instructions to M. Malvy to replace M. Laurent, the Paris Prefect of Police, with the more energetic M. Hudelo.

Vastly more important than strikes, pacifism or the growing agitation by the left-wing political parties, however, was the menace of the mutinies. The night before, the government had received a report from Colonel Herbillon, its military-liaison officer, that fresh mutinies were breaking out in the XXIst Corps—"the troops refuse to go into the trenches." So now the government was meeting to discuss this situation of multiple crisis in which, as Poincaré said, "order is menaced everywhere" and "the fever is extending itself." [16]

Had the government known the turn that the mutinies were taking within the Zone of the Armies, it would have been still more alarmed. For by these first weeks in June the revolts had assumed an even more dangerous form, and one increasingly tinged with overtones of social revolution. As rebellion picked up speed, the mutineers had begun to sense that their sheer numbers gave them virtual immunity from punishment. The mutinies were becoming bolder and more prolonged. It was now proving extremely difficult to get a rebellious unit subdued and back into the trenches. Either the mutineers refused to move up under any circumstances—and had to be "quarantined" in their camps—or else, by whole companies, battalions and regiments, they were now disappearing into the forests, to establish themselves in camps from which they could only be starved out.

One of the largest of these mutinies took place on June 2 outside Cœuvres, a modest town about eight miles southeast of Soissons and situated on the edge of the Forest of Vollers-Cotterêts. In early June Cœuvres was the depot for the 310th Infantry Regiment, which had used it for a rest camp for several weeks. In the manner of these camps, the troops had been billeted anywhere they could find space—in half-destroyed or abandoned houses, in the barns of the surrounding farms or in tents set up in the muddy fields.

The morale of the 310th was hardly exemplary, but at least discipline was good enough that the men would turn out for the endless marches and field exercises which were an exhausting feature of every "rest" camp. But everything changed on May 30 when another regiment of infantry rolled through Cœuvres on its way, supposedly, to the front. It immediately became apparent that these troops had no intention of manning the trenches. As the trucks passed down the main street of Cœuvres, each one of them was a moving hotbed of mutiny. To the watching 310th Regiment the mutineers shouted, "Down with the war! The whole corps has refused to march! Do as we do and the war will be ended tomorrow!" And, to the utter astonishment of the 310th, mixed in with the mutineers were officers, also shouting, "Throw down your arms! Liberty or death! Follow us, brothers!" [17]

Hard on the heels of the mutinous regiment a troop of cavalry cantered into the little town, towing machine guns behind the horses. The cavalrymen—who were now desperately overworked—set up their guns at the main crossroads and, with this threat, chivvied the rebellious regiment out of Cœuvres. But this, of course, left the 310th Regiment in a turmoil of revolt. Now even soldiers with outstanding combat records began to preach mutiny to their fellows. "The clamors grew louder," reported an eyewitness. "The shouts multiplied. They filled the village and threw back echoes from the distant forests. And, in the middle of these cries and whistles, there rose the chant of 'The International.' " [18]

On June 2 the 310th received orders to leave Cœuvres and march to Bucy-le-Long, a town northwest of Soissons. The troops knew what this meant—a return to the trenches. They would not go. Colonel Dussange, the regimental commander, reported later, "About three in the afternoon, one company refused to pack its gear. No acts of violence occurred, just a determined obstinacy. Immediately another company mutinied. The regiment refused to listen to me."

Pushing past their protesting colonel, the troops made their way into the woods on the south of the town. It was useless for Dussange to attempt to block the road. "The troops passed right by me on either side, without insults or pushing. Some of them saluted me." The colonel reported that his men "intended to march on Paris. Other regiments were waiting for them in the Forest of Compiègne." [19]

The revolt suddenly left Cœuvres a silent, almost deserted village. The helpless and frightened officers looked at one another. Then they gathered about them the fifty or so men who had refused to mutiny and, at daybreak the next morning, set off toward Bucy-le-Long—a thin, straggling file of officers and men who looked like a decimated regiment just returned from a disastrous battle.

The mutineers, meanwhile, had marched down the main road toward Villers-Cotterêts for a little way and then had established their own camp. Now, having revolted against their officers and Army discipline, they did what almost every similar mutinous unit was to do in these strange rebellions. They immediately elected leaders and empowered them with "revolutionary discipline" which, in its way, was far stricter than that which they had just shed. They set out sentries against surprise attack from the cavalry, which had now blocked the roads against them, and drunkenness was strictly prohibited. The mutineers of the 310th Regiment lived like this for four days—until finally their food supplies were exhausted. And then they carefully shaved and washed, formed into impeccable columns of fours and marched out of their camp to surrender to the cavalry.[20]

Probably to serve as an example to other regiments, the 310th was hurriedly reconstituted and flung into the trench system between Laffaux and Filain. Then, after it had been bloodied a bit, it was withdrawn and a court of inquiry began its work. Two thirds of the mutineers were thrown into a stockade outside Soissons; the *con-*

seils de guerre sentenced most of these to terms in penal colonies. Thirty-two others stood trial as *instigateurs* of the mutiny; half of these men were sentenced to fifteen years at hard labor, and the other sixteen soldiers were sentenced to death.

It was at this period, then, that the attitude of the mutinous troops had begun to take a subtle but discernible change. The earlier mutinies had been revolts almost solely against the futility of the Nivelle offensive. They had been uprisings of troops who refused to attack because they had lost both faith in their leaders and hope for victory. But now the French assaults had been halted and the troops were rarely being ordered to attack. All that they were being asked to do now was defend the trenches, a task which the troops had always been willing to do in the past. Why were the mutinies continuing? Why were they increasing?

The answer is twofold. First, aside from the failure of the Nivelle offensive and the crushing blow which this dealt the troops' morale, there were a vast number of subordinate military factors which entered into the picture. The miserable "rest" camps, the lack of leave, the picture of G.Q.G. which had grown up in the men's minds as a distant, indifferent monster, neither knowing about nor caring for the troops who must pay for its errors with their lives —all these bore heavily on the troops' unrest.

The second factor in swelling the mutinies, and one fully as important, was the suddenly increased attraction which the left-wing parties had for the troops. Before the war these parties—the militant Socialists, the syndicalists, the republicans of the far left—had always identified themselves with antimilitarism. At the outbreak of war they had no choice but to join the Union Sacrée, but now in the combination of civil unrest and military mutiny they saw their chance to achieve the power which had always been denied them. And so, holding out the promise of world revolution and peace, they sought to make common cause with the troops.

This, then, was the background against which the mutinies in June must be judged—and against which must be set such incidents as the revolt at Missy-aux-Bois, where, during the first week in June, a battalion of the 298th Infantry Regiment rose up and captured the town.

Poincaré, in the volume of his memoirs aptly entitled "The Troubled Year," describes how these troops sent collective letters to their officers advising that they would not return to the front and demanding that "an honorable peace be concluded without delay." [21] When the officers rejected these demands, the troops expelled them from Missy-aux-Bois, held elections to select a new "battalion commander" from among the ranks and actually established their own "government."

Everything was run in accordance with the strictest niceties of revolutionary discipline. The village was barricaded and sentries were posted to secure the men against surprise attack. The "battalion commander" even issued an order protecting the villagers' property:

> COMRADES,
> French soldiers are neither thieves nor assassins. The first man who loots or steals from the inhabitants will be immediately handed over to the Army.
>
> THE BATTALION COMMANDER

Undoubtedly these mutineers would have been happy to remain in Missy-aux-Bois almost indefinitely; but, equally obviously, this barricaded village posed such a threat to discipline that it was mandatory that they be subdued. Moreover, the mutineers were blocking the main road between Soissons and Villers-Cotterêts. A hasty screen of tightly disciplined troopers from the 1st Cavalry Division was thrown up around the village to cut off the mutineers' food supplies. Finally, on the third day of the revolt, the battalion had no choice but to surrender. Still maintaining "revolutionary discipline," the troops paraded out of the village as had their comrades at Coeuvres, to lay down their arms to the cavalry.[22]

Inevitably, news of this sensational event filtered back to Paris, where it was rumored, possibly quite correctly, that six of the mutineers were summarily executed by a picked firing squad of cavalry. "Twelve bullets were found in every body." [23]

Nor was rebellion confined to the French. As the mutinies avalanched onward, it became apparent that the two Russian brigades had become a serious menace. It was not the number of Russians in France that posed the danger—a mere fifteen or twenty thousand men were indistinguishable atoms in this war of millions—it was what they represented. For by the spring of 1917 it had been con-

clusively established that the Russian brigades in France were the
breeding grounds of mutiny.

The Russian brigades had come to France on a strange and ultimately tragic odyssey. During the winter of 1915-16 the French
government had concluded an agreement with its Imperial Russian
allies which, on the face of it, seemed to benefit both parties. The
French proposed to supply the miserably equipped Russian armies
with shiploads of armaments, but, in return, there was to be a sort
of *quid pro quo*. Alone among the embattled nations, Russia had manpower in profusion—more, really, than she could use. And thus a
bargain was struck: the French shipped munitions to Russia, and as
the ships returned to France they were to bring contingents of Russian troops.

In the beginning it had all gone wonderfully well. Two French
transports had been sent to Archangel and Vladivostok in the spring
of 1916 and four oversize Russian brigades, each of about eight
thousand men, had been loaded into them. The Russian troops had
embarked in high spirits, and their enthusiasm was rekindled when,
after a two-month voyage of nineteen thousand miles, they were welcomed by an ecstatic French crowd at the port of Marseilles.

One reason for the French joy at witnessing the arrival of the
Russians was that it was an open secret that these four brigades were
only the vanguard of a huge force which was to be ferried to France
—forty thousand men a month, it was said on good authority. But
of course it did not work out as it was planned; with the Imperial
Russian Army nothing ever went as planned. The war in Russia
deteriorated, leaving the Russians suddenly unable to spare any additional troops. In fact, of the four Russian brigades which landed at
Marseilles, two, the 2nd and the 4th, were immediately reshipped to
the Allied salient at Salonika, with the result that only the 1st and
3rd brigades—slightly less than twenty thousand men—were left in
France proper.

As the months went by, these two Russian brigades were to suffer
all the overwhelming hardships and agonies which seem to afflict any
tiny foreign force interpolated into a much larger allied army. There
were too few Russians to warrant a special ration, and they dis-
liked the French food which was fed them; they suffered from home-
sickness, and mail from Russia was almost nonexistent; they com-

plained bitterly about the French Medical Service, perhaps not realizing that the indifferent treatment meted out to them was no worse than that being experienced by the French troops themselves; and they suspected, as do alien troops everywhere, that they were being ruthlessly used as cannon fodder by their allies. Most important of all, having seen the courage and battlefield skill of the typical French junior officer, the Russians grew to loathe their own officers, regarding them as bungling cowards who were careless and indifferent toward their troops.

The Russian troops fought well enough. They were courageous under fire, although careless about such details as wearing gas masks. But from January of 1917 on they began to show unhealthy signs of unrest. Many of their problems revolved around the covey of emigré Russians who, over the years, had collected in Paris. These Russians, who had fled czardom and were mostly pacifists of extreme left-wing orientation, made it a point to meet their countrymen either in camp or when the Russian troops were in Paris on leave. So, as Imperial Russia decayed during the winter of 1916-17, the Russian troops had no difficulty in obtaining the news of the Czar's impending downfall. In fact, if anything, the Russian troops in France came to be politically more advanced than their compatriots within Russia itself. Much of the responsibility for this agitation can be laid to such prominent Bolshevik figures as Leon Trotsky, who arrived in Paris in November of 1914 and set immediately to work for the newspaper *Nashe Slovo*—"Our Word"—the voice of the revolutionary Russian exiles in France. Thus, by the early spring of 1917 the Russian brigades in France reflected an accurate, and even slightly exaggerated, picture of the Russian Army in its homeland. They had elected Soldiers' Councils which the Russian officers were either too powerless or too negligent to suppress. These councils claimed the right to approve or disapprove of any offensive in which the Russians were asked to take part. When not fighting, the troops were constantly harangued by fellow soldiers preaching the inevitability of the Socialist revolution, which would immediately be followed by peace. Gradually the majority of the Russian soldiers came under the influence of these agitators. They were even led to believe that they had been "sold" to France in exchange for arms—a charge which the Russian troops, largely ill-

educated peasants and factory workers, were prepared to accept
and which it was difficult for their officers to deny under the circumstances.

At about this time, the French high command began to be concerned about the Russian brigades. It had begun to observe that the
Russians had a peculiar ability to influence the French troops with
whom they came in contact. No French regiment was ever quite the
same after it had entered the lines alongside the Russians, who, it
seemed, literally exuded the germ of pacifism and class struggle.

At first the eroding discipline of the Russians was laid to faulty
leadership on the part of their officers, and it was proposed to stiffen
this by means of French officers fighting in Russian uniforms. This
worked out moderately well, but only temporarily. At the time of
the Nivelle offensive the Russian troops actually voted among themselves to see whether or not they would take part in the attack.
Ultimately they decided to do so, but in the offensive they were
used by the French for the attack on Fort Brimont, a heavily fortified German strongpoint on the Chemin des Dames where cannon
fodder was the prime requirement in the assault. The Russians suffered almost six thousand casualties, including half the French officers who were serving in Russian uniforms, and this was the final
blow to their morale. They flatly refused to take part in any more
offensives and had to be withdrawn to a rest camp at Neufchâteau.

Now they became a real disciplinary problem—mainly stimulated
by the political situation within Russia, where the Czar had been
forced to abdicate and the nation was in the shaky grip of Kerensky's provisional government. Amid constant strife and revolution
and counterrevolution within the Russian Army, the Kerensky government was attempting to carry on the war against Germany
while simultaneously conducting broad socialist reforms within Russia. It was a confused and desperate situation. To make Kerensky's
task even more difficult, the Germans had allowed Lenin transit from
Switzerland through Germany and across to Sweden, whence he
easily made his way back to Russia to lead the Bolshevik opposition
against Kerensky.

The position that the Russian brigades found themselves in cannot
easily be imagined. The troops wallowed in a sea of confusion and
uncertainty. On all sides they were besieged with an endless series
of speeches, propaganda leaflets and political meetings. The Keren-

sky government had sent to France a Socialist revolutionary of good credentials named Rapp, whose task was to be military commissar to the Russian brigades and to explain the position of the new government and why the war must be continued. On the other hand, the Bolsheviks had many of their representatives within the ranks who, stimulated by guidance from Lenin relayed via the emigrés in Paris, were agitating for stopping the war now and at any price. Upon this issue, war or peace, the Russian brigades split asunder. The 1st Brigade, recruited principally among the factory workers of Moscow, was politically more advanced and mostly voted to support the Bolsheviks. The 3rd Brigade, on the other hand, was recruited from among the more conservative peasantry of the Urals and generally supported the Kerensky government in its policy of continuing the war until a suitable peace could be negotiated. Among the two brigades there were roughly ten thousand men for the Bolsheviks and six thousand supporting Kerensky and his provisional government.

Amid this division and confusion, the Russian officers wandered confused and ineffectual. In attempting to discipline their men, they suffered from the crippling stigma of holding their commissions from the Czar as members of the Imperial Russian Army. Now, with no Czar and no Russian Empire, they were forced to make the best of the situation and had declared their allegiance to Kerensky's provisional government, as being both the legal government of the hour and more conservative than the Bolsheviks. Of course this meant that the officers were rejected by the majority of the Russian troops in France and were, probably rightly, regarded with suspicion by even the soldiers who supported Kerensky.

Thus, the Russian officers had succeeded in maintaining only a ludicrous fraction of the once awesome disciplinary powers which they had held over their troops. The best example of this eroding discipline occurred on May Day, when the Russian troops actually held a celebration in honor of international Socialist revolution. In previous years any attempt to conduct such a fete would have been shot down in bloody repression. But now the troops were free to march in a parade, chanting "The International" and "The Marseillaise." They had discarded their former regimental flags and carried only the red flag of world revolution, and as they passed their officers the parading troops hurled insults at them. To conclude their festivities, the troops who comprised the Soldiers' Councils seized staff cars and, with the pennants fluttering from the fenders, toured the various French Army camps surrounding Neufchâteau.

Even if there were dissension and confusion among the Russian troops as to where they stood in the spectrum of world revolution, there was no doubt in the minds of the French soldiers as to what the Russians stood for. To the countless French soldiers of left-wing political persuasion, the Russian brigades represented nothing less than the vanguard of *successful* pacifism and world social revolution. They, the French, could not see or understand the torment of indecision which was gripping the Russian brigades at Neufchâteau. They knew only that in Russia the common soldiers had seized command of their own regiments and were refusing to take part in any more attacks, and this was enough to make the Russians in France appear to be the prophets of the future.

The situation reached a head in early June. Neufchâteau was within the Zone of the Armies in an area commanded by General de Castelnau, a highly experienced officer not given to wild alarms. But Castelnau was obviously very much concerned when, upon visiting the Russian brigades on June 4, he found them on the edge of open revolt. To G.Q.G. Castelnau reported that the Russian officers had lost control over their men and that it was "mandatory to plan the return of these troops to their native country." He recommended, "If it is necessary to delay their return until arrangements have been made, then they should be sent to a camp in the interior." [24]

Clearly, there was no time to be wasted. If the Russian brigades were a focal point of mutiny, and it was obvious that they were, then they must be got out of the way promptly. Later it could be decided what must be done with them. And so, like carriers of a dread disease, the Russians were swept into boxcars and sent back to an isolated camp in the Zone of the Interior.

Much more was to be heard from these troops in later weeks. But no one could worry about that now. The situation within the French Army itself was too desperate.

Now, by mid-June, the mutinies had almost become common knowledge. True, the newspapers were muzzled by censorship, but in place of facts a flood of wild rumors had sprung up. The Zone of the Armies was swept with provocative tales of entire divisions abandoning the trenches, of wholesale executions of mutineers on such a vast scale that machine guns had to be used, and of huge clashes between the cavalry and the mutinous infantry.

Some of the rumors had, of course, a certain basis in fact. The government, desperate for soldiers who could be relied upon to fire on the mutineers, resorted to the time-tested strategem of moving foreign troops into Paris—either the giant Senagalese from Africa or the little Tonkinese from Indochina. And around the latter there built up a fresh flurry of rumor. It was asserted that these yellow troops were strangely attracted to French women and that they were making sorties from their barracks to rape Parisiennes on the streets. A later rumor, one with a grain of truth in it, was that the Indochinese had been used to suppress strikes in Paris and had fired upon and slaughtered a group of women demonstrators in the Boulevard Bessières.[25] Actually only one woman had been killed, but this story, with the number of slain women growing ever larger as it was told and retold, swept through the Army, and suddenly a feature of every rebellion was the cry, "To Paris—they are murdering our wives!"

Another persistent story which gained great credence through its constant repetition by the left wing was that many of the mutinies were actually stimulated by *agents provocateurs* from G.Q.G.'s Second Bureau in order to flush out the radicals and potential ringleaders among the troops, who could then be shot. Such a theory, that G.Q.G. was intentionally fomenting mutiny within the Army in the spring of 1917, beggars belief. There was no need whatever to search for mutineers—the Army was completely shot through with them. Even by official admission, serious cases of "collective indiscipline" occurred in fifty-four divisions of the Army, almost exactly half of the French fighting forces.[26] The Zone of the Armies was now bespread with the defeatist *papillons*, the forests were filled with deserters and mutinous units, the villages behind the lines crowded with troops either in quarantine or trembling on the brink of rebellion.

And over the battlefront there had descended an unaccountable quiet. The German attacks had ceased, and to G.Q.G. this could mean only one thing—the Germans were preparing their long-dreaded assault.

Against this bleak prospect there was yet one spark of hope. Nivelle was gone. The distraught French government, appalled at the mutinies and the failure of the Nivelle offensive—the dangers of which they had correctly predicted—had lost every vestige of confidence in the Commander in Chief. The politicians had turned against him with a vengeance, and the man who had once panicked the government with his threat of resignation was repeatedly and peremptorily summoned from Compiègne to confer with various officials in Paris, who kept him waiting in their anterooms. Although Nivelle had made every effort to shift the blame for his failure onto others, and although he had attempted desperately to ingratiate himself with any politician who would listen to him (even going so far as to seek the friendship of the Minister of the Interior, Louis Malvy, against whom he had been warned), it was now plain that his career was finished.

A replacement had been brought into the wings. On April 29, 1917, the French government had announced a new appointment: General Henri Philippe Pétain was named Chief of the General Staff and "technical adviser to the government," his headquarters to be located at the War Ministry in Paris. The appointment fooled no one, especially not Nivelle's subordinates at G.Q.G., who readily foresaw that from his newly created post Pétain would shortly be appointed Commander in Chief of the Army. And so it should have come as no surprise to Nivelle when, after the conclusion of the Chemin-des-Dames offensive in early May, it was put to him bluntly that he would make it easier for all concerned if he would resign his position. But Nivelle still possessed a perverse spark of stubbornness, coupled with a burning determination not to sacrifice his place in history. He refused to resign. If the government wanted to replace him with Pétain, they had better not look to him to make it easy for them; they would have to dismiss him.

So that was the way it had been done. By order of the Minister of War, dated May 15, 1917, General Robert Nivelle was dismissed from his command and Pétain appointed in his stead. "On the day when a choice had to be made between ruin and reason," Charles de Gaulle later said, "Pétain was promoted." [27]

And now this quiet soldier who less than three years before had been an obscure colonel suddenly found himself in command of an army which was in mutiny and expecting any day a German onslaught. It was a situation which demanded from Pétain, an officer who had always been conservative and most orthodox, a solution as imaginative and unusual as any that a military leader could possibly devise.

13

PÉTAIN AND THE SUPPRESSION: I

THE FOCUS OF OUR STORY now turns to the huge, comfortless château at Compiègne which housed General Pétain and the Grand Quartier Général.

Pétain, now sixty-one years old and white-haired, but still carrying himself with a superb military bearing, was a man of almost inhuman calm. His eyes, the feature which most impressed every observer, were of icy blueness, and he looked at his subordinates with a direct, unblinking gaze. As each day's total of mutiny was reported to him he received the information without discernible anxiety. A few blunt questions sufficed to give him the information he needed, and then the subordinate was dismissed from his presence. He seemed totally nerveless—and yet the strain must have been tremendous.

Consider now the position in which Pétain found himself. He was the inheritor of a situation *in extremis,* a general who had arrived at the summit of his career only to find that his army was decomposing in his hands. Toward the politicians who had appointed him Pétain felt no gratitude. Why should he? "They call me only in catastrophes," he was later heard to brood.[1] It was only the coldest of comfort that it had been he himself who had correctly foreseen the failure of the Nivelle offensive. No matter, now he had to retrieve its consequences. And if he failed, as seemed inevitable, history would forget Nivelle and remember only Pétain as the man who had commanded the French Army at the time of its collapse.

Could Pétain check the flood of mutiny and restore the Army to

214

health? His detractors, and there were many even then, were sure that he could not. They pointed to the notorious pessimism which had been responsible for his being relieved at Verdun. They theorized that, while he was admittedly a skillful subordinate, he lacked the moral force necessary in the supreme command. And they claimed, with a certain correctness, that he was not a brilliant strategist but simply a good tactician and a talented organizer.

To the charge that he was too much the pessimist the obvious reply is that Pétain had almost always been thrust into situations in which there could hardly be found a single reason for optimism. One of his subordinates of the time has written of those first days: "I do not know a more horrible sensation for a commander than to suddenly learn that his army is breaking up. I saw the initial disaster at Verdun and the day following [the Italian rout at the battle of] Caporetto, but on these occasions I always sensed that with some reserves and a little imagination it would be possible to caulk up the front. But there had never been anything like May 20! We seemed absolutely powerless. From every section of the front the news arrived of regiments refusing to man the trenches. . . . The slightest German attack would have sufficed to tumble down our house of cards and bring the enemy to Paris." [2]

This does not overstate the case. Pétain had taken command of a gradually shrinking Army whose fighting strength consisted principally of its 109 infantry divisions and seven cavalry divisions—about fifty thousand officers and two million enlisted men. His authority rested not on the bedrock of a powerful and determined government, but rather on the shifting silt of a crumbling political union honeycombed with treason and incipient pacifism. And, by almost any standards, the French Army was in full revolt.

To the criticism that Pétain was less of a strategist than a mere organizer, it must be answered that a talent for organization was desperately needed at the moment. And whether or not he had the necessary moral force to rise to the occasion can be judged only in the light of the results he obtained.

During the initial appalling weeks of the mutinies, Pétain remained cloistered in G.Q.G. The personal entourage which he had brought with him to Compiègne had swiftly and remorselessly cleaned out the remnants of Nivelle's senior advisers, and in their place Pétain selected principally artillerymen who were known to favor his type of warfare—abundant use of heavy guns, meticulous planning, economy in manpower. Unlike Nivelle, he experienced no difficulty in taking his subordinates firmly in hand. None of the whispers of discord which had poisoned Nivelle's relationship with the government ever emerged from Compiègne, because, amazingly for a man of his reserve, Pétain came to be immensely admired by his staff. But this was hardly a cheap popularity. It was admiration based on respect for Pétain's awesome knowledge of troops and their psychology—and for this man who, during his career, had held every possible infantry command from platoon commander to his present eminence.

Amid the work and the agonizing strain which the mutinies brought to the Grand Quartier Général, Pétain introduced an almost monastic frigidity. The personal amenities disappeared, and even generals spoke only when spoken to. The asceticism extended to Pétain's personal mess, where even to guests from outside the staff Pétain served sparse and simple meals finished off with a single slice of cheese and a solitary glass of claret. They were quiet meals, their silence relieved only when Pétain looked up to tell a story, generally an old Army tale he had told for years, which was dutifully appreciated by his overawed guests and subordinates.

But it would be a mistake to consider Pétain as merely a somber presence who cast a brooding silence over the old château at Compiègne. Beneath the sober façade he was a widely read man of great imagination and, when he chose to use it, considerable fluency, especially with his pen. And to a soldier of his enormous practical experience, the mutinies fell into a pattern which called for certain logical responses. There was probably not another officer in the French Army so well equipped to deal with the revolts.

The exact steps which Pétain took to stop the mutinies have always been somewhat veiled in secrecy—for to admit that measures had been taken to restore order would be to focus attention on the mutinies themselves. Even Pétain rarely spoke of the event in later years. Nevertheless, from a mélange of sources it is possible to trace almost exactly the steps he took in his attempts to halt the chaos.

His first move was to state the strategy he intended to pursue as Commander in Chief. Almost immediately upon taking command he issued a "personal and secret" instruction to the commanders of

his armies and army groups which was to become famous as his
Directive No. 1. It bore the date of May 19, 1917, and, predictably,
it preached the doctrine of strictly limited offenses using concentrated firepower rather than mass manpower, to achieve small successes rather than grandiose failures. And it was flavored by that
particular brand of pessimistic common sense which was Pétain's
trademark.

"The equality of the opposing forces," the directive began, "does
not for a moment permit us to envisage the rupture of the front." It
simply did not make sense, Pétain elaborated, "to mount great attacks in depth on distant objectives, spreading our initial artillery
preparations over [enemy] defenses, resulting in bombardment so
diluted that only insignificant results are obtained." No, the attacks
in the future were to be mounted "economically with infantry and
with a maximum of artillery." [3]

All along the French front, planning for offensives came to a halt.
Only on the Chemin des Dames did a fitful battle continue, and there
only because the Germans were attacking in an effort to deny the
French their pitiful fruits of the Nivelle offensive. But even in the
face of this reduced activity it was a herculean task to provide the
manpower to repel the German attacks. Pétain's staff combed and
recombed every unit on the western front in an effort to find
enough loyal troops to man the defenses. Somehow it was done;
with dismounted cavalry, a good battalion here, a sturdy regiment
there, the front was held closed. But this was a stopgap measure of
the most desperate nature. These loyal units could not hold the
trenches forever, and they could not hold the front at all in the face
of the large-scale German attack which seemed every day more
imminent. Time would soon run out, and before it did the pressure had to be removed from the French front and the mass of the
Army returned to health.

Thus a crucial question bearing on Pétain's strategy was whether
the British could be persuaded to launch an offensive to draw German pressure off the tiny group of desperate Frenchmen who were
now defending the trench lines.

Exactly how much the British knew about the French Army mutinies has never been made completely clear. Some accounts say
that they knew nothing, others that Pétain informed Haig of his

desperate straits but that Haig agreed to keep it a secret from his political superiors in London. Still others claim Haig knew all and told all to the British government.

The facts are almost surely these: At an Allied conference held in Paris on May 4-5, one which Pétain attended in his then capacity as Chief of the General Staff and military adviser to the government, the British had been told that the French Army was "exhausted" and that future offensives would have to be planned with the idea that the British would bear the burden of the attack. Although the French did not conceal the fact that they were anxious for the British to draw pressure off the French front, the mutinies were not mentioned. At this exact date, of course, the mutinies had just begun and doubtless it was considered more prudent (and less embarrassing) to withhold knowledge of their existence from the British. Nevertheless, Prime Minister Lloyd George sensed that there was much left unsaid which could explain the sudden reversal of French strategy.

The puzzlement of the British was apparent to Pétain, who, after the conference, went up to Lloyd George and said, "I suppose you think I can't fight."

"No, General," Lloyd George answered, "with your record I could not make this mistake, but I am certain that for some reason or other you *won't* fight."

Pétain turned away without replying.[4]

At any rate, convincing the British that they should mount a relieving offensive was simplicity itself. Haig had long cherished the dream of cleaning the Germans out of Flanders, and it required only a tentative promise of French assistance (which the French did not keep and which the British half suspected they would not keep) to persuade Haig to schedule a British attack as soon as it could be got ready.

This British offensive was so important that on the day after Pétain assumed command of the French Army, and amid the myriad problems which faced him, he arranged to meet with Haig at Amiens. The French general made an excellent impression on his British counterpart, who found him to be brief and businesslike in address and lucid in his thinking. Haig asked Pétain what plans he had in the making and was advised that the French were scheduling an attack at Malmaison for June 10 and a few subsidiary attacks at

later dates. This, as far as Haig was concerned, was thoroughly satisfactory, since a French attack at Malmaison would serve to divert
German reserves away from Flanders. The meeting adjourned with
Haig probably given no definite information on the state of French
morale.

But later, on June 2, after the British planning for the Flanders
offensive was well advanced, Pétain sent his chief of staff for another
meeting with Haig. The French officer brought bad news; he advised Haig that the French offensive at Malmaison was to be postponed indefinitely. The only assistance to the Flanders attack which
Pétain could offer was to fire off the pre-attack bombardment in the
hope that it would fool the Germans. Quite certainly at this meeting
the French felt compelled to reveal, in however guarded terms,
that their Army was in a state of mutiny.

With the policy of strictly limited offensives firmly established and
a major British diversionary attack on the way, Pétain could now
turn his attention to restoring the morale of the Army. The matter
of the most pressing concern was leave for the troops. Curiously,
before the war there had been no thought given to the amount of
leave which a fighting man would require. This, of course, was
due to the acceptance of the School of the Attack, which envisioned
a victory of such whirlwind speed that such amenities as leave for
the troops were hardly worth consideration. But as the trench war
slogged on, it became evident that leave for the troops was a critical necessity, and so it was decided that they were to be allowed
a pittance of seven days' leave every four months. Had this policy,
as inadequate as it was, been adhered to, all might have been well.
But the chronic shortage of troops had caused G.Q.G. to order all
leave cut off in the period prior to major offensives—as Nivelle had
stopped all leave beginning in February before his April offensive
—and there were many cases where men had had no leave for
eighteen months. It is impossible to overemphasize the importance
which leave had for the French troops. Literally, they lived for it—although the circumstances surrounding it could hardly have been
more miserable. The basic fault was that the senior officers regarded
leave for the troops not as a right but as a favor grudgingly
granted. And the conditions of travel were cruel beyond credence.
For example, once the soldier obtained his longed-for *permission*, the
dates of which might have been casually rescheduled or arbitrarily

canceled, he was expected to fend for himself completely on his journey home. Carrying his pack and his rifle, he trudged miles to the nearest railroad marshaling yard. There he counted the hours and the days which passed as he waited for a leave train. Unless he was exceptionally lucky, his wait was a long one—and all the time he had to suffer exposure to cold or rain, since there was no provision for soldiers in transit to sleep or even to wash at the stations. Even their food was difficult to come by; the pitiful pay of a French poilu would buy almost nothing in a railroad restaurant with its skyrocketing wartime prices.

Discipline for men on leave was another problem; there was either too much or too little of it. While the troops were still in the Zone of the Armies they were subject to constant harassment by tough gendarmes on the lookout for deserters, but then, suddenly, as their train finally emerged into the Zone of the Interior, the filthy and exhausted men found that discipline had almost evaporated. The situation was most pronounced at the railway stations. For example, the huge Gare de l'Est in Paris was the principal point of destination or transfer for the majority of French troops on leave. But jealousy between the Ministry of the Interior and the Army had resulted in the fractionalization of the policing of this immense station. On the railroad tracks themselves the men were under the jurisdiction of the Army; inside the station, that of the military governor of Paris; at the exits, that of the municipal police. This mélange of authority resulted in no authority at all and made possible the drunkenness and the rioting of the tormented troops in transit, inspired to desperate acts by pacifist agitators who frequented the stations.

But now, at Pétain's direction, a G.Q.G. instruction concerning leave appeared on June 2. As reiterated in the Army *Bulletin* of June 6, it announced:

> The efforts of the high command have been directed toward insuring seven days of leave every four months to everyone. The percentage of men allowed on leave at any one time, formerly fixed at 13 per cent of effective strength, will be maintained. Nevertheless, as the situation permits, this may be increased to 25 or 50 per cent in large units which have been taken to the rear to be reconstituted. The leave schedule is to be made up with the greatest of care and will be posted for inspection by those concerned.[5]

On Pétain's part, this vastly enlarged leave policy was more than a simple administrative measure; it was a daring gamble, because during this period the troops on leave were constantly rioting in railroad stations, waving red flags from trains, assaulting gendarmes, and uncoupling locomotives from the trains which were returning them to the front. But Pétain knew that without the promise of leave the Army could never be returned to discipline. It was a gamble he simply had to take.

There now followed a succession of orders designed to put the man on leave in a better frame of mind. Unit commanders were instructed to provide truck transportation from the camps to the railroad marshaling yards for the men going on leave. And at the stations themselves Pétain directed the immediate establishment of inexpensive soldiers' restaurants, barbershops, washrooms, a medical service and bunking facilities. The number of trains for the *permissionnaires* was greatly increased, and to prevent the men on leave from drifting aimlessly about he had a guidebook published for them.

Another rudimentary comfort, hitherto lacking, now made its appearance around the stations in response to an urgent appeal by Pétain: numerous gaily painted structures which housed canteens set up by the YMCA, the French Red Cross and the Foyers du Soldat.

A problem of major concern was to prevent as much as possible the news of the mutinies from getting back to the interior of France. To assist in this Pétain demanded that the captain of every company call in his men going on leave and instruct them to keep their mouths closed about what they had seen in the Zone of the Armies. Amazingly, this seems to have been fairly successful, although it must be remembered that most of the troops had little idea of the widespread nature of the mutinies and probably thought that their own unit was among a very few which had revolted.

Paris was another problem. Because pacifists literally swarmed around soldiers on leave in the capital, immediate steps had to be taken to screen the men who were allowed to journey there. Accordingly, Pétain issued orders which barred soldiers previously convicted of military offenses, certain foreign-born troops and men known to be disciplinary problems. Now, with only a more or less select group of troops allowed into Paris, he was able to appeal to them to pay no attention to the defeatists and the pacifist pamphleteers in the railroad stations. If approached by them, Pétain instructed, the soldier should have them arrested by the police; lacking police, the soldier should arrest them himself. Pétain vastly increased the number of gendarmes assigned to railway duty, and there is no question but that this display of force helped not only to drive out the pacifists but also to overawe any potentially rebellious troops.

Gradually, but definitely, the incidence of revolt among the men on leave dropped off. Pétain's gamble with the *permissionnaires* had paid off. By June 27 the riots on leave trains had dwindled away to controllable proportions, and after July 5 there were almost none to report.

By June 15 Pétain judged that it was now the time for him to take the unorthodox step of going to his troops and explaining his plans for the future. Almost every morning from that date on, he left G.Q.G. at Compiègne and drove in his command car, the white pennons of the Commander in Chief fluttering at the fenders, to the bivouac area of one or another of his infantry divisions, where he spoke to as many of the troops as he could.

First he met with the division and regimental commanders and their staffs, briefed them on his plans and, quite frankly, asked their advice in solving the problem which haunted them all. He appealed to them to air any complaints that he could rectify, all of which were carefully noted down. And when a complaint dealt with an item which should already have been handled at the division level—for example, stale bread sent up to the regiments in the front lines—he had no hesitancy in whirling on the officer responsible, no matter how senior, and reproaching him for allowing the situation to exist.

Following his conference with the senior officers, Pétain went out to speak to the troops. Every officer, every N.C.O. and a selected group of privates were gathered into an open field for an immense meeting which he addressed standing on the hood of his car or on a tree stump where all could see him. His usual procedure was first to explain to them his plans for a series of strictly limited offensives— although he was careful to emphasize that his general strategy would be to remain on the defensive until the arrival of the Americans, which would give the Allies a manpower preponderance. He promised faithfully that there would be no more *Système D*. Every battle would be meticulously prepared, with overwhelming artillery support, and he assured his listeners that the Army would soon receive a flood of new heavy guns, more shells and more tanks.

Pétain went on to explain his plans for a complete reorganization of the hitherto disgraceful Medical Service. He announced a pay raise for veteran troops and also the creation of a new decoration, a brightly colored *fourragère* shoulder cord which would be worn by the troops belonging to regiments and battalions that had been mentioned at least four times in orders of the day.

Then he turned to the junior officers. In the hearing of the enlisted men, Pétain solemnly adjured the officers to conduct a pitiless and untiring campaign against mutinous elements within the ranks. He assured them of his complete support (and, by doing so, left all his hearers with the impression that G.Q.G. would not quibble at any absence of legal niceties which might be involved in suppressing a revolt); but, he went on, the officers must, by their actions, serve as a guide for the enlisted men and would be expected at all times to be in complete charge of the troops under them. Sometimes during this talk he would spot an enlisted man who, overcome by the presence of the Commander in Chief, was weeping for shame at his past misdeeds. When this occurred, Pétain would whirl on the officers and say, "Look at these men; there is nothing the matter with them. All they require is leading, all they need is an example. Advance and they will follow you." [6]

Next Pétain turned to his listeners en masse and asked if they had any questions or advice for him. The enlisted men shuffled their feet and looked at the ground, but generally a few ideas came forth from the middle-grade officers. It had been noted, one captain would say, that most of the Croix-de-Guerre decorations went to the staff officers and the more senior ranks. Was it possible to obtain a greater percentage of these coveted decorations for the men themselves? It was, and would be done, Pétain promised. Could anything be done about the monotony of the food? Plans for its improvement, Pétain answered, would instantly be set in motion. Throughout this period for questions and answers the most meticulous notes were kept by Pétain's staff, and he always concluded it by reminding his listeners that he was known for never making promises which he could not keep.

The meeting ended with the Commander in Chief distributing

decorations to the troops, usually with a light personal comment to each man. To the poilu who was being decorated for the fifth time, "Five decorations all by yourself! What have you done?" From the embarrassed soldier the stumbling reply, "My general, I have . . . I have done what everyone else does." From Pétain with a smile, "What everyone else does? That's all there is to it, eh?"[7] Finally the troops came to attention, a band played, Pétain returned the soldiers' salute and drove off.

It is difficult exactly to estimate the number of divisions which Pétain eventually visited in this manner, but the figure certainly runs to between eighty and ninety. It is difficult, too, to put into words the immense effect he had on the troops. His visits were truly a psychological masterpiece. In one day he would succeed in assuring a whole division of his determination to hoard their lives with a miser's greed; in impressing upon them his determination to restore discipline, ruthlessly if need be; and in aligning on his side a senior private in every company, who, flattered and overwhelmed at being taken into the confidence of his Commander in Chief, was henceforth Pétain's loyal advocate among the enlisted men.

Next Pétain turned his attention to the "rest camps" in the rear areas of the Zone of the Army. It was in these camps, after all, that most of the mutinies were taking place, as, living in careless squalor, the troops found their misery compounded to the point where it was unendurable.

As in armies before and since, the French infantryman whose unit had been pulled out of the front lines and sent back to a "rest area" found that the most habitable spots had long since been occupied by rear-echelon troops who managed to live in comparative luxury. This left the fighting troops only the blasted remains of little villages which had been too often fought over and where, within the rat-infested rubble, the troops were expected to contrive their own living quarters, sanitary facilities and messing arrangements.

Compounding the troops' misery was the fact that, for transportation convenience, many of the camps were located too far forward and were subject to constant tension from the threat of German heavy-artillery harassing fire. But the ultimate indignity was the fact that the troops felt wanted by no one. The service troops in the rear felt imposed upon by the presence of the fighting troops, while the few civilians remaining in the villages were surly and embittered— except, of course, for the café proprietors, who sold oceans of wine, since the troops' sole preoccupation during rest periods was to get as drunk as possible and stay drunk as long as possible.

Into this morass, heretofore regarded as a necessary evil by G.Q.G., Pétain stepped with crisp efficiency. First, to place the camps out of even the sound of gunfire, he had the Zone of the Armies delaminated into various subdivisions: Zone of the Front, Zone of Reserve, Zone of Passage and, at the rear, Zone of Rest. In the last area he ordered the immediate construction of rough barracks with bath and laundry facilities and, most important, demanded from the services of supply the instant procurement of more than a half-million cots, a common-place amenity but one with which no one had ever thought to furnish the troops before.

But even more important than the physical improvement of the rest camps was the manner in which the troops were treated when they were in them. For the first four days after the troops had been brought back from the front lines, Pétain directed, they were to be left completely alone—*en repos absolu*—so that they could recover *physiquement* and *moralement*[8] from their experiences in the front lines. Following these four days of grace the troops were to begin training, but at first only for short periods, which were gradually lengthened.

Predictably, Pétain as a meticulous professional laid great stress on training the troops, especially with artillery. The majority of the training schools had been shut down prior to the Nivelle offensive in order to release their cadres for front-line duty, and now Pétain hastened to reopen them. The tendency of the past for the various armies to run their own schools, using their own doctrines, was checked, and instruction was centralized and unified at consolidated schools—most notably the artillery study center established at Vitry-le-François, where consideration was to be directed principally to the close support of infantry advances and improved communication between artillery and the first waves of the advance.

Another unsatisfactory aspect of the situation regarding rest camps had been that the artillery units were rarely rotated back to rest areas, the excuse having been advanced that the artillery was not suffering the proportion of casualties which the infantry did. However, Pétain recognized that the artillerymen were under frequent counter-battery fire from the Germans and that the strain on them was intense. So instructions were issued that the artillery too was to be sent into rest billets on a regular rotation scheme.

But perhaps the biggest problem the entire rest program faced was drunkenness. "The example comes from the messes of the lieutenants," Pétain stated, "where they have taken up the habit of drinking to excess. The N.C.O.s naturally follow this same error. The result is that, among the men, drink has become so important that they hesitate to begin a march of any distance without filling their canteens with wine." [9] Pétain knew that the fight against drunkenness was crucial; unless he won it his whole program of rest camps would have done nothing more than bring the men back from the trenches for a saturnalian orgy which would end in another series of mutinous explosions. He appealed to both officers and men to control their drinking, and to back up his appeal he issued orders which greatly restricted the volume of wine allowed into the Zone of the Armies, both for troops and for civilians who might resell it to the troops. Another order completely prohibited the sale of wine in the rest camps on the day before the troops were scheduled to move up to the front lines—a simple step which substantially reduced the number of drunken riots as the troops were called into ranks at the end of the rest periods.

As the weeks passed, almost every division was passed through these new rest camps. But there was one unlooked-for development which even Pétain had not forecast and which indicated the deep-rootedness of the Army malady. Curiously, although a division required at least fifteen days in rest camp to recover its morale, the troops could not under any circumstances be left in camp more than thirty days. If they were, the men generally became irritable and logy, and the incidence of mutinous acts would increase. This was drawn to Pétain's attention by such reports as a July 8 dispatch from General Guillaumat of the Second Army to the general commanding the XXXIInd Army Corps, which concluded: "I point out to you the severe effect on discipline that would result from keeping the 69th and 40th infantry divisions in their rest areas too long. This observation applies particularly to the 69th, which has been drawn back from the front since May 5, and which, for the most urgent reasons, should be brought forward as soon as possible into the combat sector." [10]

Nor was the officer corps immune from Pétain's scrutiny—especially the junior officers, the lieutenants and *sous-lieutenants*, whom he found to be of very uneven quality. Of necessity they had been hastily trained, and there were almost no regular-Army junior officers left alive. The French system of promotion from the ranks, while it had the advantage of providing officers who were battle-seasoned and undeniably courageous, had the disadvantage of producing officers who were unsure of their powers of command. For shrewd combat leadership, personal discipline and loyalty, the French junior officer was unsurpassed; but as a perceptive disciplinarian of his troops, or even, curiously, as an officer with an acute sense of responsibility toward the material welfare of his men, the young lieutenant often left much to be desired. The upshot was that the traditional almost fatherly relationship between the French officer and his men had broken down. Pétain knew this, and he exhorted the officers to get to know their men better and to demonstrate more of a feeling of personal interest in the troops' welfare—for example, in their food. A constant complaint among the men was that the food was too monotonous, or else that it had been spoiled by poorly trained cooks. Pétain instructed the officers that this was a leadership problem which must be remedied by them, and to give them the requisite technical knowledge he set up lessons in food preparation which officers under instruction were required to attend.

Another concern was to open the lines of communication upward from the junior officers to their seniors. The years of war had demonstrated to the observant Pétain that junior officers generally hesitated to report to their superiors that their troops simply could not take a certain German strong point, for to do this would invite criticism of their courage; and so an assault would be launched which both the troops and the junior officers knew was doomed to failure. Pétain made known his views on this in a directive issued on May 19.

> Over a period of almost three years, our officers have proved their heroism and courage—notwithstanding which, fearing to be accused of cowardice, they refrain from making known to their superiors any difficulties which they foresee in carrying out orders. The result of this fearful hesitancy is that the higher levels of command sometimes

keep on giving certain orders which they would quite possibly change or postpone if they had been given better intelligence. . . . I attach the greatest importance to such reports. . . .[11]

With this official benison, junior officers began to lose their feeling that it was proof of cowardice to tell their battalion commander that, for example, a certain German position could not be carried by infantry assault alone but must have more intensive artillery preparation, and the senior officers began to receive a trickle of information up the chain of command. But there were qualifications to this new doctrine; Pétain hastened to caution his officers that after their suggestions had been noted by the higher command and a decision reached, there was to be no further discussion and the orders of superior officers must be obeyed without question. And, fully as important, all complaints and suggestions must be channeled upward through the *French* chain of command and not vented to the officers of other Allied armies.

Nor were staff officers immune from Pétain's criticism. He believed, quite correctly, that many bloody offensives had been mounted merely through the staff officers' ignorance of the problems involved. He blamed the staffs of all commands for not leaving their headquarters often enough to see front-line conditions and to allow the troops, who regarded staff officers as *embusqués*, to see them. There was a good reason why the staff officers had stayed in their headquarters or, when compelled to visit the front, had removed their staff brassards: they felt that, with the troops in revolt, it was much more prudent. Pétain now demanded that they appear as frequently as possible among the troops, "wearing their brassards."

At G.Q.G. in Compiègne, where the staff had always worked long hours, the labor become even more intense. Pétain churned out directives, orders and memoranda. A section of the G.Q.G. staff was designated to investigate the rebellion in the Army at the time of the French Revolution and to report back to Pétain on the techniques which had been used to suppress this ancient mutiny. A proposal to solve the problem of obtaining enough ardent troops to launch attacks by creating *détachements d'elite* whose sole duty would be to lead offensives was flatly rejected by Pétain; he sensed, quite rightly, that an elite assault corps would succeed only in denuding the

Army of the courageous and the natural leaders who, if left in their present units, might be able to stimulate the entire Army to a renewed fighting spirit. The assault, he wrote, was "the supreme act of every soldier," and the task of the officers was "the instruction of all" to meet this challenge.[12] Pétain, reviewing the circumstances of every major rebellion, came to the conclusion that many mutinies had been triggered off by the officers' failing to make good on promises to the men that they would be sent to a rest camp. He cautioned all officers that the uncertainty of the fighting made it very dangerous to make such promises. "Nothing is more dangerous than to raise the hopes of the troops when the war can prevent them from being carried out."[13]

As the pattern of the mutinies became clearer, it was evident that many of the revolts had been stimulated by men who had always been troublemakers and who, indeed, had actually been sentenced to serve in the infantry divisions as punishment for past misdeeds. This, of course, is the crux of an age-old question in wartime military discipline: Is it right for men who are convicted of crimes to be sent to the safety of a military prison, which is where they would rather go than be at the front, and thus leave the fighting to the men who have not broken the law? Or is it better to sentence the convicted prisoner to serve in the front lines, where, at least, he is forced to endure the same hardships and dangers as the faithful soldier? French military tribunals had generally decided in favor of the latter solution, with the result that in some units the number of convicted men serving their sentences in the front lines with infantry divisions had risen as high as 7 per cent of the unit's strength. Inevitably this had a damaging effect on the morale of the rest of the troops, who could not avoid feeling that their life was almost identical with that of these troublemaking criminals. Pétain now directed that in the future all men convicted of crime must be sentenced to hard labor in the colonies and that "at the same time the suspect element" still in the infantry divisions "must be placed under close surveillance."[14]

Finally, Pétain personally undertook the project of explaining to the Army why France was fighting this war. The pacifists were whispering to the troops that France had no definite war aims, that they were fighting and dying in a capitalist war which was being waged solely for commercial profit. Neither Joffre nor Nivelle had ever bothered to rebut this; but now Pétain had a stirring article written. Entitled "Why We Are Fighting," it was run on the front page of most of the newspapers, and reprints were posted everywhere in the Zone of the Armies. In part the article said:

> We fight because we have been attacked by Germany.
> We fight to drive the enemy from our soil. . . .
> We fight with tenacity and discipline, because these are essential to obtain victory.[15]

So now Pétain had set in motion the most pressing measures for the revitalization of the Army. But it was still too early to see whether they would have any results. The British had yet to mount their relieving attack in Flanders, and the Germans could still roll through the French front.

And now still another agonizing problem had to be faced: how to punish the troops who had mutinied.

14

PÉTAIN AND THE SUPPRESSION: II

A FRENCH MILITARY execution was a dread scene: the witnessing troops drawn up on three sides of a square; the nervous firing party; gendarmes lashing a terrified, sometimes screaming prisoner to a post; then, after the rifles had done their work, a sergeant coming forward with a pistol to fire the ritual *coup de grâce* into the dead man's ear. Even for troops inured to scenes of horror by years in the trenches, the awesome spectacle of a military execution was an unspeakably frightening experience.

There has, since World War I, grown up a body of legend surrounding the suppression of the French Army mutinies. There are the tales of wholesale executions by firing squads of machine-gunners. And there are stories about hundreds of mutineers marched into no man's land and dramatically reduced to a "hash of flesh, bones, and cloth" by their own artillery.[1] But it did not happen this way at all. Neither the Army nor the nation could have endured gigantic massacres of the mutineers; nor did Pétain consider them necessary. A subtler way could be found. Of course, there had to be a certain number of executions—mutiny is much too terrible a crime to go unpunished—but Pétain's aim was to stop the revolts and restore the troops to discipline. And for this a single execution could be more effective than a blood bath. He had no intention of murdering vast numbers of these precious infantrymen.

But there was a qualification to Pétain's mercy. He was willing to allow almost any latitude to the officer whose troops were actually in a state of mutiny. And he also recognized that, after a revolt had

231

been suppressed, the prompt execution of the ringleaders would burn a lesson into the minds of the rest of the troops. So although there were probably no incidents of mass, out-of-hand slaughter, there is no question but that there were a great many trials which were hasty and somewhat offhand and which concluded with the almost immediate execution of the condemned mutineers.

Technically, many of these speedy trials and executions were illegal. Parliament, in particular the left-wing parties, had exposed the many instances of executions *pour l'exemple* which had taken place under the *cours martiales* of the early years of the war. It had demanded progressively more strict regulations regarding military justice. And so the dreaded *cours martiales* had been suppressed, and now trials could be held solely by the more circumscribed *conseils de guerre*, under which every soldier convicted of a crime had the right of appeal to a higher court and death sentences had to be personally reviewed and approved by the President of the Republic.

Although there was no question but that the old *cours martiales* had acted unjustly in many cases, there was also no doubt that the procedural delays and the appeals to higher courts permitted under the *conseils de guerre* made discipline difficult and removed the awesome example of immediate punishment. Moreover, the feeling had grown among the Army's commanders that the politicians would impair discipline by commuting the sentences of too many of the men who had been condemned to death for mutiny.

Pétain too feared that unless the Army regained the power to approve death sentences the troops would soon learn that a soldier convicted of mutiny stood an excellent chance of being pardoned. And, undoubtedly, the celebrated case of "the two syndicalists from St.-Étienne" did much to stimulate his determination to secure for himself the power of life or death over his troops.

This affair, which had its origin in one of the first of the mutinies, revolved around two corporals who had, without question, led a mutiny of their men. Ultimately the mutiny was suppressed and a *conseil de guerre* condemned the two N.C.O.s to death—a sentence which was approved all the way up the chain of command to Pétain, who then referred it to the Minister of War, Paul Painlevé, requesting his approval as well as the acquiescence of President of the Republic Raymond Poincaré.

But, surprisingly, Painlevé was obstinate in this matter, even going so far as to bring the matter up at a Cabinet meeting on June 5 which was attended by Poincaré. The Minister of War announced in no uncertain terms that he was completely opposed to the death sentence for the two corporals. To this Poincaré demurred, stating that he was willing to give his approval inasmuch as it was necessary to back the Army up in re-establishing discipline. The argument between Painlevé and Poincaré continued even after the Cabinet meeting had broken up,[2] until Painlevé succeeded in having the sentence commuted to ten years at hard labor.[3]

There are two stories as to why Painlevé was so insistent that the two corporals should not die. According to several accounts, they were influential members of powerful left-wing labor groups which the government was making a desperate effort to appease in order to preserve the Union Sacrée—a teachers' union and a trade-union council in the arsenal city of St.-Étienne. "Their execution," Painlevé is claimed to have said, "would provoke a general strike in St.-Étienne, against which the government, lacking police, would have no defense."[4] Painlevé's own version is that the men were not corporals at all, but rather were *simples soldats*, one of them a peasant from Pas-de-Calais and the other a teacher from Oise. He protested that they had always been good soldiers, that they had not been ringleaders but had been selected at random from among a mass of mutineers, that the schoolteacher was something of a mental case, and, finally, that their regiment had been restored to order and there was no compelling necessity for executions *pour l'exemple*.[5]

Regardless of which account is true, the case amply illustrates why Pétain found it necessary to demand that the government provide him with the quick trial and the immediate execution of death sentences. The situation was so desperate that only a ruthless and immediate show of force could arrest the mutinies; and so, on June 1, Pétain moved to provide his officers with this power. The first step was to authorize the armies to convene *conseils de guerre* without delay or reference to higher command; in effect, this meant that the general of almost any unit could create a *conseil de guerre* on the scene of a mutiny and immediately commence to try offenders. The second step was an urgent appeal by Pétain to Paul Painlevé asking him "in the name of the commanders of the armies" to have the government's right of review and pardon revoked. Even further, Pétain asked that the *cours martiales*, with their much more summary brand of justice, be re-established.[6]

This last demand was obviously impossible. To re-establish the *cours martiales* would require action by Parliament in open session and would necessarily involve a frank admission to the entire world that the French Army was in revolt and the situation was desperate. But Pétain had succeeded in making clear to Painlevé the fact that the power to execute mutineers without delay or pardon by the government was absolutely necessary, with the result that the Minister of War did his best for Pétain. Painlevé pursuaded the President of the Republic to give up his right of pardon "in cases where discipline and national defense require an immediate penalty." [7] Then, on June 9, Painlevé issued an order which, while retaining at least the façade of the *conseils de guerre*, abolished the right of mandatory review in cases of "collective disobedience." [8] And, to cloak these actions, which can charitably be described as only quasi-legal, instructions were issued that the newspaper censors should not permit "any comment on the changes in the Code of Military Justice," nor should they even allow reprinting of "the text of the articles modified." [9]

Later Painlevé would be bitterly assailed for these acts, which, in effect, returned the Army to the rule of the dreaded *cours martiales* with their peremptory justice and immediate executions. And he would defend himself courageously by saying, "When it is all over, you may shoot me if you wish, but now only let me re-establish order!" [10]

But the ability quickly to convene a court-martial and convict a mutineer or group of mutineers, and then to execute them almost immediately, was not, in itself, enough to halt the rebellion. Pétain sensed that many officers were not acting with sufficient vigor to quash rebellion when it first occurred. To stiffen their spines, he issued on June 5 the following order to all the officers in the Army:

> At the time of some recent incidents, officers have not always seemed to do their duty. Certain officers have concealed from their superiors the signs of adverse spirit which existed in their regiments. Others have not, in their repression, displayed the desired initiative

or energy. . . . Inertia is equivalent to complicity. The Commander
in Chief has decided to take all necessary action against these weak-
lings.

The message closed with these ominous words: *"The Commander
in Chief will protect with his authority all those who display vigor
and energy in suppression"* [11] (author's italics). The implication in
this was lost on no one. Pétain was providing his officers with full
powers. They were now permitted to take any steps which they felt
appropriate to suppress a mutiny, and, as long as it did not descend to
excesses of wholesale butchery, there would be no questions asked.

Pétain's pronunciamento to the officer corps was followed up in a
message to the commanders of armies and groups of armies dated
June 11. In it he discussed the need for forthright action in suppression and held up the actions of the commander of the XXXVIIth
Army Corps as being exemplary in this regard. His message concluded with a threat, "All officers, from the commander of a platoon
to the commander of a corps, must have the same sense of duty. It
is necessary that all realize that they must exercise their responsi-
bilities or else they will themselves be brought before *conseils de
guerre*." [12]

The commanding officer of the XXXVIIth Army Corps whom Pétain held up for emulation in the suppression of the mutinies was that
same General Émile Taufflieb who had been a witness to the Soissons riots in May. Taufflieb, an Alsatian, had dedicated his life to the
restoration of France's "lost provinces" and was possessed of an implacable Germanophobia. Though a general of only moderate tactical ability, he was a thoroughly professional officer with undoubted
personal force and coolheadedness, capable of any degree of ruthlessness necessary to suppress a mutiny.

At six o'clock on an evening in early June, Taufflieb had received
a frantic phone call from one of his subordinates, a General Bajolle,
the commander of an infantry division. Bajolle had frightening news:
a battalion of his division, stationed at a camp in Terny, had mutinied
and disappeared into the surrounding forest.

Taufflieb drove at once to Terny and listened to the story of the
affair directly from the lips of the battalion commander and the cap-
tains who commanded each of the companies. The battalion, it

seemed, had been ordered to the front and had been marched out of camp in good order. But the road by which the troops left the town of Terny passed through an area which was wooded on each side. Suddenly, and obviously by prearrangement, someone in the ranks fired a shot in the air. Instantly the column broke up and seven hundred men fled into the woods, leaving the thunderstruck officers and N.C.O.s helpless in the deserted road. In fact, the disappearance of this entire battalion had been such a shock that it was not until nearly 10 P.M. that the mutineers could be located. They had taken refuge in a large cave deep in the woods, from which they announced that they had no intention of coming out until their officers agreed to various demands which the troops intended to present.

Taufflieb drove immediately to the scene of the mutiny. By now a platoon of cavalry had been brought up to cover the entrance. Leaving his revolver in his car, and overruling the protests of his horrified officers, the general announced that he intended to enter the cave and speak to the men.

It is a dramatic picture. In the light of torches, Taufflieb stepped through the narrow entrance of the cave. Before him he saw the seven hundred mutineers, most of them lying on the floor of the cave and regarding the general with sullen disinterest. The customary command *"Garde à vous—fixe!"* (Attention!) brought no response, but a few of the troops gathered around Taufflieb, who proceeded to address the entire battalion. "It seems that you have refused to go into the trenches. . . . So I have come to find out your reasons and your grievances, so that I may then take the measures which my duty and my country demand of me."

Turning to the men who were nearest him, he asked point blank why they had revolted. He received a number of stumbling answers: "It is not our turn in the trenches, it is the turn of another battalion." "The factory workers are on strike, why shouldn't we strike too?"

Impatiently Taufflieb scorned these excuses. "This is all that you have to say to justify your mutiny? All right, then, tomorrow morning at eight I shall return—not to conduct an inquiry into the causes of the mutiny, but instead to take action." And, with a curt "Good evening, men," he left the cave.

Outside he gathered the battalion officers around him and snapped out instructions for the next morning. The troops were to be gathered in their camp at Terny and a large force of gendarmes was to be brought there. *Conseils de guerre* were to be set up immediately and held in readiness for speedy trials. But what, he was asked, if the men refused to come out of the cave? There was a pause while Taufflieb considered. And then the tough Alsatian general gave the waiting officers his reply: If the men did not come out that night, he was done with them. "Wall the cave up so that they cannot get out."

As events turned out, this technique, medieval and horrible in its simplicity, did not prove necessary. By seven the next morning the mutineers had straggled back to their camp and Taufflieb drove to Terny to address them. The battalion had been formed into ranks. The *"Garde à vous—fixe!"* was called out and this time the men came to attention. Then Taufflieb took his place before their ranks and proceeded to castigate them for their indiscipline. He drew for them the picture of the agony of the exhausted battalion which they had been scheduled to relieve and which, if subjected to a German attack, would have been cut to pieces. "You have been parties to the gravest deed which a soldier can commit in wartime. You have abandoned your flag. I have come this morning to take the necessary punishment measures called for by your act of mutiny."

With this, Taufflieb ordered the four company commanders to select five men each for punishment. The ranks stood silent as twenty men were chosen and hustled away by the gendarmes to the immediate judgment of the waiting *conseils de guerre*. The remaining troops knew what fate was intended for them.

"And now," Taufflieb promised the battalion, "tonight you *will* move up to the trenches." [13]

The mutiny was over.

While this aspect of the mutiny suppression—the arbitrary selection of victims to serve as a propitiatory sacrifice for the entire unit—seems grotesque to the mind accustomed to a different type of military justice, it must be remembered that the French Army has roots extending back to the Roman legions. And in the armies of Rome, decimation, technically the slaughter of one in ten, was an established method of dealing with units which were mutinous or had displayed cowardice in the face of the enemy. Thus to the French Army the selection of mutineers to be executed on a more-or-less random basis did not carry with it any implication of gross injustice. Indeed, it was a method which was hallowed by time.

In any reconstruction of the techniques used in suppressing the mutinies, the role of Paul Painlevé must constantly be borne in mind. It is true that he had secured virtual carte blanche for Pétain to authorize the immediate execution of mutineers convicted by the *conseils de guerre*, but at the same time it must be remembered that Painlevé was an honest and honorable man of sincere republican principles. He had little control over the more out-of-hand executions; indeed, he probably knew nothing about them. Yet Painlevé does seem to have felt acutely his responsibility in delivering the French poilu up to the *conseils de guerre*, and he must have known that these courts now consisted of frightened officers who were, in turn, under pressure from frightened superiors.

It was a burden which the conscientious Painlevé could not long tolerate, and so on June 20 the little Minister of War telephoned Pétain and asked that henceforth he refer sentences of execution to Painlevé himself for final approval. This request, of course, was unpalatable to Pétain who regarded it as "premature" and told Painlevé so.[14] The matter was finally resolved on July 14 when Painlevé issued orders abrogating Pétain's privilege of approving executions without recourse to higher authority. By then, there can be no doubt, the *conseils de guerre* had done their work and the compelling necessity for summary executions no longer existed.

Thereafter every evening messengers would appear at the Ministry of War on the Rue St.-Dominique, bearing dossiers and trial records of soldiers whom various *conseils de guerre* had condemned to death. And every evening the conscientious Painlevé would carefully review these folders and then discuss them with Pétain on the telephone or else drive to G.Q.G. to talk them over in person. But in all probability only a selected group of execution cases was actually referred to Painlevé—the delicate ones with political overtones, the trials of soldiers whose political connections were such that he would hear about their cases through other channels. Pétain, therefore, was able to suffer these time-consuming visits with a good grace. At least, this is the impression he succeeded in giving to Painlevé, who later wrote gratefully, "Pétain was not one of those commanders who were astonished at 'quibbling at a few executions' when an order given by them for an offensive could put thousands of men in their graves."[15]

Painlevé, having almost certainly seen only a few of the dossiers of men who were executed, under the delusion that he was seeing them all, was to write also that the French Army had been restored to discipline "at the price of twenty-three executions." [16] Much as it has been repeated, this figure represents only a small fraction of those actually shot, and it can be considered only the *point de vue officiel*. Without question there were many more executions than the French Army historians admitted—more, probably, than they even knew about. After all, a mutiny among the troops scarcely redounds to the credit of any commander, and when executions involved in the suppression of revolt could be covered up by listing the deaths under some category other than execution, such as "died of wounds" or "killed in an accident," there was a strong temptation to do so. Then, too, there were a vast number of charges other than out-and-out mutiny under which a soldier could quite legitimately be tried and executed. Such catch-all charges as disobedience to a superior officer, disobedience in the face of the enemy, inciting to riot and other miscellaneous military infractions all served to provide the desired result—a quick trial and execution which would serve as a deterrent to the rest of the troops.

For those not executed there were other punishments. Some mutineers were deported to various French penal colonies in Morocco, Algeria or Indochina, where they were imprisoned at hard labor. Others were sentenced to serve with disciplinary battalions such as the Zéphyrs, a unit stationed in Africa and composed of Army outcasts who were kept in discipline by methods verging on sadism and were given military tasks too dangerous and dirty even for the Foreign Legion. Some of the more fortunate offenders were lucky enough to be sentenced to serve with "punishment companies" in the most dangerous spots in the trench lines until, in the opinion of their specially trained officers, they had earned the privilege of restoration to an infantry division, which was considered much less hazardous by comparison.

In reference to this period in which he was fighting to restore the French Army to disciplinary health, Pétain has often been called "the doctor of the Army." If the analogy is as apt as it seems, it can be extended to comparing G.Q.G.'s Postal-Control section to the doctor's thermometer. Even before Pétain assumed command, Postal Control had grown to an organization of more than two hundred convalescent officers whose duty was, avowedly, censorship of the troops' mail to prevent them from sending home information which was militarily secret. But, in reality, censorship of the mail had become a relatively minor role of Postal Control. It had been discovered that this group, reading many thousands of letters a day, was ideally constituted to report on the state of morale of the Army.

Under the direction of a Lieutenant Duval, Postal Control grew greatly in size and efficiency. And, as time went on, it also became useful to open some of the mail from the interior to the troops; in particular, mail from members of Parliament to individual soldiers was greatly suspect.

The activities of Postal Control were loathed by the men and sharply criticized in the Chamber of Deputies.[17] But the information it gathered on morale, on the complaints of the troops and on the activities of pacifists were of such tremendous value that Pétain ignored all such complaints. It was a matter of agonizing necessity that he have the reports furnished by Postal Control. Pétain had begun to administer to the Army the first doses of a palliative medicine, but, to check on its efficiency, Postal Control must continue to serve as the patient's thermometer. And Postal Control showed that gradually, both through fear inspired by strict repression and through warranted concessions to the minimum requirements of the troops, the temper of the men was gradually changing for the better.

The reports from the various army group headquarters were also encouraging. In the first period of the mutinies, from April 29 until June 10, there had been ninety cases of serious mutiny reported, an average of more than two a day. But then Pétain's work began to take effect and in the period June 11 to July 1 the number had dropped to twenty, or an average of a little less than one a day. Finally, for the month of July it dropped to about one every four days.[18]

And there were other signs that discipline was returning to the Army. At the front lines, for example, there had been a time when the German Army could have sliced through the thin crust of disciplined troops holding the French trenches and taken Paris with relative ease. It had only to learn of the true state of affairs within the French Army in order to win the war. And this was the danger under which Pétain and his staff labored so furiously. It was inevitable that the Germans would learn something of the mutinies, but how much they would learn, how soon they would learn it and what they would do about it were the factors which were unknown and agonizing.

The most obvious route for information of this type was through prisoners taken in trench raids, who might under questioning blurt out what they knew. But, thanks to Pétain's skillful juggling of divisions in the front lines, the Germans took very few disaffected prisoners, and even when they did the men were sullen and silent rather than anxious to tell what they knew.[19] Ultimately, of course, by way of spies reporting to German contacts in Switzerland and inferences drawn from the bewildering numbers and types of French units holding the front lines, the Germans were able to piece together enough intelligence to indicate severe trouble within the French Army. But even then they hesitated, unable to conceive of such great good fortune.

Finally, and still only half believing what they had learned, the Germans launched a series of violent mid-July attacks on the still-disputed Chemin des Dames. But by now Pétain had succeeded in restoring the Army to at least a semblance of health, and most of the infantrymen were willing to defend the trenches even though they could not be relied upon to attack. In many cases, vigorous leadership had succeeded in bringing a division back to a very respectable fighting pitch. The 77th Infantry Division, for example, had been honeycombed with mutiny during May and June, but by mid-July it had been through the new rest camps, the worst of the troublemakers had been weeded out, and the division had been put back in the trench lines on the Chemin des Dames. On July 19 the 77th experienced a terrific German bombardment followed by an attack by four German divisions which succeeded in driving the French back a short distance. But that night, displaying magnificent vigor and *élan*, the infuriated 77th counterattacked and succeeded, amazingly, in throwing the Germans back to their original lines.[20]

It took only a few instances such as this for the German high command, which had never really been convinced of this unparalleled opportunity, to pass the whole affair off as a faulty intelligence estimate. They simply could not believe what had occurred within the French Army. "Main Headquarters," Crown Prince Rupprecht of Bavaria later apologized, "cannot be censured for taking the view that the premise for such a decision [i.e., a full-scale German attack] had not yet been realized." [21]

For the government too there was a flicker of good news. Many of the mutinies had been accompanied by shouts of "Death to the politicians!" and it was well known that the working-class districts were in a state of smoldering discontent. So it was with great apprehension that the government considered the Paris military parade which always accompanied Bastille Day, the fourteenth July, with its time-honored review of the troops by the President of the Republic. Over the years this parade had become an annual event of such tradition that to cancel it would be to admit to the populace that a disaster of the most awful proportions had taken place. Yet if it were held there was an excellent chance that the President of the Republic would be jeered at by the working populace or possibly even assaulted by the enraged troops. From all sides the government was beseeched to hold the parade on the huge grounds at Longchamp, where, at least, the person of Raymond Poincaré could be protected by a heavy screen of cavalry and the onlookers could be held at a safe distance. But, contrary to this advice, the government decided to force the issue and hold the parade in the streets of the Parisian working-class districts.

July 14, 1917, was a beautiful day. Pétain had sent only carefully selected contingents of troops into Paris for the affair, and they took their places early in the morning. Then, at 8 A.M., Raymond Poincaré, seated in an open carriage and without any escort whatsoever, reviewed the troops, after which he awarded the new *fourragères* to the units of the Foreign Legion and the 152nd Infantry Division and then led the parade.

Along the Cours de Vincennes, into the Place de la Nation, down the Avenue Diderot the troops strode. Along the route reserved seats had been set up for thousands of wounded soldiers, and behind them the sidewalks were jammed with civilian spectators. The parade tramped across the Seine at the Pont d'Austerlitz and swung down into the Place Denfert-Rochereau. The regimental bands led; the traditional marching tunes shuddered against the walls of the buildings. And behind each band, behind the regimental flags, the endless blue columns poured; the rhythmic rumble of their tread was the magnified pulse beat of a mighty nation.

The wartime French Army had never been particularly noted for its smartness on parade. But now there was something about these men, something that caught at the hearts of the spectators. As each regiment swung past, the crowds lining the streets and filling the windows broke into spontaneous cheers—"*Vive l'armée!*" and "*Vive la France!*" Flags burst forth from windows. The cheers redoubled whenever a unit marched by wearing a *fourragère*.

To the thankful Poincaré it was a scene of "indescribable enthusiasm." [22] To Georges Clemenceau it was "an unforgettable spectacle" which it was necessary to have seen "to understand the emotion . . . , the enthusiasm . . . , the love of country" that it betokened.[23]

And to Pétain, anxiously observing the parade, its success meant vindication of his efforts. The Army was a long way from being restored as a fighting instrument, but the first crisis had been passed.

Now, as the actual mutinies were on the wane, Pétain began his biggest task. Everything he had done before—the increased leave, the visits to the troops, the policy of standing on the defensive—had been essentially negative. These had been morale measures designed to quiet the Army from mutiny into obedience, however sullen. But an army which can only defend its front is doomed to defeat. Pétain knew this and realized that it was imperative that he restore his troops into a weapon which could impose its will upon the enemy.

Pétain had promised the Army that he would commit it only to "limited offensives." And now, by July, the opportunity for the first of these battles was ready-made—indeed, the opportunity was crying. The British, partly to relieve the French Army from the threat of a major German offensive, were about to launch their long-promised full-scale assault in Flanders. For Pétain there was an obligation to assist the British, as well as the perfect opportunity to demonstrate to his own troops the difference between his tactical conceptions and those of the despised Nivelle. He had to prove to his soldiers that under proper direction the French Army could be as good as or better than its German adversaries and its British allies.

So, beginning in June, Pétain funneled the French First Army into a tiny area practically on the Channel seacoast, where it was fitted in between the remnant of the Belgian Army on the north and the British mass on the south. Consisting of six divisions, several of which had experienced severe mutinies, the First Army was under the command of General Anthoine, an artillery specialist who had long been a protégé of Pétain's. Anthoine was fully aware that "an absolute success was imperiously demanded by the morale factors of the moment." To the British he wrote that his instructions from Pétain required that he undertake "the most methodical and complete preparation, as well as the duty of not knowingly launching the infantry with any chances taken on our part." [24]

The labor which Anthoine's troops expended was prodigious. All the soldiers, plus a horde of territorials brought along as laborers, lived with shovels in their hands. To prepare for an attack along a front of only a few miles, they built or reconstructed more than thirty miles of roads. They built huge ammunition dumps, set up three complete surgical hospitals, laid sixty miles of railway track and fifteen miles of water pipe.[25] Finally, more than 900 pieces of artillery were moved into the assault area.

The front which the French faced was parallel to and actually formed by the Yser Canal, running north and south. The Germans held a narrow strip of land on the French side of the canal, and it was Anthoine's intention to throw them over the canal and then to push them back as far as he could, meanwhile conforming to the British attack which was being launched on his right.

The French bombardment began with a vicious attack on the German batteries on July 15. By July 23 they had shifted to interdiction fire, preventing the Germans from reinforcing their front lines and blowing up command posts and telephone exchanges. Then, on July 27, the French trench mortars took up the attack. Unlike previous offensives, there were more than enough guns for the area to be bombarded, communications and resupply were excellent, thanks to the newly built roads, and there was no practical limit to the amount of ammunition which could be expended. "Lavish with steel, stingy with blood," was Pétain's maxim.[26]

When the assault was finally launched, on July 31, it was a phenomenal success. The German lines were only a shattered shambles of blown-down trenches and cut wire. The German artillery was virtually annihilated. The French infantry, rested and determined, sliced into this wasteland on a narrow front. Fighting was not too severe, with the result that by late afternoon they had actually captured the German third line. Then, with enemy resistance stiffening, Anthoine ordered his troops to dig in and simply hold the ground they had gained. When the French casualties were counted at the end of the day, it was found that only 180 men had been killed.[27]

The next of Pétain's clockwork limited offensives was carried out three weeks later at Verdun. He had determined to recapture the heights overlooking Verdun from the north, in particular the famous Hill 304 and its neighbor Le Mort Homme. Again huge quantities of artillery were moved up, and along a front of only fifteen miles the guns thundered for seven days and nights. A fleet of French artillery spotter planes cruised overhead and, following their instructions, gunfire was adjusted to the finest precision. Immense numbers of gas shells suffocated the German defenders.

At 4:30 A.M. on August 20, eight divisions of French infantry swept forward. By August 26 they had driven the Germans off the heights and had captured ten thousand prisoners and hundreds of artillery pieces and machine guns. The French bombardment had been overwhelming. More than a thousand Germans died when one tunnel in the Mort Homme defenses was sealed up by the accurate gunfire. And now, his objective accomplished, Pétain stopped the attack. His troops were amazed—"It has been too easy!"—and, as their trucks drove back from the victorious assault, observers marveled that men "were singing, bursting with enthusiasm, their faces radiant with hope!" [28]

Word of these limited assaults, their success, their meticulous preparation and, most important, the low casualties suffered by the attackers spread like wildfire throughout the French Army. And as it did, some of the poilu's lost confidence in himself and his leaders began slowly to return. Perhaps, he thought (but only perhaps), the pacifists and their *papillons* might be wrong. Maybe the thing could be done. Not all at once, to be sure, but perhaps the Germans *could* be beaten.

And now it was up to the politicians.

15

L'ANTIPATRIOTISME

B Y LATE SUMMER OF 1917 Pétain had succeeded in proving to his
troops and to his government that he could defend the French
front and even, perhaps, recover a bit of ground here and there by
means of one of his clockwork offensives. But he had come to realize
that this was not enough. Postal Control and the G.Q.G. Second
Bureau were constantly warning him of the dangers of a defeatism
now rampant in the interior of France. Urgent reports told Pétain of
the large quantities of defeatist newspapers and pamphlets which
were finding their way into the Zone of the Armies, and of the pacifist meetings, disguised as union meetings, which the troops were
attending when home on leave. Pétain was advised that the French
troops were being told how in Russia the command of the armies
was being taken over by Soldiers' Councils which had abolished the
death penalty and would not take part in any offensive unless they
had passed on it.

So Pétain now knew himself to be a general who was forced to
fight battles in both his front and his rear—and, though he could
fortify his front against the Germans, his rear was an unprotected
line which he could not defend with troops, but only with appeals, demands and, quite possibly, prayers.

The crux of this whole situation was the immense, but perfectly
natural, variance in the point of view between the government and
Pétain. The government, headed by Premier Ribot, dominated by
Minister of War Painlevé, and with the negligent Louis Malvy still
firmly seated as Minister of the Interior, was conducting a desper-

246

ate fight for its existence. Violently criticized for lack of vigor by such eminent figures as Clemenceau, and constantly under attack by left-wing strikes and the skillfully masked defeatism of such newspapers as the *Bonnet rouge*, the Ribot government was tottering and almost totally exhausted. The politicians in power drifted with the tides which were slowly tearing both the government and the French nation apart. They did not act, they only reacted—and even then slowly and sluggishly. And when it came to the Army mutinies, they were inclined to consider them to be solely a problem for the Army and the natural result of the failure of the Nivelle offensive, which, they comforted themselves, they had foreseen and attempted to prevent.

Equally naturally, Pétain could not be expected to see the situation in quite this light. On May 29, shortly after he had taken over the command of the Army and during the most catastrophic phases of the revolt, he had written a lengthy secret report to the government stating: "The sickness exists, it is an undeniable fact. It can have the most disastrous consequences for the Army and the nation. It is important to define the causes and then search for the remedies." He went on to outline quickly the faults in Nivelle's strategy and then turned to criticism of the government. In short, sharp sentences he found fault with the censorship of the press, which had been allowed to print extensive accounts of the mutinies in the Russian Army; he marveled that the government permitted strikes by the left-wing unions that dominated the munitions industries; he attacked the pacifist newspapers, which were permitted to be published in Paris and which had been smuggled into the hands of the troops at the front; and he condemned members of Parliament who visited the Zone of the Armies, interviewed the troops and "provoked criticism and recrimination against the high command." So, Pétain concluded, the mutinies really had two causes, "those which arose from the conditions of life at the front and those which were due to outside influences." Regarding the first, he advised that he would deal with them "to a certain point." But the others, the "outside influences," would have to be the responsibility of the government.[1]

Now, one of the most critical of these outside influences, and one in which the government could hardly avoid its responsibility, was the forthcoming Socialist International Congress to be held in Stockholm at the end of June. The occurrences at the Socialist conferences at Zimmerwald and Kienthal in 1915 and 1916 had proved that French representatives of the Marxist-oriented parties could not, with safety, be allowed to attend these conferences. Three years of war had brought the militant left to a point where it exercised immense power over the trade unions and even the mobilized workers serving in the Army. And now the Socialists had applied for passports to attend the international convention in Stockholm, where they would meet with German Socialists and would, inevitably, issue a statement condemning the war—as they had at Zimmerwald in 1915 and Kienthal in 1916.

A tricky either-or question thus faced the Cabinet. Either the Socialists got their passports and attended the meeting, where their attack on the continuation of the war would seriously demoralize the troops and where, out of reach of censorship, they would most certainly reveal the facts of the mutinies to the world (and the Socialists knew a great deal about them), or the passports were refused, the French Socialists could not attend the meeting, and the Ribot government would be faced with a bloc of violently hostile deputies, more labor strikes, and the implication that the government's position regarding the continuance of the war was so weak that it could not withstand the Socialist criticism.

It is indicative of the weak and vacillating character of the Ribot government that it deliberated too long in this matter. A final decision was prolonged, discussed and rediscussed in newspapers, in the Chamber of Deputies and in the Senate (where Clemenceau, at least, mustered enough patriotic fervor among the senators to demand that the Cabinet refuse the passports). The matter was only finally decided at a Committee of War meeting on May 31, attended by Pétain. Here, among the undecided members of the government, the question was put to the determined general, "If there is a Socialist International Congress at Stockholm and if the French delegates meet the Germans and discuss peace proposals, can you keep the Army in hand?" "No," was Pétain's monosyllabic reply. The Cabinet members stirred in their seats and looked at one another. Another point: "If the French delegates are not allowed to attend, then the Socialist congress may not be held and the Russian government may leave the war, which means that seventy-five German divisions will be released to attack us on the western front." "That danger," Pétain answered firmly, "is considerably less serious than the demoralization of our armies." There was an awed silence. Finally Painlevé spoke. "Then it is impossible to give the passports," he said.[2]

So, under Pétain's goad, the Socialists' passports were denied and it was left for the hapless government leaders to prepare themselves as best they might for the forthcoming "secret committee" session of the Chamber of Deputies.

The meetings of Parliament in what was known as "secret committee" were one of the strangest aspects of the wartime French political scene. Originally, the secret-committee sessions had developed as a means to allow the members of Parliament to ask the government of the hour various questions which bore on secret military matters and which, obviously, could not be answered in open session. At first they were single sessions lasting only one day, sometimes only a few hours, to allow a confidential military detail to be explained. But later, as the Union Sacrée gradually crumbled, the secret-committee sessions became longer and more vitriolic, with the members' inquiries taking less the form of questions and more the aspect of attacks on the government.

Even now it is still not possible to state with exactitude precisely what occurred at each of the secret-committee sessions. The members of Parliament were sworn to secrecy, forbidden even to take notes during the sessions, with the result that the only verbatim account of these meetings was the customary stenographic record which was duly transcribed and then immediately placed in the safekeeping of the government. And there seems to be substantial evidence that each of the various governments availed itself of the opportunity to alter or amend these minutes in a manner best to suit its own interests. (In response to a question as to whether the official minutes were ever altered in any way, Premier Aristide Briand once conceded with an airy wave of his hand that there were *quelques petites retouches*.)[3]

The result of these "little touch-ups" is that the subsequently published accounts of the secret committees must be viewed as what they are: not so much an account of what was actually said as a report of what each government *wished* had been said—for, indeed, the successive governments grew to dread these secret committees.

The Ribot government was no exception in this regard. Prior to its coming to power there had been seven sessions of the Chamber in secret committee and, increasingly, they had become a harrowing ordeal for the government of the day. Without question, if left to its own devices the Ribot government would never have agreed to a secret committee in the spring of 1917. It was only because of tremendous pressure from the deputies to question the government on the failure of the Nivelle offensive that Ribot and Painlevé ultimately acquiesced and scheduled the eighth secret committee for June 29. By this time, they hoped, the Nivelle failure had become a dying issue, and they counted upon being well enough prepared on the subject to fend off most of the anticipated criticism. But, apparently, Ribot and Painlevé miscalculated. They seem not to have given enough consideration to the fact that they would have to face an infuriated and influential Socialist faction which was still enraged over the government's refusal to give them the Stockholm passports, and they surely did not anticipate that the various members of Parliament would know as much as they did about the Army mutinies and that this would become the prime topic of debate.

The secret-committee session opened on June 29, 1917, and lasted for seven anxious days. In turn, deputies of all political hues mounted the tribune of the Chamber and charged the government with either incompetence, indifference or impotence. Diagne, a Negro deputy who regarded himself as the defender of all France's black colonials, took the lead with an attack on the manner in which the Senegalese battalions had been used in the Nivelle offensive. Then another deputy, Jean Hennessy, demanded that the officers responsible for the Nivelle affair be placed before a *conseil de guerre* just as would any common soldier who was derelict in his duty. But the most jarring criticism of all came not from the left wing but from the right. A Catholic soldier-deputy, Lieutenant Jean Ybarnegary, strode to the tribune to deliver a scathing account of ineptitude in the preparation of the Nivelle offensive.

"At six A.M. the battle started," the young soldier said, "and at seven A.M. it had been lost." Ybarnegary, who had taken part in the April 16 assault and who claimed to have foreseen its failure, demanded that Nivelle, whom he demolished as an officer of "petty spirit and immense pride," and three of his immediate subordinates "ought to be broken without distinction. All four," he said, "because all four have lost the confidence of the Army! . . . The penalties must be rigorous! . . . They must be conclusive! . . . They must be public!"[4]

Ybarnegary's furious speech succeeded in raising the temper of the Chamber to match his own. Following him, deputy after deputy rose to denounce the government, criticize the Army's medical services, attack the Postal Control which read their letters to their constituents in the ranks, and blast the criminal incompetence which they claimed to have witnessed prior to the April 16 attack. The multiplicity and violence of the attacks left the government grasping about for feeble defenses. Painlevé could only reply that the government too had foreseen the failure of the offensive and that it had attempted to dissuade Nivelle—a response which sounded pitifully weak in the face of these *ex post facto* onslaughts. As for punishing Nivelle and the other responsible commanders, Painlevé announced that a military commission of inquiry had already been convened and was looking into the affair to see if there were any grounds on which Nivelle could be tried—a procedure which was immediately scorned by the Socialists as a mere whitewash.

But as the days stretched on and the Chamber gave no sign of adjourning its secret-committee sessions, the subject of the deputies' attacks veered somewhat. The abortive April 16 offensive was put in the shadow by an announcement from the far left by a thirty-five-year-old Socialist deputy and attorney who had specialized in minor labor litigation, and who would later become infamous as the Fascist traitor who was Premier of defeated France in World War II. His name was Pierre Laval and he was well known in the Chamber, if for no other reason than as one of the two deputies who had been listed on the Sûreté Générale's Carnet B for immediate arrest at the outbreak of the war. Short, swarthy, wearing his habitual white bow tie and carrying in his hand a sheaf of papers, Laval spoke to a Parliament now hushed and attentive; his subject was one which the government had dreaded—mutiny.

"Messieurs," he began solemnly, "we must look at the situation for what it is. In the rear, as well as at the front, the idea has become accepted that 'we shall *not* get them' [the Germans] by military means. We are not here to lie to ourselves," he asserted, "nor are we here to create brilliant poems on the courage of France. It is necessary to state exactly what is going on—that there is, in France, a weariness of war and a pressure for peace."

Spontaneously the Chamber broke into applause, interrupted only by violent outbursts from a handful of astounded deputies of the

center and the right who demanded to know what all this was leading to. Amid the clamor Laval calmly extracted from his papers a
letter sent to him by a soldier at the front, from which after allowing the outcries to die down, he began to read: " 'An army corps has
refused to take its place in the trenches. Neither the harangues and
pleas of a colonel nor those of General Lebrun, commandant of the
Third Corps, have been able to persuade the troops to obey any order. . . . They speak of marching on Paris. . . . The Army is under
the guard of the machine-gunners.' " This last statement was read to
a Chamber now completely silent. And then Laval asked a rhetori-
cal question which ended as a slashing rebuke to the Ribot government: How to keep France in the war amid the revolt of her armies?
"The way to give hope to the troops and confidence to the workers,
whether you like it or not, is Stockholm. Stockholm is the star of
the north!"

With this, the government's house of cards caved in. One deputy
read a letter from an officer of the Tenth Army which reported
that the army commander had given the order to shoot "*sans delai*"
a number of men from the 66th and 77th infantry regiments for
"murmuring" that they had not had leave for a long time. Another
deputy claimed that most of the revolts had been started by *agents
provocateurs* in the employ of G.Q.G. itself. Even the name of
General Émile Taufflieb, the general who had put down the rebellion in the XXXVIIth Army Corps, was brought up. Deputy Paul-
Meunier claimed that when the *conseil de guerre* of the 62nd Division contented itself with giving prison sentences to seven mutineers
and acquitting four others Taufflieb threatened the senior officer of
the *conseil de guerre* with the loss of his regimental command, and
that the prosecuting officer was told, "You had before you eleven
soldiers who should have been condemned to death, and none of
them was condemned! What is more, four were acquitted. You are
going to answer to me for this!" [5]

Finally this castigation of the government and the generals wore
itself out and the desperate Ribot succeeded, in combination with
various deputies of the center and the right, in bringing the secret
committee to a close on July 6. It did the government little good
to have Painlevé assure the Chamber that the future military policy
would be one which would "have done with these bold plans, the
grandiose conception of which but thinly cloaks emptiness and lack of

preparation . . . [we] shall not demand the impossible from the human body . . . We must fight and whoever advises us now to lay down our arms is an accomplice of the enemy." [6]

So now, instead of unifying Parliament and strengthening the government to incisive action, the Secret Committee of June 29 had only brought to the forefront a condition which had begun to exist many months before. It had proved conclusively that there was within France a coalition of the left which was rapidly growing in strength, was defeatist and pacifist by nature, was historically anti-military, and, if returned to power, would almost certainly negotiate a speedy peace. Yet it was hardly necessary to have attended the secret-committee session to have learned all this. Even the unintelligent observer could see the increasing force behind the pacifist wave —in the labor movement, for example. The *bourses du travail*, the powerful hiring halls for workers located in various industrial centers, which were dominated by the Socialist-oriented Confédération Générale du Travail (C.G.T.), were increasingly under the influence of the ultra-left-wing Socialist group, with the result that the factory workers were gradually falling under the control of pacifist leadership. From the pages of manifestos the workers were implored to put themselves "at the side of the Russian and German comrades for an international protest against this war of conquest." [7] Wave after wave of strikes rippled through the munitions industry. Even the seamstresses in the Parisian dressmaking establishments erupted in vociferous unrest.

From the prefects of the big manufacturing cities the government received desperate appeals for Senegalese troops and cavalry to put down the swelling strikes. But the distraught politicians "refused to break with the workers," [8] and, anyhow, disciplined troops who could be depended to fire upon strikers were scarce indeed. Instead, the government tried to make do with stopgap negotiating teams[9] or, sometimes, simply let the strikes run their course.

And, too, the various pacifist newspapers and defeatist pamphlets were still being published with little hindrance, except for occasional censorship of their more violent attacks. A swelling flood of pacifist literature was descending on the troops in the Zone of the Armies, from such organizations as the Committee for the Resumption of International Relations, the Syndicalist Defense Committee, the huge Metalworkers' Federation and the Teachers' Union.[10] It

was noticed that the authors were generally persons whose names
had long been known to the Minister of the Interior as those listed
on the Carnet B of three years before.

Amid all this defeatist propagandizing of the spring and summer
of 1917, the office of Minister of the Interior Louis Malvy remained
conspicuously aloof. Malvy's toleration reached surprising limits.
For example, the pacifist newspaper "The Beehive," edited by the
anarchist Sebastien Faure, had long been a source of concern to the
Army. Earlier in the year Nivelle had specifically requested that it
be throttled. So it was surprising indeed that when Faure was arrested for sexual indecencies with little girls in a Paris park, Malvy's
police quashed the charge and allowed this perfect opportunity to
slip past.[11] And when one of his prefects requested permission to shut
down the *bourse du travail* in Lyons, which was a hotbed of sedition
as well as being suspected of harboring a clandestine printing press,
Malvy simply wrote one word across the face of the report—
"*Non.*" [12]

But the most amazing example of Malvy's willful negligence revolved around Miguel Almereyda's *Bonnet rouge*. Malvy had continued his subsidization of the *Bonnet rouge* until, by March of 1916,
the newspaper's pacifist campaign had become so evident that other
French journals had begun publicly to speculate on it. Under these
circumstances, the *Bonnet rouge* became too hot to permit Malvy to
keep up his secret subventions.

It required only casual observation to discern the *Bonnet rouge*
technique of treason. Under the guise of social protest and realism,
Almereyda's newspaper cleverly managed to harp on the strength
of Germany, the elusive nature of French victory, and the alleged
half-efforts of the British. It was defeatism of the most adroit nature. The frustrated censors could not really take issue with an article which pleaded for an increased French effort because the Germans were "better organized" and "better armed" and "understood
war better." [13] Nor could the censors cut out an editorial dedicated to
the mothers of French youth newly called to the colors; the mothers,
the *Bonnet rouge* sympathized on April 17, 1917, had every justification for weeping, because they would probably never see their
sons again. And when the British government condemned to death
Sir Roger Casement, who was discovered to be a German agent,

the *Bonnet rouge* of July 29, 1916, flew to his defense—"French voices join in imploring clemency."

But even though the *Bonnet rouge* was difficult to censor, and even though it staunchly defended Joseph Caillaux ("A victim of unspeakable calumnies"),[14] the Minister of the Interior had had no choice but to stop his subsidy to the paper. For most newspapers this would have been a serious blow; Malvy's payments had ranged between two and eight thousand francs per month[15]—enough to finance the entire operation of many journals. Fortunately for the *Bonnet rouge*, the newspaper had acquired another source of income. Increasingly Almereyda's behind-the-scenes political activities on top of his dissipation and drug addiction had caused him to leave the administration of the *Bonnet rouge* to a group of subordinates whose activities could not well have withstood the careful study of the counterintelligence agencies. Among them were a covey of shady left-wing journalists named Marion, Joucla and Landau. There was still another, a man named Goldschild whose alias was alternately Goldsky and "General N"—the pseudonym under which he wrote *Bonnet rouge* articles attacking the French military conduct of the war. Actually, Goldsky was a French soldier who had been mobilized as a stretcher-bearer but who, at Almereyda's request, had been transferred from the front to an office job at the Ministry of the Interior. Goldsky worked there part of the morning and then finished the day at the *Bonnet rouge*.

But the principal among the *Bonnet rouge* staff was the "business manager," a strange character named Émile Joseph Duval. Short, fifty years old, mustached and with strands of dark hair combed over a balding scalp, Duval had appeared on the scene soon after Malvy's subsidy ceased and had immediately assumed a dominant role in the editorship of the paper. How he became connected with it is unclear and can only be speculated upon. But one thing is certain: by any standards Duval was an improbable creature. He was a man who displayed an immense and authentic culture but whose previous job had been as a miserably paid clerk in the Paris poor-relief administration. He was a man who brought millions of francs into the *Bonnet rouge* but who lived a pauper's existence in a shabby little flat while his wife, a total illiterate, worked as a linen room attendant in a Paris hospital and his father remained in a charity poorhouse.

For all his strangeness, Duval had several talents to contribute to the *Bonnet rouge*. One was his ability with a pen. Although he seems to have had no previous journalistic experience, Duval emerged full-blown as the author of a series of sardonic politico-military articles which the paper ran under the pseudonym "M. Badin" (The Joker). They were the work of a genius and they lifted the *Bonnet rouge* to a literary standard it had never enjoyed under Almereyda's sole editorship. Typical was a series of articles discussing French military tactics and entitled "By Fits and Starts." In one of these, which did not get past the censor, "M. Badin" is sitting in a café. The proprietor is sweeping the floor and, with his broom, is illustrating to Badin how the French armies' new tactics will drive the enemy, symbolized by the dust, before them. "Suddenly," Duval wrote, "a gust of wind blew the dust back on the freshly swept area and at the same time the proprietor's broomhead fell off. . . . I could not help laughing at this futility." [16]

The other contribution which Duval brought to the *Bonnet rouge* was money—floods of it. Enough to satisfy all of Almereyda's now numerous vices and, moreover, to enable this little newspaper of the left to achieve an influence vastly in excess of its size. Copies of the *Bonnet rouge* were given free to troops on leave or returning to the front; the newspaper's once shabby offices were refurnished; articles by prominent left-wing writers were purchased; and a satellite weekly newspaper called *La Tranchée républicaine* was established under Goldsky's editorship to further increase the influence of the *Bonnet rouge*. *La Tranchée républicaine* was edited for soldier readership and sang the same song as its parent—attacks on the "*profiteurs de la guerre*" and constant comment on the "horrors of the war" which could not be ended because "it appears that we cannot make peace, as we would wish." [17]

With Malvy's subvention cut off, how did this journal, which had almost no advertisers, suddenly obtain the money to support its vastly expanded activities? The answer was Duval. Although this shabby little man had never managed to earn more than a pittance in his previous careers, he had, in the prewar years, been a clerk for a syndicate of French and German investors. And the principal member of this syndicate had been a German named Marx—the same Marx who was now the Germans' spy paymaster in Switzerland. Thus it was that the impoverished Duval became connected with

the *Bonnet rouge* and brought to it the money necessary to increase
the newspaper's activities.

There was only one problem to securing these German replacements for Malvy's subsidies. To get the money from Marx, Duval
had to travel to Switzerland; and the offices of the French Sûreté
Générale adjoining the Swiss border had come to take great interest
in Frenchmen who made repeated trips to Switzerland. Thus, it was
that on May 15, 1917, while returning from his thirteenth wartime
trip to Switzerland, Duval was detained and searched at the French
border control point in Bellegarde. On his person the security
police found a check for 150,837 francs for which he had only a glib
but transparent explanation—something to the effect that the check
was part of the liquidation of a prewar speculation in a Mediterranean
resort area. And why, Duval was asked, had the check come from a
German Herr Marx? Quite simple, was the reply—Herr Marx had
been one of the principals in the resort venture.

Finally the police released Duval but pointedly retained the check,
which, they advised him, would be sent to Paris for study by the
Ministry of the Interior. This posed no problem for Duval; a few
days later he called at the office of the Minister and the check was,
in the greatest confidence, returned to him by a M. Leymarie, the
chef de cabinet of Malvy himself.

It was circumstances such as these with which Pétain had to deal
in his attempt to shore up the rear of his Army and prevent it from
being eroded by pacifism from the interior. He had restored the
troops to a degree of dicipline and confidence, but a measure of
their frame of mind can be seen in the renewed popularity of a
famous cartoon by Forain which had originally appeared some time
before. It showed two worried poilus crouching in a trench with a
furious battle raging around them. One of the soldiers is saying to
the other, "I hope they can last." "Who?" asks the other. "The
civilians," is the answer.

It must be understood that the only way in which direct action
could be taken against pacifist newspapers and defeatist propagandists
was through Malvy's Ministry of the Interior. Early in the war the
Army's Second Bureau had established a counterintelligence branch
in Paris, but Malvy's violent protests had resulted in its being shut
down. So Pétain was forced to deal with Malvy, and on July 9
he wrote the Ministry of the Interior:

Recent events have thrown light on the reciprocal effects which the front has on the Zone of the Interior and the interior has on the front, due to the constant going and coming of men on leave and the frequency of correspondence. . . .

I ask your good offices in regularly communicating the following to me:

1. The intelligence data which you furnish your security services on the morale of the interior, the general frame of mind, the impressions relative to matters of the front and of the war, the disparaging reports which are circulating.

2. The intelligence data on the same subjects which you send to your prefects or which you require them to send to you.

3. The circulation figures of both Parisian and local newspapers.

4. The importance of the circulation, by region, of the newspapers which are not strictly local.

In possession of this data, I can apply at the front . . . the appropriate measures.

Only the establishment of such precise and regular co-operation can allow us to procure the information necessary to take effective action against the recurrence of incidents such as have taken place in the Army.[18]

This message was, without doubt, an oblique call by Pétain for action against the defeatists. He probably thought that if only he could get Malvy to report to him on the details of pacifism within France, Malvy would be forced to do something about it. But in this Pétain was to be disappointed.

On July 12 Malvy replied, co-operatively enough, although conspicuously denying that much of anything was wrong with the state of morale in the interior:

In response to your communication of July 9, I have the honor of informing you that I believe, like you, that it is indispensable that your services and my administration keep in close contact. . . .

Recent military events, notably the incidents which have taken place in the armies, are perhaps having an exaggerated effect on the home front because of the written and oral accounts of the fighting men.

I am agreeable, insofar as I am concerned, to send you all the information you can use. . . .[19]

But the reports which Malvy furnished were few, much delayed in transmission, and skimpy. It became obvious to Pétain that Malvy did not desire to allow the Grand Quartier Général to encroach on his prerogatives in any manner, and that he did not intend to provide any information which would leave himself open for attacks from G.Q.G. on the grounds that his ministry was not energetic enough.

This left Pétain with no place to turn but back to Painlevé, who, as Minister of War, had an obligation to assist the Commander in Chief in these matters. He sent a series of appeals to Painlevé. After "more than six weeks," he complained, G.Q.G. had received not a single report of workers' meetings and not a single copy of a pacifist leaflet, nor had any information on the pacifists been furnished to his liaison officer. "The last monthly report which I received bore a date in April. . . . I ask that you insist that the Minister of the Interior establish communications concerning the pacifist propaganda between the Sûreté Générale and my intelligence section . . ."[20]

On July 7 the strange affair of Duval and the German check which had been returned to him by Malvy's assistant had been revealed by a prominent rightist member of Parliament, Maurice Barrès, during a session of the Chamber of Deputies. Barrès had popped to his feet while Premier Ribot held the floor for a speech. Would the Premier permit a brief question? *Certainement.* In that case, Barrès had demanded, what did the government intend to do about "the swine of the *Bonnet rouge*"?[21] The stunned Premier had trouble answering this unexpected question. He stammered a reply to the effect that the whole matter was under investigation and then, inadvertently, revealed the matter of Duval's check. Now the secret was out, and from various prominent political figures there rose a storm of outraged attacks. The government had no choice but flatly to order Malvy to suppress the *Bonnet rouge*, which was done on July 13.

Still Pétain's appeals were fruitless until, on July 22, Georges Clemenceau arose in the Senate to deliver one of the most famous addresses of his career, a speech entitled "Antipatriotism." It was a monumental address, of unusual length for the normally abrupt Clemenceau, and it laid bare the bones of the *Bonnet rouge* affair as well as a series of other damning scandals which revolved around the office of the Minister of the Interior. Clearly, Clemenceau had got his information from an inside source in Malvy's offices although in this he was not alone.

Clemenceau was now an old man, and his stooped frame, sleepy eyes and heavy paunch did nothing to belie his seventy-five years. Although he was still a substantial power in the Senate, he was sincerely detested by the parties of the left, who hated his uncompromising militarism and remembered the conservatism of his government of many years before. Even among those whose attitude toward the war paralleled Clemenceau's, he probably had two enemies for every friend. But when it came to patriotism and energetic prosecution of the war, the politicians knew that the Tiger was unassailable. His articles in L'Homme enchâiné had proved that. For example, on June 29 he had attacked the government's vacillation ("There are no ministers. There is no Premier. There is no government!"). And recently Clemenceau had begun to make Louis Malvy the target of his editorial fury: on July 12 an article entitled "Dossiers Opened—Dossiers Closed"; another attack on July 15; and another on the seventeenth which concluded, "At the front, our soldiers are fighting a battle against the Boches. At the rear we are also in combat . . . against their agents." Thus, it was to an expectant Senate, with Louis Malvy present, that Clemenceau spoke on July 22.

Amid a rash of the usual comments from the floor, which he silenced with a gruff "I ask that you let me speak without interruption," Clemenceau went to the heart of the matter.

How could anyone comprehend the actions of M. Malvy? And, more specifically, how could one explain his peculiar intimacy with Miguel Almereyda and the *Bonnet rouge?* It all went back to the Carnet B of many years before, Clemenceau insisted, and he sketched for his listeners how Malvy had come to him at the time of mobilization and asked him whether he should carry out the arrests. He recounted how he had advised Malvy to make the arrests and then told how Malvy had subsequently consulted with Almereyda. The story brought cynical laughter from the Senate when Clemenceau described how Almereyda, who was himself on Carnet B, counseled Malvy in all sincerity that it was neither necessary nor desirable to make the arrests. And more laughter when Clemenceau told how, following the beginning of the war, Almereyda rushed to Malvy's office and asked the Minister of the Interior, "Where can I enlist?" Clemenceau threw his arms wide and said, "He could have asked any policeman."

Then he grew more serious. Concerning Carnet B, he did not criticize Malvy so much for not arresting the persons listed on it at the time of mobilization as he did for not keeping them under close watch. And when the "parole" which their "ambassador," Almereyda, had agreed to was violated, they should have been arrested immediately.

Next Clemenceau attacked the government for its fumbling attempts to pacify the pacifists. In a few sentences he penetrated to the core of the problem that faced Ribot and his government—they lacked courage. "And what is courage?" he answered his own question: "It is in *not* consulting this one or that one, this particular interest or that particular group, nor listening to the voices of such-and-such or so-and-so—it is in doing what one thinks right!" Not that this was an easy path, Clemenceau advised the government. "One will suffer, one will be hated, detested, scorned"—but at the end one would be able to say, "I have done my best for my country."

The Tiger then turned to what was wrong with France now. He condemned the strikes, the defeatist propaganda and the fact that Malvy's Sûreté Général was in conflict with G.Q.G. Again and again he returned to Malvy's role in these sordid affairs. He told how Malvy disregarded the warnings of his prefects of police, and how there appeared to be special laws for left-wing politicians and unionists which saved them from arrest when they agitated against the war; and he read dossiers and reports which showed that Malvy had prevented the arrest of various friends of Caillaux as well as that of foreigners of suspicious background.[22]

At this point Malvy himself, wild with rage, leaped to his feet and interrupted Clemenceau, shouting, "You reproach me for not having brought you enough heads?"

"No, no," Clemenceau cried down from the tribune, "I reproach you for having betrayed your country!"—a charge of such violence that it was later altered in the official minutes of the session to the less damning "having failed in your duty." [23]

With this exchange, Clemenceau's address drew to a close. He had done what he had set out to do. Louis Malvy was totally discredited and hopelessly compromised. Even the most loyal of governments could not possibly defend Malvy now.

In the weeks which followed, almost every newspaper and virtually every patriot joined in Malvy's denunciation, for to defend him would have been publicly to ally oneself with treason. Some of the attacks on him were untrue. For example, the royalist editor of *Action française*, Léon Daudet, wrote a letter to Raymond Poincaré formally charging, "M. Malvy has kept Germany fully informed of all our military and diplomatic plans." [24] This was ridiculous; Malvy was most certainly not a paid traitor. Nor was he stupid. He was simply a not too energetic man who habitually took the easy road of conciliation, who felt himself hopelessly compromised by past favors done him, and who was guilty of failing to realize that France was in a battle for her existence—one which she was losing. But after the Clemenceau exposé and the onslaught of attacks from the center and the right, the preoccupation of the Ribot government came to be how it could most gracefully dump Malvy.

There could be, of course, no question as to what had to be done with the *Bonnet rouge*. It was permanently suppressed and Miguel Almereyda was flung into prison. Perhaps, but only perhaps, this display of swift action might have been enough to save the Ribot government had it not been that, on the morning of August 14, Almereyda was found dead in his solitary cell at Fresnes prison. His body lay partly on the floor and partly against his cot, and around his throat there was a thin black line to show that he had been strangled.

Exactly how he died will never be known. The Ribot government claimed that Almereyda, a known dope addict who had been deprived of his morphine, had committed suicide by hanging himself from the end of his bed, using his shoelaces as a noose. But the right-wing press, perhaps correctly, scoffed at this explanation and declared that Almereyda had been murdered by members of the Ministry of the Interior who feared the revelations he might make.

A third explanation of Almereyda's death, advanced years later by an intimate of the dead man, splits the middle of the above. It was claimed that Almereyda had had a syringe of dope concealed in a pot of jam smuggled into his cell every day, and that one day the prison authorities had seized the jam pot and, eagerly anticipating his suicide over his deprivation, deliberately withheld the morphine from him.[25] But whether Almereyda died by murder or suicide, the treason scandals did not die with him—although his death hastened Malvy's exit from the scene. In mid-August Malvy went on "vacation," and finally on August 31 he resigned. Only a few days later the Ribot Ministry tottered to a fall and was replaced with one headed by Paul Painlevé.

Without question, this honest little man deserved better than he got. Unfortunately, he was committed to attempting to shore up the Union Sacrée even though not a single member of the left-wing parties could be found to accept the two Cabinet portfolios offered them, a circumstance which gave Painlevé every excuse for dismissing the left from any consideration. But the floodgates had been opened by Almereyda's death and even Painlevé was drowning in a torrent of exposed treason.

One scandal brought onto the scene the suave visage of Bolo Pasha, the international confidence man. It developed that a prominent senator, Charles Humbert, who was widely regarded as an archpatriot and a representative of the French munitions combines, had obtained control of Le Journal, France's third largest daily newspaper, with a circulation of 1,100,000. The sequence of events was complex indeed, but revolved around the fact that in 1915 the Germans, through the ubiquitous Marx in Berne, had advanced a large sum of money to Pierre Lenoir, a corrupt young Frenchman of prominent family. Lenoir had used this money to purchase the superpatriotic Le Journal, which he agreed to convert to a pacifist newspaper on signal from the Germans—probably at the time of the German assault on Verdun. The scheme went awry when Senator Humbert got wind of it and successfully blackmailed Lenoir into giving him a substantial interest in Le Journal on threat of exposure. But the association of Lenoir and Humbert bred constant friction, and so Lenoir, realizing that Senator Humbert was now himself open to blackmail, insisted that Humbert buy out his (Lenoir's) interest in the paper. Re-enter now Bolo Pasha, whom Humbert brought in to find enough money to finance his forced purchase. Bolo Pasha had an excellent idea where such funds could be obtained. Previously he had swindled the Germans, but now he made his peace with them. In the spring of 1916 the dapper confidence man took ship for the United States, where, through the German ambassador, a total of $1,638,000 was loaned to him by German-controlled banks on an interest-free basis, with the understanding that he would give them *Le Journal* stock as collateral.

When the affair was finally exposed in the fall of 1917, it became obvious that Humbert, as a leading member of Parliament and publisher of one of France's most influential newspapers, had hopelessly compromised himself with German money. It was apparent that the Germans could easily have blackmailed Humbert to follow any course they chose; indeed, since they held the stock certificates, the Germans actually owned *Le Journal*.

After an affair of such magnitude, various subsidiary treason cases—such as that involving a long-suspect deputy named Turmel, who was arrested after 25,000 Swiss francs for which he could give no explanation had been found in his locker at the Chamber—fell upon an Army and a nation satiated with scandal. However, amid all these diverse revelations, many of which were made by Clemenceau in *L'Homme enchaîné*, there was one common thread: almost without exception those charged with treason were friends of Joseph Caillaux. And almost without exception there was good reason to suppose that Caillaux knew of their activities or, if not, certainly *should* have known of their activities. All of them, including Almereyda and Bolo Pasha, had visited Caillaux at his country residence. All of them had received warm personal letters from Caillaux thanking them for their support and the pleasant conferences he had held with them. And it was established that Caillaux was the object of special concern and calculated inattention on the part of the German press, which on June 6, 1917, received this instruction from the German censorship office: "For political reasons it is urgently requested that nothing be written about the former French Prime Minister Caillaux and his name not be mentioned under any circumstances." [26]

We have now reached late October of 1917, and, with these exposés of treason within France extending even to the most prominent members of Parliament, it is small wonder that France's morale had sagged to a new low. Letters from the troops said, "What is the use of all our hardships and dangers if we are to be stabbed in the back?" [27] If the leaders themselves could not be trusted, then who was there to believe in? Increasingly, there could no longer be a "center position" in French political thought. It was as if a magnet had been inserted beneath a pan of iron filings, drawing them to one pole or another. At one extreme was Joseph Caillaux, the white hope of the pacifists, the man recognized as the single political personality who could negotiate a peace with the Germans. At the other was Georges Clemenceau, who became recognized as the man who would never negotiate, never surrender, and who would drive France either to unconditional victory or to total collapse. For the vacillating Painlevé, feverishly attempting to mollify one side or the other, there was no longer a place.

For Pétain, who had restored the Army to discipline and a certain degree of battlefield efficiency, but who knew that he could not mount a major offensive until the Americans arrived in force, there was left only dire apprehension. The Russians had completely collapsed and the Germans were furiously transporting division after division back to reinforce the western front. Then on October 24 the Germans and the Austrians fell upon the Italian Army in the mountainous region near Caporetto and opened a gap twenty-five miles wide. The Italian losses were 37,000 killed, 91,000 wounded and a phenomenal 275,000 taken prisoner. It appeared as if the Italian troops had given up, and, in frenzied haste, French and British divisions had to be sent to try to restore the front.

Under these conditions, what good had been the restoration of the discipline within the Army, and how long could it last? Would *les civiles* make peace from within or would the Army simply crack up as the result of the revelations of treason?

Nobody, Pétain included, knew the answer.

16

THE LAST MUTINY

WELL WITHIN THE CENTER of France, beginning about two hundred miles due south of Paris and approximately one hundred and fifty miles behind the 1917 fighting front, the ground begins to rise into a region of low mountains. Here, in the predominantly rural department of the Creuse, there are only a few large cities and generally the land is too cut up by hills, ravines and forests to support anything very much larger than scattered farming villages.

But occasionally the hilly land levels out into broad plateaus. It was on one of these isolated plateaus, in the town of La Courtine, that there was fought still another pitched battle to suppress Army mutiny in France. Ironically, it was a battle not among French troops but principally among the soldiers of a supposedly allied nation, Russia.

Prior to the turn of the century La Courtine, which is situated not far from the main road between Lyons and Bordeaux, had been nothing more than a little farming center; but after 1903, when it was selected as the site of a big French Army training camp capable of housing fifteen thousand men, its character began to change. In the manner of army towns everywhere, it grew up to a sizable little city full of cafés, restaurants, stores and hotels. And even after the Army mobilized in 1914 and the troops marched away to the front, many uses were found for the camp of La Courtine. Its enormous size—fifteen thousand acres—made it possible to house an immense variety of activities. In one part of the camp there was a barbed-wire stockade for captured German officers, in another a school for

266

machine-gunners, and in other sections quarters for recuperating wounded, for noncommissioned officers attending training courses, etc.

But in early June there came urgent orders from Paris: La Courtine was to be evacuated of all French troops and German prisoners and made ready to receive the two Russian brigades which were being hurriedly shipped out of the Zone of the Armies. The preparations were all in great haste, but by June 11 the evacuation of La Courtine was complete. Except for a single company of French soldiers, the vast camp stood empty.

On June 26 the rebellious 1st Russian Brigade arrived, followed ten days later by the less restive 3rd Brigade. Now all the Russian troops in France were gathered together in one camp, alone and isolated from the French Army. They moved into the two-story white-painted barracks and stabled their horses in the huge barns or pastured them on the surrounding plain. And then they simply sat and waited. Every day the supply services of the French 12th Military Region delivered rations to the camp, but in the interval between meals there was little for these troops to do but drink and talk politics—both of which they did to excess.

Just exactly what the French expected that the Russian brigades were to do at La Courtine has never been quite clear. What is apparent is that, with mutiny sweeping through the French Army, Pétain had absolutely no intention of allowing these thunderheads of social revolution back into the Zone of the Armies. At that time probably all that was desired of the Russians was that they stay out of harm's way until their transportation back to Russia could be arranged. But this was less easy than had been supposed. The German submarine campaign was near its zenith and transport vessels were in agonizingly short supply. Moreover, every ship left afloat was urgently required to ferry to France the American troops who had just begun to cross the Atlantic. The problem was further complicated by the fact that before the Russian troops could be shipped back the permission of the Russian government had to be obtained, and this permission was proving to be surprisingly difficult to get.

Amid all this delay and confusion there was, however, one man who had a plan. General Nikolai Lochvitsky, the forty-nine-year-old Russian commander of the 1st and 3rd brigades, viewed the situation as humiliating both for Russia and for himself and determined that he and his officers would restore discipline to the brigades.

This was a project of the first magnitude, because, in truth, discipline at La Courtine had rapidly deteriorated, especially within the 1st Brigade, whose Moscow factory workers had become increasingly Bolshevik and pacifist. The 1st Brigade troops now flatly refused to participate in any military drills whatsoever, and the only working parties in which they would take part were those connected with the distribution of the daily food ration. All pretense of discipline by their officers had been given up, and routine police duties were in the hands of a cadre of "militiamen" selected by the enlisted men themselves on the basis of two per company.

But all of this was as nothing compared to the turmoil within the camp caused by the conflict between the two brigades. Their political differences had widened and hardened to the point where each group viewed the other as being traitors. Major Le Long, a French liaison officer attached to Lochvitsky's staff, summed up the basic difference between the two brigades: the 1st claimed that it would fight only if it was returned to Russia, while the 3rd "hopes to return to Russia, if at all possible, but agrees to take part in fighting on the French front if ordered to by the provisional government." [1]

Within days after the troops had arrived at La Courtine, the conflict was brought to a head by the arrest of a captain of a 3rd Brigade machine-gun company by soldiers of the 1st Brigade. The men of the 3rd interpreted this as an oblique attack upon themselves, and the captain's company threatened to come get him if he was not immediately released. Finally, through the intercession of a committee of soldiers of both brigades, the captain was released. But now the 3rd Brigade refused to remain in the same camp with the Bolshevik 1st Brigade, who outnumbered them. So on the afternoon of July 8, notwithstanding the appeals of Lochvitsky and the orders of General Louis Comby, the French commander of the 12th Military Region, the troops of the 3rd Brigade packed their baggage. Amid the jeers of the 1st Brigade, they marched out of La Courtine.

Ultimately they made their way a few miles north to Felletin, where they made camp on a broad plateau. They had been joined by Lochvitsky and his staff and by five hundred dissidents from the 1st Brigade plus almost all the 1st Brigade officers, and, now totaling about 6,500 men, they flatly refused the orders of the French to return to La Courtine. Instead they pitched tents, set out pickets to guard against a surprise attack by the 1st Brigade and began to lead a sort of gypsy life in the warm summer. In a rough way discipline had been re-established in the 3rd Brigade. The men permitted their officers to give strictly military orders, although the officers had been stripped of most of the old privileges and prerogatives of Czarist days. The soldiers received the delegates of the Kerensky provisional government, Rapp and Svatikov, staged a parade in their honor and listened attentively while these two men harangued them about the necessity of doing their duty for Russia and its French ally.

But all was different with the 1st Brigade back at La Courtine; there a complete state of anarchy prevailed. The troops flatly refused to take orders from the provisional government. Across the front of the former headquarters building they had stretched a huge banner inscribed "A bas la guerre." A busy Bolshevik committee published various Communist leaflets attacking the "bourgeois" war, reprints of old antimilitarist articles by Tolstoi and a pronunciamento sent from Russia entitled "Declaration of the Rights of the Soldier." So when Rapp and Svatikov appeared at La Courtine to attempt to speak on behalf of the provisional government, they were greeted only by stormy cries of revolution and furious demands by the troops that they be returned to Russia.

Virtually driven out of La Courtine, Rapp and Svatikov returned to Paris to decide what could be done. Obviously everything was at an impasse. One way out was submitted by a committee of officers of the 3rd Brigade, who proposed that the 3rd send an ultimatum to the 1st Brigade ordering it to give up its arms and surrender its leaders; once this had been done the problem of restoring discipline would obviously be much simpler. On the other hand, two leaders of the 1st Brigade who were interviewed by Rapp and Svatikov presented an impressive case. The 1st Brigade, they claimed, would definitely agree to fight against the Germans, but they demanded that it be returned to Russia first. "You are the representative of the new regime," they said to Rapp and Svatikov. "Just give the order to send us back to Russia—then you will see how order re-establishes itself and how discipline is restored." [2] Reluctantly, Rapp and Svatikov made their decision. They telegraphed to Petrograd recommending that both brigades be brought back to Russia and predicting that unless this was done promptly there would be a "bloody collision" [3] between the rebels and the loyal troops.

The month of July passed in the exchange of telegrams between Petrograd and Paris. At Petrograd the matter was handled by M. Noulens, the French ambassador, whose government was becoming daily more anxious to repatriate the Russians. The whole affair had got completely out of hand. At first it had been supposed that the Russian brigades were like quarreling children who could be shunted out of sight and mind at La Courtine. But now the situation had changed entirely. The children had suddenly produced knives and were about to have at one another. Vastly more important was the fact that, despite censorship, the mutiny at La Courtine was becoming well known throughout France; and events had transformed the gray-clad 1st Brigade troops into a symbolic vanguard of worldwide proletarian revolution. No one knew where this mutiny might lead to and so, although shipping was still in desperately short supply, the French attached such urgency to the matter that they now gladly offered to make transportation available at once to remove this dangerous mutiny deep in the heart of the nation. But Noulens found that the Russian provisional government had a far different view of the situation. Kerensky categorically refused to take these troops back. He had plenty of mutinous troops of his own within Russia, and the provisional government seemed to fear that the troops of the 1st Brigade in particular would become a storm center of Bolshevism if returned to their homeland. Instead, Noulens was advised the 1st Brigade must be dealt with in France, "an energetic repression having become indispensable." [4] And in a separate telegram the Russian commander in France was ordered to reestablish discipline "with the utmost severity" and employ the death penalty wherever necessary.[5]

Now the battle line had been drawn. Inevitably the French became involved, and General Comby received orders to begin concentrating cavalry and infantry in the neighborhood of La Courtine. He threw up pickets in a wide arc around La Courtine and refused to allow the 1st Brigade to leave camp. Abruptly the 3rd Brigade was ordered out of the way, and on August 10 it was loaded into fifteen trains and shipped to a camp near Bordeaux, 150 miles to the east. Only the Russian staff was left, and the empty city of flapping and deserted tents at Felletin.

As the rebels at La Courtine realized that they were being gradually encircled, they too made plans. The troops of the 1st Brigade, now totaling about eight thousand men, elected as their leader a tall, energetic Bolshevik soldier named Globa, who lost no time in reestablishing a rough revolutionary discipline. Globa, in civil life a Moscow factory worker, had the conviction and oratorical fluency of a fanatic. Somehow he had contrived to charm a Frenchwoman from La Courtine, the wife of a soldier at the front, to live with him as his mistress. Globa's love affair interfered not at all with his effectiveness as the leader of the rebels. He put a stop to the excessive drinking, ordered the rust cleaned from rifles and machine guns, and flatly rejected an ultimatum by Lochvitsky that the 1st Brigade surrender its weapons; to the ultimatum Globa scornfully replied, "We are not children." [6]

While the 1st Brigade dug trenches and sited machine guns around the perimeter of its camp, a mysterious unit of Russians moved into Aubusson, twenty miles north of La Courtine. Known as the "2nd Special Artillery Brigade," it was a force of only 750 men consisting of a battalion of infantry, two companies of machine-gunners, and a six-gun battery of 75s, complete with a large number of French "instructors." Supposedly, this unit was newly arrived from Russia and was "passing through" France.[7] More probably it had been drawn from the more reliable units of the Russian brigades already at Salonika and merely served as a mask for the French, who directed this "Russian" artillery and wished, insofar as possible, to avoid direct participation in the repression.[8] In early September this force was joined by another Russian unit, the "2nd Special Regiment," consisting of 2,500 men hand-picked from the 3rd Brigade. To distinguish these Russians from the rebels of the 1st Brigade, they wore yellow-and-blue armbands on their right sleeves.

Now General Comby moved in his carefully selected French troops. Most of the privates were eighteen-year-olds who had just finished their training and were uncontaminated by the mutinies in the Zone of the Army. Their N.C.O.s were well-disciplined and reliable instructors from the various training schools in the vicinity. The French divided up the area surrounding La Courtine into three sectors, established command posts for each sector and set up a reserve. All told, they numbered about three thousand men, including infantry, cavalry, artillery and machine-gunners.

By September 14 the ring of Russians and French had begun to tighten around the 1st Brigade. The town of La Courtine was ordered evacuated of its civilian population, and a final ultimatum was sent to Globa by the Russian general commanding all Russian troops in France, demanding that the 1st Brigade stack its arms in the camp and then march in small groups to various collection points which had been established. Soldiers attempting to leave the camp bearing arms would be "met with fire." If the rebels did not surrender on their own by 10 A.M. on September 16, they would be treated as "traitors to their country" and discipline would be reestablished by force.[9]

While the rebels were considering this proposal, a circle of loyal Russians was drawn up around the camp; these troops occupied the hills surrounding the plateau on which La Courtine was situated and then filtered into the town itself. The "Russian" artillery was set up in full view of the camp on a height known as Hill 795. Behind the Russian ring, and acting as a sort of backstop, was a larger circle of French troops, who blocked the roads and strung telephone wires between the command posts. All of the French and loyal-Russian dispositions were complete by nightfall of September 14, and the troops, with weapons loaded and machine guns ready to fire, awaited the decision of the 1st Brigade.

The first night passed without event. The watching French and Russians could clearly make out that within the camp a huge meeting was taking place. Bathed in the glare of arc lights, Globa was haranguing the 1st Brigade. The French cannons that the rebels could see on the skyline were only dummies, Globa said. And he promised that the Russians and the French would never attack in earnest—their troops would never fight against fellow workers and revolutionaries.

On the morning of September 15 the situation remained unchanged. Since the rebels had not surrendered, General Comby ordered all food deliveries to them to cease. The rebels had rejected the ultimatum, and they countered with a statement of their own, addressed to General Comby and delivered at 3 P.M. by Father Laliron, a local priest who was held in great respect by the rebels.

The rebel statement, which was, in turn, scorned by Comby, accused certain Russian officers of being German spies and contained, Comby said, "only the poor ordinaries of this sort of missive." [10] Father Laliron, disregarding Comby's warning that the rebels might hold him hostage, carried the news of the French rejection back to the 1st Brigade and urged Globa and his revolutionary committee to consider carefully the gravity of their decision to withstand the French and the Russians. "Tomorrow there will be men killed," Laliron admonished the leaders, "and it will be you who must bear the responsibility before God and man." [11] But the 1st Brigade was determined, and, as sun set, the priest walked out of the camp and back down the road to the town.

A little before 10 A.M. on September 16, Comby and a group of his officers mounted a small hill which commanded a perfect view of the camp. The whole plateau was bathed in sun from a cloudless sky. Around the perimeter of the camp they could see the rebel trenches, held only by a few sentries and surrounded by the double ring of the attackers' trenches. Almost all the rebels, it seemed, were remaining in the barrack buildings; only a few men could be seen hurrying about the camp streets. A complete and total silence had spread throughout the hills and over the camp. Only from below, where Father Laliron was saying Mass in his chapel, was there the sound of bells to interrupt the stillness.

Comby looked at his watch, looked down again at the camp. And at precisely 10 A.M., from a hill to the west, there came the flat reports of four spaced shots from the battery of 75s. The battle for La Courtine had begun.

The first artillery shot had been a blank, but the next three were exercise projectiles, nonexplosive metal slugs "less deadly than regular field projectiles but dangerous nevertheless," [12] observed Comby. The three shells landed against a hill flanking the rows of barracks and sent up warning plumes of dirt.

There was a period of silence to let the threat implied by these warning rounds sink in upon the rebels. Then from the barracks the watchers heard a strange sound. The rebels were singing "The Marseillaise"—followed by Chopin's "Funeral March."

The 75s began to fire again, slowly and drawing closer to the barracks. It was superb shooting, but continued for only a few minutes. Then firing ceased, and for the next four hours the artillery was silent to give the rebels a chance to surrender.

But there were no white flags; not even troops sortieing from their barracks for an attack. The 1st Brigade's strategy was *rester en place*, to put the Russians and French in the position of having to massacre "helpless troops" and hope that the besiegers would themselves revolt against this slaughter. So they stayed in their barracks and sang their defiance. At 2 P.M. their song was a defeatist tune from the trenches, "It is in Vain That You Make These Attacks, My Boy," when the artillery began again.

This time the 75s were firing shrapnel, aiming not directly at the barracks but at the ground alongside them. As each round landed it made a bright flash and a black puff of smoke, and a scattering of steel slugs swept through the barracks. Suddenly the streets of the camp were filled with running men who were abandoning the wooden barracks in favor of masonry buildings. Abruptly, the 75s checked their fire. Then, when the rebels had found shelter, the artillery resumed again. Sometimes the guns fired singly, other times in a four-gun salvo, but always there was a lengthy interval between shots to allow the rebels to surrender if they would. Several times the gunfire lifted to permit the besieged to carry wounded to the camp gate, where French ambulances waited to take them to a hospital in nearby Ussel. When night fell, at eight, the cannonade finally ceased.

Slowly then the rebels began to turn on the lights in the camp. Under their glare the watchers could see men milling around in the streets. Occasionally a few would slip away into the surrounding darkness, and occasionally, too, there would be the flash of a rebel sentry's rifle as he fired at a comrade fleeing the camp. All told, about two hundred rebels escaped from the camp that night to give themselves up to the besiegers. One was shot down and mortally wounded at the camp gate. Neither side would rescue him, and, in the loom of the arc lights, he was watched by both rebels and loyalists as he writhed and died in the dirt of the road.

Later in the night a few sporadic shots were fired from the rebel camp in the direction of the encircling trenches. The fire was instantly returned by rifles and machine guns and within seconds built up to a volume fully equal to that of an active sector at the front. The lights of the camp flicked off while Russian fought Russian in a fratricidal conflict; then gradually the fire waned and died away.

Promptly at ten the next morning the artillery bombardment resumed—only to be checked immediately by a peculiar incident. In the fields surrounding the barracks were nearly a thousand horses which had not been fed for twenty-four hours. Now the rebels herded them together and drove them riderless down the road to the town of La Courtine, where they were collected and put out to pasture by the French. The artillery began again.

The firing did not stop until 2 P.M. And then from the stone barracks, now windowless and with their roofs pierced in a thousand places, white flags began to wave. From the barrack doors there poured a flood of men, all carrying their personal baggage but none bearing arms. Under white flags they formed into columns of fours and slowly trudged off down the streets and into captivity. Seventy-five hundred of the rebels surrendered. They were split up among three collection points and then marched to camps in groups of two hundred. So beaten and docile were they that each group required only two French privates and a corporal to guard it.

At La Courtine there remained only five hundred hard-core rebels. They had fortified themselves within the hospital and the former officers' mess building, from which they had viewed with contempt their comrades' surrender. Now they resolved to put up a stubborn defense. The loyalist Russians were equally determined to take them without delay. Throughout a cold, rainy night the 75s fired and the encircling Russians drove in the handful of rebels still manning the trenches. Then, in the morning, after a heavy barrage of small-arms fire, the attackers charged the remaining rebel strong points, split them up and drove the defenders into the surrounding woods, from which they were hunted the next day.

Thus the battle for La Courtine was over. Discounting the French artillerymen who surely must have secretly directed the 75s, General Comby could say truthfully that the French had not actively participated in the fighting.

There remained only the punishment of the rebels. Almost all of them had been caught; even Globa was picked up by a patrol of Russian lancers as he and his French mistress were fleeing down the road to St.-Sétiers. In time the rebels were herded into ranks, where, under French bayonets, they endured a tongue-lashing from Rapp, and following this they were split up into three groups, depending upon their assessed degree of culpability in the rebellion. The hard core of the rebels, consisting of eighty-one men, was delivered up to the jurisdiction of Russian authorities at Bordeaux, where, it appears, most of them were secretly shot. Another 549 hard-case men were sent to prison camps, where they suffered all the manifold horrors of a French prison, and were ultimately shipped to the dreaded penal battalions in Africa.

But the mass of the rebels, about 7,500 men, by an incredible error of judgment were returned to La Courtine, where they served under French or Russian officers and were guarded by a battalion of French infantry. Within a week they again rose in rebellion, but this time it was quickly suppressed and the men were split up to be sent to munitions factories as "volunteer" workers or shipped to North Africa, well out of harm's way.

So the Russian mutiny had been smashed and its leaders scattered to the winds. There was no longer any danger of these troops serving as a rallying point for a new wave of French mutinies. At the cost of a few score anonymous Russians dead and eight hundred rounds of 75-mm. ammunition, the last military mutiny in France had been buried.

17

"I WAGE WAR!"

THE ARMY was now completely redisciplined. There had not been a single incidence of mutinous revolt since September. Pétain had achieved the best that could be done. Although the troops could scarcely be described as ardent, at least they were willing. "Morale varies from good to quite satisfactory," Postal Control reported in October; "it is the product of resignation rather than enthusiasm. But each man knows his patriotic duty and knows that he must do it." [1] Yet, although revolt had been quelled in the Army, the rot had transferred itself to the interior of France, where a different kind of mutinous wave was cresting within the civil population.

"Peace now!"—these were the words on too many mouths. Peace, to end the "nibbling" at the German lines which had almost invariably cost more in French lives than German. Peace, to end the meatless days, the inflation, the spectacle of profiteering war contractors wallowing in luxury. Peace, to bring the fathers, husbands, brothers and sweethearts back from the trenches. What did it matter if Alsace and Lorraine remained in German hands? They had been Germany's for forty-five years and somehow France had survived. Just exactly what, it was openly asked, were France's war aims? Why not conclude peace now? It was obvious that Germany too was sick of the war, and surely she would give generous terms. And even if she would not, what difference would it make? Revolution had now descended upon Russia and, in the eyes of many, would soon batter down the thrones of Central Europe. Any territorial concessions would be only temporary; when revolution gripped Germany, the fruits of conquest would be relinquished by a proletarian government. Only let the war stop now and end the agony at whatever price.

A Parisian diarist spoke of the war as the "Vintage," with the "younger generation flung into the winepress, crushed, with the incessant gurgle of streaming blood—pale, frightened mothers looking on—while the levers of this winepress would be forced down by the unwearied arms of the ambitious politicians, the Chauvinists, the profiteers . . ." [2]

This, then, was the current of defeatism running rife through Paris and all the great French industrial cities. It was the *cafard*—a kind of sullen civil mutiny born of war-sickness and nurtured by disgust for political leadership which was either weak or treasonous. In a way, the exposure of the *Bonnet rouge*, the resignation of Malvy, and the glare of publicity upon the pacifism espoused by paid traitors or the parties of the left had been a good thing. True, it had broken up the political unity of France, but this had long been a feeble fiction anyhow. At least now, in the fall of 1917, the road ahead was becoming more or less plain. If the nation demanded a negotiated peace, then its Parliament would permit the formation of a government headed by Joseph Caillaux. He would come to power backed by a coalition consisting of the Radical Socialists (over whom Caillaux still wielded great authority) plus both wings of the Socialist party, which regarded Caillaux as the candidate from the left who stood the best chance of becoming Premier. And to make the pill of defeat easier for the deputies to swallow, they could even salve their consciences with the thought that Caillaux was publicly denying that he would conclude anything but a victorious peace. He challenged those who accused him of defeatism to make their charges more specific—"Where? When? How? Who?" [3] But despite Caillaux's denials, everyone knew that once in office he would be compelled to do the bidding of the left-wing parties to whom he was beholden.

On the other hand, if the nation could summon the strength to continue the war, Parliament would have to select another government to conduct it, a government of an entirely different character from the present Painlevé Ministry, hedged about as it was with compromises and concessions, hazy war aims, lip-service patriotism, and sniping from the outermost wings of both left and right.

The Painlevé government had been formed in September. In its initial test of strength it had been supported by a vote of 386 to none in the Chamber of Deputies, but there had been 131 deputies who had abstained from voting—an ominous figure that included 86 Socialists. And as the weeks passed it became obvious that the Painlevé government could not last: it was too weak to suit the right, too warlike to suit the left. Frantically Painlevé scurried between the various political camps, giving a promise here, making a concession there, in his well-meaning attempts to present a façade of political harmony to the watching world. But time and events were running out for this government. Painlevé had arrested the traitors exposed in the *Bonnet rouge* affair and in the *Journal* treason, and he had been instrumental in forcing Malvy's resignation. Nevertheless, the right wing charged him with responsibility for these episodes. Useless for him to complain that he had been bequeathed "a dreary record of arrests and scandals to clear up, almost all of which were from the distant past." [4]

Events were now racing to a conclusion. The tension had become unendurable; wolf packs had begun to form around the dying Painlevé Ministry and soon they would bring it down.

In early November an insignificant dispute broke out within the Chamber of Deputies. A right-wing member who was also an infantry lieutenant serving at the front accused a Socialist soldier-deputy of cowardice in the face of the enemy. This being a serious charge, a motion was made to investigate the affair. Painlevé deprecated the event and asked for a week's delay. Using this petty issue as an excuse, the right and the left of the Chamber rose up on November 13 and voted him down 277 to 186. Painlevé was "the victim of his friendships"; [5] his attempts at conciliation had cost this mathematical genius dearly.

The fall of the Painlevé Ministry was the first instance of a French government actually losing a vote of confidence during the war (the other Premiers—Viviani, Briand and Ribot—had resigned to permit the formation of more powerful ministries), and it was an indication of what was to follow. A tremor of cataclysmic change was in the air. Unsensed by its allies, whose perception was dulled by their own problems and their lack of understanding of the real nature of the political situation, France had almost come to the point of quitting the war.

Now that there was no government, it was the task of President of the Republic Raymond Poincaré to turn up a member of Parliament who was capable of forming one. One such member was leaving no doubt as to his availability—Joseph Caillaux, who in recent months had come out of the semiseclusion in which he had lived in the years following Madame Caillaux's acquittal for the murder of Gaston Calmette. Whatever his defects may have been, Caillaux knew the temper of the times; he knew that the superpatriotism of the first year of the war had waned and that he was now in no danger whatever of being mobbed again as a suspected German spy.

With the passage of time, Caillaux's physical appearance had changed. He had added more weight, and his face was covered with purplish veins. His voice had grown hoarse and his manner was, if anything, more abrupt and more arrogant. But he had lost none of the shrewdness or the consuming personal ambition which had always been the volcano within this dynamic man. Caillaux knew that France was not prepared to accept an out-and-out pacifist as its Premier, and he wrote numerous speeches and polite letters to newspapers denying accusations that he proposed making peace with the Germans. (In L'Homme enchaîné Clemenceau printed Caillaux's letter following it with the cynical comment, "Has he not been the colleague of Cavallini and Scarfoglio [well-known Italian traitors]? . . . And has anyone heard him say that he would pursue the war at all costs?") [6]

In his cynicism, the Tiger was undoubtedly correct. For, although Clemenceau could not know it at the time, Caillaux had long since drafted his plan for a coup d'état. This draft, a series of notes written principally during 1914 and 1915 and hidden in his "Reynouard" safe-deposit box in Florence, was in several sections. In one part, entitled "Les Responsables," Raymond Poincaré was accused of being actually responsible for the war, while he, Caillaux, was portrayed as a force for peace which Poincaré and his friends had struck down with a vicious blow. Another memorandum was entitled, quite aptly, "The Rubicon" and consisted of a plan to be implemented when Caillaux had been asked to form a government. In brief, his outline called for either the dissolution of or an extended holiday for Parliament; for the promotion of the pro-left General

Sarrail from commander of the French troops in Greece to Commander in Chief of the Army; for the occupation of Paris by selected regiments, principally those who had been recruited in Caillaux's home district; and for the appointment to key positions of such persons as Almereyda.[7]

All these documents were not to come to light until later. But they reveal Caillaux for what he was—a man distorted by ambition, half certain that his hour would come, half in agony that it would not.

Never before had Raymond Poincaré experienced so difficult a time finding a candidate able to form a government. To the Élysée Palace he summoned all the old names, but it was obvious that none of them could, or none would, attempt to form a government. It was as if forty months of war had emasculated all the once potent political figures. As the field narrowed down, only two names kept recurring—Caillaux and Clemenceau.

Poincaré was a dedicated patriot who believed ardently in the vigorous continuation of the war, yet he hesitated to call on Clemenceau. One reason was that he and Clemenceau hated each other (it was to Poincaré that the Tiger had referred when he said, "There are two useless organs: the prostate and the Presidency of the Republic"[8]). Quite aside from personal enmity, Poincaré was sincerely frightened of what Clemenceau might do once he got into office. When the Tiger had been Premier before the war it had become evident that his vaunted republicanism was paper-thin and lasted only as long as it suited him; his government had turned out to be one of the most reactionary since 1870. And now he was much older, even more irascible, even less inclined to suffer the intrusions of Parliament. A Clemenceau government might become such a tyranny that, rather than tolerate him, the nation would make peace with Germany. A respected adviser counseled Poincaré that a Clemenceau government would be "a great risk." But something had to be done soon. "The crisis is grave," Poincaré admitted to his diary. The same day he wrote of Clemenceau, "That devil of a man has the patriots behind him."[9]

Finally Poincaré made his decision. There was no help for it. "It is necessary to choose between Caillaux and Clemenceau. My choice is made." At three o'clock in the afternoon of November 14, Poincaré summoned Clemenceau to the Élysée Palace and invited him to form a government.

The submission of a Clemenceau government to the Chamber of Deputies was, quite definitely, France's last card. Through its deputies the nation was being asked to accept, as the leader who would help them win the war, an old man whose enemies were ranked in legions before him, a man whom it knew to have only two saving graces: a hatred of Germany and the energy of a fanatic. Indeed, if the Chamber rejected Clemenceau there was no one who could be called upon to take his place—except Joseph Caillaux. So when, on the afternoon of November 20, the Tiger confronted the Chamber of Deputies to obtain the necessary vote of confidence, even the aisles were jammed with listeners; people were "sitting, standing, suffocated, nearly torn to bits, and looking around them in a kind of silent stupor." [10]

Clemenceau read his ministerial declaration; "We have accepted the government in order to conduct the war with redoubled energy. . . . We shall carry on this program. . . . There will be no consideration of persons or partisan passions . . . , there will be neither treason nor half-treason—only war. Nothing but war! . . . For these measures, without turning back, we seek, gentlemen, the sanction of your vote." [11]

The Tiger stepped down from the tribune. There were a few questions, a couple of statements. And then the Chamber balloted. By a vote of 419 to 65, Malvy and Caillaux abstaining, France accepted the government of Georges Clemenceau.

Winston Churchill has best described the effect which Clemenceau had upon the members of Parliament during the first days of his rule: "He ranged from one side of the tribune to the other, without a note or book of references or scrap of paper, barking out sharp, staccato sentences as the thought broke upon his mind. He looked like a wild animal pacing to and fro behind bars, growling and glaring; and all around him was an assembly which would have done anything to avoid having him there, but having put him there, felt they must obey. The last desperate stake had to be played. France had resolved to unbar the cage and let her tiger loose upon all foes, beyond the trenches or in her midst. With snarls and growls, the ferocious, aged, dauntless beast of prey went into action." [12]

The aim of Clemenceau's government was set forth in the Tiger's famous ministerial declaration of March 1918. In response to a question concerning the government's policies he leaned forward from the tribune and shouted hoarsely, "But I, messieurs, *I wage war!* . . . In domestic policies, I wage war. In foreign policies, I wage war. Always, everywhere, I wage war. . . . Russia has betrayed us, and I continue to wage war. Unhappy Roumania has been forced to capitulate, but I still wage war. . . . And I shall continue to wage war until the last quarter of an hour!" [13]

And the moment the Tiger went into action, democracy temporarily died in France. And died unmourned.

There is a curious streak in the politics of the French nation. These unusual people, the nation which gave birth to the first European republic and which constantly demands adherence to the strictest "republican" principles, seem always to long for a man on horseback who will lead them out of the chaos into which their own racing intelligence and their own republicanism has led them. This peculiar nation which, left to itself, will never grant its leaders sufficient power even to conduct its routine affairs is constantly tempted to deliver up *every* power to one strong man in the moment of ultimate crisis.

Georges Clemenceau sensed this strange quirk within the French nation, and he seized upon it with consummate skill. Once he had assumed the government, he immediately turned it into a species of dictatorship. He ran roughshod over opposition, used any tactics, any technique, any method as long as it got results. The end was victory and it justified any means—police spies, private threats, blackmail. There was a dossier on everyone of importance and Clemenceau never for a moment hesitated to use it. He was determined to drive France, both the Army and the interior, into waging war with the utmost resolution. And a long lifetime of political in-fighting had taught this ferocious old man how to handle recalcitrant politicians.

The Tiger ran a government of very few. To himself he reserved not only the premiership but also, to ensure that the war effort would be pursued dynamically, the Ministry of War. As for the rest of his ministers, they were ciphers—"not a single man of the first rank," it was observed.[14] This was precisely what Clemenceau wanted. He had not selected his ministers to curry favor with Parliament; he had selected them solely to obey his orders and, anyway, he despised most of them. These cowed mediocrities bore endless indignities from their master; for instance, of Jules Pams, his Minister of the Interior, Clemenceau had once said, "Pams is not a name, it's a noise." [15]

The actual business of the government was concentrated in the hands of Clemenceau and two young assistants. General Jean Mordacq had been plucked by the Tiger from the command of the 24th Infantry Division. Clemenceau recognized him as an exceedingly bright officer and made him his *chef de cabinet* for military matters. Now, with first-class professional advice of his own, Clemenceau was independent of G.Q.G., whose views he could (and did) dispute at any time it suited him. He reorganized the Army's staff system, fired older generals and abolished various committees and commissions which had long since lost their usefulness except as snug berths for *embusqués*.

Clemenceau's other aide was Georges Mandel, about whom more must be said. Mandel, the son of a Jewish tailor in the Sentier district of Paris, had had one ambition since his early youth—to serve Georges Clemenceau. Around the turn of the century, when he was twenty-one years old, he had appeared at Clemenceau's office and asked to work for him, and the Tiger had taken him on. Now Mandel assisted Clemenceau in a variety of capacities—as his *chef de cabinet* for political matters, as director of censorship, as the unofficial Minister of the Interior, but principally as Clemenceau's "eyes and ears." [16]

There was, most certainly, nothing attractive about Mandel. One observer described him as "small, twisted, pale, with a long thin nose planted askew, to either side of which a glaucous green eye glinted, hard and steady. On his forehead hung a damp wisp of hair. He was always cold for the same reason one expects a fish to be." [17] Another saw Mandel differently—as "an adder . . . poised and alert." [18] But no matter; this unappetizing person with the flat, expressionless voice was completely devoted to the Tiger. Clemenceau, in turn, reposed more confidence in Mandel than he did in any other human being, and scores of times every day he drew upon Mandel's remarkable intelligence and his truly phenomenal memory.

An officer of a British military mission, visiting Clemenceau to discuss a difficulty the British were having with a troublesome French politician, had occasion to see how Clemenceau and Mandel worked. The question of how the politician could best be dealt with arose. "Let us ask Mandel," Clemenceau proposed, and he pressed a concealed button on his desk. Almost instantly the curtains against one wall parted and revealed a small side door, through which Mandel entered.

"Tell us, Mandel," Clemenceau requested, posing the question.

Mandel's reply was precise, frigid and unhesitating. "The gentleman in question served in the Chamber of Deputies from 1894 to 1899. He narrowly escaped being prosecuted in 1902 over the issue of some rather doubtful shares . . . There is a dossier on him."

"Good," Clemenceau replied cheerfully. "Then we shall have no further difficulty from him." [19]

In his capacity of chief of censorship, Mandel speedily and ruthlessly suppressed the pacifist newspapers and pamphleteers. The presses were carted off, the publishers thrown into jail on any pretext or charge which seemed convenient. Any prefect who showed signs of laxity or negligence was swiftly dismissed. Gone were the days when agitators could frequent the railway stations to press pacifist pamphlets into the hands of soldiers on leave. Now there were no more pacifist pamphlets, just as there were no more agitators.

And as the unofficial Minister of the Interior (Pams was little more than a figurehead), Mandel served as Clemenceau's alter ego, as a whip which galvanized into action all the miscellaneous security apparatus which Malvy had allowed to function in low gear. A witness has described how Mandel accomplished this. At the Ministry of War on the Rue St.-Dominique there were frequent meetings of top police officials, at which he presided. He squatted with twisted legs at a small Louis XV table and issued his directions, and it was obvious that his audience was terrified of him.

"*Le Matin* will be suspended for four days and the editor warned. *Warned*—he will understand what that means."

"*Certainement*, Monsieur le Chef de Cabinet, *certainement*."

"Has the evidence against So-and-so been completed? Why not? The Premier will be angry. You know what that implies for you, Monsieur le Prefect."

And with quivering voice the prefect would answer, "*Mais oui,* Monsieur le Chef de Cabinet, *mais oui.*" [20]

Clemenceau drove France as a hard master. But he drove no one harder than himself.

The old man started his day early, generally arising about 5 A.M. and working for a couple of hours in the study of his apartment on the Rue Franklin, in the suburb of Passy. After this he received a visit from a gymnastic instructor who put him through a brisk workout.

By quarter to nine, Clemenceau was at his office in the War Ministry. As if to emphasize his statement "I wage war!," he generally operated from here rather than from the more elaborate offices maintained for the Premier. There he donned a gray skullcap, seated himself at an immense desk in a room which looked out into the courtyard of the Ministry, and began to shuffle through the papers strewn in a disorderly heap in front of him. Then he summoned Mordacq, who briefed him on the military situation, and a few minutes later Mandel, to give an oral digest of the political situation. Peculiarly for an old journalist, Clemenceau almost never read the day's newspapers, preferring to receive his news distilled and concise from Mandel.

In the late morning Clemenceau either presided over a meeting of the Supreme War Council or, more rarely, dictated orders at a meeting of his rubber-stamp Cabinet. Then luncheon at his apartment, following which he returned to his office to receive callers until late afternoon, when it was time for him to appear at the sitting of Parliament. Then, in the evening, he went back to his office to work at his desk or consult with Mandel until about nine, when he returned to his bachelor apartment for dinner and bed.

Although Clemenceau had maintained bachelor quarters for many years, he actually became a widower only during 1917. Mary Plummer Clemenceau, the American schoolgirl whom he had married in 1870 and who had left him only a few years later, had died. She had never divorced Clemenceau, nor had she ever returned to the United States. Since leaving Clemenceau she had lived in the Paris suburb of Sèvres, where, unknown or forgotten by everyone, Clemenceau's wife had existed by means of a small allowance from relatives in the United States, a pittance from Clemenceau himself and a meager income as a guide for American tourists to the Paris museums. Always an unwilling expatriate, Mary Plummer had never learned to speak more than a little French. After her death it was found that she had made scrapbooks of newspaper clippings about Clemenceau, even though she could read them only with the aid of a dictionary.[21] Although she and her husband had lived in Paris for more than thirty years, they had rarely set eyes upon each other in all that time.

The only times Clemenceau varied his daily Paris routine were when he visited the troops at the front, which he did as often as three times a week. On these occasions he left by car at 4 A.M. Wearing a shabby tweed coat and a disreputable felt hat, he toured the trenches, talking with the troops and getting his own perspective on the battlefront situation. Frequently, and needlessly, he exposed himself to enemy gunfire. Jumping up on a parapet one time, he shook his fist at the startled Germans only a few hundred feet away and screamed, "*Cochons! Salauds!* We'll get you in the end!" [22]

All this gives a clue to the technique used by this old man to lead France. Clemenceau's stunning success as a wartime leader lay not so much in what he did as in the spirit in which he did it. It was a monumental demonstration of the effect which one totally determined man can have upon a huge mass—who, it developed, needed only to be led. All France, soldiers and civilians alike, now knew that there would never be a surrender, never be a negotiated peace. Suddenly the nation realized that it had delivered itself irrevocably into the hands of a man who, before he would give up, would bankrupt the country, send every soldier to his death, and then, if driven from the soil of France, would continue the war from France's colonies.

Faced with this sort of determination, Parliament quailed before Clemenceau. At any time the Chamber of Deputies, most of whose members detested Clemenceau, could have cast him from his post by an adverse vote of confidence, but they did not dare. Only occasionally did Parliament attempt seriously to dispute the Tiger's power. Once the Senate and the Chamber formed a joint committee to investigate certain aspects of the conduct of the war. In a group, the delegation visited the Ministry of War, where they were received with deferential attention by Mordacq. All their questions were answered, but in vast detail and with the greatest complexity.

Mordacq summoned witnesses who droned on at stupefying length. Enormous and confusing masses of imprecise and undigested data were placed at the committee's disposal. Mountains of records were assembled by the attentive Mordacq who urged the politicians to study them closely. Finally the exhausted and utterly bewildered members retreated and Clemenceau was bothered no more.

Regarding Joseph Caillaux, Clemenceau claimed, "It is probable that Caillaux is the only man with whom I have never had a controversy—it is strange but true—except perhaps for a fortnight before I came into power." [23] But now he set out to ruin Joseph Caillaux. He made this clear to an American newspaperman who interviewed him shortly after his government was formed. "I intend to accomplish two things," the Tiger said. "One, I intend to destroy the German Empire. Two, I intend to destroy Joseph Caillaux." [24]

Louis Malvy, Caillaux's pilot fish, had fallen into Clemenceau's net early and easily. Léon Daudet, a royalist editor and self-appointed spy hunter, had flatly accused Malvy of giving the plans for the Nivelle offensive to German agents—a ridiculous charge which was believed by almost no one. But this accusation had to be investigated, and on November 22, only two days after Clemenceau had come to power, it was announced in the Chamber of Deputies that a committee of thirty-three deputies was to be formed to investigate the charges of "crimes committed by M. Malvy in the exercise of his functions." Malvy apparently had no doubt that he would be able to defend himself, and he jumped to his feet in the Chamber to demand that the committee meet as quickly as possible to investigate the charges and give him an opportunity to clear his name.[25] Six days later the committee assented to his request and recommended to the Chamber that Louis Malvy be brought to trial before the Senate, which for this occasion would sit as a high court. Under Clemenceau's gaze, the motion was adopted—and now the Tiger knew it was time to go after Malvy's master, Joseph Caillaux.

But to prosecute Caillaux on grounds of treason was to be a more difficult matter. Clemenceau's representatives in the Chamber of Deputies reported that their associates were frightened that a trial of Caillaux would be the signal for a wholesale bloodletting of Clemenceau's political opposition. And the Chamber was in a position to block the Tiger's attack on him. Caillaux, still a deputy, possessed the customary parliamentary immunity to arrest and trial, and the Chamber would have to be persuaded to suspend that immunity in his case before any legal action could be taken against him; since Caillaux was the leader of the left and still wielded great power, Clemenceau knew that the Chamber would not willingly act on this matter. The only way he could force its hand would be to gather such an overwhelming body of evidence of Caillaux's treason that no deputy could resist the Tiger's pressure.

Clemenceau commissioned General Dubail, the military governor of Paris, to gather this evidence. It was all done in the most thorough manner. Caillaux's safe-deposit box was located in the bank in Florence, and its contents, the draft plan for a *coup d'état*, were brought to Paris. The incautious letters which Caillaux had written to Bolo Pasha and to Almereyda ("My best regards and sincere thanks, my dear editor and friend, for your Sunday issue . . .") [26] were gathered up, and the files of the security organizations were ransacked to bring forward various long-buried reports of Caillaux's travels to Italy and his meetings with Italians who had subsequently been arrested as traitors.

On December 12 the Dubail report was made public and the Clemenceau government asked Parliament to withdraw Joseph Caillaux's immunity on the grounds that he "endangered the security of the state." Dubail had stated, "It is a serious matter that a statesman such as M. Caillaux, who has occupied the highest offices in the state, who has had the honor of directing the policy of his country and who has enjoyed the position of leader of a great party, should be on terms of indisputable intimacy with French and foreign adventurers." [27] Under the pressure of the documentary proof brought out in the report, the Chamber of Deputies voted to convene a committee of eleven under Deputy André Paisant to examine these charges and make a recommendation to the Chamber.

On December 22 the Paisant committee made its report to a packed Chamber of Deputies and recommended that Caillaux's immunity be withdrawn. This was an event of the greatest significance; the London *Times* described the whole affair as "the most important non-military event in France since the beginning of the war." [28] To have Parliament consider withdrawing the immunity of one of its most prominent members was almost unheard of. Where would this all end? The history of French politics had amply demonstrated that when parliamentary immunity was once withdrawn the debating chamber could turn into an abattoir. And if the hallowed immunity could be stripped from Joseph Caillaux, then it could be infinitely more easily taken from the less important members. If the deputies acquiesced in this step, however guilty Caillaux might be, they would be delivering up their lives to Clemenceau, the ruthless Tiger who now sat impassively on the government bench of the Chamber.

The Paisant report had been read, and now there was a stir in the Chamber. Down the aisle strode Joseph Caillaux. Mounting the tribune, he commenced an address which, for eloquence and lucidity, remains one of the greatest in the history of the French Parliament. For, indeed, the man was talented. With genius Caillaux played upon the fears of his fellow deputies, protested his own innocence and then, turning to the seated Clemenceau, recounted how, years before, he had supported the Tiger when Clemenceau had been attacked in Parliament. "You honored me then by allowing me to aid you," Caillaux declaimed. "Yes, I stood by you. Have you forgotten?" [29]

But Clemenceau was pitiless. Mandel was watching, ready to make note of any deputy who failed in his duty. The Chamber was intimidated. The deputies sensed that the Tiger had France at his back and they could not deny him the opportunity to try Caillaux. By an almost unanimous vote they suspended Caillaux's immunity.

On January 13 an order was issued for Caillaux's arrest. Additional evidence of treason had been delivered to Clemenceau by the United States government, which provided deciphered copies of German diplomatic dispatches stemming from Caillaux's South American visit in 1915.[30]

The story of these deciphered messages is a fascinating one in itself. It all stemmed from the first days of the war, when, as part of the British mobilization plan, cable ships pulled up the German transoceanic telegraph lines. Thus the Germans were forced from the outset to radio their communications to and from overseas diplomatic stations. To take advantage of this happy situation, the British established a network of radio intercept stations which monitored the German coded transmissions and forwarded these intercepts to the office of the director of Naval Intelligence, where they were turned over to a hastily improvised team of cryptoanalysts known as "Room 40." Although even the most experienced of the British cryptographers had never had any more elaborate prewar training than attempting the solution of the Sunday *Times* word puzzles, these amateurs soon developed into a formidable team of code breakers.

Yet for many months the intercepts of the German diplomatic code, a series which generally bore the prefix "13040," defied decoding—until, in February of 1915, a strange event occurred. A German named Wilhelm Wassmuss had been sent by his government into Persia to stimulate the desert tribes into a holy war against the British—a sort of T. E. Lawrence in reverse. But shortly after his arrival in Persia he had been arrested by a pro-British official and had escaped his captors only by the greatest good fortune, leaving his personal effects which had fallen into British hands. The most suspicious feature of the event was Wassmuss' profound anxiety over his lost baggage, which he made numerous unsuccessful attempts to recover through diplomatic channels.

Late in the summer of 1915 these attempts came to the attention of Admiral William Hall, the British director of Naval Intelligence and a man of sheer genius at his job. Hall, nicknamed "Blinker" Hall because of his habit of twitching his eyelids when excited, decided that Wassmuss' inordinate desire to recover his luggage was curious indeed and gave orders that the bundles should be sent to his London office.

There exists a marvelous description of the sequel to Hall's order: The German baggage is delivered to Hall's office, and, eyelids twitching furiously, the admiral cuts open the bundles with his pocketknife. Seconds later, Hall has in his hands the codebook for the German "13040" code.

Now it became simple. The accumulated stacks of German diplomatic messages were speedily decoded; and when the United States entered the war, the codebook was made available to them for their own use.[31] In this manner, then, the codes were broken and the long-buried evidence of Joseph Caillaux's treason was resurrected and delivered to Clemenceau. At 8 A.M. on January 14, 1917, a group of police officers arrived at Caillaux's home on the Rue Alphonse de Neuville. The accused man was still asleep and his valet had to be sent to arouse him. But it was not until 9:45 that he descended the stairs, an immaculate figure, bathed and massaged, his valet behind him carrying his overcoat. The waiting officers placed him under arrest, and without further ado this former Premier of France was tossed into a cell at the prison La Santé.

With Malvy and Caillaux now awaiting trail, Clemenceau had no further trouble with the parliamentary left wing. Curiously, the hatred they bore him probably aided Clemenceau more than it hindered him. His was the first wartime government which did not have to undergo the emasculating compromises which every previous Premier had felt compelled to make in an effort to placate the left. On February 10, 1918, the Tiger demanded and obtained authorization to enact economic legislation by simple decree; this gave him personal and total power over French industry, agriculture and finance. Parliament now was Clemenceau's tool. There were no more secret-committee sessions, no more spectacles of a harried Premier juggling interruptions from scoffing deputies. Now only the Tiger spoke, and Parliament obeyed.

Clemenceau did, however, extend a few compromises. He purposely failed to arrest Adolphe Merrheim, the pacifist chief of the Metalworkers' Federation, and he released from Army service a few other union leaders. Clemenceau regarded them as unimportant sops thrown to the left. Since he now wielded full power and had united the nation behind him, he could easily afford to joke about the Socialists. "These fellows make a great deal of noise when they're permitted to," he later expounded, "but if you tell them, 'That's enough!' they keep quiet. . . . I didn't even have to engage in a struggle with them. They melted away like pale shadows." [32]

Clemenceau was somewhat lenient in matters of censorship too —especially when it came to personal attacks against himself. "The right to slander members of the government," he observed cynically, "should be beyond all restriction." [33] The day after he was called to power, Clemenceau's newspaper, *L'Homme enchaîné*, had reverted to its previous title, *L'Homme libre*.

But Clemenceau would tolerate nothing which interfered with the war effort. When a group of strikers' delegates called at his office, the old man heard them out and then dismissed them politely, even went so far as to offer them transportation in his official automobile. "But I warn you," he cautioned, "it is only going to Vincennes"— the execution grounds for traitors.[34] The warning was not lost upon the strikers.

Why, then, was Clemenceau loved—why, then, was France prepared to follow him to the death? For only one reason. In the glow of Clemenceau's determination a faltering nation had again found itself. Some enemies would carp with the quatrain;

> Though he's already one foot in the grave,
> The grim Clemenceau cries, "I wage war!"
> Alas! humanitarians deplore,
> He's not alone to face the German wave! [35]

But this criticism was a feeble sob compared to the blast of white-hot patriotism which Georges Clemenceau stimulated. He made Frenchmen proud and determined. Perhaps even more important, he snatched from them the option of peace or war. This made all the difference. Now it was only war.

To Pétain, and to the troops individually, it became apparent that at last there was a civil force behind them which for resolution and discipline would match their own. Clemenceau was instrumental in establishing a unified command among the Allies—and got a Frenchman, Foch, accepted as its generalissimo. He even dismissed General Sarrail from command of the army at Salonika, a step which no government had ever dared take before for fear of the left-wing reaction.

Most important, Clemenceau virtually stopped the feud between the Army and the government. There were no more instances such as Joffre's making G.Q.G. a state within a state, no more disgraceful exhibitions such as when Nivelle terrorized the Ribot government with threats of resignation. When there was a conflict between Foch and Pétain over the use of the Army's strategic reserve, old Clemenceau blurted out, "I will arrange all that. . . . The organization of the army of maneuver [the reserve] is scarcely defensible in itself. But I will be there. At the moment of attack, I will be there. If there is a question, I will decide it." [36]

No, far more than with any previous government, the French war effort was totally and completely under the personal management of Georges Clemenceau, the man who believed that "war is too serious a matter to leave to soldiers." [37]

Only at the end of World War I did the immense scope of the French war effort really become evident. This was a nation which mobilized for battle a greater percentage of its population than any other nation; this was a land which had been predominantly agricultural before the war and yet, even though deprived of its richest provinces by German occupation, managed to alter its economy to become an industrialized power which supplied not only its own needs but much of the requirements of its allies.

And this was an Army which was almost overwhelmed at first, which lost most of its career officers, which rewrote its doctrine on the march, and which survived four years of almost barren battering at a solidly entrenched enemy.

It is against the background of these phenomenal accomplishments that this story of treason and mutiny must be set. The Army and the people faltered—but only for a moment. The nation brought to its head two men, Pétain and Clemenceau, who knew how to cut out the diseased tissue and make France well again. A nation which can do this has an enduring claim on greatness.

18

AFTERWORD

THIS IS A STORY without a climactic epilogue. A tale which trails off into silence, with its central characters dying either unknown or despised. Curiously, only their antagonists, Caillaux and Malvy, ever again attained a measure of public esteem.

Georges Clemenceau, of course, proved to be exactly the man to lead France to victory, but his craving for personal power, his raging nationalism and his unbending hatred of Germany made him poorly suited for a world at peace. He proved more capable of fighting enemies than winning friends, and in January 1920 the French Parliament refused to continue a Clemenceau government. The Tiger spent his last years in travel and writing. The fall of his government had embittered him to the point where he felt that even his close friends had betrayed him. When they came to console him on his defeat and assure him of their devotion, he put his hand to his ear and remarked, "Did I hear a cock crow?" [1]

Clemenceau died in Paris on November 24, 1929, at the age of eighty-eight. His life came within a decade of spanning that of the Third Republic which, in his way, he had so faithfully served.

Pétain too lived to a tremendous age. And, like Clemenceau, he suffered from the defects of his greatness. Pétain continued the war as Commander in Chief of the French armies on the western front, but he was denied the pinnacle of military achievement, the Supreme Command of the Allied Armies.

The strain of latent pessimism which was a part of Pétain's make-up seemed always to curse him. When the Germans' offensive of March 1918 nearly broke the Franco-British lines and it seemed that they would capture Amiens, it became a matter of the utmost necessity for the Allies to agree on a single commander for their forces. To select this man, the Allied generals and politicians met in urgent session in the city hall of the town of Doullens. Outside they could hear the shuffle of thousands of feet as the retreating Allied divisions poured to the rear.

Probably Clemenceau had gone to the Doullens meeting prepared to insist that Pétain be given the job. But he changed his mind when Pétain drew him to one side and, pointing to the British Field Marshal Sir Douglas Haig, whispered, "There is a man who will be obliged to capitulate in the open field within a fortnight, and we shall be lucky if we are not obliged to do the same." General Foch, on the other hand, electrified the conference by crying, "You aren't fighting? I would fight without a break. I would fight before Amiens. I would fight all the time!" On this, Clemenceau shifted his support to Foch and he was selected as the Allied Generalissimo.[2]

But Pétain's subsequent wartime record was good. He was made a marshal of France and was widely heralded as one of the saviors of the nation. His contribution to victory had been immense, not only in the suppression of the mutinies but in his theories of the predominant role of firepower. When Pétain was received into the French Academy, the speech of welcome said, "You have discovered this: that fire kills." [3]

In the years after World War I, Pétain served in a variety of capacities—as Minister of War, as a member of the Superior War Council, and later as ambassador to Franco's Spain. He was an old man now, and with age the innate conservatism engendered by his peasant upbringing and Army background had hardened to the point where he interpreted any political change whatever as an encroachment of Bolshevism. The aged marshal grew to admire Mussolini, Hitler and Franco for the "order" which they had brought to their nations. Moreover, both Pétain's conservatism and his influence on military affairs were so strong that he could, and did, block France's rearmament with new weapons to meet the coming German threat.

Finally when the German blitzkrieg of 1940 crushed France, Pétain was called to power, and he negotiated his nation's surrender. During the wartime years, as the self-appointed "Chief of State," Pétain ruled France as the Vichy minion of Nazi Germany. He appointed Pierre Laval, of Carnet B notoriety, as Premier and "in the Nazi 'order' they were merely the tawdry managers of a nation in misery." [4] In Pétain's defense it must be said that, although he was not exactly senile, he apparently needed daily injections to make him alert enough for a few hours in the morning, but this left him in the world of a very old man for the balance of the day.

At the end of World War II he was tried and, for his wartime treason, was sentenced to death by the government of Charles de Gaulle, although de Gaulle himself commuted the sentence to life imprisonment. Sorrowfully de Gaulle wrote later, "Monsieur le Maréchal! You who had always done such great honor to your arms, you who were once my leader and my example, how had you come to this?" [5]

Pétain died in 1951 at his prison on the tiny Île d'Yeu, twenty miles off the western coast of France. He was ninety-five—a dazed relic who had lived so long that he had outworn his deserved glory. It has been said of him, probably quite correctly, that "he was a subordinate of great value, but never possessed the moral fiber of a supreme commander in the highest conception of the term." [6] Nevertheless, there is still a French right-wing group, the Association pour Défendre la Mémoire du Maréchal Pétain, which is active and which finances the publication of laudatory biographies of Pétain.

As for Joffre, after he was deposed in 1916 to make way for Nivelle he was banished to Paris, where he was given a tiny staff, an empty office and nothing to do. But later, when the United States entered the war, Joffre was sent on a mission to Washington to coordinate Franco-American military activities. This was his last wartime service. He died in 1931.

Nivelle fared somewhat better than Joffre. After the failure of his April 16 offensive and his subsequent dismissal, he was made to appear before an Army court of inquiry which investigated charges of culpable negligence against him. The commission's report, the essence of which was that the failed offensive was all the fault of the politicians, whitewashed Nivelle of blame. The Chamber of Deputies was furious, but could do nothing about it. In late 1917

Nivelle was made military commander of French North Africa, a surprisingly good position for a general who had fallen into such universal disrepute. He died in 1924.

Louis Malvy was tried before the Senate, sitting as a court. Although Léon Daudet's charge that he had given the Germans the plans for the offensive of April 16 could not be sustained, Malvy was found guilty of culpable negligence in the performance of his duties and was sentenced to five years' banishment from France. He passed this time in Spain and then returned to French politics, where his still-excellent connections earned him re-election as a deputy. Once he even served briefly as Minister of the Interior, but this was too much even for France, and he hastily resigned. Malvy died in Paris in 1949.

Joseph Caillaux enjoyed a similar example of the leniency of French justice when meted out to politicians. Fortunately for him he was not brought to trial until February 1920, at which time a left-wing tide had filled the Senate with friends who were inclined to view Caillaux's wartime deeds with understanding. He was found innocent of "plotting against the security of the state abroad," but was found guilty on a less serious charge and was sentenced to three years' imprisonment and ten years' loss of civil rights. Since he had already passed three years in prison awaiting trial, he was released immediately and later, in 1924, was granted an amnesty.

In later years Caillaux again returned to politics. He was elected a senator, served as Finance Minister in various cabinets, and rebuilt much of his power within the Radical Socialist party. He died in 1944.

It is interesting to theorize what might have happened had Caillaux become Premier instead of Clemenceau. Although most certainly Caillaux could not have made an immediate peace with Germany (the Army and the right wing would have still been strong enough to prevent this), it is equally certain that he would never have infused France with the vigor necessary to continue the war. Sometime in 1918, probably in March when the Germans burst through the Allied defenses, France would have collapsed; and then, notwithstanding the fury of Britain and the United States, a negotiated peace would have been arranged. If this had happened, perhaps today Caillaux would be regarded as a great statesman, the "first

European," and a man of peace. Treason, after all, is a transitory crime and must be set within the context of the time.

For the others, the small fry such as Bolo Pasha, Duval and the members of the *Bonnet rouge* staff, the courts were not so kind as they were to Malvy and Caillaux. They were tried before a *conseil de guerre*, the Third Military Court of the Seine, and received the sort of sentence to be expected from such a court.

Bolo Pasha was found guilty of treason. On April 17, 1918, immaculate in new suit and white gloves, freshly shaven and still the dapper figure of a confidence man, Bolo stepped to the stake at Vincennes and was shot.

Duval, Marion, Joucla and Goldsky of the *Bonnet rouge* were given varying sentences. Duval was shot, the others were condemned to long prison terms. Lenoir, the young Frenchman who had conspired to buy *Le Journal* with German money, was also sentenced to death. He died less well than Bolo; in fact, it seems evident that he actually perished from fright just before the execution and that it was a corpse which was tied to the stake to await the firing squad.

All the foregoing are events of public knowledge, amply documented, suitably recorded. There now remains only one element in this story of mutiny and treason which still must be told. It is the tale of the Army mutineers and what happened to them after May and June of 1917, and it must be considered one of history's best-kept secrets.

There could be only two possible sources for complete details of the mutinies and the punishment given the troops who rebelled. One of these sources would be Pétain—and Pétain is dead. He had promised the officers of the Army that he would "protect with his authority all those who display vigor and energy in suppression," [7] and he was true to his word. He rarely spoke of the mutinies, never wrote his memoirs, and died still silent on the affair. From a despised grave, Pétain, who never made a promise he could not keep, still protects the Army.

The other source of complete details would obviously be the French Army itself. Granted, no military organization *wants* to publicize mutinies within its ranks, but it would seem that after

more than forty years these events could safely be revealed to
the public. However, with the exception of one short chapter in the
immense multivolume French official history of World War I, the
Army has chosen to remain silent regarding any details on the mutinies. And probably even this sketchy chapter would not have been
written if it were not for the fact that various political personalities,
such as Poincaré and Painlevé, whose eminence was such that
they could scarcely be prevented from writing as they pleased had
mentioned the mutinies in their memoirs. But, aside from this single
acknowledgment of the mutinies in the official history of the war,
the Army has remained mute. Inquiries concerning them are politely
referred to the civilian libraries with the advice that the records of
the *conseils de guerre* which tried the mutineers will not be made
public until fifty years after the date of the mutinies. Very possibly they will not even be available then. For secrecy's sake, most of
the records concerning the mutinies have probably long since been
destroyed, in addition to those which were incinerated in May 1940,
when the French Ministry of War, about to flee Paris before the
German occupation, burned its files in a huge bonfire.

Why does the French Army take this stand? How has it been able
to keep these mutinies, an event which involved scores of thousands
of men, a secret? The answer is complex, but basically it is this:
The French Army is and always has been a great power within
France. Over the course of many decades it has accumulated an
influence which is unknown and unsuspected in nations which have
grown up in the tradition of "no large standing armies." Within certain limits, the French Army reveals what it wishes to reveal and
keeps secret what it wishes to keep secret. Occasionally the Army
grossly abuses its power, as in the Dreyfus Affair, and then it cannot conceal its error. But when there is some reasonable excuse for
military secrecy, then the Army can and does hide the affair. Thus it
is with the mutinies. During World War I it was a matter of compelling necessity to keep the mutinies secret. In the years after World
War I the Army saw no reason to publicize the event, which scarcely
redounded to the glory of French arms. Moreover, a few months
after the end of World War I a naval flotilla and a small force of
French troops were sent to the Black Sea to assist the "White" Russian armies in their attempts to overthrow the Bolshevik government. But after only a short while in Russia the French soldiers and

sailors became so infected with Communism and outright mutiny that the whole force was hastily withdrawn. To the Army command in the years after World War I it must have seemed that its troops had somehow become infected with a latent germ of rebellion. If this was the case, it was a matter of authentic importance to keep secret any facts regarding mutiny in the Army. And now in recent years the climate within France has not been such that revelation of past military revolts would be received in an agreeable light.

So when it comes to precise figures and individual details on the mutinies, the only sources are those which, as they were charitably described to the author by a French historian, reflect *le point de vue officiel*. It has been officially admitted that there were 110 cases of "grave collective indiscipline" and that these occurred within 54 different divisions.[8] It has never been made clear just what criteria were used to select the "grave" mutinies from the less grave, but judging from the supporting data given it must be inferred that these mutinies were *at least* on a battalion scale and, more probably, on the order of almost a full regiment. Assuming this to be the case, it would not be too much to say that there were *at least* 100,000 men in active mutiny, and probably many more.

The fate of these active mutineers and their less active comrades is also a matter of conjecture. Again, it is officially admitted that during the six-month period from May to October 1917 the *conseils de guerre* found 23,385 men guilty of various crimes, and that of these 412 were condemned to death, with only 23 mutineers actually shot.[9] But this figure is obviously far too low. Granted, the repression of the mutinies never degenerated to a bloodbath; however, the figure of twenty-three executions obviously does not include men shot out of hand during the course of suppression, nor, despite declaimers to the contrary, is it conceivable that it includes mutineers who were executed under various charges other than mutiny.

As for the remainder of the mutineers, they were generally sent to the viciously disciplined punishment battalions in Africa or else shipped to the prison colonies, from which those who survived returned to France only in 1924 when a general amnesty was passed by Parliament.

The fate of the Russian brigades, both the mutinous 1st Brigade as well as the 3rd Brigade, is better known. Among the rebels, as we have seen, eighty-one ringleaders were imprisoned on the Île d'Aix, where, apparently, most of them were secretly shot. The 500-odd "hard" cases were sent to French prisons or the penal battalions in Africa, from which few of them ever returned. The remaining 7,500 men of the rebellious 1st Battalion were, in a sense, victims of the Bolshevik revolution of November 1917, because after this event the French refused to allow them to return to Russia, since they suspected that the troops would only join the Red armies against which the Allies had aligned themselves. As a result, the French offered these Russians a choice of "voluntary" labor within France or deportation to prison camps in Africa. Many of them chose labor, but about three thousand of them refused and were deported to Africa, where they were treated as prisoners of war. It is doubtful if more than a handful of these ever made their way back to Russia.

The fate of the loyal Russians is equally obscured. The phantom "2nd Special Artillery Brigade" disappeared back into the limbo from which it came. Subsequent attempts to trace it have failed. From the remaining loyalists a "Russian Legion" was formed, principally of much-decorated soldiers with monarchist leanings, and it fought with considerable valor on the western front in the closing days of the war. Of the rest, many stayed in France after the war and still live there to this day. Those who wanted to return to Russia had to wait until 1919 or 1920, when they were finally repatriated as part of an exchange of prisoners with the Communist government. There remains only one more group to account for among these unhappy troops. One unit had been allowed to return to Russia immediately after the armistice so that it might fight against the Red Army in the "White" forces of General Wrangel. They were overpowered in 1919 in the Crimea and, presumably, paid the ultimate penalty.

A logical question to ask concerning the secrecy surrounding this biggest of all military mutinies is why, despite Army secrecy, there have not been articles about it in the newspapers. It would seem to be a topic of great interest to readers, a subject which, with interviews of surviving mutineers, would be a journalistic coup. But there is a reason why this has never been done, and it is wrapped up in the peculiar character of French journalism. For some reason the French have always been indifferent and immune to newspaper advertising, even though newspapers are generally conceded to occupy positions of substantial influence within France. Accordingly, deprived of the income (and the relative independence) which advertising revenue would give it, the French press must turn elsewhere for funds—for "subventions" to meet the deficit between production cost and the revenue from the newsstand sale. These subventions have been provided on a quasi-secret basis from a variety of sources. Before World War I the French press was subsidized largely by Russian money which sought to create a climate favorable to investment in Russian railroads by French capital and to the furtherance of the Franco-Russian alliance. After World War I, the press was generally subventioned by the large moneyed families, by the Comité des Forges, by the government and, most probably, by the Army itself.

But what of the newspapers of the far left, the journals which the Army and its friends cannot or will not buy? For these newspapers there is always the threat of censorship in the event that "unsuitable" subjects are pursued too avidly by the editors. However, this threat would probably be unnecessary. The newspapers of the left touched upon the mutinies briefly in the period immediately after the war and then, apparently realizing that the part played in these events by the left wing sat poorly with their readership, dropped the subject.

It is now, even forty-five years later, difficult to get Frenchmen to talk about the mutinies. Those who are wise do not discuss military mutinies in France. As in the case of the German occupation of 1940-44, there seems to be a sense of collective guilt about this event. And anyhow it has passed into the realm of history. The youngest men who could have taken part in the mutinies are now in their middle sixties, there are not so many of these left, and those who are still alive do not like to think of themselves as former mutineers.

In a way, all this secrecy is a little extreme and, perhaps, not at all necessary. Nothing could tarnish the glory of the French soldier's role in World War I, and it is even possible to build a case around the argument that if it had not been for the mutinies another Nivelle type of offensive would have been restaged and the Army would have collapsed in a bloody heap. Perhaps the Army revolts of 1917 had their uses. Maybe it is unfair to label this convulsion of exhausted troops a "mutiny." At any rate, none dare call it treason.

Now there is only one final scene. The scar of the main trench system still cuts its furrow across northeastern France. In large sections the industrious farmers have filled in the trenches, have leveled the shell holes and have somehow made the soil yield crops. But in many fields, notably at Verdun, nothing useful will grow. The earth has been too badly infected by the shellfire, and the ground is covered only by an ugly metallic-green weed. The visitor to Verdun can see a concrete shed which covers the "Trench of Bayonets" where the earth caved in on a unit of the 137th Infantry Regiment, burying the men alive and leaving only the bayonets on their rifles protruding above this mass grave. The visitor can look out at the desolate battlefield from which, until 1932, ten cartloads of bones were collected each day. And he can visit the huge, ugly mortuary of Douaumont which is built over the skeletons of thousands of unknown bodies collected from the surrounding fields.

This is at the eastern edge of France. Beyond Verdun is Germany. And from the center of France, from the west, the wind comes endlessly, keening and moaning through the ugly monuments.

AUTHOR'S NOTE

THE WRITING of this book has been a labor of love. For a number of years I have been fascinated by World War I and, in particular, by the French Army mutinies and the political pacifism which accompanied them.

For the sketchy character of the first half-dozen chapters, I make no apology. They are, after all, merely outlines of the events. Other authors have written at vastly greater length and with much more competence on such topics as the birth of the Third Republic, the Dreyfus Affair and the Battle of Verdun. My only reason for including them here is to give the reader background in the politico-military history of the Third Republic and, later, to show the awesome casualties which the French Army suffered in the three years of war leading up to the spring of 1917.

The feature of the events described in this book which is most intriguing to me is the eerie quality of the political treason coupled with the secrecy in which the mutinies have been shrouded. To reduce these to relatively contemporary equivalents, it is as if during World War II a former President of the United States were conducting secret conversations with known traitors in the pay of Nazi Germany; as if the editors of a prominent New York liberal newspaper were secretly subsidized by the Germans; and as if the Attorney General and his director of the F.B.I. were winking at the whole affair. Moreover, it is as if a large part of the U. S. Army fighting in Europe mutinied but, so tight was secrecy and so closely was the press watched, that no full account of the mutinies was published in the newspapers of the United States either during or after the war.

ACKNOWLEDGMENTS AND NOTES

WITHOUT THE KIND assistance of many persons, this book would most certainly never have been written. In particular, I wish to acknowledge the manifold kindnesses of Evan Hill of Newport, New Hampshire, without whom it would not have been started, and to my friend Donald M. Murray of Glen Ridge, New Jersey, without whose experience and guidance it would not have been completed.

The list of those whose time and facilities I shamelessly imposed upon is embarrassingly long and could not possibly be printed here in its entirety. However, foremost among them would be Mrs. Agnes F. Peterson of the Central and Western European collections, Hoover Institution on War, Revolution and Peace, Stanford University; Dr. John Finch of the French Institute, New York; Monsieur F. Debyser of the Bibliothèque de Documentation Internationale Contemporaine et Musée de la Grande Guerre, Paris; also the patient staffs of the New York Public Library, of Butler Library, Columbia University, of the U. S. Military Academy Library, U.S.M.A., of the Library of Congress, of Baker Library, Dartmouth College, of Littauer Library, Harvard, and of the Glen Ridge Public Library, Glen Ridge, New Jersey.

Many busy persons have given me the benefit of their knowledge of the subject about which this book revolves. Foremost among them are Major-General Sir Edward Spears, London; Cyril Falls, London; and Janet Flanner, Paris. In addition, I owe thanks to Captain Morrell of the Institut für Militärgeschichte, Freiburg, Germany, and Lieutenant Colonel Stamey of the Office of the Chief of Military History, Department of the Army, Washington, for their assistance in searching for German intelligence analyses of the French Army mutinies.

Regarding translations, I assume full responsibility for all translations from the French. For translations from German and Russian, I must acknowledge my debt to Robert Cloos of North Plainfield, New Jersey, and Michael V. Korda of New York City.

And, finally, my particular appreciation to Madame Michele Lapautre, who researched for me in Paris; my editors at Simon and Schuster; and, most especially, my wife, Sandra, who endured three years of my fascination with the subject of this book.

307

In the notes to the various chapters, I have indicated my sources for direct quotations, for all references to specific mutinous incidents and for any fact which it seems to me would be particularly helpful (or possibly debatable) to a student of the events of the period.

Regarding my sources generally, I offer the following prefatory comment. When dealing with affairs such as military mutiny and civil treason in France, it is helpful always to ask oneself the question, In whose interest is it to reveal the facts? Neither French journalism nor French official military history is written with an eye toward absolute truth. Almost everything is written to advance a certain political aim. Once the above is securely fixed in the researcher's mind, much becomes clear. Certain aspects of the political treason described in this book were well publicized, especially in the years immediately after Clemenceau came into office. There is, of course, a good reason for this. The Clemenceau government (and the right-wing parties) was quite anxious to expose the treason of the opposition and to build up a body of public opinion which would insure Joseph Caillaux's conviction in his 1920 trial before the Senate. If Caillaux was not convicted, the Clemenceau government, which was still in power, would be badly embarrassed. Thus it was to *someone's* interest to throw considerable light on the affair, and the numerous accounts of Caillaux's wartime activities and the *Bonnet rouge* must be judged with this in mind.

The Army mutinies of May and June 1917 are a different matter. Here it is to no one's advantage to publicize the event: not to the Army's (for the various reasons mentioned in the Afterword); not to that of the right wing, whose opinions jibe with the Army's in affairs of this sort; nor, even, to that of the left wing, whose connection with the mutinies would be difficult to explain to a nation which is intensely proud of its World War I victory. Little, therefore, has been written of the mutinies. Perhaps even less would be written if it were not for certain top political figures who mention in their memoirs their own roles in the suppression of the mutinies. In this case it *is* to their interest to comment upon the mutinies, because they can do so in such a manner as to throw a favorable light upon themselves (e.g., Painlevé describes his daily trips or telephone calls to G.Q.G. to intercede on behalf of mutineers sentenced to death).

Since the mutinies were revealed as fact, the French Army's Service Historique was compelled to insert a fairly skimpy account of them in its official history of World War I, *Les Armées françaises dans la Grande Guerre*. Probably it was felt that there was no help for it and, moreover, that it gave an excellent opportunity to "set the record straight" and toss most of the blame upon basically nonmilitary causes. In addition, the mutinies could now be described in the more delicate term "collective indiscipline."

Even when it comes to the biographies which describe the role of key figures involved in the suppression of the mutinies, the yardstick "In whose interest is it to reveal the facts?" must again be applied. The case of Pétain is a good ex-

ample. All his biographies are more or less suspect. Those which were written
in France during the Nazi occupation of World War II (such as Laure's
Pétain) are frankly adulatory and obviously written to win popular support
for the Vichy "Chief of State." The biographies written outside France (such
as Lavalade's *Pétain?*) reflect the Free French point of view and attack Pétain
violently. Others, written since the war (such as Carré's *Les Grandes Heures
du général Pétain*), carry the imprint "Published under the patronage of the
Association for the Defense of the Memory of Marshal Pétain."

Almost no one in France, it seems, writes modern history simply to tell the
facts of an event. Everything is subsidized. Everything has its *point de vue*.

How, then, to find what are the facts amidst this sea of slanted misinforma-
tion? Again the test "In whose interest is it?" is applied, this time in a negative
manner. If it is *not* to the author's interest to cover up, slant or otherwise distort the facts, we may look at a source with an only faintly jaundiced eye. And
if several more-or-less-distinterested sources arrive at the same conclusion or
state the same events, it is possible to use the "fact" with some degree of confidence. This is the policy I have attempted to follow in this book—to test for
interest and then, whenever possible, qualify by multiplicity.

This does not mean, however, that every "fact" in this book is actually that
—a fact. I may have unintentionally maligned an occasional regiment or person. But it does mean that I have traced every source I could find and have
tried to cross-check it. For example, every instance of mutiny has been checked
against the French Army order of battle for the date mentioned to ensure that
the unit mentioned could actually have been in the place described at the time
stated. When I began this book I believed many of the tales which have been
current for years concerning the mutinies. I believed that whole divisions had
abandoned the trenches and that countless officers had been murdered by their
rebellious troops. I no longer believe this. The stories which tell of events such
as these are not true. The actual mutinies were less theatrical, but dramatic
enough all the same.

In this connection, the reader with some background in or knowledge of the
French Army mutinies will doubtless be surprised at the omission of the material contained in the famous magazine article "The Bent Sword," by
"A.M.G.," which appeared in *Blackwood's Magazine* for January 1944. Many
works dealing with World War I have credited this article with providing
theretofore unpublished facts about the mutinies. My research has led me to
believe otherwise. A.M.G.'s article discusses, among other revolts, a mutiny in
the "21st Division of Colonial Infantry"; the author implies that the sources for
this data are "two slim monographs published by the German General Staff."
However, this tale of the 21st D.I.C.'s mutiny was actually published earlier in
Mutiny, a book by the British Communist Tom Wintringham (London, Stanley Nott, 1936). Moreover, there was no such division as the "21st Division of
Colonial Infantry." In addition, neither the U. S. Army Historical Service nor
the German Army Institut für Militärgeschichte can find any record of "two
slim monographs" on this subject having been published by the German Gen-

eral Staff subsequent to World War I. Thus, pending clarification of these
seemingly major discrepancies in the "A.M.G." article, I considered it more
prudent not to include it.

Nor, for similar reasons, have I given credence to Henri Barbusse's famous
story, in his *This and Thus*, of 250 mutineers who were supposedly driven
about in trucks at night until they lost their sense of direction, and who were
then guided into no man's land, where they were told to sit down on the
ground and face the German trenches. "Close up tight," Barbusse says they
were ordered, "and mind you don't stir." Then the guarding troops departed,
"crawling away very cautiously," following which all 250 troops were murdered by the French artillery. *Incroyable*.

There are several elements of style which were used in the interests of clarity. For example, the technical title of the head of the Third Republic Ministry
was, of course, the *Président du Conseil*. To avoid confusion between the
President of the Republic and the *Président du Conseil*, I have chosen to refer
to the latter as the Premier. For similar reasons (to avoid confusion between
an individual minister and the collective Ministry), I have generally referred
to the Ministry as "the government."

One final note will, perhaps, be of interest to the reader. The whole question
of the "executions for example" which took place, principally in 1915, when
the *cours martiales* were permitted has attracted considerable attention, although relatively little has been written on it. My source was the magazine
Crapouillot, which, in turn, quotes as its source a speech made by a French
deputy, M. Jade, before the Chamber and reported in the *Journal officiel* of
April 24, 1921. Supplementing the acknowledged van Passen account of the
executions in the 45th Brigade is the New York *Times* for July 2, 1934. These
events, which should not be confused with the mutinies of the spring of 1917,
were the basis for the well-known novel *Paths of Glory* (New York, 1935), by
Humphrey Cobb, who, in a note to the reader on p. 265, gives several additional references, including the book *Le Fusille*, by Blanche Maupas, the widow
of one of those executed.

After the war a long series of little-publicized "revisionary trials" was held
in which troops who had been illegally executed were "rehabilitated." In the
case of the four corporals, a monument was erected to their memory in the
town of Sortilly, in the department of Manche. Their widows were awarded a
token compensation—one franc.

CHAPTER ONE

Of great help in the preparation of this chapter were various biographies of
Clemenceau not mentioned in the following notes—in particular, Brunn's
Clemenceau, Martet's *Georges Clemenceau* and Hyndman's *Clemenceau: The
Man and His Time*. Also helpful was Weyer's *The Decline of Democracy in
France*.

1. Brogan, *France under the Republic*, p. 117.
2. Hyndman, *Clemenceau: The Man and His Time*, p. 208.
3. Williams, *The Tiger of France*, p. 76.
4. Curtis, *Boulanger: The Original Man on Horseback*, p. 59.
5. Maurice Barrès, quoted in Jackson, *Clemenceau and the Third Republic*, p. 71.
6. Ratinaud, *Clemenceau, ou La Colère et la gloire*, p. 96.
7. Brogan, *op. cit.*, p. 281.
8. De Gaulle, *France and Her Army*, p. 81.

CHAPTER TWO

1. Paléologue, *An Intimate Journal of the Dreyfus Case*, pp. 204-6.
2. Halasz, *Captain Dreyfus: The Story of a Mass Hysteria*, p. 20.
3. Brogan, *France under the Republic*, p. 386.
4. Halasz, *op. cit.*, pp. 237-38.
5. De Gaulle, *France and Her Army*, p. 84.
6. Ardant du Picq, *Études sur le Combat*, pp. 154-155.
7. Flanner, *Pétain: Old Man of France*, p. 13.
8. Foch, *Mémoires*, p. lvii.
9. Falls, *The Great War*, p. 35.
10. Flanner, *op. cit.*, p. 5.
11. *The Times History of the War*, Vol. I, p. 15.
12. *The Times History of the War*, Vol. I, p. 233.
13. Goerlitz, *History of the German General Staff*, p. 142.

CHAPTER THREE

Unreferenced but helpful in providing background for this chapter was Aulard's *Histoire politique de la Grande Guerre*.

1. Moltke, "Mobilization Mornings," in *Living Age*, for Jan. 20, 1923, p. 134.
2. Schmitt, *The Coming of the War, 1914*, p. 18.
3. *Ibid.*, p. 19.
4. *The Times History of the War*, Vol. II, p. 441.
5. Allard, *Les Énigmes de la guerre* p. 36.
6. Renouvin, *Forms of War Government in France*, pp. 1-10.
7. *Ibid.*, p. 30.
8. Albert, *Le Procès Malvy*, p. 79.
9. Sancermé, *Les Serviteurs de l'ennemi*, p. x.
10. *Les Procès de trahaison*, p. 180.
11. Terrail, *Nivelle et Painlevé*, p. 184.
12. Renouvin, *op. cit.*, p. 36.
13. Malvy, *Mon Crime*, p. 39.
14. Géraud, *Gravediggers of France*, p. 95.
15. Lyon, *The Pomp of Power*, p. 178.
16. *Ibid.*
17. *Figaro* for March 13, 1914 (facsimile reproduction of letter).
18. Caillaux, *Agadir: ma politique extérieure*, p. 132.
19. Johnson, *The Enemy Within*, pp. 284-5.
20. *Times* (London), July 27, 1914.
21. Raphael, *The Caillaux Drama*, pp. 17-22.

22. Adam, *Treason and Tragedy*, p. 132.
23. *Bonnet rouge* for July 30, 1914.
24. *The Times History of the War*, Vol. II, p. 438.
25. Brogan, *France under the Republic*, p. 483.
26. De Gaulle, *France and Her Army*, pp. 90-91.
27. *Figaro*, July 29, 1914.

28. Joffre, *Memoirs*, Vol. I, p. 126.
29. *The Times History of the War*, Vol. II, p. 440.
30. Schmitt, *op. cit.*, p. 21.
31. *Bonnet rouge* for Aug. 3, 1914.
32. Jackson, *Clemenceau and the Third Republic*, pp. 163-64.
33. *Ibid.*, p. 164.
34. *Journal officiel* for Aug. 5, 1914.
35. Renouvin, *op. cit.*, p. 11.

CHAPTER FOUR

Valuable in background for this chapter, although not referenced below, have been the following: Joffre's *Memoirs*, King's *Generals and Politicians*, Recouly's *Joffre*, Messimy's *Mes Souvenirs*, Adam's *Paris Sees It Through*, Esposito *et al.*, *The West Point Atlas of American Wars*, Vol. II, Gallieni's *Mémoires: Défense du Paris 25 aôut-11 septembre 1914* and, most especially, Spears's *Liaison, 1914.*

1. Liddell Hart, B. H., *Reputations*, p. 7.
2. Churchill, *The World Crisis*, Vol. III, p. 24.
3. *The Times History of the War*, Vol. II, p. 146.
4. De Gaulle, *France and Her Army*, p. 92.
5. Ducasse *et al.*, *Vie et mort des Français, 1914-1918*, p. 38.
6. *Les Armées françaises dans la Grande Guerre* (hereafter *L.A.F.*), Tome I, Vol. I *Annexes*, No. 352.

7. *The Times History of the War*, Vol. II, p. 459.
8. *Ibid.*, p. 460.
9. De Gaulle, *op. cit.*, pp. 93-94.
10. Goerlitz, *History of the German General Staff*, p. 161.
11. Galtier-Boissière, *Histoire de la Grande Guerre*, p. 225 (facsimile reproduction of announcement).
12. Churchill, *op. cit.*, pp. 37-38.
13. Edmonds, *A Short History of World War I*, p. 61.
14. Churchill, *op. cit.*, pp. 289-92 (appendices).

CHAPTER FIVE

The number of contemporary accounts of trench life by members of the French, British and German armies is endless. Unfortunately most of them dwell so heavily on the humor and the fighting spirit of their respective soldiery that these "diaries" are almost worthless (an exception to this is Henri Barbusse's *Le Feu*). I found it far more rewarding to consult various Army technical manuals, foremost among which were the 1918 French *Manuel de chef de section d'infanterie* and the U. S. Army's translation of the 1917 edition, *Manual for Commanders of Infantry Platoons*. Also helpful were the charts showing French Army platoon and company organization and assault formations found in the appendices to Spears's *Prelude to Victory*, pp. 522-26.

Techniques of trench warfare varied, of course, from year to year, and even from army group to army group within the French Army itself. In this chapter I have attempted to give a generalized picture of trench tactics as they were in 1915 and in the years which followed.

1. From *Achievements of Cavalry* (London, 1897), quoted in Ropp, *War in the Modern World*, p. 184fn.
2. Edmonds, *A Short History of World War I*, p. 431fn.
3. Falls, *The Great War*, p. 12.
4. Joffre, *Memoirs*, Vol. II, p. 590.
5. Liddell Hart, B. H., *Through the Fog of War*, pp. 163-64.
6. Spears, *Prelude to Victory*, p. 302.
7. *Manual for Commanders of Infantry Platoons*, p. 15.

8. *Ibid.*, p. 355.
9. *Ibid.*, p. 155.
10. Spears, *op. cit.*, pp. 524-25.
11. *Manual for Commanders of Infantry Platoons*, p. 29.
12. De Gaulle, *France and Her Army*, p. 100.
13. Corday, *The Paris Front*, p. 96.
14. *Ibid.*, p. 107.
15. Liddell Hart, B. H., *Reputations*, p. 29.
16. Churchill, *The World Crisis*, Vol. III, p. 290.

CHAPTER SIX

Among the works most valuable in the preparation of this chapter, although unreferenced below, were Liddell Hart's *Reputations*, Bolton's *Pétain*, Flanner's *Pétain: Old Man of France*, Serrigny's *Trente Ans avec Pétain* and Lavalade's *Pétain True to Scale*.

Partisans of General Charles Lanrezac may, perhaps, feel that I have dealt unfairly with him in this chapter. However, I elected to use Joffre's *Memoirs* and Spears's *Liaison, 1914* as my guides.

Concerning the "executions for example," details as to additional sources will be found on pages 235-38.

1. Ferry, *Les Carnets secrets d'Abel Ferry, annexe 7.*
2. Spears, *Liaison: 1914*, pp. 483-84.
3. Churchill, *Great Contemporaries*, p. 194.
4. Pierrefeu, *French Headquarters, 1915-1918*, p. 34.
5. Renouvin, *The Forms of War Government in France*, pp. 33-39.
6. Jean Bernier, "Les Fusilés 'par erreur,'" in *Crapouillot* for October 1960, pp. 41-43.
7. Paassen, *Days of Our Years*, pp. 155-56.

8. *Annuaire de l'armée française pour l'année 1914*, table of seniority of infantry colonels.
9. Laure, *Pétain*, pp. 7, 14.
10. Géraud, *Gravediggers of France*, p. 318.
11. Laure, *op. cit.*, p. 15.
12. *Ibid.*, pp. 28-29.
13. Joffre, *Memoirs*, Vol. II, pp. 355, 450.
14. Spears, *op. cit.*, p. 535.
15. Poincaré, *Au Service de la France*, Vol. VI, *Les Tranchées* (1915), pp. 331-32.

CHAPTER SEVEN

There are two works which contribute so substantially to an understanding of the interrelationship between G.Q.G. and the French government that they must be specially acknowledged. Pierrefeu's account (referenced below in both French and its English translation) is the appraisal of G.Q.G. by an observant French journalist who was brought to Chantilly to write the daily communiqués. King's *Generals and Politicians* is a definitive account of the clash between the Army and the politicians.

1. Pierrefeu, *French Headquarters, 1915-1918*, p. 115.
2. Gallieni, *Mémoires: Défense du Paris*, p. 51.
3. Brogan, *France under the Republic*, p. 512.
4. Joffre, *Memoirs*, Vol. II, p. 397.
5. *Ibid.*, p. 398.
6. Gallieni, *Mémoires*, p. 172.

7. Herbillon, *Souvenirs d'un officier de liaison*, Vol. I, p. 139.
8. Renouvin, *The Forms of War Government in France*, p. 32.
9. Quoted in King, *Generals and Politicians*, p. 50.
10. Pierrefeu, *G.Q.G., Secteur 1*, p. 52.
11. Herbillon, *op. cit.*, p. 171.

CHAPTER EIGHT

There is, of course, an immense mass of source material available on the Battle of Verdun. For a physical picture of the battlefield I found the Michelin Tire Company's illustrated guidebooks to the battlefield, published in 1920, to be most valuable. Also helpful were the Verdun volumes of Palat's *La Grande Guerre sur le front occidental* and Ducasse *et al.*, *Vie et mort des Français, 1914-1918*.

1. This and the preceding quotations from Falkenhayn's report are from his *General Headquarters, 1914-16*, pp. 209-14.
2. Gallieni, *Les Carnets de Gallieni*, p. 233.
3. *Ibid.*, p. 234.
4. Jobert, *Souvenirs d'un ex-parlementaire*, p. 133.
5. Joffre, *Memoirs*, Vol. II, p. 440.
6. *Ibid.*

7. Pétain, *Verdun*, p. 93.
8. Churchill, *The World Crisis*, Vol. III, p. 97.
9. Serrigny, *Trente Ans avec Pétain*, p. 82.
10. Buchan, *The Battle of the Somme: First Phase*, map pp. 12-13.
11. Boraston, *Sir Douglas Haig's Despatches*, pp. 22-23.
12. Churchill, *op. cit.*, p. 179.
13. *Ibid.*, p. 290.

CHAPTER NINE

Unreferenced below but of the greatest value in the preparation of this chapter are various accounts, many of which are politically suspect but serve to give the background on the treason of the time. Among them, all contemporary with the event, are Sancermé's *Les Serviteurs de l'ennemi*, Marchand's *L'Offensive morale des Allemands en France*, Dejean's *Casque à pointe et Bonnet rouge*.

Espousing their own defense are Malvy's *Mon Crime* and Caillaux's *Devant l'Histoire: mes prisons*.

Other, more dispassionate works of great value are the *Histoire politique de la Grande Guerre*, by Aulard *et al.*, and *Les Procès de trahaison* (*Revue des causes célèbres*), especially sections 6 through 11, which deal with the *Bonnet rouge*. Peculiarly, however, many of the accounts of Caillaux's treason were not published *in extenso* in France, and the best contemporary sources are British.

1. Hyndman, *Clemenceau: The Man and His Time*, p. 262.
2. Corday, *The Paris Front*, p. 97.
3. Galtier-Boissière, *La Grande Guerre*, p. 306.
4. *Ibid.*, p. 307.
5. Ducasse *et al.*, *Vie et mort des français, 1914-18*, p. 270.
6. Trotsky, *My Life*, p. 249.
7. Ducasse *et al.*, *op. cit.*, p. 258.
8. *L'Homme enchaîné* for Feb. 2 and Jan. 23, 1917.
9. *Ibid.* Feb. 20, 1917.
10. *Ibid.*, various dates in January 1917.
11. Poincaré, *Au Service de la France*, Vol. V, *L'Invasion*, pp. 188-91.
12. *Bonnet rouge* for August 1, 1916.
13. Johnson, *The Enemy Within*, pp. 135-36.
14. *Bonnet rouge* for Oct. 22, 1914.
15. Johnson, *op. cit.*, p. 63.

16. Gallieni, *Les Carnets de Gallieni*, p. 187.
17. Joffre, *Memoirs*, Vol. I, p. 194fn.
18. Johnson, *op. cit.*, p. 54.
19. Maxse, "The Strange Case of M. Caillaux," in *The National Review* for February 1918, p. 740.
20. *Ibid.*, pp. 740-41.
21. *Ibid.*, p. 741.
22. Adam, George, *Treason and Tragedy*, p. 157.
23. Corday, *op. cit.*, p. 192.
24. Adam, *op. cit.*, p. 165.
25. Jean Ybarnegary, quoted in Torres, *Pierre Laval*, p. 72.
26. Malvy, *Mon Crime*, pp. 227-28.
27. Pierrefeu, *French Headquarters, 1915-1918*, p. 179.
28. *Times* (London), Dec. 22, 1917.
29. *Ibid.*, Dec. 13, 1917.

CHAPTER TEN

Among all the accounts of the Nivelle offensive, the works of Painlevé and Spears stand out to such an extent that I have used them almost exclusively in the notes below. Nevertheless, many other works give valuable insight into one or another of the aspects of this offensive. Davis' *Reservoirs of Men* is the definitive study of the Senegalese troops. Other works consulted include *The War Memoirs of David Lloyd George*, Terrail's *Nivelle et Painlevé: la 2ᵉ crise du commandement*, Herbillon's *Souvenirs* (Vol. II), Mangin's *Comment finit la guerre*, Ratinaud's *1917, ou La Tragédie d'avril* and various French "trench papers" of the period.

1. Spears, *Prelude to Victory*, p. 20.
2. Corday, *The Paris Front*, p. 154.
3. Joffre, *Memoirs*, Vol. II, p. 450.
4. *Ibid.*, p. 451.
5. Palat, *La Grande Guerre sur le front occidental*, Vol. XII, p. 264.
6. Spears, *op. cit.*, p. 32.
7. *Ibid.*, p. 102.
8. Falls, *Military Operations, France and Belgium, 1917*, Appendix 19.
9. Gallichet, *L'Offensive français de 1917*, pp. 117-21.
10. Spears, *op. cit.*, pp. 130-31.
11. *L.A.F.*, Tome V, Vol. I, p. 277.
12. Painlevé, "La Vérité sur l'offensive du 16 avril 1917," in *La Renaissance*, 1919, special issue, p. 20.
13. Spears, *op. cit.*, p. 338.
14. Ducasse *et al.*, *Vie et mort des Français, 1914-1918*, p. 312.

15. Painlevé, *op. cit.*, p. 27.
16. *Ibid.*, p. 29.
17. *L.A.F.*, Tome V, Vol. I, p. 579.
18. Carré, *Les Grandes Heures du général Pétain*, p. 38.
19. Spears, *op. cit.*, p. 373; all other quotes in this section on the April 6 meeting are from Painlevé *op. cit.*, pp. 31-32.
20. Churchill, *The World Crisis*, Vol. III, p. 280.
21. *Journal officiel* for June 24-July 1, 1922, *annexe* on the session of June 29, 1917, p. 333.
22. William, *My War Experiences*, p. 637.
23. *L.A.F.*, Tome V, Vol. I, p. 637.
24. Pierrefeu, *French Headquarters, 1915-1918*, p. 157.

CHAPTER ELEVEN

1. Carré, *Les Grandes Heures du général Pétain*, pp. 51-52.
2. *L.A.F.*, Tome V, Vol. I, p. 704.
3. Palat, *La Grande Guerre sur le front occidental*, Vol. XII, p. 422.
4. Painlevé, *Comment j'ai nommé Foch et Pétain*, p. 135.
5. *L'Humanité* for May 24, 1921.
6. Carré, *op. cit.*, p. 110-11.
7. Ratinaud, *1917, ou La Tragédie d'avril*, p. 13.
8. Sources for the revolt of the 2nd Colonial Division: Terrail, *Nivelle et Painlevé*, pp. 169-70; Palat, *op. cit.*, p. 424; Bathe, *Frankreichs schwerste Stunde*, p. 170.
9. *L.A.F.*, Tome V, Vol. II, pp. 422-23.
10. Sources for the revolt at the XXXIInd Corps depot: Allard, series entitled *Les Mutineries dans l'armée française*, in *L'Œuvre* for Aug. 29, 1932; Palat, *op. cit.*,

p. 426; Terrail, *op. cit.*, p. 171; Bathe, *op. cit.*, p. 174.
11. For the revolt in the 158th Division: Allard, *Les Dessous de la guerre révélés par les comités secrets*, p. 175; Terrail, *op. cit.*, p. 171.
12. The account of the Soissons revolt witnessed by Taufflieb is based on his *Souvenirs d'un enfant de l'Alsace*, pp. 337-38.
13. Sources for the Soissons revolt of the 370th Regiment: Bathe, *op. cit.*, pp. 175-79; Painlevé, *op. cit.*, p. 141.
14. For the Fère-en-Tardenois mutiny: Ratinaud, *op. cit.*, pp. 11-14; Palat, *op. cit.*, pp. 426-27; Allard, *op. cit.*, p. 175; Terrail, p. 172.
15. Painlevé, *op. cit.*, p. 138.
16. With the exception of the above quotation, the revolt of the 128th Regiment is from Allard, *op. cit.*,

p. 201; Palat, *op. cit.*, pp. 425-26; and Jobert, *Souvenirs d'un ex-parlementaire, 1914-19*, p. 267.

17. Lloyd George, *War Memoirs*, Vol. IV, p. 338.

18. Pierrefeu, *French Headquarters, 1915-1918*, p. 167.

19. *L.A.F.*, Tome V, Vol. II, p. 193.

CHAPTER TWELVE

1. Terrail, *Nivelle et Painlevé*, pp. 172-74.
2. Painlevé, *Comment j'ai nommé Foch et Pétain*, p. 138.
3. Terrail, *op. cit.*, p. 217.
4. Painlevé, *op. cit.*, p. 143.
5. Poincaré, *Au Service de la France*, Vol. IX, *L'Année trouble*, pp. 148, 161.
6. Jobert, *Souvenirs d'un ex-parlementaire*, p. 265.
7. Gallichet, *L'Offensive français de 1917 (avril-mai) de Soissons à Reims*, pp. 235-36.
8. Painlevé, *op. cit.*, p. 143.
9. Terrail, *op. cit.*, p. 637.
10. *L.A.F.*, Tome V, Vol. II, p. 194 (total taken by lumping together the separate figures for "desertions to the enemy or in front of the enemy," "desertions to foreign soil" and "desertions to the interior").
11. These units and figures were announced by Jobert in the secret-committee session of the Chamber on June 29, 1917. Since no notes were allowed to be taken at these secret meetings, the figures and precise unit designations vary slightly in the various accounts of the event. I have accepted the data in Jobert (*op. cit.*, p. 261) except in the case of the 61st Battalion,

which Jobert does not mention in his memoirs but upon which the following agree: Allard, *Les Dessous de la guerre révélés par les comités secrets*, pp. 189-90, and Palat, *La Grande Guerre sur le front occidental*, Vol. XII, p. 428.

12. *L.A.F.*, Tome V, Vol. II, pp. 193-94.
13. Corday, *The Paris Front*, pp. 256-57.
14. *La Tranchée républicaine* for the weeks April 24-May, 31, 1917.
15. Poincaré, *op. cit.*, p. 153.
16. *Ibid.*, pp. 152-53.
17. Jolinon, "La Mutinerie de Cœuvres," in *Mercure de France*, Aug. 15, 1920, p. 75.
18. *Ibid.*, p. 78.
19. Allard, *op. cit.*, p. 198.
20. Jolinon, *op. cit.*, p. 83.
21. Poincaré, *op. cit.*, p. 178.
22. Sources for the seizure of Missy-aux-Bois: Jobert, *op. cit.*, pp. 25, 262-65; Gallichet, *op. cit.*, pp. 234-36.
23. Corday, *op. cit.*, p. 260.
24. Poitevin, *La Mutinerie de la Courtine*, pp. 32-33.
25. Bathe, *Frankreichs schwerste Stunde*, p. 212.
26. *L.A.F.*, Tome V, Vol. II, p. 193.
27. De Gaulle, *France and Her Army*, p. 103.

CHAPTER THIRTEEN

In addition to those referenced below, the following sources have been helpful in preparing this chapter: Herbillon's *Souvenirs*, Laure's *Pétain*, Pierrefeu's *French Headquarters, 1915-1918*, and Ratinaud's *1917, ou La Tragédie d'avril*.

1. Flanner, *Pétain: Old Man of France*, p. 21.
2. Serrigny, *Trente Ans avec Pétain*, p. 146.
3. *L.A.F.*, Tome V, Vol. II, pp. 85-87, and Vol. II *Annexes*, No. 235.
4. Lloyd George, *War Memoirs*, Vol. IV, p. 335.
5. *Bulletin des armées de la République* for June 6, 1917.
6. Spears, *Liaison, 1914*, p. 536.
7. Carré, *Les Grandes Heures du général Pétain*, p. 137.
8. *Ibid.*, pp. 130-31.
9. *Ibid.*, p. 134.
10. *L.A.F.*, Tome V, Vol. II *Annexes*, No. 662.
11. *Ibid.*, Tome V, Vol. II, pp. 195-99, and Vol. II *Annexes*, No. 237.
12. *Ibid.*, *Annexes*, No. 1038.
13. *Ibid*, No. 759.
14. *Ibid.*, Tome V, Vol. II, p. 203.
15. Carré, *op. cit.*, p. 153.

CHAPTER FOURTEEN

In addition to those sources shown below, I used Renouvin's *The Forms of War Government in France*, Laure's *Pétain* and *Le Commandement-en-chef des armées françaises*, and Herbillon's *Souvenirs* as especially valuable background material for this chapter.

1. Barbusse, *This and Thus*, p. 79.
2. Poincaré, *Au Service de la France*, Vol. IX, *L'Année trouble*, p. 156.
3. Terrail, *Nivelle et Painlevé*, p. 159fn.
4. *Ibid.*, pp. 176-77.
5. Painlevé, *Comment j'ai nommé Foch et Pétain*, pp. 168-69.
6. *Ibid.*, p. 144.
7. *L.A.F.*, Tome V, Vol. II, p. 205.
8. Painlevé, *op. cit.*, p. 145.
9. Allard, *Les Dessous de la guerre révélés par les comités secrets*, p. 200.
10. Painlevé, *op. cit.*, p. 146.
11. *L.A.F.*, Tome V, Vol. II, p. 197.
12. *Ibid.*, pp. 197-98.
13. All quotes by Taufflieb are from his *Souvenirs d'un enfant de l'Alsace*, pp. 339-42.
14. *L.A.F.*, Tome V, Vol. II, p. 206.
15. Painlevé, *op. cit.*, pp. 146-47.
16. *Ibid.*, p. 147.
17. Allard, *Les Dessous de la guerre*, p. 196.
18. *L.A.F.*, Tome V, Vol. II, p. 192.
19. Nicolai, *The German Secret Service*, p. 187.
20. Carré, *Les Grandes Heures du général Pétain*, p. 172.
21. William, *My War Experiences*, p. 279.
22. Carré, *op. cit.*, p. 145.
23. *L'Homme enchaîné* for July 15, 1917.
24. Both Anthoine quotes are from *L.A.F.*, Tome V, Vol. II, p. 653.
25. Carré, *op. cit.*, p. 173.
26. *Ibid.*, p. 176.
27. *L.A.F.*, Tome V, Vol. II, p. 675.
28. Carré, *op. cit.*, pp. 174-75.

CHAPTER FIFTEEN

The sources mentioned in the notes to Chapter 9 were again helpful in preparing this chapter.

1. All quotes in this paragraph are from Carré, *Les Grandes Heures du général Pétain*, pp. 79-92.
2. Poincaré, *Au Service de la France*, Vol. IX (L'Année trouble), p. 149.
3. Jobert, *Souvenirs d'un ex-parlementaire*, pp. 247-48.
4. *Journal officiel* for June 24-July 1, 1922, *annexe* on the session of June 29, 1917, pp. 334-36.
5. All of this section, including the Laval speech and the section on Taufflieb, is from Allard *Les Dessous de la guerre*, pp. 171-79. The only exception is the sentence on shooting men from the 66th and 77th R.I., which is from Jobert, *op. cit.*, p. 267.
6. *Times* (London), July 9, 1917.
7. Ducasse *et al.*, *Vie et mort des Français, 1914-1918*, p. 335.
8. Painlevé, *Comment j'ai nommé Foch et Pétain*, p. 160.
9. *Ibid.*
10. Gallichet, *L'Offensive française de 1917*, p. 117.
11. Adam, *Treason and Tragedy*, p. 106.
12. Clemenceau, *Antipatriotisme: devant le Sénat 22 juillet 1917*.
13. *Bonnet rouge* for November 18, 1916.
14. *Ibid.*, February 12, 1915.
15. Terrail, *Nivelle et Painlevé*, p. 185fn.
16. *Bonnet rouge* censored article for July 13, 1916.
17. *La Tranchée républicaine* for week of May 1-9, 1917.
18. *L.A.F.*, Tome V, Vol. II *Annexes*, No. 669.
19. *Ibid.*, No. 697.
20. *Ibid.*, No. 820.
21. Quoted in King, *Generals and Politicians*, p. 183.
22. All the preceding are from Clemenceau, *Antipatriotisme, devant le Sénat 22 juillet 1917*, the published transcript of the speech.
23. The interchange between Malvy and Clemenceau does not appear in the official transcripts of Clemenceau's speech; however, it definitely did occur. Among the many who make reference to it is Brogan in his *France under the Republic*, p. 536.
24. Daudet, *Le Poignard en le dos*, p. 19.
25. Galtier-Boissière, "L'Affaire du *Bonnet rouge*," in *Crapouillot* for October 1960, p. 47.
26. Maxse, "The Strange Case of M. Caillaux," in *The National Review* for February 1918, p. 741.
27. Corday, *The Paris Front*, p. 294.

CHAPTER SIXTEEN

In addition to the works referenced below, other sources have been most helpful in researching this chapter. Among them have been Obey's "Camarades Rouski," in *La Revue de Paris*, December 1920; Micheler's *Le Général Alfred Micheler*; and Poitevin's *Une Bataille au centre de la France en 1917*.

1. Poitevin, *La Mutinerie de la Courtine*, p. 63.
2. *Ibid.*, p. 78.
3. *Ibid.*, p. 81.
4. *Ibid.*, p. 89.
5. Danilov, *The Russian Detachments on the French and Macedonian Fronts* (in Russian).
6. Poitevin, *op. cit.*, p. 103.
7. *Ibid.*, p. 112.
8. Reed, *Ten Days That Shook the World*, Appendix 7 to Chapter 2, in which Reed reports having vainly searched the provisional government's files for some record of a "2nd Special Artillery Brigade" which was supposedly on its way through France.
9. Poitevin, *op. cit.*, p. 124.
10. *Ibid.*, p. 138.
11. *Ibid.*, p. 140.
12. *Ibid.*, p. 145.

CHAPTER SEVENTEEN

Although not cited in the notes to this chapter, the following sources were extremely valuable: Caillaux's *Devant l'Histoire: mes prisons*, Malvy's *Mon Crime*, Mordacq's *Le Ministre Clemenceau: Journal d'un témoin* and his biography, *Clemenceau*, Foch's *Mémoires*, Michon's *Clemenceau* and Bruun's *Clemenceau*. King's *Generals and Politicians* again proved most helpful.

1. Carré, *Les Grandes Heures du général Pétain*, pp. 186-87.
2. Corday, *The Paris Front*, p. 276.
3. *L'Homme enchaîné* for January 17, 1917.
4. Painlevé, *Comment j'ai nommé Foch et Pétain*, p. 220.
5. Corday, *op. cit.*, p. 293.
6. *L'Homme enchaîné* for November 15, 1917.
7. Adam, *Treason and Tragedy*, p. 169-75.
8. Ducasse *et al.*, *Vie et mort des français, 1914-1918*, p. 348.
9. The Poincaré quotes here and in the next paragraph are from his *Au Service de la France*, Vol. IX, *L'Année trouble*, pp. 366-67, 370.
10. Martet, *Clemenceau*, p. 134.
11. *Ibid.*, pp. 134-35.
12. Churchill, *Great Contemporaries*, p. 272.
13. Clemenceau, *Discours de guerre*, p. 215.
14. Aulard *et al.*, *Histoire politique de la Grande Guerre*, p. 288.
15. Jackson, *Clemenceau and the Third Republic*, p. 161.
16. Ratinaud, *Clemenceau, ou La Colère et la gloire*, p. 179.
17. Spears, *Assignment to Catastrophe*, Vol. I, p. 57.
18. Williams, *The Tiger of France*, p. 146.
19. Spears, *op. cit.*, p. 58.
20. *Ibid.*
21. Williams, *op. cit.*, pp. 280-82.
22. Martin, *Statesmen of the War*, p. 323.
23. Martet, *op. cit.*, p. 79.
24. Williams, *op. cit.*, p. 153.
25. *L'Homme enchaîné* for November 23, 1917.
26. Dubail report, quoted in *Figaro* for Dec. 13, 1917.
27. *Ibid.*
28. *Times* (London) for Dec. 13, 1917.
29. *Figaro* for Dec. 23, 1917.
30. Aulard *et al.*, *op. cit.*, p. 292.
31. Tuchman, *The Zimmerman Telegram*, pp. 15-21.
32. Martet, *op cit.*, p. 194.

33. Jackson, *op. cit.*, p. 173.
34. Corday, *op. cit.*, p. 347.
35. Ducasse *et al.*, *op. cit.*, p. 350fn.

36. Poincaré, *Au Service de la France,* Vol X, *Victoire et armistice*, p. 58.
37. Jackson, *op. cit.*, p. 288.

CHAPTER EIGHTEEN

1. Brogan, *France under the Republic*, p. 568fn.
2. Clemenceau, *Grandeur and Misery of Victory*, p. 39.
3. Valéry, *Discours de réception de M. le maréchal Pétain a l'Académie française*, p. 83.
4. Géraud, *The Gravediggers of France*, p. 481.
5. De Gaulle, *War Memoirs*, Vol. II, *Unity*, p. 360.
6. Lavalade, *Petain?*, p. 8.
7. *L.A.F.*, Tome V, Vol. II, p. 197.
8. *Ibid.*, pp. 192-93.
9. *Ibid.*, p. 206.

BIBLIOGRAPHY

FRENCH OFFICIAL PUBLICATIONS

Annuaire de l'armée française pour l'année 1914.

Les Armées françaises dans la Grande Guerre, 95 vols. Paris: Imprimerie Nationale, 1922-25. The official history of World War I by the Service Historique of the French Army.

Bulletin des armées de la République.

Journal officiel: Débats parlementaires. Paris: Imprimerie Nationale.

Manuel de chef de section d'infanterie. Paris: Imprimerie Nationale, 1918. An English translation of the 1917 edition was made by the U. S. Army and published under the title *Manual for Commanders of Infantry Platoons* (Washington: Government Printing Office, 1917).

PUBLISHED WORKS

ADAM, H. PEARL, *Paris Sees It Through.* London: Hodder and Stoughton, 1919. An Englishwoman's view of Paris during World War I.

ADAM, GEORGE, *Treason and Tragedy.* London: Jonathan Cape, 1922. Despite the fact that the author consistently misspells the name of the *Bonnet rouge* editor as "Almeyreda," this is the eyewitness account of an experienced reporter who saw the treason trials from beginning to end.

ALBERT, FRANÇOIS, *Le Procès Malvy: Examen critique.* Paris: Ligue des Droits d'Homme et du Citoyen, 1919. An account sympathetic to Malvy.

ALLARD, PAUL, *Les Énigmes de la guerre.* Paris: Éditions des Portiques, 1933.

——, *Les Mutineries de l'armée française,* appearing serially in *L'Œuvre* (Paris) for Aug. 26-Sept. 1, 1932.

——, *Les Dessous de la guerre révélés par les comités secrets.* Paris: Éditions de France, 1932.

ARDANT DU PICQ, CHARLES, *Études sur le Combat* (Seventh Edition). Paris: Chapelot, 1914.

AULARD, A. (with E. Bouvier and A. Ganem), *Histoire politique de la Grande Guerre.* Paris: Quillot, 1922. A valuable history of French politics of the period.

BARBUSSE, HENRI, *Le Feu: Journal d'une escouade*. Paris: Flammarion, 1918. Barbusse, a writer of thoroughly left-wing convictions, gives an excellent account of trench warfare and the war as seen by the French enlisted man.

———, *This and Thus*, trans. Brian Rhys. London: J. M. Dent & Sons, 1929.

BATHE, ROLF, *Frankreichs schwerste Stunde*. Potsdam: Protte, 1936. An account of the French Army mutinies by an experienced German military historian.

BERNIER, JEAN, "Les Fusils 'par erreur,'" in *Crapouillot* for October 1960.

BOLTON, GLORNEY, *Pétain*. London: G. Allen, 1957.

BORASTON, J. H., *Sir Douglas Haig's Despatches*. New York: Dutton, 1919.

BROGAN, D. W., *France under the Republic: The Development of Modern France (1870-1939)*. New York: Harper, 1940.

BRUUN, GEOFFREY, *Clemenceau*. Cambridge: Harvard, 1943.

BUCHAN, JOHN, *The Battle of the Somme—First Phase*. Edinburgh: Nelson, 1917.

CAILLAUX, JOSEPH. *Agadir: ma politique extérieure*. Paris: Michel, 1919.

———, *Devant l'Histoire: mes prisons*. Paris: Éditions de la Sirène, 1921. This and the foregoing work are, naturally, Caillaux's defenses.

CARRÉ, LT. COL. HENRI, *Les Grandes Heures de Pétain et la crise du moral*. Paris: Éditions du Conquistador, 1962. Although publication of this work was sponsored by a pro-Pétain group, Lt. Col. Carré's credentials as a historian of World War I are beyond dispute. Among his other works, he was one of the officers who wrote the French official history of the war.

CHURCHILL, SIR WINSTON S., *The World Crisis*, 6 vols. London: Butterworth, 1927.

———, *Great Contemporaries*. New York: Putnam, 1937.

CLEMENCEAU, GEORGES, *Grandeur and Misery of Victory*, trans. F. M. Atkinson. New York: Harcourt, 1930.

———, *Antipatriotisme: devant le Sénat 22 juillet 1917*. Paris: Payot, 1917. Clemenceau's speech in the Senate attacking Louis Malvy and the Ribot government.

———, *Discours de guerre*. Paris: Plon, 1917.

CORDAY, MICHEL, *The Paris Front*. New York: Dutton, 1934.

CURTIS, MICHAEL, "Boulanger: The Original Man on Horseback," in *History 3* (a Meridian Books periodical) for September 1960.

DANILOV, GENERAL G. N., *The Russian Detachments on the French and Macedonian Fronts* (in Russian). Paris: Association des Officiers Russes Anciens Combattants sur le Front Français, 1933.

DAUDET, LÉON, *Le Poignard dans le dos*. Paris: Nouvelle Librairie Nationale, 1918.

DAVIS, SHELBY CULLOM, *Reservoirs of Men: A History of the Black Troops of French West Africa*. Geneva: Kundig, 1934.

DEJEAN, GEORGES, *Casque à pointe et Bonnet rouge*. Lausanne: Martinet, 1917.

DUCASSE, A., MEYER, J., and PERREUX, G., *Vie et mort des Français, 1914-1918*. Paris: Hachette, 1959. Particularly valuable for its collection of anecdotage and extended quotations from contemporary accounts.

EDMONDS, SIR JAMES E., *A Short History of World War One*. London: Oxford, 1951.

ESPOSITO, COLONEL VINCENT J., *et al, The West Point Atlas of American Wars, Vol. II*. New York: Frederick A. Praeger, 1959. The marvelous clarity and detail of both maps and text make this work exceedingly valuable. There are 70 pages of maps dealing with every World War I front and all battles of importance.

FALLS, CYRIL, *The Great War*. New York: Putnam, 1959.

———, *Military Operations, France and Belgium, 1917*, Vol. I and Appendices. London: Macmillan, 1923. Part of the British official history.

FALKENHAYN, GEN. ERICH VON, *General Headquarters, 1914-16, and Its Critical Decisions*. London: Hutchinson, 1919.

FERRY, ABEL, *Les Carnets secrets d'Abel Ferry: 1914-18*. Paris: Grasset, 1957. Ferry was a prominent and outspoken soldier-deputy who was killed in action during the closing months of the war.

FLANNER, JANET, *Pétain: Old Man of France*. New York: Simon and Schuster, 1944.

FOCH, MARSHAL FERDINAND, *Mémoires*, 2 vols. Paris: Plon, 1931.

GALLICHET, HENRI (pseud. "Galli"), *L'Offensive française de 1917*. Paris: Garnier, 1919. Recollections of a deputy who toured the front at the height of the mutinies.

GALLIENI, GEN. JOSEPH SIMON, *Les Carnets de Gallieni*. Paris: A. Michel, 1932.

———, *Mémoires: Défense du Paris 25 aout-11 sept. 1914*. Paris: Payot, 1920.

GALTIER-BOISSIÈRE, JEAN, *Histoire de la Grande Guerre 1914-18*. Paris: Crapouillot, 1959.

———, "L'Affaire du *Bonnet rouge*," in *Crapouillot* for October 1960.

GAULLE, CHARLES DE, *France and Her Army*, trans. F. L. Dash. London: Hutchinson, 1945.

———, *The War Memoirs of Charles de Gaulle*, Vol. II, *Unity*, trans. Richard Howard. New York: Simon and Schuster, 1959.

GÉRAUD, ANDRÉ (pseud. "Pertinax"), *The Gravediggers of France*. Garden City: Doubleday, 1944.

GOERLITZ, WALTER, *The German General Staff, 1657-1945*, trans. Brian Battershaw. New York: Praeger, 1959.

HALASZ, NICHOLAS, *Captain Dreyfus: The Story of a Mass Hysteria*. New York: Simon and Schuster, 1955.

HERBILLON, COL. ÉMILE, *Souvenirs d'un officier de liaison pendant la Guerre Mondiale*, 2 vols. Paris: Tallandier, 1930. The memoirs of an officer who served as go-between for G.Q.G. and the government.

HYNDMAN, H. M., *Clemenceau: The Man and His Time*. London: Richards, 1919. A contemporary account of Clemenceau's Ministry by a prominent British Socialist who knew Clemenceau well.

JACKSON, J. HAMPDEN, *Clemenceau and the Third Republic*. New York: Macmillan, 1948.

JOBERT, ARISTIDE, *Souvenirs d'un ex-parlementaire, 1914-1919*. Paris: Figuière,

1933. Jobert was a member of the left wing who said much more about the mutinies during the secret-committee session of June 29, 1917, than was subsequently reported in the *Comptes rendu in extenso.*

JOFFRE, MARSHAL JOSEPH J. C., *Personal Memoirs of Joffre,* trans. Col. T. Bentley Mott, 2 vols. New York: Harper, 1932.

JOHNSON, SEVERANCE, *The Enemy Within.* New York: McCann, 1919. Although a few sections of this work are fictionalized, the greatest part contains extensive quotations, documents, etc., the authenticity of which is beyond doubt.

JOLINON, JOSEPH, "La Mutinerie de Coeuvres," in *Mercure de France* for Aug. 15, 1920. The account of an eyewitness to this mutinous incident.

KING, JERE CLEMENS, *Generals and Politicians.* University of California Press, Berkeley and Los Angeles: 1951. A scholarly and absorbing analysis of the conflict between the Army and the government.

LAURE, GEN. A. M. L., *Le Commandement en chef des armées françaises.* Paris: Berger-Levrault, 1937.

———, *Pétain.* Paris: Berger-Levrault, 1941. A documented propagandistic effort patently written to whip up popular enthusiasm for Pétain as head of the Vichy government.

LAVALADE, GEN. CHADEBEC DE, *Pétain?* Rio de Janeiro: Atlantica Editora, 1942.

———, *Pétain, True to Scale.* Rio de Janeiro: Atlantica Editora, 1943. Both of the above are debunking accounts of Pétain written by a Free French officer during World War II. As such, they provide the other side of the coin to the works of Pétain's apologists.

LIDDELL HART, BASIL H., *Reputations: Ten Years After.* Boston: Little, Brown, 1928.

———, *Through the Fog of War.* New York: Random House, 1938.

LLOYD GEORGE, DAVID, *War Memoirs of David Lloyd George.* Boston: Little, Brown, 1934.

LYON, LAURANCE (pub. anonymously), *The Pomp of Power.* London: Hutchinson, 1923.

MALVY, LOUIS, *Mon Crime.* Paris: Flammarion, 1921.

MARCHAND, LOUIS, *L'Offensive morale des Allemands en France.* Paris: La Renaissance du Livre, 1920.

MARTET, JEAN, *Georges Clemenceau,* trans. M. Waldman. New York: Longmans, 1930. The reminiscences of Clemenceau's private secretary.

MARTIN, WILLIAM L., *Statesmen of the War,* New York: Minton, Balch & Co., 1928.

MANGIN, GEN. CHARLES M. E., *Comment finit la Guerre.* Paris: Plon-Nourrit, 1920. The account of the general known as "the Butcher," whose command was greatly reduced after the Nivelle offensive but who by the war's end was again in a top command.

MAXSE, L. J., "The Strange Case of M. Caillaux," in *National Review* for February 1918. An analysis of the Dubail report as interpreted by a contemporary British political observer.

MESSIMY, GEN. ADOLPHE, *Mes Souvenirs.* Paris: Plon, 1937.

MEUNIER, FERNAND, *Les Crimes des conseils de guerre*. Paris: Association Républicaine des Anciens Combattants et des Victimes de la Guerre, 1922. A left-wing version of the suppression of the mutinies.

MICHELER, GEN. ALFRED (with Col. Émile Herbillon), *Le Général Alfred Micheler*. Paris: Plon, 1933.

MICHON, GEORGES, *Clemenceau*. Paris: Rivière, 1931.

MOLTKE, GEN. HELMUTH VON, "Mobilization Mornings," in *Living Age* for Jan. 20, 1923. An account of the beginning of the war, taken from Moltke's memoirs.

MORDACQ,GEN. JEAN J., *Clemenceau*. Paris: Éditions de France, 1939.

———, *Le Ministère Clemenceau*, 4 vols. Paris: Plon, 1930-31. These accounts by Clemenceau's military adviser throw much light on the Tiger's method of dealing with Parliament and G.Q.G. during his Ministry.

NICOLAI, COL. W., *The German Secret Service*. London: Stanley Paul, 1924. Written by the German officer responsible for collecting intelligence of French morale.

OBEY, ANDRÉ, "Camarades Rouski," in *Revue de Paris* for December 1920. A quasi-fictionalized account of the battle at La Courtine by a writer who evidently was there at the time.

PAASSEN, PIERRE VAN, *Days of Our Years*. New York: Dial, 1946.

PAINLEVÉ, PAUL PRUDENT, *Comment j'ai nommé Foch et Pétain*. Paris: Alcan, 1923.

———, "La Vérité sur l'offensive du 16 avril 1917," in *La Renaissance* for November 1919 (special number). Painlevé's indictment of Nivelle and defense of his own role in the April 1917 offensive.

PALAT, GEN. BARTHÉLEMY E., *La Grande Guerre sur le front occidental*, 14 vols. Paris: Chapelot and (vols. 9-14) Berger-Levrault, 1920-27.

PALÉOLOGUE, MAURICE, *An Intimate Journal of the Dreyfus Case*. New York: Criterion, 1957.

PÉTAIN, HENRI PHILIPPE, *Verdun*, trans. Margaret MacVeagh. New York: Dial, 1930.

PIERREFEU, JEAN DE, *G.Q.G., Secteur 1*. Paris: Édition Française Illustrée, 1920. English edition, translated by Maj. C. J. C. Street and amended somewhat, *French Headquarters, 1915-1918* (London: Bles, 1924).

POINCARÉ, RAYMOND, *Au Service de la France*, 10 vols. Paris: Plon, 1926-33. Since Poincaré played a far larger role in events than Presidents of the Republic were accustomed to playing, these memoirs are invaluable as source material for the political aspects of the war.

POITEVIN, PIERRE, *Une Bataille au centre de la France en 1917*. Limoges: Impr. Soc. des Journaux & Publ. du Centre, 1937.

———, *La Mutinerie de la Courtine*. Paris: Payot, 1938. An excellent and detailed account of the suppression of the Russian revolt.

Les Procès de trahaison, in *Revue des causes célèbres* (Paris), 1919. An account, complete in eleven parts, of the trials of Bolo Pasha and various members of the *Bonnet rouge* staff, from the stenographic records of the court proceedings.

RAPHAEL, JOHN, *The Caillaux Drama*. London: Max Goschen, 1914. Written just before the trial of Madame Caillaux for the murder of Gaston Calmette. The author, a British newspaperman who was living in Paris, offers about the only account of the shooting not wildly distorted by political bias.

RATINAUD, JEAN, *Clemenceau, ou La Colère et la gloire*. Paris: Fayard, 1958.

———, *1917, ou La Tragédie d'avril*. Paris: Fayard, 1959.

RECOULY, RAYMOND, *Joffre* (Eng. trans.). New York: Appleton, 1931.

REED, JOHN, *Ten Days That Shook the World*. New York: Boni and Liveright, 1919. An appendix contains data on the Russian mutiny in France gathered by the author in Petrograd at the time of the Russian Revolution.

RENOUVIN, PIERRE, *The Forms of War Government in France*. New Haven: Yale, 1927. An invaluable handbook to many aspects of French politics and military justice during the war.

ROPP, THEODORE, *War in the Modern World*. Durham: Duke, 1959.

SANCERMÉ, CHARLES, *Les Serviteurs de l'ennemi*. Paris: Victorion, 1917.

SCHMITT, BERNADOTTE, *The Coming of the War*, 2 vols. New York: Scribner's, 1930.

SERRIGNY, GEN. BERNARD M., *Trente Ans avec Pétain*. Paris: Plon, 1959. The memoirs of Pétain's long-time *chef de cabinet*.

SPEARS, GEN. SIR EDWARD L., *Assignment to Catastrophe*, 2 vols. New York: Wynn, 1954. The author's reminiscences about French political figures whom he knew well during World War I are notable for their marvelous detail of events.

———, *Liaison, 1914*. London: Heineman, 1930. General Spears, a lieutenant at the time, was assigned as a British liaison officer to the French Army. His observations are fascinating.

———, *Prelude to Victory*. London: Cape, 1930. In this the author witnesses at first hand the French preparations for the Nivelle offensive.

TAUFFLIEB, GEN. ÉMILE, *Souvenirs d'un enfant de l'Alsace*. Strasbourg: Imprimerie Alsacienne, 1934. Taufflieb's army corps was stationed in and around Soissons during the height of the mutinies. This tough general was, apparently, fully competent to suppress rebellion among his troops.

TERRAIL, GABRIEL (pseud. "Mermeix"), *Nivelle et Painlevé—2ᵉ crise du commandement*. Paris: Ollendorf, 1919.

TIMES, *History of the War, 1914-18, The*. Published contemporaneously in the London *Times* in 273 parts and later bound in 22 volumes plus index (London: 1914-19).

TORRES, HENRI, *Pierre Laval*. New York: Oxford, 1931.

TROTSKY, LEON, *My Life*. New York: Scribner's, 1930.

TUCHMAN, BARBARA, *The Zimmerman Telegram*. New York: Viking, 1958. Contains a complete account of the breaking of the German diplomatic code.

VALÉRY, PAUL, *Discours de réception de M. le maréchal Pétain à l'Académie française et réponse de M. Paul Valéry*. Paris: Plon, 1931. The speech of welcome when Pétain was received into the French Academy in 1929.

Verdun and the Battles for its Possession. Clermont-Ferrand: Michelin, 1920.

This guidebook to the battlefield is valuable for its many photographs and maps of Verdun made during and immediately after the war.

WEYER, MARY, *The Decline of French Democracy*. Washington: American Council on Public Affairs, 1940.

WILLIAM, CROWN PRINCE of the German Empire, *My War Experiences*. London: Hurst and Blackett, 1922.

WILLIAMS, WYTHE, *The Tiger of France*. New York: Duell, 1949. Conversations with Clemenceau by an American newspaperman who knew the Tiger quite well.

NEWSPAPERS

Le Bonnet rouge, Paris.
Le Figaro, Paris.
L'Homme enchaîné, Paris.
L'Humanité, Paris.
Times, London.
La Tranchée républicaine, Paris.

INDEX

A

Action française (newspaper), 262
Africa, 211
Agadir Affair, 47–48, 49–50
Agriculture, 16
Aisne, River, 155–156, 158, 159, 164, 166
Almereyda, Miguel, 42–43, 44, 45, 53–54, 55, 56, 135–137, 141, 143, 254, 255, 256, 260–261, 262–263
Alsace Province, 3, 4, 60, 177, 178, 277
Anarchists, 11, 14, 17, 39, 132, 153
André, General, 25
Anthoine, General, 244
Anti-clericalists, 22, 26
Araguaya (steamer), 141
Archangel, Russia, 206
Ardant du Picq, Charles, 27–28
Ardennes Forest, Battle of, 60
Army *Bulletin* (newspaper), 220
Army of France, The
  "affair of the four corporals at Suippes," 99–100

Army of France, The (*cont.*)
  birth rate and, 16–17
  "butcher" generals, 96–100
  casualties in, 70, 71, 85, 91, 92, 130, 146
  chef de cabinet in, 154
  conscription and, 18, 19, 25, 35
  contrasted with the German Army, 31–33, 63–64, 91
  desperation of, 210
  discipline in, 89, 97–98, 186, 231–239, 277
  Dreyfus affair and, 6, 18, 19, 20–24, 26, 40, 97–98
  18th Infantry Regiment of, 177, 179, 183, 192
  Fifth Army in, 65, 95
  First Army in, 243
  1st Colonial Infantry Division of, 176
  foreign troops employed by, 157, 172, 211
  Freemasonry and, 25
  generals in, 93–105
  General Staff of, 20–22, 24, 27–30, 35, 36, 37, 55, 59

Army of France, The (*cont.*)

Grand Quartier Général
(G.Q.G.) in, 65, 80, 85, 90,
97, 106–114, 117, 119–121,
142–143, 147, 150, 154, 160–
161, 163, 165, 166, 168, 169,
173, 175, 176, 183–185, 197,
198–199, 204, 210, 211, 212,
238, 239, 293

Group Armies of the Center
(G.A.C.) in, 155

Group Armies of the East
(G.A.E.) in, 155

Group Armies of the North
(G.A.N.) in, 155, 164, 176

Group Armies of Reserve
(G.A.R.) in, 155, 156, 157, 159,
163, 176

June Mutinies in, 197–213,
299–301

justice in, 231–239

maneuvers and, 93–94

May Mutinies in, 174, 175–196,
235–236, 299, 301

medical service in, 90, 172, 190,
207, 223

method of fighting of, 61–62

mobilizes for World War I,
35–38, 55

mutiny within, 214–216, 231–241,
242, 247, 299–301

officers in, 89–90, 93–105

137th Infantry Regiment, 304

128th Regiment of, 192–193

Plan XVII and, 30, 32, 36, 38, 59,
60, 62, 63

plans for 1916, 114–115

Postal control and, 239–240, 246,
251, 277

Army of France, The (*cont.*)

reserves and, 18, 19, 25, 35, 38, 55

retreat of, 62, 63

"School of the Attack" in, 26–31,
58, 59, 61, 62, 63, 64, 219

Second Army in, 105

2nd Battalion of, 177–179

Second Bureau of, 20–22, 29, 35,
37, 40, 60, 120, 142–143, 150,
246, 257

2nd Colonial Infantry Division
of, 180, 182–183, 194

"Section of Statistics" in, 20–21

Senegalese in, 157, 172

77th Infantry Division in, 241

siege of Paris, 57, 65

Sixth Army in, 65, 66, 67, 69,
171, 185, 195

soldier-deputies in, 112–113, 185

structure of, 38

system of trial, 97–98

Tenth Army in, 104, 173

territorial army and, 18, 19, 38

Third Bureau of, 35, 163

3rd Zouaves in, 167

XXXII Army Corps of, 185,
226–227

XXXVIIth Army Corps of, 188

33rd Infantry Regiment of, 103

310th Infantry Regiment of,
202–203

Triple Entente and, 33, 48

trusted with control of France
(1914), 57

XXIst Army Corps of, 185, 188,
189, 201

298th Infantry Regiment of,
204–205

Zone of the Armies and, 111, 142,

Army of France, The (*cont.*)
158, 198, 201, 211, 220, 221,
224, 225, 226, 246, 247
Zone of the Interior and, 111
Association pour Défendre la
Mémoire du Maréchal Pétain,
297
Augagneur (Deputy), 201
Austria, 36
Austria-Hungary, 33
Austro-Hungarian Empire, 3

B

Bajolle, General, 235
Balfourier, General, 122
Balkans, 144
Ballad of the Sword, The (poem),
19
Bambara (tribe), 157
Barrère, Camille, 143, 144
Barrès, Maurice, 259
Bastian, Madame, 20
Bastille Day, 242
Bazelaire, General, 122
Beauvais, France, 154
Beehive, The (newspaper), 254
Beekeeper's Journal, The, 14
Belgian Army, 243
Belgium, 59
Belleville Height, Battle of the, 126
Bérube, Colonel, 99
B List, *see* Carnet B
Boer War, 73
Bois Camard, Battle of the, 126
Bolo, Paul Marie, 137–138, 141, 143,
263–264, 289, 299

Bolsheviks, 208, 209, 270, 302
Bonapartists, 11
Bonnet rouge, Le (newspaper), 43,
135-136, 143, 200, 247, 254–257,
259, 260, 262, 278–279, 299
Boulanger, Georges Ernest Jean
Marie, 10, 30
appointed to the military command of Tunisia, 11
characteristics of, 12
death of, 13
elected to Chamber of Deputies,
11
enters public prominence, 10–11
flees to Belgium, 13
indicted for treason, 13
named Minister of War, 11
plan of, 12
Boulanger Affair, 6, 10–13
Boulevard Bessières, France, 211
Bourgeois, Léon, 144
Briand, Aristide, 142, 143, 145, 147,
151, 161, 249
Bruecker, Monsieur, 21
Brunicardi, Monsieur, 143
Buat, Colonel, 112
Bucy-le-Long, France, 203
Bülow, Karl von, 66, 67, 68–69

C

Caillaux, Madame Gueydan, 47
Caillaux, Joseph, 139, 142, 201, 255,
261, 264–265, 278, 280, 281,
288–289, 290, 295, 298–299
achievements of, 45
Agadir crisis and, 47–49, 50
Almereyda and, 53, 54

Caillaux, Joseph (*cont.*)
  anti-British attitude of, 49
  Army paymaster general, 54
  background of, 45
  Cabinet member, 45, 51
  Chamber of Deputies and, 45, 47
  characteristics of, 51
  contacts Germans in South
    America, 140
  death of, 298
  defends second wife, 53
  divorces first wife, 47
  fears assassination, 141
  German secret negotiations with,
    49
  Green Dispatches and, 49, 52
  investigated by Senate, 50
  married, 47
  married to second wife, 47
  Minister of Finance, 45, 51
  political intrigue and, 50
  political shifts of, 46–47
  Premier, 48–51
  pro-German attitude of, 48–49,
    51
  Radical Socialist leader, 45–46,
    51
  resigns cabinet post, 53
  scandal and, 47, 51–52
  subversive visitors to, 141
  Ton Jo letters and, 47, 52
  under surveillance, 142–145
Caillaux, Léo Raynouard Claretie,
  47, 52, 53–54
Calmette, Gaston, 51–54, 280
  exposes Joseph Caillaux, 51–52
  murdered, 53
Cambon, Ambassador, 49
Canal Company, 13–14, 15

Carnet B, 38–44, 55, 142, 251, 297
Casement, Roger, 139, 254
Castelnau General de, 145, 155, 210
Ceccaldi, 139
Chantilly, France, 107
Chauvinists, 278
Chef de cabinet, 257, 284
Chemin des Dames, Ridge of the,
  159, 168, 173, 175, 176, 178,
  182–183, 187, 190, 195, 197,
  208, 212, 241
Churchill, Winston, 96, 129, 170,
  282
Claretie, Léo Raynouard, *see*
  Caillaux, Léo Raynouard
  Claretie
Clemenceau, Georges, 5–6, 12,
  56–57, 111, 134–135, 243, 247,
  248, 259–261, 262, 265, 280–
  286, 287, 288, 289, 292–294,
  295
  advises Malvy on Carnet B list, 42
  appointed mayor in Paris, 6
  attacks Army leadership, 24–25
  birth of, 6
  characteristics of, 9–19
  comments on Boulanger's death,
    13
  death of, 295
  dishonored and defeated, 14–15
  education of, 6
  elected to Chamber of Deputies, 7
  elected to Paris Municipal
    Council, 7
  elected to Senate (1902), 41
  family background, 6
  flees Paris, 7
  forms a Ministry (1906–1909),
    41

Clemenceau, Georges (*cont.*)
  leader of Radical party, 10
  lives in U.S., 6
  marriage of, 6
  Mrs. Clemenceau leaves, 10
  names Boulanger Minister of
      War, 11
  pro-Dreyfus, 22
  refuses offers of the premiership,
      10
  returns to Senate and journalism
      (1910), 41
  supports Paris Commune, 7
  turns to writing, 15
  wins success as wartime leader,
      287
Clemenceau, Mary Plummer (Mrs.
    Georges), 6, 10, 286–287
Clericalists, 22
Coeuvres, France, 202, 203, 205
Comby, Louis, 268, 270, 271–273,
    275
Comité des Forges, 303
Committee for the Resumption of
    International Relations, 133
Communists, 17
Compiègne, France, 189, 212, 214,
    215, 216, 222, 228
Confédération Générale du Travail
    (C.G.T.), 253
Cordonnier, Private, 179
Croix de Guerre, 181
Cronau, Corporal, 179

D

d'Alenson, Colonel, 154–155, 161,
    162, 163, 166, 168

Daudet, Léon, 262, 288, 298
de Gaulle, Charles, 103, 297
Delatoile, General, 100
Déroulède, Paul, 14–15
Deserters, 199
d'Esperey, Franchet, 155, 176, 185,
    198–199
Diagne (Deputy), 250
Didier, Private, 179
Dormans, France, 198
Douaumont, mortuary of, 304
Dreyfus, Alfred, 21–23
Dreyfus Affair, 6, 18, 19, 20–24, 26,
    40, 89, 97–98, 300
Driant, Émile, 117, 119, 121
Dubail, General, 289
Duchêne, General, 122, 180
Dussange, Colonel, 203
Duval, Lieutenant, 240
Duval, Émile Joseph, 255–257, 259,
    299
Duverger, Madame, 141
d'Uzès, Duchess, 11

E

East Prussia, 66
École Polytechnique, 24
Elting, John R., v–vi
Élysée Palace, 200, 282
Ethe, battle of, 61
Études sur le Combat (du Picq), 28

F

Falkenhayn, General von, 115, 116, 125
Faure, Félix, 23
Faure, Sebastien, 154, 254
Fayolle, Monsieur, 28
Federation of Metals, 133
Fère-en Tardenois, France, 192
Figaro, Le (newspaper), 51–52
Filain, France, 203
Flanders, 218, 219, 230, 243
Foch, General, 28, 148, 296
Fondère, Monsieur, 49
Foreign Legion, 239, 242
Forest of Vollers-Cotterêts, battle of, 202
Fort Brimont (France), 208
Fort Douaumont (France), 121, 148–149, 152
Foyers du Soldat, 221
France, The Third Republic of
   Anarchists in, 11, 14, 17, 39, 132, 153
   Anti-clericals in, 22, 26
   Army Commissions, 111, 119
   Army receives full authority from, 57
   Bonapartists in, 11
   Boulanger Affair and, 6, 10–13
   Cabinet of, 44, 200–201, 212, 248
   capital moves to Bordeaux, 63
   capital returns to Paris, 108–109
   Carnet B and, 38–44, 55, 251, 254, 260, 261
   Chamber of Deputies and, 4–5, 46, 57, 110–111, 119, 131, 147, 197, 201, 240, 248–249, 251,

France, The Third Republic of (cont.)
   252, 259, 279, 282, 288–289, 290
   Clericalists in, 22
   conflicts with Army over authority, 109–113
   Dreyfus Affair and, 6, 18, 19, 20–24, 26, 40
   Foreign Ministry and, 49
   foreign policy of, 48
   formation of, 8, 9–10
   German subversives and, 137–138
   military government in, 65
   Minister of the Interior and, 39–40, 142, 143
   Ministry of War in, 37, 142, 153, 199, 285, 287
   Monarchists in, 22
   Nationalists in, 11
   newspapers and, 134–137, 302–303
   Pacifists in, 44, 45, 131, 133, 137, 142, 143, 153–154
   Panama Scandals and, 6, 13–15, 18
   Parliament and, 109, 110, 142, 190, 191, 200, 247, 253, 264–265, 278, 284, 290, 293
   Party friction ceases for World War I in, 55
   passes measure curtailing Army's power, 111
   Prefects and, 39
   Pro-Germans in, 44, 45
   Proletarians in, 4–5, 17
   Radicals in, 10, 11, 39
   Radical Socialists in, 45–46, 51, 142

France, The Third Republic of
(*cont.*)
Republicans in, 4–11, 14, 16, 22,
24, 25, 26
Royalists in, 4–5, 8, 11, 24
Senate in, 4–5, 110–111, 147
Socialists in, 25, 39, 132–133, 135
soldier-deputies in, 112–113
"State of Siege" declared by
(1914), 57
structure of government in,
39–40
symbol of, 8, 9–10
Syndicalists in, 39, 40, 42, 44, 132
Trade Unionists and, 133, 153
treason within, 264–265
Union Sacrée and, 131, 132, 133,
204, 233, 249
United Socialist Party, 131
Zone of the Interior and, 111,
210, 220, 258
Francis Ferdinand, Archduke,
33–34, 36
François, Colonel, 145
Franco-Prussian War (1870), 2, 3,
73
Freemasonry, 25
French Infantry Manual, 84
French Red Cross, 221
French West Africa, 157
Freycinet, Charles de, 163

G

Gallichet, Henri, 199, 202, 203
Gallieni, Joseph, 59, 65–66, 109,
110, 118, 137

Gambetta, Léon, 6
Garrel, Private, 179
Gasparri, Cardinal, 144
Gastinne-Renette, Monsieur, 52
German Army, 3, 6–7, 28, 73, 155,
158, 159–160, 163, 164, 165,
168, 170, 172, 240, 243, 244,
296
Battle of Chemin-des-Dames and,
197–198
Battle of Verdun and, 120–127
casualties in, 129, 183, 265
contrasted with French Army,
63–64
crosses Belgian frontier, 59
General Staff of, 27, 32, 36, 64, 69
invades France, 61–66
Junker aristocratic officers in,
31–32
Kaiser as Supreme Warlord, 31
mobilization of, 35–37
plans for 1916, 115–116
population increase and, 16, 91
prestige in, 31
"Race to the Sea," 70
reserves in, 60
Schlieffen Plan, 32–33, 36, 62, 65,
66, 69
Supreme Headquarters of, 66–68
Twentieth-century methods of,
61
Germany, 16, 17, 20, 31, 33, 50, 55,
132, 138–139, 141, 144, 296,
297
Girard, Corporal, 99–100
Globa (soldier), 271, 272, 275
Goldsky, Monsieur, 299
Grand Condé Hotel (Chantilly),
107

Grand Quartier Général (G.Q.G.),
     The conflicts with govern-
     ment, 109–113
  formula of, 114
  headquarters of, 107
  military police in, 107
  Postal Control and, 150
  power of, 108, 109–110, 111
  Second Bureau of, 120, 142–143,
     150
  Service du Moral, 143
  system of selection for, 106
  transferred to Beauvais, 154
  Verdun and, 117, 119-120, 121
  Zone of the Armies and, 111, 142
  Zone of the Interior, 111
Grandmaison, Loiseau de, 28, 29, 64
Great Britain, Army of, 66, 69, 71,
     73, 79, 155–156, 159, 243, 244,
     285, 290
  battle of the Somme and, 127–130
  casualties in, 129
  8th Division of, 129
  formula of, 114
  General Headquarters of, 127
  Imperial General Staff of, 152
  "New Armies" of, 127
  plans for 1916, 114–115
Green Dispatches, 49, 52
Guarantee Trust Company of New
     York, 140
Guerre Sociale (newspaper), 56
Guesde, Jules, 55
Gueydan, Madame, see Caillaux,
     Madame Gueydan
Guillaumat, General, 122, 226–227

H

Haig, Douglas, 96, 114, 128, 129–
     130, 151, 152, 296
Haig, William (Blinker), 291
Heidessen, Lieutenant von, 63
Hentsch, Richard von, 68–69
Herbillon, Colonel, 201
Herr, General, 117
Herz, Cornelius, 14
Hill 304, Battle of, 126, 245
Hill 795, 272
Hilmi, Abbas, 138
Hindenburg Line, 159, 168
Hohenberg, Duchess of, 33–34
Hohenzollern, William, 3
Hubert, 154
Hudelo, 201
Humbert, Charles, 263–264

I

Indochina, 211
"International, The" (song), 185,
     189, 202, 209
Italian Army, casualties in, 265
Italy, 48, 144, 151, 164, 165

J

Jaurès, Auguste, 56, 131
Jobert, Aristide, 198
Joffre, Joseph, 80, 91, 95, 103, 104,
     146, 148, 150, 151, 152, 153,
     163, 229, 293, 297
  alters method of fighting, 62–63

Joffre, Joseph (*cont.*)
appoints Gallieni as military governor of Paris, 64–65
characteristics of, 66, 97, 108
conference at Chantilly and, 114
death of, 297
forms Sixth Army, 65
leads expeditionary force (1894), 58
made Commander in Chief of all the French Armies, 112
methods of dealing with the government, 109–110, 111
orders attack, 67
power of, 107–110
prepares for attack on Paris, 65
promoted to rank of Marshal, 147
retired as the Commander in Chief of the French Armies, 147
sanctions Plan XVII, 59, 60
selected Commander in Chief of French Army (1914), 59
soldier-deputies and, 112–113
Verdun and, 117, 119, 122
Joucla, Monsieur, 299
Justice, La (newspaper), 15

K

Kerensky, Alexander, 208–209
Kluck, Alexander von, 66, 67, 69

L

Lac, Father du, 24
Lacaze, Admiral, 145

La Courtine, France, 266–267
battle of, 273–276
Laffaux, France, 203
Laliron, 272–273
Lanrezac, Charles, 95
La Placette, Private, 179
Laurent, 201
Laval, Pierre, 39, 251–252, 297
Lebel Rifle, 30
Le Bois Camard, battle of, 126
Lebrun, General, 252
Lechat, Corporal, 99–100
Lefoulen, Corporal, 99–100
Legion of Honor, 138
Le Mort Homme, battle of, 126, 245
Lenin, Nikolai, 132, 138, 208
Lenoir, Pierre, 263, 299
Leseyeux, 137
Lesseps, Ferdinand de, 13–14
Leymarie, M., 257
L'Homme enchâiné (newspaper), 134–135, 264, 280, 292
L'Homme libre (newspaper), 56, 134, 292
Lloyd George, David, 79, 151, 218
Lochvitsky, Nikolai, 267–268, 271
London *Times* (newspaper), 56, 134, 289, 291
Longuet, Jules, 132
Lorraine Province, 3, 4, 60, 277
Luxburg, Count von, 140–141
Lyautey, Louis, 144, 163

M

Maginot, André, 165
Malike (tribe), 157

Malmaison, France, 218–219

Malvy, Louis, 39–45, 53, 135, 136, 137, 139, 142, 153, 161, 201, 212, 246, 258–261, 262–263, 278, 279, 282, 288, 292, 295, 298
    French counterespionage and, 142

Mandel, Georges, 284, 285, 286, 290

Mangin, Charles M. E., 96, 148, 156, 171, 174, 176

Marianne, 8, 9–10

Marion, Monsieur, 299

Marne, battle of the, 67–71

"Marseillaise, The," French National Anthem, 181, 209

Marseilles, France, 206

Martini, Monsieur, 143

Marx (spy), 137, 141

Marx, Herr, 257

Marx, Karl, 17

Marxists, 17

Maudhuy, Monsieur, 28

Maupas, Corporal, 99–100

May Day, 209

Medical Service, 223

Merrheim, Adolphe, 154, 292

Messimy, Adolphe, 58, 139

Meunier, Paul, 252

Michel, General, 58

Micheler, Alfred, 155, 163, 164, 174, 176

Migone, Monsignor, 144

Military discipline, 89, 97–98

Millerand, Alexandre, 110, 111

Minotto, James, 140

Misciatelli, Monsignor, 144

Missy-aux-Bois, France, 204–205

Moltke, Helmuth von, 36, 65, 66, 67, 68

Monarchists, 22

Mont Spin, battle of, 192

Morange, 100

Mordacq, Jean, 284, 286-288

Mort Homme, battle of the, 126

Moscow, 209

Moulia, Corporal, 179

N

Napoleon III, 6

Natchalo (newspaper), 154, 207

Nationalists, 11

Neufchâteau, 208, 210
    battle of, 61

Nicholas II, Czar, 162, 207

Nivelle, Robert, 100–101, 148, 154–156, 158–171, 173–174, 175, 176, 178, 180, 183, 192, 195, 204, 212, 214, 215, 216, 225, 229, 243, 247, 250, 297–298
    appointed Commander in Chief, 150
    battle at Fort Douaumont and, 148–149
    given authority over British Army in France, 153
    outlines offensive to Lloyd George, 151–152
    promoted to general, 148
    turns attention to troop morale, 153–154
    Verdun Method of, 149, 150, 151
    visits London, 151–152

Noblemaire, Major, 144

No Man's Land, 124
Noulens, Monsieur, 270

O

"Operation Alberich," 159
Ourcq, Battle of the, 101, 148
Ovillers Ridge, 129

P

Pacelli, Monsignor, 144
Pacifists, 44, 45, 131, 133, 137, 142, 143, 153–154, 221, 253, 258
Painlevé, Paul Prudent, 161–166, 168, 170, 232–234, 238–239, 246, 250, 251, 252, 263, 265, 278–279, 300
Paisant, André, 289
Pams, Jules, 284, 285
Panama, 13
Panama Scandals, 6, 13–15, 18
Paoli, 137
Papillons, 180, 193, 194, 200, 211
Paris, France, 185, 189, 190, 192, 199, 203, 207, 211, 212, 215, 218, 221, 278
first air raid in, 63
siege of, 57, 65
Paris Commune, 4, 7, 17
Pasha, Bolo, *see* Bolo, Paul Marie
Pau, Paul Marie, 59
Pax Britannica, 73
Pernant, France, 189
Peul (tribe), 157

Pétain, Henri Philippe Benoni Omer Joseph, 28, 101, 121, 148, 155, 164, 169, 212–213, 238, 239, 242, 243, 246–247, 257, 258–259, 265, 267, 277, 293, 294, 295–297, 299
Battle of Verdun and, 122, 125–126
birth of, 102
briefs Staff on new plans, 222
characteristics of, 101, 102, 104–105
commander of French Army, 214–230
death of, 297
education of, 102
efficiency of, 225
establishes headquarters at Souilly, 122
military background of, 102–103
military theory of, 102–103
plans new means of attack, 217
promoted to brigadier general, 103
promoted to commander of the Second Army, 104
promoted to commander of the Sixth Division, 103
promoted to commander of the XXXIIIrd Army Corps, 104
promoted to command the Group Armies of the Center (G.A.C.), 148
promoted to general, 104
psychological effect on troops of, 224–225
restores Army as a fighting force, 243–244
restores disciplinary justice to the

Pétain, Henri Philippe Benoni
    (*cont.*)
    Army, 231–235, 240–241
    takes command of the Battle of
        Verdun, 122
    talks with British about new
        strategy, 218
    uses limited offensives, 244–245
Pius XII, Pope, 144
Plan XVII, 30–31, 32, 36, 38, 59,
    60, 62, 63, 108
Plummer, Mary, *see* Clemenceau,
    Mary Plummer (Mrs. Georges)
Poincaré, Raymond, 49, 52, 57, 104,
    131, 135, 169–170, 201, 232–
    233, 242, 243, 280–282, 300
Pont, General, 188
Postal Control, 150, 175, 239–240,
    246
Postards, 24
Princip, Gavrilo, 33–34
Pro-Germans, 44, 45
Proletarians, 4–5, 11
Prussia, 2, 3

R

"Race to the Sea," 91
Radicals, 10, 11, 39
Radical Socialists, 45–46, 51, 142,
    278
Rapp, Delegate, 209, 269, 276
Raynouard, Léo, *see* Caillaux, Léo
    Raynouard Claretie
Reinach, Jacques de, 14
Rendeau, General, 191
Renouard, Colonel, 163

Republicans, 4–11, 14, 16, 22, 24,
    25, 26
Reveilhac, General, 98–100
Ribot, Alexandre, 142, 161, 165,
    170, 198, 200–201, 246–247,
    248, 249, 250, 252, 259–261,
    262–263, 293
Richard, Monsieur, 42, 44, 137
Rivière, Séré de, 26
Rod-and-Line Fisherman, The
    (magazine), 14
Roman Catholic Church, The, 5,
    24, 25
Rossignol, battle of, 61
Royalists, 4–5, 8, 11, 24
Rupprecht, Crown Prince of
    Bavaria, 170, 241–242
Russia, 33, 36, 48, 55, 144, 163,
    164, 165, 246, 266, 283
Russian Army, 66, 158, 267–276,
    301–302
    brigades of the, 203–206, 207
    casualties in, 265
    hardships suffered by, 206–207
Russian Revolution, 195, 199, 201,
    277

S

Sacred Way, 122, 126
St.-Cyr, 26, 70, 89
Saint-Pair, G. de, 143–144
Salandra, Premier, 143
Sapeigneul, France, 167
Sarrail, Maurice, 112, 139, 280–281,
    293
Schlieffen, Count von, 32–33
Schlieffen Plan, 95

School of Fire at Châlons, 102
School of the Attack, 26–31, 58, 59, 61, 62, 63, 64, 101, 102, 116, 219
Schwarzkoppen, Max von, 20, 21
Selves, Monsieur de, 49–50
Senegalese, 157, 172, 211
Serbia, 36
Socialist International Congress, 247
Socialist Party, 200–201, 278–279
Socialists, 248–249, 251
Soissons, France, 177, 180, 187, 188, 191, 192, 199, 205
Soldier-Deputies, 112–113
Somme, battle of, 127–130, 146, 153, 155, 156
Sonis, Madame de, 103
Sonnino, 144
Souilly, France, 122
Steinheil, Madame, 23
Suez Canal, 13
Sûreté Générale, 39, 40, 257, 259, 261
Svatikov, Delegate, 269
Syndicalists, 39, 40, 42, 44, 132, 200
Système D, 79, 134, 176, 222

T

Taufflieb, Émile, 188–189, 235–237, 252
Third Republic, see France
Tolstoi, Leo, 269
Ton Jo letters, 47, 52
Tonkinese, 211
Tranchée républicaine, La (newspaper), 200, 256

"Trench of Bayonets," 304
Trench Warfare (1914–1918)
    artillery in, 74, 78, 85, 86
    assault wave in, 86
    attack in, 86–88
    barbed wire and, 74, 80, 85
    communications trench, 78
    conditions in, 79
    cover trench, 77
    factors behind stalemates in, 74
    firing trench, 76
    hand grenades, 85
    infantry life in, 80–84
    machine guns and, 74, 80
    magazine rifle in, 74
    "moppers up" in, 86
    pillboxes and, 79–80
    "redoubt" and, 78
    reserve trench, 78
    stretcher bearers, 87
    "strong point" in, 76
    supplies to, 85
    supporting wave, 86
    support trench, 77
    tactics of, 85–87
Triple Entente, 33, 48
Trotsky, Leon, 133
Troyes, France, 200
Tukulör (tribe), 157
Turkey, 33

U

Union Sacrée, 131, 132, 133, 204, 233, 249
United Socialist Party, 56, 131–132

United States of America, 163, 165, 291

V

Vaillant, 132
Verdun, France, 116, 215, 245, 304
    battle of, 117, 119–127, 128, 146, 148, 153, 156
    condition of defenses at, 117, 119–120
    fortress at, 116–117
Verdun Method, 150, 152, 156
Versailles, France, 200
Vigo, Eugene Bonaventure Jean-Baptiste *see* Almereyda, Miguel
Villers-Cotterêts, France, 191
Virton, battle of, 61
Vitry-le-François, France, 225
Viviani, Premier, 40, 142
Vladivostok, Russia, 206

W

Wassmuss, Wilhelm, 291
Wood, Evelyn, 73
Wrangel, General, 302

Y

Ybarnegary, Jean, 250–251
YMCA, 221
Young Republican Guard, 43

Z

Zéphyrs, 239
Zone of the Armies, 111, 134, 142, 158, 175, 184, 187, 198, 201, 210, 211, 220, 221, 224, 225, 226, 246, 267
Zone of the Interior, 111, 142, 210, 220

MAPS

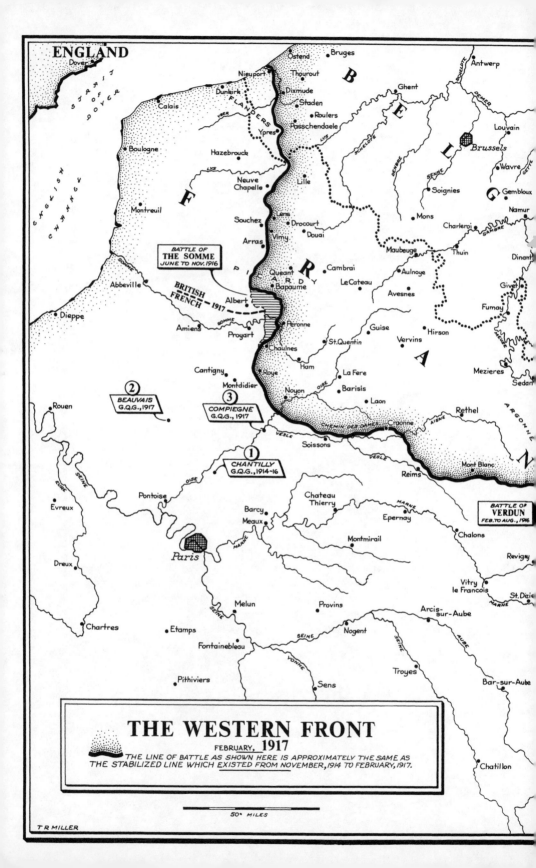

THE WESTERN FRONT

FEBRUARY, 1917

THE LINE OF BATTLE AS SHOWN HERE IS APPROXIMATELY THE SAME AS
THE STABILIZED LINE WHICH EXISTED FROM NOVEMBER, 1914 TO FEBRUARY, 1917.

50± MILES

T R MILLER

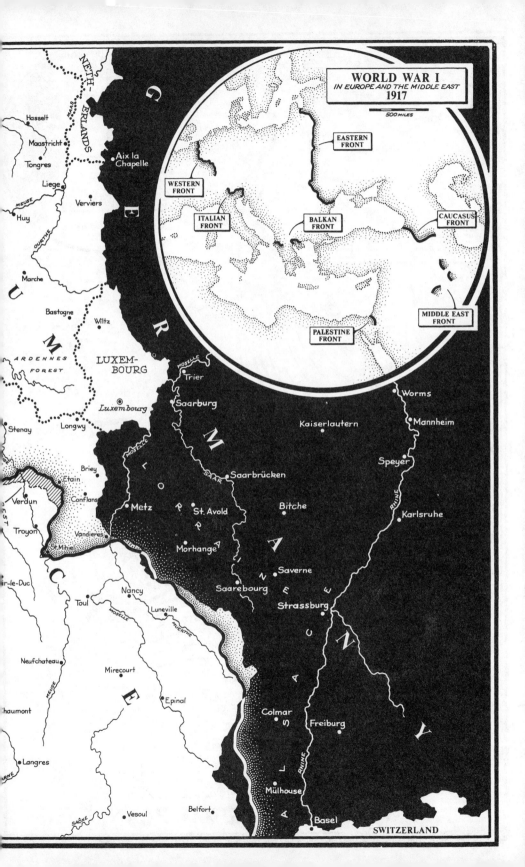

WORLD WAR I
IN EUROPE AND THE MIDDLE EAST
1917

500 MILES

EASTERN
FRONT

WESTERN
FRONT

ITALIAN
FRONT

BALKAN
FRONT

CAUCASUS
FRONT

MIDDLE EAST
FRONT

PALESTINE
FRONT

Hasselt

Maastricht

Tongres

Liege

Huy

Verviers

Marche

Bastogne

Wiltz

ARDENNES
FOREST

LUXEM-
BOURG

Luxembourg

Stenay

Longwy

Aix la
Chapelle

MEUSE

OURTHE

MEUSE

NETH-
ERLANDS

GERMANY

Trier

Saarburg

MOSELLE

Worms

Mannheim

Kaiserlautern

Speyer

Briey

Etain

Conflans

Verdun

Troyon

St. Mihiel

Vandieres

Metz

St. Avold

Morhange

Saarbrücken

SAAR

MOSELLE

Bitche

Saverne

Saarebourg

Strassburg

RHINE

Karlsruhe

LORRAINE

ALSACE

Nancy

Toul

Luneville

MOSELLE

MEURTHE

Neufchateau

Mirecourt

Epinal

MEUSE

Langres

Colmar

Freiburg

RHINE

Mülhouse

Basel

SWITZERLAND

Vesoul

Belfort

Chaumont

SAÔNE

MARNE

ar-le-Duc

Stenay

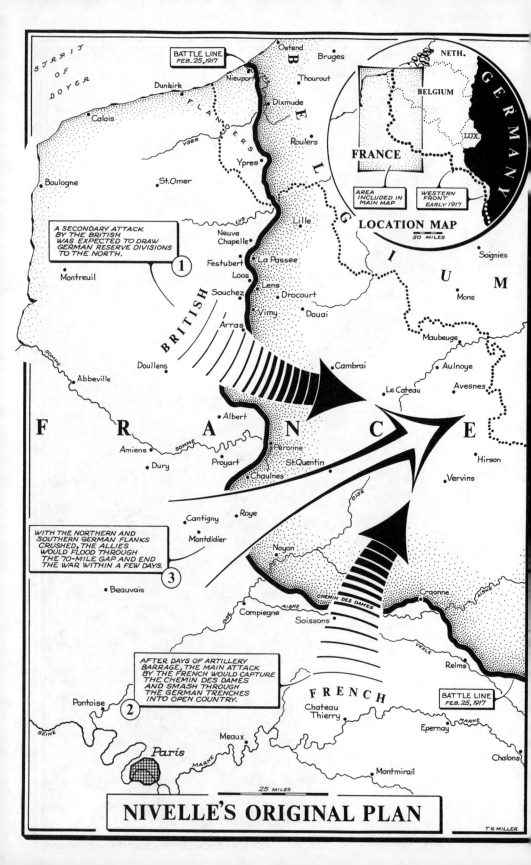

NIVELLE'S ORIGINAL PLAN

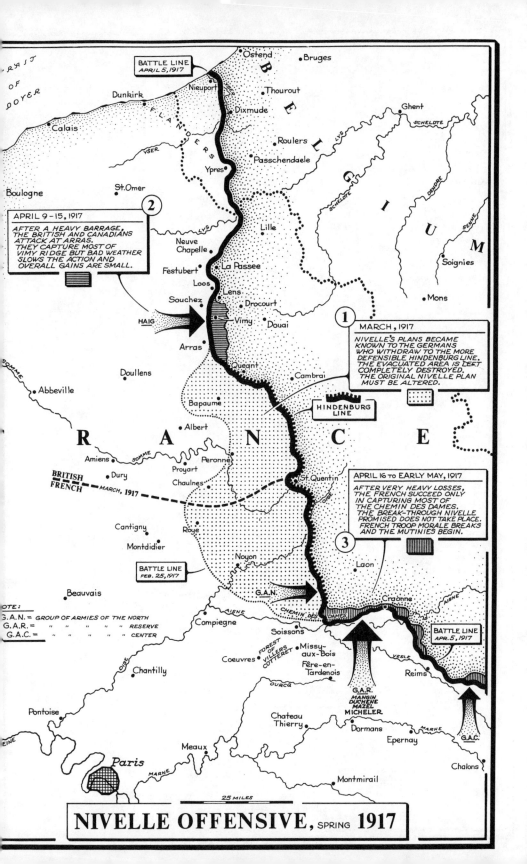

STRAIT OF DOVER

Ostend • Bruges

BATTLE LINE
APRIL 5, 1917

Nieuport

Thourout

Ghent

Dunkirk

Dixmude

SCHELDT

Calais

B E L G I U M

Roulers

Passchendaele

YSER

Ypres

Boulogne

St.Omer

Lille

Soignies

2

APRIL 9–15, 1917
AFTER A HEAVY BARRAGE,
THE BRITISH AND CANADIANS
ATTACK AT ARRAS.
THEY CAPTURE MOST OF
VIMY RIDGE BUT BAD WEATHER
SLOWS THE ACTION AND
OVERALL GAINS ARE SMALL.

Neuve
Chapelle

LYS

Festubert

La Passee

Loos

Lens

Mons

Souchez

Drocourt

HAIG

Vimy

Douai

Arras

Queant

Cambrai

1

MARCH, 1917
NIVELLE'S PLANS BECAME
KNOWN TO THE GERMANS
WHO WITHDRAW TO THE MORE
DEFENSIBLE HINDENBURG LINE.
THE EVACUATED AREA IS LEFT
COMPLETELY DESTROYED.
THE ORIGINAL NIVELLE PLAN
MUST BE ALTERED.

SOMME

Doullens

Abbeville

Bapaume

HINDENBURG
LINE

F   R   A   N   C   E

Albert

Amiens

SOMME

Peronne

Dury

Proyart

St.Quentin

BRITISH
FRENCH   MARCH, 1917

Chaulnes

OISE

APRIL 16 to EARLY MAY, 1917
AFTER VERY HEAVY LOSSES,
THE FRENCH SUCCEED ONLY
IN CAPTURING MOST OF
THE CHEMIN DES DAMES.
THE BREAK-THROUGH NIVELLE
PROMISED DOES NOT TAKE PLACE.
FRENCH TROOP MORALE BREAKS
AND THE MUTINIES BEGIN.

Cantigny

Roye

Montdidier

3

Noyon

Laon

Beauvais

BATTLE LINE
FEB. 25, 1917

Craonne

AISNE

NOTE:
G.A.N. = GROUP OF ARMIES OF THE NORTH
G.A.R. =   "   "   "   " RESERVE
G.A.C. =   "   "   "   " CENTER

G.A.N.

CHEMIN DES DAMES

Compiegne

AISNE

BATTLE LINE
APR. 5, 1917

OISE

Soissons

FOREST OF VILLERS COTTERET

Missy-
aux-Bois

Chantilly

Coeuvres

Fère-en-
Tardenois

VESLE

Reims

OURCQ

G.A.R.
MANGIN
DUCHENE
MAZEL
MICHELER

SEINE

Pontoise

Chateau
Thierry

Dormans

Epernay

MARNE

G.A.C.

Meaux

Chalons

Paris

MARNE

Montmirail

25 MILES